D1552725

TEACHING NEW HISTORIES OF PHILOSOPHY

PUBLISHED BY
THE UNIVERSITY CENTER FOR HUMAN VALUES
PRINCETON UNIVERSITY

Teaching New Histories of Philosophy

Proceedings of a Conference

UNIVERSITY CENTER FOR HUMAN VALUES
PRINCETON UNIVERSITY
APRIL 4–6, 2003

EDITED BY
J. B. SCHNEEWIND
PROFESSOR EMERITUS
JOHNS HOPKINS UNIVERSITY

Copyright © 2004 by the Trustees of Princeton University
Published by the University Center for Human Values
306 Louis Marx Hall
Princeton University
Princeton, NJ 08544
All rights reserved.

Library of Congress Cataloging-in-Publication Data
ISBN 0-9763726-0-6

Printed in the United States of America

Contents

Preface

J. B. Schneewind

During the academic year 2002/03 I had the privilege of being Laurance S. Rockefeller Visiting Professor of Distinguished Undergraduate Teaching in the Princeton University Center for Human Values. As part of my responsibilities in that position I organized a conference called Teaching New Histories of Philosophy. The conference papers and comments, as well as a record of some of the discussion, are published here.

In the past few decades a large amount of work has been done to set the major works of modern philosophy in their varied contexts. Historical classics have been reinterpreted in the light of their relations to the works of authors we have generally considered minor, to nonphilosophical writings, and to religious, social, political, and scientific changes and events. No definitive synthesis of new interpretations has emerged, and perhaps none is to be expected. But the new material should affect the ways in which we teach the history of philosophy from Montaigne and Descartes to today.

Undergraduate courses on the history of modern philosophy are among the most widely used offerings of college philosophy departments. They present the subject to those who want to know more about philosophy than they have gotten from a general introductory course. They often satisfy distribution requirements. They are usually required for a philosophy major. It is therefore important that these courses should incorporate the best understandings we now have of the works we teach in them. But the dual role of the courses—(1) general introductions to the subject and (2) mandatory preparation for advanced work in philosophy—poses a problem. Teachers suppose that those doing advanced work will have learned in the Descartes to Kant course about philosophical arguments on major topics in epistemology and metaphysics. But if we spend time on what the new history tells us about the relations between modern philosophy and its many contexts, we have much less time for careful analysis and discussion of the arguments. Are we then still preparing students for the usual array of upper-division courses?

At the conference this issue was discussed at length, as were similar issues about teaching 19th-century history and the history of more recent, largely analytic, philosophy. The transcription of the discussions on the last morning of the conference will give the reader some idea of how lively the exchanges were on the other days as well.

I went over the transcript of the final discussion to extract from it the sections of the conversations that were fully enough preserved to make sense. I have not edited any of the papers; nor have I checked references.

I know that the conferees and the large audience attending all four sessions will join me in expressing gratitude to the Princeton Center for Human Values and to the Shelby Cullom Davis Center for the generous support they provided. The conference would not have been possible without their substantial contributions. Will Gallaher and Kim Girman were marvels of efficiency and patience in making arrangements for the many speakers, the recording of the final session, the refreshments and dinners, and everything else concerning the logistics of the conference. Dr. George Leaman of the Philosophy Documentation Center has provided us with one of his mailing lists for the distribution of this volume; I am most grateful to him for this generosity. I am additionally grateful to Dr. Gallaher and the Center for Human Values for taking on the extra and very large task of preparing the papers for distribution.

I hope that readers will find the volume useful in thinking about their own teaching of the history of modern philosophy.

June 5, 2003

Philosophy and the Scientific Revolution

Daniel Garber

THE SUBJECT of this conference is Teaching New Histories of Philosophy. I have been studying the history of philosophy for some years now, trying to push the limits of the older approaches to the subject. I have also been teaching it for quite a while too. It is strange, then, that I have found it difficult to combine the two. In my graduate seminars I have been proselytizing for newer approaches, but I have found it difficult to figure out how to introduce some of these newer approaches into my basic lecture courses. While my own scholarly work in the history of philosophy has evolved considerably over the years, I don't know that I teach the *Meditations* to undergraduates and beginning graduate students that much differently now than I did 25 years ago. Shocking. So, inspired by this conference, I have decided to try to put the different pieces of my life together in a course that I am teaching right now. The main theme of this paper will be a description of the outline of the course and its conception and will include some remarks about how it actually worked in practice. (As I write this paper I am at the beginning of the semester; by the time of the conference itself I shall be somewhere in the middle of the term.) Before I begin talking about the course, I would like to talk a bit about what these new histories of philosophy are that we are supposed to be teaching.

There is a tendency in these kinds of discussions to talk in the singular about *the* new history of philosophy, as opposed to *the* old history of philosophy. This, of course, is nonsense. There never was a single, old history of philosophy against which my generation of young Turks was reacting in the late 1970s and 1980s; nor is there a single new history of philosophy that we intended to replace it with. (This parallels a theme in my course as well: there was neither a single scholastic philosophy nor a single new philosophy in the early 17th century either.) For that reason it is important to read the title of this conference carefully: it is about teaching new histor*ies* of philosophy, and not *the* new history of philosophy.

What my generation of historians of philosophy was reacting against was a bundle of practices that characterized the writing of the history of philosophy in the period: the tendency to substitute rational reconstructions of a philosopher's views for the views themselves; the tendency to focus on an extremely narrow group of figures (Descartes, Spinoza, and Leibniz, Locke, Berkeley, and Hume in my period); within that very narrow canon the tendency to focus on just a few works to the exclusion of others—those that best fit with our current conception of the subject of philosophy; the tendency to work exclusively from translations and to ignore secondary work that was not originally written in English; the tendency to treat the philosophical positions as if they were those presented by contemporaries; and on and on and on. In the prospectus for the *Cambridge History of Seventeenth-Century Philosophy,* Michael Ayers and I wrote the following passage, which drew fire even before the volume was finished:

> …[O]ur view of philosophy as a discipline has in large part been shaped by a standard account and critique, in many respects tendentious and oversimplified, of the various philosophical positions for which the great names of the early-modern period are the supposed spokesmen. Commentators in the analytic tradition in particular, writing very much out of their own philosophical interests and preconceptions, have often lost sight of the complex context in which seventeenth-century philosophy was written. In doing so, they have not only distorted its achievements but have denied themselves the tools necessary for the interpretation of the very words and sentences they continue to read and expound.

We ourselves were surely guilty of some exaggeration here; what we presented was a kind of cartoon version of the "analytic" history of philosophy as it existed at that time. Not all historians of philosophy were like that even in the period. Even so, the old history of philosophy was a useful demon to posit, even if it didn't altogether fit the practice.

We were up to something different, something that other scholars working in the history of philosophy were not doing at the time—at least not those who were working in English. We were rebels then, sometimes striking out on new paths, boldly going where no one had gone before—at least not for a long time. Sometimes we were recovering older and forgotten secondary literature. Most of all we were doing something different from what we had been taught as the history of philosophy: intellectual parricide. It was heady stuff. My own particular heresies in the history of philosophy derived from my acquaintance with the history of science. I was a graduate student at Harvard, enamored of Quine's program for naturalizing everything. At the same time I was assisting in a course in which we were reading Descartes. Reading about Descartes, I learned of his importance for the history of science. This was particularly interesting to me, given my Quinean tendencies. If Descartes was both a philosopher and a scientist, then how did he turn up as the villain in Quine's story rather than the hero? This made me curious to read some of Descartes's scientific writings and to try to figure out how they related to his more straightforwardly philosophical writings. I had the feeling that Quine was reacting to the Descartes of lore and legend and not to the real, flesh-and-blood philosopher. At the same moment, I was becoming interested in the philosophy of John Locke and discovered the wonderful essays of Maurice Mandelbaum.[1] Mandelbaum made the convincing case (convincing to me, in any case) that Locke's philosophy had to be read in the context of the mechanical philosophy as developed by Robert Boyle. All of this stirred my imagination. I began reading more and more in the history of science, trying to link the history of science to the history of philosophy. (A coconspirator in this enterprise but from the other direction was Raine Daston, then a graduate student in the Department of History of Science at Harvard, and part of this conference.)

This took me in a number of directions. First of all, it convinced me of the importance of reading the whole corpus of a philosopher and not just the more obviously philosophical bits. Second, it took me outside the great philosophers and into a literature in the history of science, figures generally considered not very relevant to the history of philosophy. It also took me to other aspects of the background. For example, when working on Descartes, I became curious about what

Descartes learned in school and how his later thought was affected by it. More generally, I became more and more curious about the scholastic background to 17th-century philosophy. This, in part, is what led me to some of the non-English literature in the history of philosophy. Much of what I was interested in also interested other commentators, such as Martial Gueroult, or Henri Gouhier, or Etienne Gilson. From them I also was led to other non-English literature that my teachers had not told me about. But it also led me farther afield, outside texts and ideas and into the world. One of the important trends of history of science in the 1980s and 1990s was its interest in the social background to science. There was the extreme group that thought it was all sociology and that content and argument had no interesting role to play in the process. (This isn't strictly true, insofar as argument itself can be given a sociological gloss.) But whether or not you thought that it was all sociology, it was hard not to be impressed by the increasing role that sociological factors were playing in histories of science. To focus on texts and the transmission of ideas began to seem downright old-fashioned. I began to wonder if as a historian of philosophy I shouldn't be paying more attention to those sorts of factors as well. And so, I made some stabs at trying to integrate aspects of these more sociological approaches into my work in the history of philosophy.

Which brings us back to a central question: what are the "new" histories of philosophy anyway? What characterized the new attitude that my generation brought to the study of the history of philosophy was the more serious emphasis on the "history" in the history of philosophy. We were (and still are, I suppose) accused of neglecting the "philosophy" part, of being "mere" historians of ideas (or even antiquarians) as opposed to *real* philosophers. This is not the place to defend the philosophical importance of the approaches to the history of philosophy that I favor, and I do think that they are philosophically significant. My interest in making the history of philosophy more genuinely historical did lead me in the direction of my colleagues in history and in the history of science and did lead me in the direction of research that, at least on the surface, didn't look as if it had much immediate philosophical payoff. But just as there is no single correct way of approaching the history of a period or a place or an event, there is no unique way of making the history of philosophy historical. In this way the new histories of philosophy in my domain constitute a grab bag of different approaches that have in common only the idea that the history of philosophy should grapple with philosophy in a seriously historical way. Whatever that means exactly.

But how can that be translated into an undergraduate course? There are constraints on what can be done. Students (and colleagues) have expectations that certain texts and authors will be covered. One can stray outside the canon from time to time and perhaps supplement canonical authors with other, more obscure texts, but there is a legitimate expectation that as the historian of philosophy in a department of philosophy, I will teach the students what they need to know about Descartes and Leibniz and Hume in order to prepare them for other courses in philosophy. A second constraint is student interest. I may be fascinated by the minutiae of 17th-century epistolary practices, or by Sir Kenelm Digby's eccentric theories of the dense and rare, or by the organization of social services in Paris in the 1630s, but I can't necessarily expect that students who sign up for a class in the Department of Philosophy will feel the same way. Another constraint is language. Few undergraduates (not to mention graduate students) feel comfortable working in foreign languages such as French and German, and it has been a long time since you could count on your students to be able to read, write, and speak Latin.

What I decided to do was a course on philosophy and science in the 17th century called Philosophy and the Scientific Revolution. The core of the course is a reading of some of the canonical writers of the period. On the syllabus are the following: Descartes, Bacon, Galileo, Boyle, Locke, Leibniz, and Newton. This by itself is hardly innovative. What is new about this part of the course is this. Now, the older histories of philosophy read philosophical figures such as Descartes, Locke, and Leibniz in isolation from their scientific contemporaries. This course, of course, puts them together with some important scientific texts. In addition, I am asking the students to read scientific texts written by people who are generally considered philosophers, such as Descartes's *Le monde* and some of Leibniz's dynamic writings.

This is a new history of philosophy, in a way, but kind of an *old* new history of philosophy—something that was being done years ago. But while I am using some canonical texts from the history of philosophy and the history of science, I am trying to reorient them in a significant way. In recent years a certain master narrative of the period has emerged. On that narrative, the rise of the so-called mechanical philosophy is seen as the main alternative to the Aristotelian philosophy of the schools; the scientific revolution is seen as a battle between these two titans, with the mechanical philosophy winning in the end. (On this, see Westfall or Dijksterhuis.) On this view of the period, characters such as Descartes and Galileo and Bacon represent a united front against the Aristotelianism of the schools, attempting to substitute explanations in terms of size, shape, and motion for explanations in terms of substantial forms and real qualities of their opponents. This is not entirely false; it is, for example, very close to the way in which Descartes presents himself and his own historical situation. But it is a kind of caricature of the real historical situation. There are, on one hand, significant differences between different strains of Aristotelianism, though they do have a great deal in common. But it isn't too much of an exaggeration to see the Aristotelianism of the schools as a kind of unitary opponent. On the other hand, there were considerable differences among the opponents of Aristotelianism. In addition to the mechanical philosophers, there were Platonists, and alchemists, and magicians, and those, like Fludd, who were very difficult to put into a single category. In a genuine history course, I would emphasize the variety of the scholastic traditions and the variety of the alternatives available through much of the 17th century. But there isn't time to do that here: in a course offered in a department of philosophy I still feel some obligation to cover a certain number of canonical texts. My strategy is to use a smaller number of the canonical texts to tell a different story, teaching many of the same texts but giving them a rather different spin and trying as much as possible to include some background material that is a bit different.

The story I want to tell is this. There is such a thing as Aristotelianism, as codified in the textbooks that every educated person had to study. There are differences among Aristotelians, but there is also a common heritage, something that every educated person could be assumed to know, if not necessarily to believe. And it was against this that a number of people in the period reacted.

But—and this is the crucial thing—they didn't always react against it in the same way. Descartes maintained the form of scholastic learning in many ways, but the content he poured into that form was very different. He questioned the senses and made them subordinate to reason, and he substituted for a world grounded in the senses a world of purely geometrical bodies governed by laws of nature—a world built by a solitary thinker. Bacon, too, rebelled against the schools, but in a very different way. His conception of science was grounded in natural histories, observations sorted into tables and then sifted into empirical regularities—a conception of science suited for a corporate science situated in a scientific society. And Galileo, too, rejected the Aristotelian model, but in a different way still. His view of the world starts not from the classroom and the Aristotelian textbook, but from the arsenal. Largely uninterested in the foundations of philosophy or the theory of method, Galileo attacked problems in understanding nature with the tools of the mathematician, which included optics, astronomy, and above all, mechanics. The point is that these three fathers of modern philosophy—Descartes, Bacon, and Galileo—don't represent a single alternative to the Aristotelian philosophy, mechanical philosophy or otherwise: they are competing programs, alternative ways of seeing the brave new world of post-Aristotelian thought. The so-called mechanical philosophy arises only later, in the thought of Robert Boyle. Boyle took these competing accounts (and others as well), put them together, and dubbed the result the mechanical or corpuscular philosophy. By setting aside points of difference among competing camps of anti-Aristotelians and by emphasizing commonalities, Boyle created a new program in the 1660s. Even then, it wasn't the only alternative to the Aristotelian program around. It was visible, though, and it did capture the imagination of other philosophers such as Locke and Leibniz, who in different ways elaborated on it. But it was also rather short-lived. By the late 1680s, there was a new kid on the block, Isaac Newton, whose program represented a serious repudiation of the mechanical philosophy that Boyle had cobbled together.

This is my story. It isn't altogether original, of course. The texts I am teaching are much the same as the texts that have been taught for years in courses of this sort, though I am orienting them a bit differently, telling a different master narrative than is usually taught. But if there is an innovation, it is in where I begin the story. I want to begin by giving the students some sense of what it was like to be a student in 1600 or so, what an educated person could have been expected to know, the classroom experience that they could have been expected to share. If I were more theatrically inclined, I could dress in an academic robe and lecture them in Latin while they copied my lectures into their copybooks with quill pens. But I am not, so I have to content myself with lecturing in my normal academic garb in English. We began by discussing the early-17th-century classroom: who was there, how old they were, what they did in the classroom. Here I am greatly aided by my vade mecum: Laurence Brockliss's superb book *French Higher Education in the Seventeenth and Eighteenth Centuries*.[2] This I supplemented with a translation of the Jesuit *Ratio studiorum* of 1599, which I found on the Internet at a Jesuit site.[3] I think that students are quite interested in finding out how students of the past lived, what it was like to sit in the classroom, how they were taught and learned. What is remarkable is how little things had changed. It was amusing to watch them as I stood on the dais, lecturing them in fixed seats, describing how their early-17th-century counterparts attended classes in similar circumstances. Even the discussion section existed in the period. Large classes divided into sections of 10 each, led by an advanced student (a decurion), who drilled them and corrected their lessons.

The *Ratio studiorum* gives an outline of the curriculum. Using the *Ratio studiorum*, we talked about what it meant to study philosophy in the period, the general contents (logic, physics or natural philosophy, metaphysics, and ethics), the period of time spent on philosophy (two years at the University of Paris, three in the Jesuit schools), and the fact that the physics seemed to take up the bulk of the curriculum. We also talked about the place of mathematics in the curriculum and the way in which it was studied as a supplement to the physics curriculum. But for any real content, one has to go to the textbooks themselves. In a way, this is easy: many textbooks of the period survive. A number of them are also available on the Internet. For example, through the Web site Early English Books, one can download a complete copy of Eustachius a Sancto Paulo's widely used textbook the *Summa philosophiae quadripartita*, first published in 1609 but widely reprinted. (The edition I used was Cambridge, 1648.) The problem, of course, is that it is in Latin, as were almost all of the classroom materials. The compromise I made is this. I made available to the students the table of contents of the "physics" section of Eustachius's textbook in Latin. Thanks to the Internet, it was easy to post it on the course Web site for them to download. In addition, I posted the tables of contents of two mathematics textbooks: Bartholomaeus Keckermann's *Systema compendiosum totius mathematices hoc est geometriae, opticae, astronomiae, et geographiae* (published in Oxford, 1661, though it is the record of a course given in 1605) and Petrus Galtruch's *Mathematicae totius* (London, 1683), also in Latin. Both are later than my target period but representative of what would have been taught in the mathematics part of the curriculum earlier in the century. Even though they are in Latin, it was easy enough to go through them in class and show students the general structure of the physics as it was taught. In Eustachius I emphasized the distinction between the general part of physics and the discussion of particulars (cosmology, terrestrial physics, etc.), particularly the fact that living things and their souls were discussed as a part of the physics unit. In the mathematics textbooks I emphasized how little pure mathematics they get. Galtruch gives about 30 pages of elementary arithmetic (whole numbers, fractions, ratios, and a couple of pages on logarithms) followed by 20 pages of pure geometry and 30 of practical geometry. Keckermann dispenses with the arithmetic altogether and begins with about 70 pages of geometry. Neither treats algebra. In both, the emphasis is on "mixed mathematics," what we might call applied mathematics: optics, geography, astronomy, and music.

This gives us the bare outline of the course in natural philosophy and the supplementary course in mathematics. However, to appreciate the new philosophies that follow, it is necessary to have a more detailed knowledge of the course. For this the Latin of Eustachius was a real obstacle. After some searching about on the Web, I found in Early English Books two texts that looked like they might be appropriate. The first was a curious book by one Daniel Widdowes (or Woodhouse) called *Natural Philosophy, or, a Description of the World and of the several Creatures therein contained* (London, 1631). This is a short book, a paraphrase/translation/adaptation of a book published about 50 years earlier: *Rerum naturalium doctrina methodica* by Wilhelm Adolf Scribonius (1579).

Widdowes gives a whole course in natural philosophy in just 65 pages, with very short definitions and copious dichotomies, in the style of Ramus. This isn't exactly what a textbook would have looked like, but I had high hopes that it would quickly give students an idea of what the world looked like to an educated person in 1600. It didn't work, for a number of reasons. First of all, it was just too short and didn't give enough detail. But more important, it didn't have the style of argument one finds in a textbook of the period, the constant references and appeal to authorities. Much better in this regard, I found, is a book by Daniel Sennert, *Thirteen Books of Natural Philosophy* (London, 1660). The first eight of those books turn out to be a translation of his *Epitome naturalis scientiae*. (The other five books are translations of later essays on natural philosophy.) While not exactly a textbook, the Sennert is rather close in both form and content to what would have been used in a classroom. Sennert, of course, was an original thinker of the period, an alchemist, an atomist, and a physician who had his own distinctive point of view. But in the *Epitome* he is less the original thinker and more the teacher, transmitting the basics of Aristotelian natural philosophy to the student. Again, through the miracle of modern Internet wizardry, I was able to download the book, and post generous selections on the course Web site for students to download. We used Sennert as the basis of discussions of some of the basic issues in scholastic natural philosophy: matter and form, the four causes, the concept of motion, the distinction between the celestial and terrestrial realms, the four elements, etc. But with the text, they could see something about the style of philosophizing that would be difficult to communicate through a lecture.

Sennert typically begins any discussion by canvassing the variety of opinions that others held, citing their views and comparing them before finally arriving at his own. The cast of characters is somewhat different than one finds in Eustachius, for example; Sennert constantly cites Aristotle, with whom he agrees most often, but Scaliger seems to come up rather often as well. But even so, the constant citation of authorities, the idea that philosophy is done in the context of a deep tradition, and the scholastic method of weighing what others have said before expressing one's own position all come out loud and clear. This, as much as the content, is what these young students were expected to absorb. And it is this, as much as the content, that the revolutionaries of the 17th century were reacting against.

So there it is: my attempt to teach one of the new histories of philosophy, ironically enough by trying to teach the old philosophy in the old-fashioned way, trying to return to early-17th-century practice in the teaching of philosophy.

For your reading pleasure I am including an appendix with the syllabus of the course. The supplementary materials can be found on the Web, on the Blackboard site for my course, and can be downloaded at will.[4]

Appendix: Course Syllabus
phi332, Spring 2003
Philosophy and the Scientific Revolution

This course will focus on philosophy and the scientific revolution of the 16th and 17th centuries. We will read a mixture of philosophical texts, scientific texts, and contemporary philosophical texts. We will discuss both the relations between what we now call science and what we now call philosophy in the period of the scientific revolution, as well as the way in which these historical episodes are reflected in more recent literature in the philosophy of science. The material is divided into the following five parts.

1. We will begin with a survey of what an educated person would have believed about the physical world circa 1600–1650, a view of the world grounded largely in the philosophy of Aristotle. We will try to use contemporary materials to re-create something of the classroom experience during that period. This will constitute a kind of baseline against which we will be able to measure some of the innovations that we will examine later in the course.

2. We will then look at a group of three important innovators in natural philosophy from the early 17th century: Descartes, Bacon, and Galileo. While all three rejected the traditional Aristotelian teaching of the schools, they represent different and largely incompatible programs for natural philosophy.

3. We will then turn to some of the writings of Robert Boyle and John Locke. While Descartes, Bacon, and Galileo represent competing visions for natural philosophy, Boyle represents an attempt to consolidate a number of different alternatives to Aristotelianism into one coherent program—what he called the corpuscular or mechanical philosophy. Locke represents a philosophical elaboration of this program, which came to dominate natural philosophy in the later part of the 17th century.

4. We will end the historical part of the course with a discussion of the magisterial systems of Leibniz and Newton, which draw on the mechanical philosophy but step well beyond.

5. The final unit of the course will treat the larger historical and philosophical questions of what a scientific revolution is and whether the changes that took place in 17th-century Europe constitute such a revolution. We will read and discuss Thomas Kuhn's seminal *Structure of Scientific Revolutions*.

The following books are on order for the course and will be available at the Princeton University Store:

Required

Bacon, Francis. *The New Organon*. Cambridge University Press, paperback.

Boyle, ed. Stewart, *Selected Philosophical Papers of Robert Boyle*. Hackett, paperback.

Descartes (ed. Stephen Gaukroger). *The World and Other Writings*. Cambridge University Press, paperback.

Galileo (tr. Drake). *Discoveries and Opinions of Galileo*. Anchor Books, paperback.

Galileo (tr. Drake). *Two New Sciences*. Wall and Emerson, paperback.

Kuhn, Thomas. *The Structure of Scientific Revolutions*. University of Chicago Press, paperback.

Leibniz (Ariew and Garber, eds.). *Leibniz: Philosophical Essays*. Hackett, paperback.

Locke. *Essay concerning Human Understanding*. Oxford University Press, paperback.

Newton (ed. H. S. Thayer). *Newton's Philosophy of Nature*. Macmillan USA, paperback.

Supplementary

Cohen, I. B., and George Smith, eds. *The Cambridge Companion to Newton*. Cambridge University Press, paperback.

Cottingham, John, ed. *The Cambridge Companion to Descartes*. Cambridge University Press, paperback.

Jolley, Nicholas, ed. *The Cambridge Companion to Leibniz*. Cambridge University Press, paperback.

Machamer, Peter, ed. *The Cambridge Companion to Galileo*. Cambridge University Press, paperback.

Peltonen, Markku, ed. *The Cambridge Companion to Bacon.*
Cambridge University Press, paperback.

Some additional material will be available at the Blackboard Web
site. All required reading will be in English, though some foreign-
language materials may be made available for students who would
like to use them.

Papers

There will be two papers due during the term—a shorter one (four
to six pages) due on March 12—and a longer one (seven to
eight pages)—due on April 14. Students will have a choice among
several topic questions. In addition, there will be a take-home
final examination, due on May 13. There is a grade penalty of 1 point
(on a scale of 100) per weekday to a maximum of 10 (or one full
letter—for example, from A– to B–) for unexcused lateness.

Readings

Week 1 (Feb. 3/5)
Introduction: what every smart person knew in 1600
Reading:
Texts on Blackboard Web site in Course Documents, under
"Scholastic Textbooks, etc." Read the Widdowes and Sennert in their
entirety; the other documents will be discussed in class. (Don't worry
that some of the reading is in Latin: it will be explained in class.) Print
out all *except* the Jesuit "Order of Studies" and bring it to class.

Week 2 (Feb. 10/12)
Introduction, continued (M).
Descartes's New Philosophy (W)
Reading:
Discourse on the Method I–III (on Web)
The World: Treatise on Light (in Gaukroger, ed., *The World and
Other Writings* and on Web)
Other selections to be announced.

Week 3 (Feb. 17/19)
Descartes, continued.

Week 4 (Feb. 24/26)
Bacon's New Method
Reading:
Great Instauration and *New Organon* (in Sargent, ed., *Selected Philosophical Works*)
New Atlantis (in *Selected Philosophical Works* and on Web)
Other selections to be announced.

Week 5 (March 3/5)
Bacon, continued (M).
Galileo's New Sciences (W)
Reading:
1. Observational astronomy: *Starry Messenger* (in Drake, ed., *Discoveries and Opinions*)
2. Copernicanism and theology: *Letter to the Grand Duchess Christina* (in *Discoveries and Opinions*)
3. Matter theory: *Assayer* (in *Discoveries and Opinions*, pp. 272–9), *Two New Sciences*, day 1.
4. Motion: *Two New Sciences*, days 3 and 4, selections to be announced.
First paper topic distributed: March 3

Week 6 (March 10/12)
Galileo, continued.
First paper due: March 12

Week 7 (March 24/26)
Boyle and the Mechanical Philosophy (M)
Reading:
Origin of Forms and Qualities (in Stewart, ed., *Selected Philosophical Papers*)
Locke and the Philosophical Elaboration of the Mechanical Philosophy (W)
Excerpts from the *Essay Concerning Human Understanding*, selections to be announced.

Week 8 (March 31/April 2)
Locke, continued (M).
Leibniz (W)
Readings:
Excerpts from Ariew and Garber, eds., *Philosophical Essays*, selections to be announced.

Week 9 (April 7/9)
Leibniz, continued.

Week 10 (April 14/16)
Newton
Excerpts from Thayer, ed., *Newton's Philosophy of Nature*
Second paper topic distributed: April 14

Week 11 (April 21/23)
Newton, continued (M).
Kuhn, *The Structure of Scientific Revolutions* (W).
Second paper due: April 23

Week 12 (April 28/30)
Kuhn, continued.
Take-home final examination distributed: April 30
Take-home final examinations: Due May 13 (dean's date).

NOTES

1. *Philosophy, Science, and Sense Perception.* Baltimore: Johns Hopkins University Press, 1964.
2. Oxford University Press, 1987.
3. The translation used can be found on the course Web site mentioned below, with complete directions for accessing it.
4. The Web site is on the Princeton Blackboard site. To get there, go to https://blackboard.princeton.edu/. To the left of the main log-in box, there is a button that reads "preview." Press it. Then follow the links: click the "Courses" tab on the top of the page; then click "Spring 2003," then "Humanities," then "PHI," then the "Preview" button to the right of the "PHI332" entry. That gets you into the course Web site. On the course Web site, click "Course Documents," and within that, "Scholastic textbooks etc." That will give all of the texts that I mentioned in this essay.

Old History and Introductory Teaching in Early Modern Philosophy: A Response to Daniel Garber

LISA DOWNING

I VERY MUCH admire the beautiful syllabus Dan has designed here, and I also appreciate his forthright acknowledgment that this course represents a new effort on his part to create an undergraduate course that fully embodies the historical spirit that animates his work. When I first read Dan's paper, I was much relieved to find his confession that the newer trends in history of philosophy, to which his own research has contributed so much, had not in fact greatly transformed his pedagogy in lecture classes. I was relieved, of course, because when I had asked myself, inspired by this conference—Do I teach the "new histories of philosophy"?— my initial answer was: "Mmm, not so much, not so obviously, at least in lower-level courses." I'd like to devote my comments today to reflecting on this situation: To what extent does my teaching reflect old history? Why is this the case? and What, if anything, ought I to do about it?

As Dan acknowledged, of course, it would be irresponsible to go on about old versus new histories without some attempt to say what is meant by these categories. I'm going to eliminate the plurals, by the way, and speak of old and new history, for the sake of convenience. I acknowledge the point behind the pluralization, which, I take it, is that there is no one set of necessary and sufficient conditions for inclusion in either category but that each is characterized, rather, by a number of overlapping characteristics or, as Dan put it, by a bundle of practices. I'll begin with Dan's list of some of the characteristics of old history: "The tendency to substitute rational reconstructions of a philosopher's views for the views themselves; the tendency to focus on an extremely narrow group of figures (Descartes, Spinoza, and Leibniz, Locke, Berkeley and Hume in my period); within that very narrow canon the tendency to focus on just a few works to the exclusion of others—those that best fit with our current conception of the subject of philosophy; the tendency to work exclusively from translations and to ignore secondary work that was not originally written in English; the tendency to treat the philosophical positions as if they were those presented by contemporaries...." And I'll add a couple of my own: The tendency to mine the philosophical past for theories and ideas with contemporary application, or to use the arguments of past philosophers for target practice.

I think this list provides a good first approximation of at least our stereotype of old history. New history may be characterized negatively, as attempting to avoid these pitfalls. To what extent are these in fact pitfalls, however, when it comes to undergraduate pedagogy? A little reflection suggests that many of the characteristics of old history serve *some* purposes of undergraduate philosophy teaching. In some cases, this is simply for practical reasons: of course one must typically consider a limited number of figures, work from translations, and ignore untranslated secondary literature in undergraduate classes. More substantially, and more controversially, if we are trying to introduce students to the discipline of philosophy, as an ongoing enterprise, via historical texts, it will be useful to choose texts that still seem to us, from our current perspective, to be philosophically rich and to include theories and arguments still worth taking seriously, and it may be useful to stress continuities between these texts and our current concerns. Further, the students need philosophical target practice, meaning, practice in evaluating arguments, and one must show them how to get it with the texts that one assigns them. When I teach early modern texts, as I often do, as part of a Philosophy 100, Introduction to Philosophy, class, I am trying to provide this sort of introduction to an ongoing enterprise, which I think helps explain why my syllabus looks suspiciously "old." This explanation, however, is incomplete, it leaves many questions unanswered. In order to further clarify the rather delicate problem of the role of history in introductory philosophical teaching, I want to explore the category of old history at some length.

I will do so by making a distinction among three different kinds of practices that all fit this stereotype to some extent or other. The first of those practices I want to illustrate with a reminiscence: When I was a graduate student at Princeton in the late '80s, there was an occasional practice of attaching asterisks (pronounced as "stars") to the names of the great, dead philosophers, to allow one to speak of their views without being responsible for historical accuracy about them. Thus, one sometimes heard talk of a character called "Locke star". The idea was that while scholars might still be debating the views of John Locke, Locke* could be freely stipulated to have held exactly such-and-such a kind of simple-minded dispositionalism about color. One sort of "old history," in line with this starring practice, simply appropriates historical figures, texts, and views for some contemporary purpose, without any real interest in the historical questions of what views were actually held by these figures and what doctrines they actually intended to express by the words they wrote. The starring practice was meant to put this sort of appropriation beyond criticism by ensuring that it made no false historical claims. And surely it did do that, though there was still something somewhat galling to the historian about the practice, a point to which I shall return momentarily. Nevertheless, I have to agree that the starring practice is not intrinsically problematic; it makes quite clear that what is going on is not history, and the main point of the appropriation seems clear: convenient illustration. Though one might wonder why Locke's name is being invoked at all: what is being added to the dispositionalist view by associating it with Locke through the medium of the fictional Locke*?

The starring practice is in keeping with what is sometimes called philosophical history (for example, by Robert Sleigh), or perhaps with a certain extreme subset of what goes on under that name. It is unclear that this sort of "old history" should be called history at all, since what defines it is a lack of concern with the historical question of what the historical actors actually believed and actually intended to express with the words that they wrote.[1] The virtue of the starring practice is that it makes this explicit. I will label this kind of "old history" *quasi-history*. The purposes behind quasi-history are not always easy to identify, but they may include the project of mining a text for philosophical ideas— while also improving on them—to produce something more philosophically illuminating or plausible than anything actually considered by the author.

Quasi-history, as I have already suggested, is not problematic *as history*, because it is not history. The practice, however, does have its associated hazards, among which are the following three.

First hazard: As Sleigh has nicely pointed out, the point of quasi-history is not always clear, and it may degenerate into "an exercise in a priori reasoning to no clearly defined end."[2] However, I agree with Sleigh (and Wilson and others) that quasi-history *can* succeed as philosophy, with Mackie's *Problems from Locke* being a canonical example I endorse. Quasi-history may sometimes produce genuine historical insights as well, if, for example, the Spinoza* in question turns out to genuinely share some important characteristics with Spinoza.

Second hazard: It is very often ambiguous whether a work or a particular reconstruction of an argument is quasi-history or attempted history. Claims to state what a philosopher didn't exactly hold but nevertheless "dimly perceived" are often in this category. I think this ambiguity is a problem despite the fact that I also think that genuine history and quasi-history *can* be successfully combined. For instance, the question of what X *should have thought* about Y, in keeping with her most-central philosophical commitments, can in many cases be asked and answered in a way that improves our historical and philosophical understanding of what X did think.

Third hazard: Quasi-history may seem to imply the irrelevance of actual history to philosophy. This, I think, is what I found aggravating about the easy invention of Locke*. The implicit suggestion may seem to be that the disputes of "scholars" can be bracketed, while philosophers concern themselves with what's important—the logical structure of particular theories, whether or not they were held by any actual historical figures. I will have a little more to say about this shortly; for present purposes, I think it is enough to observe that while the irrelevance of actual history might seem to be suggested by some uses of quasi-history, it certainly does not necessarily follow from the category in general. That the concerns of historians can for some purposes be bracketed does not, of course, imply that they ought always to be bracketed.

A second category of old history one might call lazy history. It is distinguished from quasi-history in terms of its intentions. This sort of history does intend to attribute views to actual historical authors; it intends to discuss Locke rather than Locke*. However, because it naively assumes too much continuity between present and past philosophical concerns, fails to acknowledge important aspects of the historical context, works from English translations instead of the original language texts, etc., it fails in its intentions. It gives us Locke*, but not intentionally, and the asterisk goes unacknowledged. This, I take it, is the most obviously criticizable form of old history; it is history, but bad history.

I do not suppose, however, that every history of philosophy that fits some of the earlier listed stereotypical characteristics of old history thereby fails as history. A work of history of philosophy that considers only canonical figures and a small number of texts, even one that considers issues selected for their contemporary appeal, need not thereby fail in its historical ambitions. A piece of history of philosophy that focuses exclusively on the internal dynamics of Hume's *Treatise* or Spinoza's *Ethics* may well succeed in telling us something true and illuminating about Hume's or Spinoza's thought. The product will be partial history, or limited history, but of course all history is partial and limited. Here I will mean specifically by *limited history* the history of philosophy, which is limited along some of the lines indicated in the stereotype of old history. Whether a work of history is lazy history or *limited history* requires well-informed judgment to determine and may in some cases be a matter of degree. For example, in my opinion, no work that considers Locke's primary/secondary distinction and fails to acknowledge a role for mechanism in informing the distinction can come close to capturing Locke's thought on the subject. This is lazy history par excellence. On the other hand, someone who discusses Berkeley's philosophy of science in the context of his idealism but not in the context of his Newtonianism may succeed in providing a limited history, true enough as far as it goes, despite neglecting much of what is most interesting about Berkeley's thought in this area. To put the point another way, although many works of history of philosophy may be successful without stressing historical context, it is obviously precarious to do such history without some grounding in the context that goes beyond present philosophical concerns, since only someone familiar with the context can accurately judge its relevance to the topics at issue.

Thus, the central hazard associated with limited history, in the sense of history limited along some of the lines of the "old history" stereotype, is that if the author is not well-informed or lucky, it might fail as history and thus end up as an example of lazy history. A second important hazard, however—one that I think has fueled much of the criticism of old history—is that this sort of history, because, of course, it fits neatly with the concerns of contemporary philosophers and thus receives institutional support, has dominated and might continue to dominate work in the history of philosophy, almost to the exclusion of all else. The resulting problem, then, would be that all of our limited history of philosophy is limited in much the same way. A more desirable state of affairs, surely, is that histories of philosophy should be written from a variety of perspectives, taking into account the many interrelated contexts in which a particular philosopher, school, doctrine, or idea operated.

I take it that it is obvious why this would be more desirable from a historical point of view, as it would generate a more complete understanding of the historical situation in the early modern period. I am committed to the position that it is desirable from a philosophical point of view, as well, although, influenced by Margaret Wilson, I doubt that there's a single story to tell about why this is the case. Dan, in his earlier paper "Does History Have a Future?" proposed that new history gives us perspective on our philosophical beliefs and that the uncovering of genuinely different philosophical starting points might allow us to question some of our own. Margaret, with her characteristic matter-of-fact iconoclasm, suggested that one of the values of contextual history may be to *free* contemporary philosophy from its past by revealing that we have *retained* assumptions that are no longer justified in our current context. Both of these are ways in which history might reform philosophy. (Other proposals on this topic are explicit or implicit in several of the papers assembled here.) Margaret also implied that the reverse might already have happened—that is, that philosophy has reformed history of philosophy: specifically, that the interest in examining historical connections between philosophy and science has certainly been facilitated by, perhaps even fueled by, shifts in contemporary philosophy, such as the prominence of philosophical naturalism (a thought that fits well with my own experience, as well as with Dan's autobiographical remarks about his transition from Quinean naturalism to a new approach to Descartes). One might optimistically imagine philosophy and history of philosophy's spurring each other forward in an "evolving sequence of interactions"—something like Michael Friedman's model of the relations between philosophy and science, an ideal that requires that each side function partially independently of the other.

After this long excursion into varieties of old history, I want to return to pedagogy. As I said earlier, what's going in my lower-level courses looks suspiciously like old history. Now we can ask: What sort of old history is it? Is it quasi-history? It certainly isn't explicitly so. There are no asterisks on the syllabus. But of course it might effectively be quasi-history nonetheless. I think what goes on in standard introductions to philosophy may often fall into this category: the instructor wants to discuss epistemological issues such as foundationalism and skepticism, she deems most contemporary literature too difficult, and she assigns the students Descartes's *Meditations* instead. Representing Descartes's actual views doesn't really make the list of her pedagogical goals. Although I've committed myself above to the claim that quasi-history can be blameless and even worthwhile, this use of it makes me queasy for a couple of reasons: (1) If it is self-conscious, it involves, well, *lying* to the students. (2) If it is un-self-conscious, then what's being taught is lazy, false, and misleading history. Both problems could be avoided, of course, by wheeling in the asterisks. My instinctive reaction to that thought is: surely no instructor would actually do that! But why not? Here we get to subtler questions about the role of historical texts in introductory teaching. Teaching Descartes* instead of Descartes, while it would satisfy some of the purposes of my introductory teaching, would violate others. I've never done the experiment, but I suspect that given the choice, students would request Descartes and object to Descartes*, if only because they are overly invested in the great man/great books view of intellectual history. Nevertheless, I think they'd be right to object. They'd be right to object because in assigning these texts, I implicitly represent to the students that they are worth reading not merely for what can be done with them or for what we might draw from them that would be better expressed in some other form but for what they were in their own time, in the hands of their author. And very often, I present these texts as crucial in the shaping of our discipline, where appreciating their force requires treating them as historical texts.[3]

If I am not teaching quasi-history, that leaves me with lazy history or limited history. Obviously, I'm trying to avoid the former. In the case of a Philosophy 100, Introduction to Philosophy, this leaves me teaching canonical works but trying to devote enough time to them to indicate what they were in the hand of their author: Descartes's *Meditations* as a work of metaphysics and epistemology, but also as a crucial support for the reform of Aristotelian science, and Berkeley's *Principles* as genuinely motivated, just as he insists, by opposition to skeptics and atheists. As for my teaching of modern philosophy sequences, I think that there has been a gradual evolution, almost unnoticed by me until I was forced to reflect on it for this occasion, from what was effectively lazy history, overly influenced by the epistemological paradigm toward a much more flexible mixture of old and new histories, unconstrained by any master narrative, except for the idea of the early modern conversation, the evolution of philosophy through the communication and critique of ideas. It has been my interest in the real debates of the period, along with my sense of the pedagogical possibilities of these debates, that has led me to expand my syllabus beyond the limits of old history, an expansion that I think I can and should consider pushing further. The modest notion of tracking real historical debates has many advantages: It allows us to observe what early modern thinkers in fact thought important enough to argue and dispute about, it facilitates the inclusion of women as participants in many conversations, it exhibits philosophy as dynamic and evolving, and it shows students examples of effective philosophical criticism. A syllabus influenced by this idea will likely include many canonical works and figures but must also discuss more neglected ones, such as Malebranche's *Search after Truth,* Bayle's *Dictionary,* Boyle's *Origin of Forms and Qualities,* or Rohault's *System of Natural Philosophy.* It will likely include issues related to contemporary philosophical concerns, such as the nature of mind or the status of causation, but must also address issues now considered, as Susan Neiman notes, passé or perhaps even embarrassing, such as the relation between God and creation (an issue unabstractable from debates about causation).

There are, of course, many interrelated conversations going on in the period, from which one might take many different courses. My own early modern teaching has been converging on a course one might call Cartesianism and Its Critics, focusing mainly on metaphysics and natural philosophy. Last semester, I tested the hypothesis that an excellent Leibniz syllabus can be constructed entirely out of correspondence and public disputes; I'd like to try something similar for the early modern sequence soon. From the papers for this conference, I've already acquired many new ideas about how to capture and communicate various important topics of early modern conversation, including Dan's innovative proposal about how to represent the content of late scholastic education, and I've no doubt that more will be forthcoming from our discussion.

NOTES

1. I do not mean to suggest naively that access to the intentions of historical authors is ever unproblematic. I do suppose, however, that we can make sense of the project of trying to determine what authors meant to express by their words and that we can often make well-grounded judgments about which interpretations are more or less successful at pursuing that project.
2. Sleigh, p. 3.
3. Though as Neiman and others have emphasized in their papers, sometimes a later, mistaken, or one-sided interpretation of a text may be what most influences philosophical development. But making full sense of this requires more history, not less.

BIBLIOGRAPHY

Garber, Daniel. "Does History Have a Future? Some Reflections on Bennett and Doing Philosophy Historically." In *Doing Philosophy Historically*, ed. P. H. Hare. Buffalo, N.Y.: Prometheus, 1988, 27–43.

Sleigh, Robert. *Leibniz and Arnauld: A Commentary on Their Correspondence*. New Haven, Conn.: Yale University Press, 1990.

Wilson, Margaret. "History of Philosophy in Philosophy Today and the Case of the Sensible Qualities." *Philosophical Review* 101 (1992), 191–243.

Meaning and Metaphysics

Susan Neiman

I'D LIKE TO ASK YOU to begin with an act of imagination: you're an
18th-century man of little means who is by nature an inquirer. You
live in a provincial city that is often affected by, but always distant
from, the motor of history. Apart from the pleasures of friendship
and the table, the one thing that really moves you is the restless urge
to advance ever further in the pursuit of truth. In your 40s the
discovery of Rousseau takes you back to your roots: the pursuit of
truth without benefit for humankind in general now strikes you as a
less productive activity than making saddles. So you renew your
devotion to pursue truth *and* goodness, and you ignore everything
else in their wake. Your schedule is grueling: lecturing four hours
every day on subjects ranging from anthropology to military strategy
and a range of academic duties after that. There are no grants or
sabbaticals; on the side, as it were, you sit in your study, for 12 years
denying yourself even the pleasure of communicating your still
inchoate thoughts. In late middle age you finally pull your notes
together, send them off to the publisher, and wait for an echo.
(You've proved that you're patient; you know that digesting a work
this hard will take time. Lots of time.) Eighteen months go by without
a hint of reaction, and when reaction finally comes, it's not even that
praise that Nietzsche called the voice of disappointment, but—the
Garve-Feder review.

I suspect that even the patient and wise among us would be
inclined to rage, for the Garve-Feder review (thus bequeathed to the
annals of the history of philosophy because it was so bad that neither
Garve nor Feder wanted, in the end, to take credit for it) wasn't only
bad—though it was hostile, and dismissive, and inaccurate, and
flawed in all the ways reviews can be flawed; it completely missed
the point. In attacking Kant for being a Berkeleyan idealist, the
review failed to see that Kant was not even concerned about the

reality of objects; it was the reality of ideas that was in question. (Nor was he worried in the first instance—as later variants would have it— about the foundations of natural science, which served him as a marvel and a model for what human knowledge can be; it was other branches of knowledge whose stability was in question.) The Transcendental Deduction, indeed most of the Aesthetic and the Analytic— themselves comprising only slightly more than a third of the *Critique of Pure Reason* in bulk—were needed to establish a structure in which one could ground and understand the things whose reality seemed truly problematic: ideas of God and justice and freedom. These are matters that every thinking person of the 18th century worried about and to which a driven and conscientious person might well devote 12 silent years of his life. By contrast, the questions of idealism and skepticism over which Garve-Feder spilled their successive ink concern nothing other than "...the ridiculous despotism of the Schools, which raise a loud cry of public danger over the destruction of cobwebs to which the public has never paid any attention, and the loss of which it can therefore never feel" (KrV Bxxxv).

It's not hard to see that Kant was still in a rage several years later when he wrote the preface to B—which, like most of the changes in B, and most important, like the *Prolegomena* itself, were motivated by the desire to refute Garve-Feder. For as Kant wrote to Schulze, he experienced the fact that nearly no one understood him as an insult (*Kränkung*) and worried that his inability to make himself comprehensible meant all his work was for nought. To be sure, some descriptions of the book that followed Garve-Feder held extravagant praise: a late 1782 notice called the first *Critique* an honor to the German nation, indeed a monument to human reason itself, while a 1784 reviewer regretted that the book hadn't been written in French or Latin, so that foreigners could be aware of just how great an honor the German nation had received.[1] The same reviewer even called the book the most noble and useful product the human spirit had ever discovered for the general good (*zum allgemeinen Besten*). But he, like all reviewers, acknowledged that the book was very difficult. And praise without an echo is just what Nietzsche called it. Several years after its publication, readers were bitterly arguing about why the Critique was so hard to understand. The editor of the Gottingschen Anzeigen, source of the Garve-Feder review, printed this arch notice: "Herr Prof. Kant of Königsberg has printed a *Prolegomena to any future Metaphysic* with Hartnoch of Riga, which contains an explanation and defense of the *Critique of Pure Reason* that was discussed by us. He elegantly complains that the reviewer of the *Gottingschen Anzeigen* didn't understand him. If the worthy and profound man weren't floating too much in the clouds, if he didn't choose his own terminology...he would be less subject to this danger" (*Rezensionen*, 34). Other reviewers were no less snide, but their ire was directed toward the colleagues they considered too lazy to make the effort to grasp something really new.

But the damage had already been done, because Kant himself had written the *Prolegomena*, and the vast majority of reviewers preferred to tackle the shorter book. Now scholars may continue to disagree about the merits of the latter. I found its discussion of the nature of metaphysics deep and helpful—as I was finishing my own Kant book and had thus spent more than 10 years thinking about the subject. As an introduction to—or more honestly, a substitute for—the first *Critique*, for which it serves today no less than in the 1780s, it's a miserable failure. For what Kant meant as a study aid turned into a polemic. And no wonder: at the time he wrote the *Prolegomena*, the only feedback his work had been granted was courtesy of the miserable *Gottingschen Anzeigen*. What had been for him a side issue and a *Selbstverständlichkeit*—the material reality of physical objects—took center stage, with increasing frustration and even an edge of bitterness.

Can we imagine the history of philosophy without the Garve-Feder review? Villains make for easy narratives, and it would be too simple to blame them alone for the way the epistemological paradigm captured our attention. Note that it didn't capture our attention immediately. Once Garve-Feder had raised it, the question of whether Kant was a Berkeleyan inevitably played a major role in the post-*Prolegomena* discussion. But Kant's early readers were far more aware than later ones of the issues he thought were not scholastic cobwebs—for example, "materialism, fatalism, atheism, free-sprited unbelief, *Schwärmerei* and superstition" (KrV Bxxxiv). A Garve-Feder-less history would surely have been less epistemologically centered. Here it should be emphasized that the domination of philosophy by questions of m & e in fact turns out to be very largely questions of e. It's usually Kant himself who's given blame, or responsibility, for this shift. Didn't he (usually) tell us that (most) questions of metaphysics were beyond the range of human knowledge, so that the only matters worth sensibly discussing were matters of knowledge themselves? I've argued at length elsewhere that this was not Kant's primary goal.[2] What does Kant himself say in his most central discussion of the history of philosophy—three pages tacked on to the end of the first *Critique*, one feels, in the breathless urge to get the damned book done?

There Kant sketches three historical controversies that gave rise to what he calls the chief revolutions in metaphysics. The last one concerns matters of method; the second is indeed about the question of whether knowledge is derived more from reason or the senses, which takes up most of the time and space in normal undergraduate introductions to philosophy. But the controversy Kant names as first is quite another. This is the question of "whether reality is to be found solely in the objects of the senses, and all else is fiction"—a position he attributes to Epicurus—or whether, rather, as Plato had it, the objects of the senses are the source of illusion, while only the intellect gives us truth (KrV A854/B882).

Why do people worry about the distinction between appearance and reality? Don't we learn very early that we're blessed with enough senses to provide checks and balances if we're uncertain about the data one of them offers? (If we really want to know whether the stick in the water is as bent as it looks from a distance, we can walk to the pond and pull it out.) Wasn't Descartes the first to tell us that only madmen really wonder whether all their perceptions might be dreams? Don't we find these kinds of philosophical concerns dissipating like Hume's, with or without a glass of sherry and a conversation about *anything*—be it backgammon or tenure or mortgages or carpools, not to mention love and death—that reminds us the external world presents other challenges than that of proving its existence? I believe that metaphysical worries about the difference between appearance and reality have, since Plato, been far less often driven by the worry that appearances will not turn out to be what they seem to be but, rather, the fear that they will. I will sketch an argument for this belief briefly in what follows.

The use of counterfactuals in the history of philosophy is only slightly less suspect than the use of counterfactuals in history proper. Why try to imagine the history of philosophy without Garve-Feder, when if it hadn't been Garve-Feder, it might well have been something else? Introducing this sort of speculation could lead us to a slope whose length is endless—and endlessly irresponsible. It is only productive if it enlarges the scope of imaginative possibility. Since this itself is one of the tasks of philosophy proper, such an exercise may be allowed even by those who are skeptical of its use in history itself. To encourage our imagination, and to discourage the sort of piety that leads to misguided applications of the principle of charity, I've insisted on the obvious: that even the very greatest of books is also just a book, with a history, which like all history is subject to ordinary and devastating accident. It's a joke, but not a bad one, to remind ourselves that awful first reviews of world-historical books might be an instance of that contingency Hegel thought philosophy's *sole* task was to eliminate.[3]

Common to all of those engaged in writing new histories of philosophy is a turn away from the rational reconstruction of mid-20th-century philosophy, which insisted on describing the great philosophers of the canon in terms of what mid-century philosophers cared about at Oxbridge or in a couple of departments in the Ivy League. Reacting against practices that would be illicit, even embarrassing, in real historical disciplines (besides history proper I think of history of art or science or literature), new historians of philosophy insisted on basic historians' virtues—like reading whole books rather than parts of them or checking multiple translations if not actually mastering more languages. This sort of thing could simply count as doing one's homework. But far more fundamentally, new historians of philosophy proposed to read the canon in light of what its authors actually cared about. Once again, such a proposition might seem self-evident to most historians, but was radical and provocative for philosophers—for reasons, I will argue, that aren't entirely wrong. This historicized, contextualized perspective reminded us that the giants of the history of philosophy were also major players in the scientific and political controversies of their times, and our knowledge of the history of philosophy has been vastly improved by the research based on this reminder—much of it done by participants in this conference. Among other things, their work reminds us of how very much early modern philosophers cared about. The would-be Newtons of the mind moved between poetry, physics, and history with a blithe devotion that can only make us wistful—and should remind us of how recent and unstable our own ways of cutting up interests and subjects may be.

Given our new understanding of the range and full-bodiedness of earlier philosophers' interests, it would be silly to propose another unidimensional model to replace the epistemological one. But I'm continually struck by the relative absence of discussion of one large subject that earlier philosophers really, really cared about—namely, questions now considered to belong to religion.[4] A combination of politeness and embarrassment leads most 20th-century readers confronted with an earlier text to go scurrying behind its manifest content to dig up something they hold to be more intellectually respectable than what it actually says. So we tend to rush over the obvious fact that even the *Meditations*—not my choice, by the way, for where to begin the study of modern philosophy—is in the first instance a complex proof that God is not a deceiver. In contrast to the brain-in-vat stories sometimes told in an attempt to make Descartes's concerns compelling to contemporary students, the idea that the world might be controlled by a force that does not want our good was not a sci-fi fantasy but an ever-present nightmare. Descartes lived in a world of people who regularly tortured each other to death over differing opinions on the matter. The attempt to sanitize his work by reading out the theology and the argument that the *Meditations* is really about general skepticism or the foundations of modern science are in danger of forgetting the obvious: that for Descartes, it really was (also) about God and devils, with gnosticism looming temptingly in the background. And a God whose omnipotence requires his ability to do anything whatsoever— as Descartes's voluntaristic God does—comes perilously close to an evil demon himself.

We're generally in danger of forgetting the obvious—forgetting to explain it. (Once asked to prepare a paper about the foundation of ethics, I went looking for encyclopedia entries and index references to the word *foundationalism* and discovered that even those authors who held the battle for or against it to be the central one of modern philosophy thought the topic too large or too obvious to deserve a separate entry.) I suspect something similar occurs with words like *religion* or *Providence:* they loomed so large in the consciousness of earlier philosophers that separating them out individually from other questions seemed too violent and daunting a task. But a few of the highlights of the 19th century should nonetheless suffice. Hegel wrote that philosophy should become theodicy—and described his own work as the completion of Leibniz's.[5] Long after you may have thought it would be superfluous, Marx wrote that the criticism of religion is the first premise of all criticism, and he described Prometheus's hatred of the gods as the fundamental confession of the philosopher.[6] Heine couldn't write a history of philosophy without writing a history of religion at the same time as well. And Kierkegaard's, Schopenhauer's, and Nietzsche's preoccupations with questions now generally consigned to darker ages are too manifest to allow for much esoteric scurrying (though inevitably, studies have been written trying to turn Nietzsche into a good epistemologist concerned—or rather unconcerned—with the foundations of knowledge). What about soberer 19th-century philosophers? Across the English Channel, John Stuart Mill wrote descriptions of metaphysical and natural evil that might have been lifted from Sade, who whiled away his time in prison writing works that are not only exercises in pornography but also attempts to invert the argument from design.[7]

The centrality of these sorts of questions for 19th-century philosophy may be a reason for the relative absence of 19th-century philosophy in standard curricula. For confronted with the sorts of passages I've mentioned, a good student of the 18th century is likely to wonder, Didn't they read their Kant? Just as Kant is held to be responsible for consolidating the epistemological paradigm, so is he thought to have put religion beyond the pale. (It was Mendelssohn, after all, who called him "all destroying.") Anyone interested in arguing for the philosophical centrality of questions now assigned to religion must say something central about Kant. In fact it is quite easy to show that such questions were never far from his mind—in popular as well as academic treatises, in pre-Critical as well as Critical periods—and hence that it was perfectly natural that they would remain on the minds of his immediate heirs, who read and remembered his thoughts on the subject quite well. Again, a few instances will have to suffice here. The first is his claim that Rousseau deserves the sought-after accolade "Newton of the mind" for justifying Providence and refuting the objections of King Alfonso and the Manicheans.[8] (King Alfonso was a 13th-century Castilian monarch whose study of Ptolemaic astronomy brought him to the blasphemous conclusion that God should have asked his advice before creating the universe.) This quote is a pre-Critical reflection. Those who prefer to take evidence of Kant's concerns from a more central point in the Critical Philosophy should be struck by the fact that Kant's example of a hypothetical proposition that will become the basis in the Metaphysical Deduction for his interpretation of the principle of sufficient reason is, "If there is perfect justice, the obstinately wicked are punished" (A73/B99ff). This might, of course, be a slip that reveals old obsessions without providing a key to mature ones—though the fine, popular essays from *Idee einer allgemeinen Geschichte in weltbürgerlichen Absicht"* to *"Über das Mißlingen aller philosophischen Versuche in der Theodizee"* suggest it is not. But perhaps most decisively, his argument for the Highest Good—elaborated and repeated throughout all of his mature writing, but never fundamentally changed—is a constant and central point by which to measure Kant's driving concerns.

Once one begins to look for it, it's quite easy to find evidence that Kant began with questions about Providence—in three 1756 essays about earthquakes, following the devastating one at Lisbon, published at his own expense in the *Königsbergischen wöchentlichen Frag- und Anzeigungsnachrichten*—and didn't let them go through his last helpless essay about contingency and the supposed right to lie.[9] But to make this point too close to the way Heine made this point would be a historian of philosophy's Pyrrhic victory. In the funniest history of philosophy ever written, Heine provided a masterly description of a Kant more fearless than Robespierre in storming the heavens, but wimping out and repopulating them out of pity for his servant Lampe, who couldn't be happy without God. Fifty years earlier, the *Berlinische Monatsschrift* anticipated Heine by correctly prophesying that Kant's backdoor revival of Providence would provide material for satire and comedy (*Rezensionen*, p 83). Among other things, such a passage should remind us that talk of Providence was no mindless conventional 18th-century formula but a most controversial subject of constant debate.

Heine's discussion should remind us that there were good reasons for invoking the principle of charity. It wasn't a matter of condescension but respect. These are the giants whose shoulders we stand on. How we conceive and teach the history of philosophy determines how we conceive and teach its present and future. The mid-20th-century philosophers who used the principle of charity to ignore past philosophical issues they found embarrassing weren't merely philistines or pointlessly anachronistic. To be sure, some people will always want to study and teach the history of the subject—like the history of many subjects—for its own sake. But a crucial function of studying and teaching the history of philosophy is to show us how to go on *in philosophy*. If closer historical investigation shows that our giants were more worried about Providence than about most things, aren't we doing them—and, more importantly, ourselves—a favor by politely overlooking their time-bound obsessions? If we decide this to be the case, then studying the history of philosophy will be less compatible with studying philosophy proper than the past decades have confidently assumed. Careful concern for what actually moved our forebears would conflict with the need to see them as forebears—ancestors struggling with problems that are, importantly, ancestors of our own.

It isn't often that we get to eat our cake and have it, but in fact I think that here we can. Attention to the kinds of questions about Providence that drove most of the classics of the history of philosophy actually takes us closer to the point where most people begin the study of philosophy. For in looking at standard philosophical education, I am not only troubled by the gap between the manifest concerns of most classic philosophers and what students are told they were really concerned about but also at least as troubled by the gap between the expectations with which most students approach philosophy and the experience they get in the classroom. I trust Dan Brudney wouldn't mind my quoting a story from his biography that we often discussed in graduate school. Asked on a tour of prospective graduate programs why he'd chosen philosophy, he answered "Well, like most people, I read Nietzsche and Sartre in high school and just wanted to go on." His interlocutor, a hard-nosed defender of classic analytic philosophy, responded, "Yes, but most people grow out of that."

Responses like that reveal the subtext of what we're actually teaching in the standard D to K e & m course with which most people enter the subject. We teach them to confuse seriousness with pedantry. We teach them that it's a sign of good taste to turn their intelligence toward puzzles, and a sign of naïveté, or even vulgarity, to want it turned toward the world. Rejecting such messages needn't end in a plea for Stalinism in the academy. Beauty is in short enough supply in the world to make creating and preserving it a great good in itself. (If you find this tone too bathetic, you can simply ask whether life is really long enough to leave room for boredom.) So I don't think the primacy of the practical—from which not just Kant but most students begin—precludes devotion to forms of truth and beauty that may not be directly connected to it. Nor do I think that the purpose of teaching philosophy, historically or otherwise, is to give students answers about how to live their lives. I do think it reasonable to expect that we, and they, and the people we tell them to read, be talking about the same kinds of questions. And I remember my own sense of utter bewilderment upon finally reaching college, overjoyed to be at a place where someone could help me make sense of the questions I'd been mixing with my own reading of bits of Nietzsche and Sartre and the like and wondering what they had to do with the piece of wax.

Students confident enough to voice their bewilderment (I wasn't) are usually sent to do ethics. But apart from the very problematic fact that many ethics courses are themselves dominated by questions about foundations, this suggestion underscores the way in which ethics, and the history of ethics, are not seen as the cores of the field but as something of a sideline offered to fill up atavistic needs for relevance. At that point many students simply take up subjects like history or politics or literature, which have clearer connections to the questions about meaning, and how to live, that sent them to philosophy. Sometimes I wish I'd joined them. But a mixture of diffidence and stubbornness left me in the field trying to figure out what my own questions had to do with—if not exactly the piece of wax—the themes of appearance and reality that form the core of classical metaphysics.

The order is thus a tall one. Rousseau insists that education begin with children's own interests. I'd like to begin teaching philosophy at the place where 18-year-old students approach it, and at the same time attend more to what moved 18th-century philosophers. Having said that the latter were obsessed with Providence, these look like irreconcilable demands. George W. Bush's faith that Providence will right what all the odds say will go wrong is a terrifying example of the sort of thing that gave Providence a bad name. If we reject such faith—or even more thoughtful versions of faith *tout court*—how can we ask our students to take 18th-century appeals seriously?

In *Evil in Modern Thought* I've argued for looking more closely at what was at stake in those appeals. Doing so enables us, first, to dismiss the widespread idea that they were driven by timidity or prudence.[10] So it's sometimes said that ever-present censorship forced 18th-century thinkers to profess the forms of traditional faith in order to keep their jobs, or their heads, but provides no key to their real beliefs. Views like this were stated in early works of 20th-century history of philosophy like Russell's *Leibniz* and taken over without much serious reflection. A more subtle and pernicious form of cowardice was alleged by authors like Heine. Unable to overlook the evidence that many of the greatest philosophers not only talked about Providence but also took their talk seriously, Heine (and Marx, and Nietzsche, and lesser critics) accused them of failure of nerve. Bold enough in their starting points, thinkers like Kant and Hegel drew back when they grasped the conclusions to which their work led. Nor were they honest enough to leap straightforwardly into faith, like Jacobi, when he saw the unfettered use of reason lead to nihilism. Equally unable to face the thought of a world void of order and comfort and unwilling to abandon a formal commitment to reason and argument, the greater philosophers muddled through with talk of *als-ob* and *Weltgeist*.

It's striking to note how many readers prefer to see Kant and Hegel as floundering in bad faith rather than lacking what they consider to be courageous secular good sense. But a closer look at 18th-century discussions of Providence reveals suppositions so bold as to make

20th-century assertions of simple nonexistence look bland and cautious. The best-known of such texts, Hume's *Dialogues*, invites us to imagine God as an ostrich or a spider, a child making mud pies, or a washed-up old fool. Bayle's *Dictionary*, called the arsenal of the Enlightenment, said traditional conceptions of God gave us a father who breaks his son's bones to show his own skill at healing and a vicious mother who allows her daughters to go to a ball she knows will spell their doom. And Sade only made explicit the image of God that Descartes raised as a nightmare: a Being whose goal is to deceive us *and* to set an example of the cruelty we regularly experience at the hands of smaller forces. Now all of these texts, and considerably less provocative ones, were indeed subject to the censorship that every 18th-century author learned to evade by posthumous or anonymous publication or even change of venue. But this meant that texts were read more, not less, often and inevitably taken more seriously. When writers like Kant or Voltaire wrote about Providence, it wasn't for lack of imagination. The 18th century could imagine almost anything.

One thing uniting new historians is the reminder that earlier philosophers wrote in response to events in real time. We might rather ask why 20th-century analytic philosophy didn't. Trying to discuss all the answers to this would lead us too far afield, but one misguided reason for projecting the historical vacuum backward must be addressed. This is the well-intended supposition that students might overlook the timelessness that makes classic texts classic if we emphasized that earlier philosophers wrote in response to specific historical problems. My own teaching experience suggests just the opposite. Showing students how earlier philosophers responded to particular events in their world makes it easier to see how later philosophers can do the same. (When analytic teaching of philosophy seeks its examples from science fiction, European teaching naturally turns to historical context. It's a turn English-speaking philosophers would do well to emulate, for I think it has direct consequences for the present. Europeans cannot imagine philosophers who don't react historically or a history that doesn't seek its philosophers. In this context it may be of interest that last month's *Frankfurter Allgemeine Zeitung*, the German cultural equivalent of the *New York Times*, ran an essay applying Rawls's condemnation of Hiroshima to current debates about just wars—a condemnation one fears was read in America only by the audience of original readers of *Dissent.*)

One central historical example I've found particularly useful in teaching is the Lisbon earthquake, the watershed event that divided the early from the late Enlightenment. Initially, contemporary students are surprised to learn that the 18th century reacted to Lisbon with shock, despair, and intellectual disorientation. Any conceptual trauma caused by the earthquake must, they feel, be the result of a worldview that assumes God oversees not only every step of the people of Lisbon but every sparrow's fall. In fact, the view that God directly intervenes in every event had already been attacked in Leibniz's *Theodicy*, which argued that subjection to natural law was one of the things that made ours the best possible world. Should God suspend the law of gravity to spare frustration to the owner of a fragile vase? Such questions had long formed the basis of an argument for general Providence, toward which even impious thinkers like Voltaire inclined.[11]

Traditional orthodox thinkers thus weren't the ones disturbed by the earthquake; they viewed it as a gift from heaven. For years they had battled Deism, natural religion, and the general Providence they viewed as the first step toward the denial of Providence, and hence religion, *überhaupt.* Enlightenment thinkers, by contrast, viewed nature itself as a wonder—and our increasing ability to understand it as one more piece of evidence for the argument from design. They saw the commitment to naturalistic explanation not as a threat to the most-general claims of religion but precisely as their confirmation. But orthodox theologians thought Enlightenment attempts to penetrate the order of the universe threatened the veil of mystery and the demand for humility, which piety requires. The occurrence of vast, unprecedented violence—15,000 people and one of the West's major cities destroyed in about 10 minutes— seemed a message to the Deists that God does indeed intervene directly in history and to anyone else inclined to naturalism that the ways in which he does so are hopelessly mysterious.

Thus it wasn't faith in miracles and wonders that was shattered by Lisbon, but liberal views about the miracle and wonder of nature itself. Lisbon shocked not those who were particularly benighted but those who had good grounds to be sanguine about the capacities of human reason. No interesting 18th-century thinker accepted the naive view of progress Voltaire lambasted in *Candide*. But expectations for a world that made increasing sense seemed well-founded. The natural sciences had combined to make the universe systematically intelligible. (Indeed, this was one of the arguments for dropping particular Providence in favor of general Providence, for a perfectly constructed order doesn't require a God who keeps jumping in and out of it.) And the beginning of the end of the feudal order, with its revolutionary attempt to replace tradition by principles of natural law, provided glimpses of a social world both transparent and just. With both the natural and social worlds making more sense all the time, who could be blamed for supposing that the world as a whole would follow? Here Voltaire's reaction was at once extreme and exemplary. Hardly a defender of traditional religion, he thought the earthquake put the principle of sufficient reason in doubt. Without a ground for the fact that the citizens of equally dissolute Paris and London had been spared the disaster visited on Lisbon, Voltaire thought the babies lying shattered in their mothers' arms called philosophy itself into question.

Contemporary readers who wonder what conception of philosophy could be shaken by an earthquake should remember Hegel's claim, nearly a hundred years later, that philosophy's sole task was to eliminate contingency. Even more moderate aims of making general sense of the world and the concepts we use in navigating it may seem threatened in the face of massive inexplicable suffering, because the problem of evil (underscored for the 18th century by Lisbon but presented on sufficient other occasions to make it the subject of constant discussion) is not just one more mystery about the world; it is so central to our lives that if reason stumbles there, we are apt to conclude—as Hume wanted us to conclude—that reason is no use at all.

In this context, Lisbon was once the central reminder of something everyone would rather forget: the gap between *is* and *ought* that runs through human experience. The distinction is at least as crucial a part of our experience as that between cause and effect or substance and accident. For Kant, the distinction between *is* and *ought* is just the distinction between categories of the understanding and ideas of reason. But you needn't be a Kantian to use it. Every form of moral critique, every visceral reaction of indignation or despair in the face of injustice, depends on our ability to distinguish between the way the world is from an idea of the way the world ought to be. (Of course we make mistakes about both, as we make mistakes about what caused what—but we normally respond with an effort to improve our application of the distinction, not by abandoning it.) One needn't go as far as Schopenhauer, who thought no one would have ever begun to philosophize if the world was always as it should be, to view the gap between *is* and *ought* as one crucial point at which philosophy begins. It is clearly the point at which metaphysical and moral questions emerge as separate questions—and demonstrate how deeply they are connected.

Philosophers can be divided according to the ways they respond to the fact that the world is so often far from the way it should be. On one side are those who insist on the existence of some truer, deeper reality behind the appearances, in which—contrary to the superficial chaos and misery we experience—everything turns out to be as it ought to be. Plato, Leibniz, and Hegel offer the clearest examples of such a view, but one can also include those like Rousseau and Marx, who believed that structures behind appearances allow for change through the course of history. Now all their proposals for redesigning Creation could lead to the charge that their authors were taking over prerogatives best left to the divine. Even more troubling was the worry that the search for a better order behind appearances was an attempt to flee the relentlessness of the appearances—and thereby deny the reality of evil and misery. So an opposing line of thought including philosophers as different as Hume and Schopenhauer insisted that intellectual honesty requires acknowledgment that reality is just as bad as it seems. Note that while both sides are driven by moral convictions, the moral concerns quickly issue in metaphysical ones.

The division I've drawn is rough around the edges, and it joins together philosophers who would have been surprised to learn they had much in common. Grouping thinkers as I've done surely leaves out important differences between them. But it's no cruder than the division of philosophers into rationalists and empiricists—a schema with which it's partly coextensive. (Interestingly enough, Kant fits into neither schema but is perfectly torn between them.) Those who view the foundations of knowledge to be the guiding problem of modern philosophy will divide philosophers according to whether they thought knowledge comes from reason or experience—and view other differences to be inessential. The division I've proposed is neither more nor less exact than the familiar one, but it does have the merits of being more faithful to the tradition's overriding metaphysical (as opposed to epistemological) interests and of being more interesting to students as well, for once we group philosophers this way, it becomes easier to see that what was at stake in these debates was not religion in any sense that can be narrowly stated. One example will have to suffice to suggest why: Bayle and Hume were central figures in the group of thinkers who insist on the final reality of appearances. While Hume often expressed admiration for the French thinker, most scholars agree that Bayle was the committed fideist he claimed to be, while holding Hume to be the sanguine atheist described in Adam Smith's portrait. As the *Dialogues* themselves stated, differences between atheism and theism were not major differences but matters of degree and tone. What united Hume and Bayle were not their views about God but their views about reason. For when reason contrasts the appearances, in which history is little but a series of crimes and misfortunes, with its own ideas about what should be, it can find no ground for the difference. Faced squarely with this evidence of reason's impotence, either one can, like Bayle, maintain belief in God's existence and benevolence despite all the grounds for doubting them or one can, like Hume, use those grounds as a reason to abandon faith altogether. The only faith that cannot survive such argument is the faith that reason is of use in making sense of the world.

Showing how metaphysical positions undercut or override theological ones in the history of philosophy is one way to show that our concepts of reason are more centrally at stake in the underlying question of the problem of evil than our concepts of God. (Since all three major Western religions had both rationalist and fideist traditions, battles about the authority of reason were fought out within religious frameworks as well as apart from them.) Another route is to show how traditional questions of the problem of evil reappear in the work of even those contemporary philosophers deeply committed to leaving God out of matters entirely. While this is easiest to do with the existentialists, I've argued that it can be done for Critical Theory, Arendt, and Rawls. I won't repeat those arguments here but will conclude with some remarks about teaching philosophy in the light of those views.

I've sketched my own view of the main underlying narrative of the history of metaphysics at some length—not at enough length, surely, to convince anyone outright but hopefully enough to convince some to read more. Doing so was part of an answer to Jerry Schneewind's question—early on in the e-mail discussions that preceded this conference—as to whether I really wanted to do away with the standard D to K m & e course on which most of us were raised. I really do. I don't think the standard course can be redeemed by supplementing it with new material or even by requiring students to take a history of ethics course as well. Or, because committing courses to oblivion is only slightly less unnerving than committing books to the flames, let me rather say that I have no interest in teaching such courses and that I hope to interest others in teaching philosophy differently. Obviously, nothing should prevent those who want to teach or take some version of the standard sequence qua history of epistemology from doing so. But to offer the standard sequence as an introduction to the history of *philosophy* is not much better than reading Kant through the eyes of the *Gottingschen Anzeige*.

Instead, I've sketched an alternative that takes place on grounds where we can meet our students and the historical classics at once. These involve questions that unite moral and metaphysical concerns and show why each of them matters. Rather than permitting us to put such questions behind us, I suspect that growing up makes us more aware of the role of contingency and luck in human life and more concerned about whether it's to be celebrated or mourned. We wonder whether explaining things comes too close to justifying them, and if so, where we should stop. We worry about how to maintain values of fairness and decency when the world as a whole does not. We ask about the sense of making theoretical sense of the world when we cannot make sense of misery and terror. We think more and not less frequently about whether history presents anything but grounds for despair and whether hopes for progress are based on anything but wishful thinking. We may do it with brilliant irony, like Hume, or with spare and careful dryness like Rawls, but we find one way or another to be engaged with some piece of the problem misprized as the meaning of life.

Any well-trained analytic philosopher (and all it takes is a stray Heideggerian to get me to answer to this description) will worry that introducing such questions permits sloppy good intentions to replace the critical thinking we're in business to promote. In fact, the subject provides an enormous wealth of texts through which students can learn analytic skills. I don't know of a sharper collection of arguments in one place than those contained in Hume's *Dialogues*. (Hume judged it to be his own best work. I find it unquestionably the best introduction to his work as a whole, as well as a far better key than the rest to why Kant found that work so decisive.) But even without the *Dialogues'* breathtaking rigor and concision, there are scores of other texts with which students can learn to think clearly, deeply, and in dialogue. For beginners, it's probably simplest to teach such a course chronologically, precisely because it offers a narrative in which earlier philosophers argued with each other. I have also taught the course according to the distinction drawn earlier, beginning with the views of those who sought reality behind the appearances before turning to those who insisted that appearances are final. The problem of constructing a syllabus is not a dearth of first-rate and demanding texts but of choosing among them.

The number and variety of texts available should be sufficient to dispel any concerns that such a course would degenerate into the promotion of banal pieties or *Weltweisheiten*. The problems are too hard, the texts are too difficult, for this to be very likely. A cynic might rather say that in offering the problem of evil as alternative narrative to the problem of skepticism, I've merely substituted one insoluble problem for another. But there's a brighter view of the enterprise. This would see it as a way of teaching philosophy that puts the first sentence of the *Critique of Pure Reason* in the foreground of philosophical thinking (and finally accepts, as Kant himself never quite did, that this is the last word on the subject of the final solution of major philosophical problems). The question of the sense and meaning of the world as a whole is paradigmatic of those questions that transcend all of reason's powers to answer. Too often, analytic philosophers forget the claim that these are questions reason cannot ignore—and leave them to those who believe they can be answered with silly or dangerous kitsch. If we dismiss altogether what Kant saw as reason's need to confront such questions, our students are likely to get reason's needs met elsewhere.

In various stages of my own work on these subjects I've taught this material to undergraduates at Yale, Tel Aviv University, and Humboldt-Universität zu Berlin. At Yale I used the material for a large lecture course that served both as an introduction to philosophy and as an upper-level course for majors who'd already had some background in more standard histories of philosophy. More than once I began with the *Book of Job*—a text well-known and discussed, of course, throughout the 18th century and a sheer delight to teach—before leaping over millennia to the modern. But if one wants to remain within a stricter historical framework, the place to begin is Bayle's *Dictionary*—a great, lively, and influential text in itself and a necessary preparation for Leibniz's *Theodicy*. The article "Manicheans" is often enough to convey what Bayle is doing, and excerpts from the *Theodicy* are relatively easy to choose. I like to supplement the latter with Pope's *Essay on Man*, both because it's far more appealing than the *Theodicy* and because it's importantly different. Comparing the two gives students a chance to think about fine differences in argument and about the differences between forms of persuasion in literature and philosophy. I devote somewhat more time to Rousseau, reading the whole of the second *Discourse* and excerpts from the *Émile*. Time permitting, *Candide* is a great text to teach, but in any case, Voltaire's poem "The Lisbon Earthquake" and Rousseau's letter in response to it provide terrific examples of philosophers engaged in debate with each other about contemporary events. Hume's *Dialogues* come next, virtually teaching themselves. There are various ways to put Kant into such a course—none of them ever entirely satisfactory but all of them compelling. The most successful I've tried used the two prefaces to the *Critique of Pure Reason* along with the Canon of the first *Critique* and the Dialectic of the second. This can be supplemented by some of the *Berlinische Monatsschrift* essays, particularly "What Is Orientation in Thinking?" "The Idea of a Universal History," and "On the Impossibility of Every Future Attempt at Theodicy."

One could teach all of this material comfortably within one semester and stop with Kant. I've preferred not to do so but to race on. (Ideally, of course, one should take two semesters, but it's possible to give students a reasonable idea of how the story goes on in one.) I have included the first 150 or so pages of Sade's *Justine*. (A note on teaching Sade, for those who've never done it: it's both more boring and more painful than expected, but he's important enough so that leaving him out altogether seems wrong. The first time I taught him was in a small advanced seminar to which I assigned *Juliette*—partly to make sure I read the entire book myself as preparation for reading Adorno and Horkheimer's discussion of it—and deeply regretted having required students to read texts containing unspeakably violent images.) Following Sade I have introduced Hegel—through the *Introduction to the Lectures on World History*, possibly supplemented by chapter four of the *Phenomenology*—and Marx—via the beginning of the *Critique of the Philosophy of Right*—and selections from the *German Ideology*. Time permitting, Schopenhauer, who can be conveyed well in excerpts, comes next. Nietzsche provides a natural point at which to end the course and is probably easiest to introduce through the *Geneaology of Morals*. There are dangers in ending an introductory philosophy course with Nietzsche, of course; students can find him too compelling to think further. This is one reason I haven't finished the course with Nietzsche but either structured the material nonchronologically (according to the schema I suggested) or continued into selections from the 20th century. And now that it's finally finished, I've assigned my own book, which students found a helpful guide.

I'm well aware that acceptance of the sort of narrative I propose, or some better version of it, would affect not only the teaching of introductory history courses but many other sorts of teaching as well. It's a consequence that would delight anyone who believes, as I do, that philosophy itself took a wrong turn in 1782 and that it would do well to stop short and reconsider its directions. Should such a process occur, it would be, of course, a very long one. As temptation for undertaking a part of it, I close by mentioning a few of my own experiences teaching such a course. I've seen, for example, two different Tel Aviv students plead to be allowed to mix their analyses of Hume in one case, and Leibniz in the other, with the analysis of a film they swore was crucial to our discussion, a claim about which I was skeptical till I saw the film, *Breaking the Waves*. I remember the Yale student so delighted with the argument for the Highest Good that she interrupted discussion to say, "I'm quitting English and majoring in Kant." As of this writing I am still receiving papers from students at Humboldt—accustomed to read a fraction of the amount per course that we expect from Ivy League under-graduates—who insist that it wasn't enough to read the immense body of literature I forced on them; they want to do extra work on Schelling or Feuerbach or Freud. At the three very different universities where I offered it, this way of approaching the history of philosophy provoked *both* more intense and more lively discussion—and more hard work and engagement—than any other course I taught.

NOTES

1. *Rezensionen zur kantischen Philosophie*, herausgegeben von Albert Landau. Albert Landau Verlag, Bebra, 1991. Hereafter: *Rezensionen*, 18, 74.

2. See Neiman, *The Unity of Reason: Rereading Kant.* New York, N.Y.: Oxford University Press, 1994. And Neiman, *Evil in Modern Thought: An Alternative History of Philosophy.* Princeton, N.J.: Princeton University Press, 2002.

3. See Hegel, *Introduction to the Lectures on World History,* trans. H. B. Nisbet. Cambridge, England: Cambridge University Press, 1975, 28.

4. J. B. Schneewind's *Invention of Autonomy* is the best exception I know about; of course I may have overlooked others.

5. Hegel, ibid., 43.

6. Marx, Critique of Hegel's *Philosophy of Right,* and Marx, *Dissertation.*

7. Mill, "Nature" In *Three Essays on Religion, Collected Works of John Stuart Mill,* ed. J. M. Robson. Toronto: University of Toronto Press, 1969, 385.

8. Kant, *Reflexionen*, 58.12.

9. For a longer argument to this effect, see my *Evil in Modern Thought,* chapter 1. Volker Gerhardt's recent *Immanuel Kant: Vernunft und Leben* (Reclam, 2002) argues that Kant was necessarily and systematically more concerned about God after he showed the impossibility of proving God's existence.

10. I suspect many of the same claims (and counterclaims) could be made about earlier centuries but will confine my discussion to the one I know best.

11. See the astoundingly moving argument for Deism in *Candide*'s discussion of El Dorado.

Evil and Wonder in Early Modern Philosophy: A Response to Susan Neiman

MARK LARRIMORE

IT'S A GREAT PLEASURE to be back at Princeton and to be invited to reflect on the place the problem of evil might have in a curriculum in the history of philosophy. I can think of no better way into this subject than the work of Susan Neiman, who has opened up an exciting trajectory for teaching the history of modern philosophy. In my remarks today I want to suggest that we can go even farther along the path she has opened up. Early modern philosophy was not just shaped by the problem of evil but also helped give the problem of evil its modern shape. Approaching early modern philosophy as Neiman invites us to can thus do more than just acquaint us with forgotten responses to questions about evil and Providence. It can also revive other, perhaps better, questions—questions vital if we are to really come to terms with the challenges of evils.

After indulging in a few thoughts about the place of the history of philosophy in philosophy and its pegadogy, I want to explore the ways an approach to the history of philosophy through the problem of evil can aid in our quest for good questions. I will end by proposing a course in early modern philosophy that sets the emerging problem of evil against the backdrop of early modern attempts to articulate the wonder of the world and our powers to make theoretical and practical sense of it.

WHY DO PHILOSOPHY?
WHY DO HISTORY OF PHILOSOPHY?

I am surprised at the timidity of some of our participants' answers to the question of the relevance of the history of philosophy for philosophy in general. It seems to me that the history of philosophy is not only germane to the aims of philosophy but indispensable. Especially, as I will try to show, if we are troubled by the problem of evil.

What do we teach when we teach philosophy? How to think clearly, respect for argument, reflectiveness, rigor, and a sense of responsibility for the concepts we use. But not only this. We teach students to ask questions. The big questions (if you believe in them), the questions of the day (if you don't)—in any case, better questions. For this, the history of philosophy is essential. This is not only because the history of philosophy is a kind of bank of conceptual biodiversity, although it certainly is that, too. More fundamentally, the history of philosophy is essential to philosophy because we find ourselves in history, too. Students won't learn to think outside the box until they know they're in a box.

A big part, then, of what we do is to teach questions and that questions have histories. Like the concepts designed to address them, questions are invented, forgotten, and sometimes remembered. And for students, what could be more exciting than the idea that Western philosophy, far from being mere footnotes to Plato, is a history of inventions? The philosophy of the 18th century becomes more interesting, not less, when students learn that Leibniz invented theodicy (or at least the word), that Kant invented autonomy, and that Schleiermacher invented religion. And even more interesting when they learn that the inventor of theodicy also helped invent the modern individual, that the inventor of autonomy helped invent race, and that the inventor of religion invented hermeneutics.

TEACHING EARLY MODERN PHILOSOPHY

That and how we teach early modern philosophy is especially important, because the boxes we think inside nowadays are very largely inventions of the past two centuries—although not without important debts to earlier periods, as I'll mention in a moment.

Susan Neiman's suggestion that we approach modern thought through the problem of evil seems to me a very good one, for the reasons she mentions. It takes us closer to the philosophers we study, and it brings us closer to our students. Much is opened up by the suggestion that "metaphysical worries about the difference between appearance and reality" may be driven not by the worry that appearances are deceiving but rather by the worry that they are not—that the world actually is as disorderly or callous or indifferent or absurd as it seems to be. Among other virtues, this approach helps us see that and why normative and epistemological questions can and do coincide.

It is also true that the problem of evil is immediately intelligible to students. Questions about our very capacity to make sense of the world—especially moral and practical sense—confront all young people, perhaps especially now that vulgar poststructuralism and relativism are so powerful. Even the most theory-besotted student who will quote (probably without having properly read) Nietzsche and Foucault on every other occasion will pause before saying that pain is culturally constructed, not to mention genocide.

But it seems to me that the Neimanian *Fragestellung* illuminates post-Kantian philosophy better than the pre-Kantian. It shines a way back, but the light cast is pretty dim by the time you get to the 17th century. The early modern philosophers wrote a lot about Providence, but they were not asking the questions that structure work on the problem of evil in the 19th and 20th centuries.

By and large, our students aren't either. The recent efflorescence of academic writing on evil concentrates on "moral evil" and regards the problem of "natural evil" as moot. Not so our students, who are horrified at moral evils but also grieve illnesses, deaths, and the depression-induced suicides of their friends. Further, they realize that one of the biggest questions bridges the distinction between "natural evil" and "moral evil": the world seems so fertile for evil that a single madman can lead a nation to a war which kills 50 million or, to take this beyond the fetishization of human wills, that a single badly designed presidential ballot can... You could call this metaphysical evil, but you needn't. I prefer to see it as a backward way of recognizing that moral evils wouldn't bother us nearly so much were we not so vulnerable to being hurt by them and other evils. (Neiman recognizes something like this in *Evil in Modern Thought* but sees it as an artifact of the 20th century; she doesn't connect it to our vulnerable existence as social animals on the third rock from the sun.) It is because goodness is fragile that evil so troubles us.

HISTORICIZING THE PROBLEM

I, too, have taught many courses on the problem of evil, including the Bayle-to-Kant sequence Neiman describes. Frankly, I have lost my enthusiasm for it. My own research into the sources and precursors of 18th-century theodicy has led me to see Leibniz, inventor of the word *theodicy*, as seeking not to ground a philosophical discourse on Providence but rather to drive it into the ground as fruitless and unnecessary, a distraction not only from science and piety but also from ethics (which are, for him, much the same thing). The Bayle-to-Kant story line now seems to me like reading only the second half of *Wuthering Heights*, where Heathcliff destroys Kathy's kids. The best part of the story is over before we even begin.

But this is precisely not a reason not to approach early modern philosophy by means of the problem of evil. It is only a warning that it matters how we teach it or, to put it another way, that it has much to teach us even about what questions to ask, if we let it.

One thing coming at early modern philosophy from the problem of evil does is show that it is irresponsible to teach early modern philosophy as if it's sui generis. As Jill Kraye has reminded us, we sever the early modern period from the Renaissance at our peril. Early modern philosophy not only arose in the face of the breakdown of ecclesiastical authority, the scientific revolutions, the emergence of the autonomy of politics and ethics, and empire but also was articulated in the context of the revival of ancient philosophies, especially the Hellenistic philosophies of Stoicism, Epicureanism, and Skepticism.

(One question any course on early modern thought should raise is what the early moderns thought was new about what they were doing and whether it really was. For this reason, the course I will propose starts with Hume's *Dialogues* but goes directly back to its model, Cicero's *On the nature of the gods*, and then assigns enough of *City of God* for students to realize that cogito ergo sum isn't new—but also that what Descartes does with it is.)

Nowhere is the Hellenistic flavor of modern discussion more evident than in reflection on evil, because, as Hume wisely noted in characterizing the problem as "Epicurus's old questions," the modern problem of evil is a Hellenistic one. Almost every claim made in 17th-

and 18th-century discussions of evil is scooped by debates between ancient Skeptics, Epicureans, and Stoics on Providence.

Neiman doesn't highlight this, because she doesn't sufficiently historicize her questions. She suggests that "our concepts of reason are more centrally at stake in the underlying question of the problem of evil than our concepts of God" (17). But this claim too has a history. The claim is that "theodicy is really logodicy," to borrow a term from Foucher de Careil over a century ago. And the turn of the 20th century is where Neiman's *Fragestellung* comes from. Her trajectory of texts and figures can be traced to the largely Neo-Kantian histories of philosophy written to face down the threats of Schopenhauerian pessimism and Nietzsche's alternative at the start of the 20th century. (This is presumably why Neiman has to tweak her syllabus in order not to end with Nietzsche.)

One can go in very interesting directions with the Neo-Kantian approach. Think of the extraordinarily illuminating account of the development of religious ideas Max Weber develops out of the idea that intellectuals, motivated by the desire to see the world as a "meaningful cosmos," rub up against the "ethical irrationality of the world" and so shape and reshape religious ideas. Like Neiman, Weber thinks the end of the process is the utter disenchantment of the world.

But this is not the only story one could tell. The American contemporaries of Windelband, Lempp, and Cassirer were also obsessed by the problem of evil, but they were haunted not by Schopenhauer and Nietzsche but by Schopenhauer and Darwin. From the perspective of their concern, the alternatives of Schopenhauer, Nietzsche, and (Neo-)Kant are just too few. All are forms of flight from the fact of our vulnerability to the world—Stoic sour grapes at a cosmos shown to be indifferent to us and our values or, at least, resistant to our attempts to make sense of it as a whole. One of the contributions of *Evil in Modern Thought* is its frank admission that this Neo-Stoic approach ends in conceptual bankruptcy. After Arendt's Eichmann, the world we too hastily threw away has claimed our humanity, too.

To avoid this dead end, one might approach early modern philosophy's wrestlings with the problem of evil through the work of

Hans Blumenberg. When Blumenberg links Epicurus, Marcion, nominalism and the modern age, it is not in the interest of presenting the modern as derivative. Precisely the opposite. The modern is "legitimate" because it takes a fundamentally different approach to the world than its theological predecessors: the world is not designed for us, but it is a place we can up to a point make our own, if we figure out how. This Epicurean alternative is tempting after the spontaneous combustion of Kanto-Stoic views in the crucible of 20th-century history.

Blumenberg's questions strike me as more pertinent than Windelband's, but I'm not throwing my lot in with them, either. Epicureanism is a refreshing alternative to the head trip of modern Stoicism, not to mention to its meltdown, but one thirsts for a richer sense of evils and of goods than the Hellenistic philosophies, in ancient or modern form, offer. One thirsts for Aristotle, for Plotinus, or even for Augustine. I want my world back, with all its heartbreak. I worry that the hegemony of Hellenistic questions and Kantian answers in modern normative reflection prevents us from doing justice to the horror of nonmoral evil and so, unintentionally, feeds the paralyzed complacency toward evil that is one of the plagues of our times.

QUESTIONING EVIL AND GOOD TOO

So, what can we do? I've mentioned three ways of approaching evil and modern thought: Neiman's Neo-Kantian view, Blumenberg's Neo-Epicurean one, and the broader claim that modern thought on evil is framed in Hellenistic terms. An alternative account of the problem of evil is afforded by seeing it as a dualist question with origins in Manicheanism. (Both the Neo-Kantians and Blumenberg think they've acknowledged this, but I think they have not really realized its significance.)

Bayle claimed to find the explanations Manichean dualism offers for the mix of good and evil in the world more persuasive than Catholic natural theology (who wouldn't?), but he was no Manichee. He was a thoroughly modern mix of skeptic, Epicurean, and fideist. As Neiman helps us see, he is concerned not with the nature of God but with reason. Reason's inability to make its mind up between monism and dualism shows its insufficiency. Mani is just a character in Bayle's skeptical spectacle of the self-immolation of reason. Bayle was not really tempted by metaphysical dualism. He was haunted not by the thought that God faces an evil enemy but by the worry raised already in the Book of Job—that God himself is evil. A frightening thought, even after Descartes despatches the evil genius, but not a Manichee one.

The Manichee question, the dualist question, is fundamentally different from this. It's not about the fact that there is evil that is hard to account for. It's about the fact that there's also good and that this is every bit as hard to account for as evil— maybe even harder, since there is so much evil. The nicest formulation of this question that I know of appears in Boethius's *Consolation of Philosophy* (although Boethius himself is too Stoic to pay it much heed): "If there be a God, from whence proceed so many evils? And if there be no God, from whence cometh any good?" Epicurus's old questions represent only half the problem for the questioner astonished, troubled, and provoked to wonder and philosophy by evil and good.

It is the near unintelligibility to us of what one might call the problem of good that makes late modern reflection on evil a dead end, trapping us with the Hellenistic philosophers but without the world. We live in times for which the reality of evil is more compelling than that of good. Darwinian ideas and the market have between them explained away what used to be the wonders of function and order in our experience of the world and of ourselves. They have redefined the joys of human flourishing as expendable commodities ("goods") of ultimately indifferent value, perhaps because everyone is thought to have a slightly different, restlessly wandering, and ultimately insatiable appetite. Evil alone seems real, permanent, final, universal, objective.

I cannot count the number of times students have told me that evil is necessary in order that we be able to recognize good by contrast, as though we're apt to misrecognize goodness or order or beauty or justice. Goodness not self-evident? From the perspective of most of the early modern philosophers, this is backward and inside out. Evil and good are not simple contraries. More fundamentally, evil is parasitic on good. Good alone is real, if fragile. As Leibniz saw, a proper understanding of any given evil leaves you at the doorstep of the mystery of there being anything at all.

Already at Leibniz's time, the idea that evil was privation seemed to many little more than a rather tasteless play on words. It is easy to point to the substantiality of evil—the malicious will, the distended belly of the malnourished child, the gated community—which seems more than the absence or perversion of good. (It's harder to spell this out.) But who talks anymore about the ways in which good exceeds the absence of evil? The world is heartrendingly fertile for evil, but is it not also astonishingly fecund of good?

We don't even know how to think this anymore.

Happily, there is early modern philosophy to help us. Arguably, articulating the wondrous fecundity of good, indeed of being, of substance itself, is part of what Spinoza's necessity discloses. It is what the fertility of the general wills of Malebranche's God reveals. It is part of what Leibniz (and predecessors like the Cambridge Platonists) meant by harmony. It is in the precritical Kant, and in the analogical effusions of Herder. Crucially, none of these is about making the world as a whole into a "meaningful cosmos."

A COURSE

The course on early modern philosophy I envision narrates how Hellenistic philosophy's inert ways of making sense of the world won out over the many expressions of wonder that characterized the ages of discovery. Tracing the shifting typology of evils is an important part of this. But equally important is probing the kinds of goods these evils were thought to compromise. The key lies in good questions. The problem of evil will draw us toward less familiar but more fundamental questions about the problem of good—and why it no longer seems problematic to us.

Let students see why it could have been thought that goods are things that grow in being shared, that good is something you participate in, or that being itself is good. Jerry Schneewind has shown how important the standoff between voluntarism and its critics was for the emergence of modern moral philosophy. Students need to see that both voluntarists and antivoluntarists, while in the end chasing God from the world, intended to reinforce a wonder at the world they thought their opponents too easily took for granted. Let them see why (or at least that) wonder was dropped from the philosophic menu.

I hope this is more than nostalgia for views of the world that have bceome irretrievably lost—not because I wish to turn back time but because I fear our resources for facing evil in our own time are woefully thin without them. The problem of evil cannot stand on its own. If our purchase on good is lost, then so, surely, is our purchase on evil. One can be approached in as "postmetaphysical" a way as the other, or neither can.

Suggestion for a Syllabus: Evil and Wonder
in Early Modern Philosophy

The course is designed to introduce great and less-well-known works of philosophy from the early modern period, to raise questions about the newness of the modern, to historicize questions and categories we take for granted (like the distinction between *is* and *ought*, the coherence of the problem of evil, etc.), and to make students aware of the importance of dialogue.

- Hume, *Dialogues concerning natural religion* (esp. bks. 10 and 11)
- Cicero, *On the nature of the gods*
- Augustine, *City of God* xi.16-xii.8
- Descartes, *Meditations* (excerpts)
- Thomas Traherne, *Centuries of meditation* (excerpts)
- Anne Conway, *Principles of the most ancient and modern philosophy*
- Spinoza, Ethics (excerpts including appendix to Book 1)
- Malebranche, *Dialogues on metaphysics and religion* (excerpts)
- Bayle, *Historical and critical dictionary* ("Epicurus," main text and rems. N, R, S, T; "Manichees," main text and rem. D; "Paulicians," rems. D, M)
- Leibniz, *Theodicy* (excerpts including preface and Myth of Sextus)
- Leibniz, "Principles of nature and grace"
- Pope, *An essay on man* (only if you keep Traherne)
- Voltaire, "Zadig," "Poem on the disaster of Lisbon," "Letter from J. J. Rousseau to M. de Voltaire"
- Rousseau, *Discourse on the arts and sciences*
- Kant, *The only possible argument in support of a demonstration of the existence of God* (excerpts)
- Kant, *Critique of judgment* (introduction, antinomy of teleological judgment and its resolution, etc.)
- Herder, *Ideas* (excerpts)
- Kant, "On the failure of all philosophical efforts in theodicy"

The Forgetting of Gender

Nancy Tuana

When one reads historical works covering long spans of time there are no more traces of our names to be found than there are traces to be found of a vessel crossing the ocean.

—*Anna Maria van Schurman*

As WE DESIGN our courses in the history of modern philosophy, whether done as a survey in one or two semesters for our beginning majors or as more intense author/theme courses for our advanced majors and graduate students, there are a series of values and beliefs embedded into the structure of our courses. These include decisions about which individuals count as the great philosophers and those whose work was influential on the development of their work. Though the canon shifts historically and is often an issue of some dispute between the traditions within philosophy, we seldom make this fact a theme of our courses.[1] Our course design also embeds values concerning which texts and which topics are the most important to study and why. Woven into our courses are assumptions concerning the purpose of teaching the history of philosophy. Are these courses designed to prepare the student for more detailed historical work, or are they intended to provide an introduction to contemporary philosophical concerns? And if the latter, which contemporary concerns are our focus?[2]

One of the questions for which feminist philosophy (and other forms of feminist theorizing) has become famous is the *whose* question. Whose science? Whose knowledge? And particularly relevant to the concerns of the new histories of philosophy, Whose history?

Feminist philosophy proceeds from the premise that gender is an important lens for analysis. Our work begins with attention to women, to their roles and locations: What are women doing? What social/political locations are they part of or excluded from? How do their activities compare with those of men? What do women's roles and locations allow or preclude? How have their roles been valued or devalued? To this we add attention to the experiences and concerns of women: Have any of women's experiences or problems been ignored or undervalued? How might attention to these transform our current methods or values? And from here we move to the realm of the symbolic: How is the feminine instantiated and constructed within the texts of philosophy? What role does the feminine play in forming, through either its absence or its presence, the central concepts of philosophy?

Although hardly unique in this respect, contemporary history of philosophy is complicit in a wider societal pattern of attention to men and the masculine role.[3] Women, though never fully ignored, are often relegated to a minor role, located in realms considered less important or influential, rendered a "helpmeet" to man, and then forgotten. The history of philosophy has played a large role in the forgetting of gender in the realm of philosophy. Our canon almost completely excludes the writings of women, and little attention has been given to the experiences or concerns of women or to the role of the feminine.

Feminist work in the history of philosophy is dedicated to evoking gender. In the case of the history of philosophy, this focus bifurcates along the axes of (a) attention to women and (b) investigation of the symbolic imaginary related to feminine/masculine. This essay is a plea to undo the forgetting of gender by theorizing its absence and presence in the teaching of the history of philosophy. My essay is designed to provide an overview of the complexity of this task, as well as a sense of what is gained in the process. It will be my contention that the issue of gender is not simply a question of equity. Recalling gender calls into question models of philosophy and philosophical concepts that emerge from and rely on the forgetting of gender. Adding gender to our history of philosophy courses enriches them by helping us recover the value(s) of our task.

THE QUESTION OF WOMEN

The question of canon formation is one that can be and has been raised without attention to gender. Similarly there are far more reasons than that of gender for the exclusion of philosophers from the history of philosophy text or classroom. But what happens when we bring gender to these concerns?

One response of feminist philosophers is to decry the forgetting of women philosophers and to recover their voices and contributions to the history of philosophy. Therese Dykeman in her introduction to *The Neglected Canon: Nine Women Philosophers—First to the Twentieth Century* invokes "truth" as a justification for the study of women philosophers.

> The challenge of history here ruffles the waters of "truth" capsizing false assumptions about women's contributions to the philosophical canon. Denied ready access to education, ill recognized, and often, therefore, wielding little influence, women have been, however, philosophers, and in the face of impossibility, by using innovatively every philosophical and rhetorical method available to them, women have written philosophy. These anthologized works are testaments to their achievements and to philosophy's fuller "truth." Hence they mandate careful and rigorous study (1999, xvi).

For Dykeman, the recovery of the work of philosophers like Mary Astell, Sor Juana Inés de la Cruz, Judith Sargent Murray, and Anna Maria van Schurman is part of an effort to convey a more accurate picture of the chronicle of philosophers and their contributions to the fundamental philosophical questions of their time.

There is significant controversy over the enterprise of writing the history of philosophy. For some, it is a chronicle of worthies, those great minds whose work shaped philosophy. The problem here is, of course, the evaluative. Genius and influence are not self-evident. So we often try to clarify and justify the basis of our evaluation by defining the history of philosophy as a story of the emergence and development of philosophical commitments and concerns that manifests a progression of order and clarity. There are problems here too, of course, many of which have been addressed by the scholars who are part of this symposium, including the issue of how we go about defining which questions and concerns are the most central to the doing of philosophy.

Despite the controversy, I doubt there would be significant disagreement about the influence or impact of philosophers like those chronicled by Dykeman. History classes are all too brief—and often, few and far in-between in the education of the typical philosophy major. How can we justify devoting time to, say, the work of Anna Maria van Schurman when there is hardly time to cover the work of Descartes or Spinoza, not to mention Gassendi? True, her work was influential in her time, but it has hardly passed the test of time. So perhaps her exclusion and that of many other women philosophers is simply justified.

If the task of a course in the history of philosophy is simply to chronicle those whose work has most informed our contemporary concerns, then I would be at the end of my essay.[4] But there is more to say here, a more that has to do with canon formation and the process by which certain voices are omitted from the canon.

I hope it goes without saying to our 21st-century students that the fact that the contemporary philosophical canon includes only the work of men (and primarily those of certain social standings) is a reflection of the social ordering of society and not the intellectual capacities of women. Few of us now debate the questions prevalent in the modern period concerning whether women were even capable of higher intellectual endeavors or whether efforts to educate women would lead to their physical or spiritual downfall, indeed perhaps even the devolution of society. We now take for granted that the reordering of society to allow for more equity between women and men will result in our future canons' including the work of women philosophers. Even if our students do not know the details, I predict they would surmise, if asked, that the exclusion of women from higher education and the gendered expectations of a life devoted to the private realm explain the exclusion of women from the history of philosophy. Though I like this sensibility far better than the long-standing belief in women as the less noble sex, it too presents a distorted lens.

The nature of this distortion has become apparent only as contemporary historians of philosophy have devoted their attention to the work of women. Feminist philosophers of history, like Mary Ellen Waite, Therese Dykeman, and Eileen O'Neill, who have devoted their attention to women philosophers have identified the work of more than a hundred women philosophers from the ancient period to the 19th century whose work was published and preserved.

If our students conclude from the absence of women philosophers in their texts and classes to the general exclusion of women from the practices of philosophy because of social conditions, they will have internalized a distortion that has been relatively recently constructed.

O'Neill in "Disappearing Ink: Early Modern Women Philosophers and Their Fate in History" turns her attention to an explanation for women's almost complete absence in contemporary histories of philosophy, identifying the 18th and 19th centuries as pivotal to their disappearance. Noting both the relatively robust presence of women philosophers in 17th-century standard histories of philosophy, O'Neill examines the reasons the list of women narrows to a small handful by the 19th century and the reasons women philosophers are virtually absent from histories of philosophy written after that time. Arguing that their absence in 19th-century histories is not reflective of ignorance of the work of women philosophers, O'Neill identifies other factors. First is the "purification" of philosophy. "By allying philosophy motivated by religious concerns with an unreflective mysticism, 18th-century historians excised whole philosophical schools, and the work of many women, from philosophy proper" (1998, 34). Second, the work of other women, such as Schurman and Conway, disappeared because their ideas or worldview did not win out. But equally important, O'Neill says that philosophy that becomes "unfashionable" is often characterized as feminine and thus worthy of forgetting. "The alignment of the feminine gender with the issues, methods, and styles that 'lost out,' together with a good deal of slippage between gender and sex, and the scholarly practice of anonymous authorship for women, led to the almost complete disappearance of women from the history of early modern philosophy" (1998, 36).

Although the above-mentioned three factors explain much of women's "disappearing ink," O'Neill argues that to explain the striking absence of women's philosophical contributions in the 19th century, we must look outside philosophy to the aftermath of the French Revolution and anxieties about how to maintain a system of male rule predicated on sexual difference in the context of ideals of a common humanity and an egalitarian social order.

Hence, the common inability of current students of philosophy, not even to mention practicing philosophers, to list 10 women philosophers from the modern period has nothing to do with the absence of women from the practice of philosophy but with complex values that inform the narratives of philosophy. I hope it is becoming clear that by continuing to engender the opacity of these values in our history of philosophy courses we are being epistemically and ethically irresponsible.

THE QUESTION OF STYLE

A lesson that feminists have been trying to teach us for centuries is that to the extent that a profession or calling is defined in terms of practices gendered male, it should be no surprise that women's activities in this realm will be deemed less worthy. What if we take seriously the fact that women were for the most part excluded from the institutions central to philosophical training in the modern period—the university, the scientific academy, and the seminary—and look to those locations where women's erudition was cultivated? Rather than identifying only those exceptional women who gained entrance to the university or the scientific academy, what if we looked for alternative sites?

John J. Conley in his *Suspicion of Virtue: Women Philosophers in Neoclassical France* argues that if we limit our histories of 17th-century philosophy to the realm of the university, then women philosophers will end up maintaining only secondary roles to male philosophers—Descartes's correspondent, Spinoza's critic.[5] Conley argues instead for exploring "the distinctively feminine sites of philosophy, like the salon and the convent" (2002, 16). It is his position that if we are to accurately understand women's contributions to philosophy, then we must foreground the venues in which women pursued philosophical inquiry. In the 17th century this means taking the salons seriously and understanding the impact of women's education in convent schools.

Conley's text is devoted to a study of the critique of virtue developed by five women philosophers of the neoclassical period: Madeleine de Souvré, Marquise de Sablé; Antionette du Ligier de la Garde, Mme Deshoulières; Marguerite Hessein, Madame de la Sablière; Françoise d'Aubigné, Marquise de Maintenon; and Louise-Françoise de la Baume Le Blanc, Mademoiselle del al Vallière. Conley traces in their writings a sustained argument about the nature of virtues and an account of the moral dispositions.

He argues that one of the impacts of this different site of philosophy is the preference for a literary rather than a scientific mode of argument. Rather than the treatise of the university and seminary, members of the salon perfected the letter, the memoir, the novel, maxims, poetry, tales, and devotional works. "Reflecting the education curriculum for women and the dominant concerns of salon debate, these works focused on moral philosophy, especially questions of moral psychology: the problem of moral freedom, the virtues, the will" (2002, 11). Conley defends the inclusion of these texts as public, systematic works in moral philosophy that compose "an alternative to, and not only a derivation of, the philosophy produced by the canonical male theorists of the period" (2002, 16).

These nontreatise works present the contemporary philosopher with a particular challenge. Trained as we are to embrace and evaluate a particular style of writing—the treatise, the journal article, the professional presentation—we, and our students, are often ill equipped to fully comprehend, much less assess, these genres. Indeed, to the extent that we have elevated the rational, objective, universal style of much of contemporary philosophy, the personal, situated, individual style of such writings renders their philosophical status questionable. But this fact in itself calls into question the contemporary enterprise of teaching the history of philosophy. Surely no one would argue that a tradition and its value should be excluded simply because its genre is currently unfashionable.

Although it is certainly not the case that nontreatise works have been completely excluded from the canon of modern philosophy— we need only remember the prayers of Pascal or the dialogues of Berkeley—those advocating the inclusion of women's philosophical writings must deal with the fact that the majority of women doing philosophy in the modern period used literary genres. This fact presents a cluster of questions typically ignored in many histories of modern philosophy: When and why did certain genres come to be designated as unsuitable for philosophical reflection? Is there any correlation between a genre's being marked suitable or unsuitable for philosophical reflection and that genre being typed as either feminine or masculine? Do the various genres that have been excluded provide resources for doing philosophy, or do they affect the content of philosophical concerns in ways that are lost when we shift to the treatise format? What is lost, for example, when we no longer expect the emotions that the form of the writing produces in us to be part of the overall argument of the author? Are the contemporary demarcations between philosophical and non-philosophical works simply reflections of contemporary models of philosophy being imposed on past philosophical practices, and should that fact call into question the adequacy of our contemporary models of philosophy?

Granted these are complex questions that cannot be fully addressed in our classes, but to simply ignore them is to close off our students to these crucial issues. What should be clear at this point is that we cannot approach the issue of adding women philosophers to the canon without also rethinking the values and models embedded in current practices of canon formation and norms informing our history of philosophy courses.

THE STANDPOINT OF WOMEN

In their book *Presenting Women Philosophers,* Cecile T. Tougas and Sara Ebenrick say that many of the contemporary women studying and teaching philosophy:

> have found that the traditional "canon" of academic philosophy in the West does not satisfy us. In seeking what was missing from it, we—and sometimes our male colleagues, too—have turned to examine the work of women thinkers. In doing so, we wondered if there were women philosophers before the 20th century whose writing could help fulfill our need for what we felt was missing (2000, xv).

For some, a quote like this rings a warning bell. To assume simply because a philosopher is a woman that she will do philosophy differently from a man is to invoke an essentialism concerning differences between men and women. Many feminist theorists have critiqued the long history of such essentializing, demonstrating that women's alleged difference is too often (always already?) marked as inferior. Doesn't a claim like that of Tougas and Ebenrick simply fall into the same trap feminists have been decrying for centuries? To answer this, let me return again to Conley's argument. Part of his thesis is that the "feminine site of philosophy" marked these women's texts in a manner far more profound than mere style.

Gender analysis not only identifies certain traits of tone or style as reflective of women's experience; it clarifies why certain virtues, such as fortitude or glory, recede in these authors' works, and why other virtues, such as civility, are in the ascendant. It also explores sex-specific reasons that these authors criticize certain virtues esteemed by men (Maintenon) and why they distance themselves from a distinctively male critique of virtue (Sablé) (2002, 18).

In other words, a careful study of the philosophical work of women philosophers leads to the surprising conclusion that the sex of the philosopher can be epistemically significant. However, it is equally important to understand that this significance is not the result of some essential nature separating women and men but that it arises from the fact that the questions and concerns we have as philosophers are not divorced from the values we inherit from our social locations or from our experiences.[6]

Though interesting in itself, this insight provides another answer to the question of why we should consider opening our histories of philosophy and—I would argue, our courses—to the work of women philosophers. If the dominant model of philosophy privileges the experiences and concerns of certain groups of men, then we have a basis for questioning the adequacy of this model (not to mention an explanation for the reason that women and some groups of men have the experience of something being missing from standard philosophical courses). Although I do not deny the value of tracing the history of the exclusion of women's (and some men's) experiences and concerns from the canons of philosophy, it is not this topic that I think is most relevant to our courses in the history of philosophy. Rather, I would strongly advocate the inclusion of the positive project of employing women's philosophical work as a lens to interrogate and potentially improve the dominant model of philosophy—a task well worthy of our courses in the history of philosophy.

Catherine Villanueva Gardner, in *Rediscovering Women Philosophers: Philosophical Genre and the Boundaries of Philosophy*, argues that recovery of the work of women philosophers, particularly in the realm of moral thought, can provide resources for enhancing contemporary moral theory. Gardner argues that the dominant model of moral theory emphasizes concerns associated with the public sphere and is focused on the roles and ideals of socially advantaged men, which "lend themselves well to being addressed or dealt with through the creation and use of sets of rules, principles, or beliefs…for agent behavior" (2000, 6). She claims that this model leaves little room for the role of the emotions or the imagination in moral decision making and demands an impersonal approach in moral activity, calling certain genres and topics into question and thereby becoming mutually reinforcing. Gardner examines the work of five women philosophers—Catharine Macaulay, Christine De Pisan, Mary Wollstonecraft, George Eliot, and Mechthild of Magdeburg—and argues that the form and content of their writing can be used to present a challenge to the dominant model of moral philosophy. It is her contention that their delineation of the sphere and concerns of the moral realm "has its roots in their experience as women, of their awareness of themselves as women, or of their awareness of the social imitations of their sex" (2000, 181).

Gardner argues that Mary Wollstonecraft presents such a challenge to the dominant model of contemporary moral philosophy in that a complex notion of genuine sensibility is central to her view of morality: "…sensibility becomes intertwined with the creative imagination, moral and social progress, and the equality of women. Yet this notion of sensibility is not simply the subject of her work, it is also a part of her work in the sense that it is expressed through the form of her work" (2000, 13). Wollstonecraft employs a writing style that exemplifies sensibility in order to invoke in the reader an understanding of its importance. Gardner argues that if we define the genres of philosophy in such a way as to exclude texts like those of Wollstonecraft's, we will thereby exclude important resources for understanding the role the passions play in moral philosophy. Wollstonecraft is thus a resource for enhancing or transforming contemporary moral philosophy in that she offers a model of virtue in which reason and sensibility mutually strengthen and support one another.

Gardner's overall point is that the initial delineation of the sphere of morality grounding the currently dominant model of moral theory itself arises from a particular standpoint and is not morally neutral.

She argues "that the valuing of, and desire for, neutrality and objectivity are themselves moral judgments grounded in a particular view of the world, a view that…is male biased" (2000, 180). The inclusion of the previously forgotten standpoints of some women philosophers provides a speculum for revealing and perhaps questioning the moral judgments underlying contemporary moral theorizing.

Once again we see that the inclusion of the philosophical writings of women in our histories of philosophy is far more than an issue of equity; it is an issue of the adequacy of our contemporary models and genres.

THE ISSUE OF WOMAN

That there were women in philosophy refracts our original question—Whose history?—in a multifaceted manner. The fact of women's presence suggests that philosophy was more open to women than contemporary histories of philosophy have led us to believe. This realization requires complex investigations to fully understand this aspect of the forgetting of gender. But then we are left with the concern that perhaps the problem was not the exclusion of women from philosophy but the denigration of that realm and those characteristics associated with women. And indeed, one feminist approach to the history of philosophy is to suggest that the problem is far more complex than a mere prohibition of women. Those of us who raise the question of women and the history of philosophy turn our attention to the received canon to examine philosophers' accounts of women and the related question of their conceptions of femininity.

One does not have to look far to find examples of philosophers who viewed women as inferior to men. I have argued that the Aristotelian conception of women as lesser or misbegotten men has had a profound structuring impact on the history of philosophical conceptions of men as the true form and women as inferior (Tuana, 1993). Similarly, Luce Irigaray (1985a) has argued that woman has been defined not in terms of true difference from men but in terms of lack according to an A (male) –A (female) logic. Men are the true form; woman the deviation. Men are rational animals; women, less capable of reason. As just one example as illustrative of a genre:

Women are capable of education, but they are not made for activities which demand a universal faculty such as the more advanced sciences, philosophy, and certain forms of artistic production.... Women regulate their actions not by the demands of universality, but by arbitrary inclinations and opinions (Hegel 1973, 8).

Not only will those reading philosophy find numerous instances of women being judged to be inferior to men; they will also find women are often presented as "other" rather than as the subject of the text. Again, just one instance:

Woman, who is weak and who sees nothing outside the house, estimates and judges the forces she can put to work to make up for her weakness, and those forces are men's passions. Her science of mechanics is more powerful than ours: all her levers unsettle the human heart. She must have the art to make us want to do everything which her sex cannot do by itself and which is necessary or agreeable to it (Rousseau 1979, 387).

It is to a man, albeit a man of the white European upper class, that Rousseau addresses this passage. This fact situates the reader of philosophy along the lines of gender. For the man who reads this text, whether or not he agrees with Rousseau, whether or not the foregoing passage represents his experience, the discourse constructs him as Subject. It is he to whom Rousseau speaks. The woman reading Rousseau realizes immediately that she is the Object of the discourse; she is presented as Other. The woman philosopher/ philosophy student reading Rousseau finds herself confronted by a paradox. She is, on one hand, being defined as Other; on the other hand, as a philosopher, she is invited to identify herself as subject, yet a subject that is defined as male.

It is tempting when coming across a philosopher's sexism to argue that they were, after all, simply men (and women[7]) of their time. It thus is not surprising or philosophically relevant that these philosophers would internalize and reproduce such societal biases. The problem with this response is that it assumes that their sexism has not been inscribed on the central categories of their theories—what it is to be rational, to be moral, to be a political agent. As feminist philosophers began to pay attention to canonical philosophers' views on women, we discovered that the sexism ran far deeper than false beliefs about women. We discovered that certain traits or abilities were being defined as gendered, that is, marked as masculine or feminine.

Feminist reading strategies not only of focusing attention on a philosopher's views of women but also of attending to how concepts are marked as either masculine or feminine offers another response to Tougas's and Ebenrick's experience of philosophical texts' not being satisfying to women. If, as Genevicvc Lloyd argues, "rationality has been conceived as the transcendence of the feminine; and the 'feminine' itself has been partly constituted by its occurrence within this structure" (1984, 104), then the gender bias cannot simply be ignored or judged philosophically insignificant. To the extent that the central categories of philosophy have been inscribed in this way, not only is philosophy *not* the objective, universal practice many philosophers have believed it to be; it is also complicit in a social organization that impoverishes the lives of women as well as men.

THE EXCLUSION OF THE FEMININE

One of the common themes in feminist histories of philosophy is the contention that many of the central categories of philosophy are formed through the exclusion of the feminine. In a complex, two-step process, concepts like reason, morality, and agency are produced through the prioritizing of masculine characteristics and the forgetting of gender. The concepts so constructed are then posited as objective and universal rather than gendered and particular. To give you a sense of this reading strategy and of its complexities, consider feminist investigations of the maleness of reason.

Given the widespread acceptance of the view within philosophical and other contexts that rational abilities are at the core of what it is to be human as well as our conceptions of what it is to be of good character or live a good life, conceptions of reason quickly became a central axis for feminist investigation. The question of the maleness of reason may be what is behind common judgments of women as less capable of rational thought, but the question itself is far more complex. To investigate the maleness of reason, we must consider the extent to which conceptions of rationality have privileged traits historically associated with masculinity. In other words, we must consider the extent to which the attainment of rationality has been perceived as involving the control or transcendence of attributes historically identified as female—the body, the emotions, the passions, the appetites, sensuousness. If it is the case that what Michèle Le Dœuff has called the philosophical imagery of gender (1989) is inscribed onto a philosopher's conception of reason, then we cannot simply ignore his—or her—sexism, for it is at the core of the values from which this central category emerges.

An obvious example here is Descartes, who makes a distinction between reason, on one hand, and the "fluctuating testimony of the senses" and the "blundering constructions of imagination" on the other (1955c, 157). The senses and the imagination are excluded from the realm of reason because these faculties are subjective and thus, according to Descartes, only impede the quest for certainty. Descartes did not deny that the ability to be rational was difficult to attain; he advocated rigorous discipline and training to develop it. But not only is there nothing overtly sexist about this conception of reason; Descartes did not perceive this capacity as limited to men. Indeed, he saw his method as opening the way to a new egalitarianism in knowledge. "The power of forming a good judgment and of distinguishing the true from the false, which is properly speaking what is called good sense or reason, is by nature equal in all men" (1955b, 356). "Even those who have the feeblest souls can acquire a very absolute dominion over all their passions if sufficient industry is applied in training and guiding them" (1955a, 81). A woman, just like a man, through training and careful attention, is capable of learning to ignore her emotions, her appetites, and all things relating to the body. But feminists do not conclude from this that Descartes's "man" of reason is gender neutral. Indeed, in this we take our cue from Elisabeth, Princess Palatine, Abbess of Herford, correspondent of Descartes.

Elisabeth in her correspondence with Descartes called attention to a problem with his method:

[T]he life that I am constrained to lead does not allow me enough free time to acquire a habit of meditation in accordance with your rules. Sometimes the interests of my household, which I must not neglect, sometimes conversations and civilities, I cannot eschew, so thoroughly deject this weak mind with annoyances or boredom that it remains, for a long time afterward, useless for anything else (Blom 1978, 111, Princess Elisabeth to Descartes 10/20 June 1643).

Genevieve Lloyd in *The Man of Reason: "Male" and "Female" in Western Philosophy* argues that "it is not just impinging social realities, however, which militate against sexual equality...there are aspects of Descartes's thought which—however unintentionally—provided a basis for a sexual division of mental labour whose influence is still very much with us" (1984, 49). She argues that the sharpness of his separation of the ultimate requirements of truth seeking from the practical affairs of ordinary life reinforced already existing distinctions between male and female roles, "opening the way to the idea of distinctive male and female consciousness" (1984, 50). Women, historically defined by qualities that directly contradict Descartes's requirements for rationality—passion, body, sensuousness, emotion, passivity—would have to both transcend their female characteristics and reject their female roles (maternal feelings, attachment to individuals, etc.) to attain a rational life. It makes little sense, given this, to argue that Descartes's conception is gender neutral.

To make this point is not, of course, the end of the story but, rather, the beginning. Once we have overcome the forgetting of gender and have begun to trace the contours of its inscription on the history of philosophy, we can begin to reassess not only these categories but also the very purpose of writing and rewriting histories of philosophy.

THE STANDPOINT OF FEMINISTS

Feminist philosophy in attending to the denigration of the feminine in the history of philosophy presents an important step, but one that must be seen as a first step of a much larger inquiry. Our chronicles of the gendering of the central concepts of philosophy are not to be taken as subscribing to a view of past history as a series of errors that current philosophers can now correct or as a justification for simply rejecting philosophy as unredeemably sexist. What feminist historians of philosophy discovered is that we could not defend female capabilities without challenging the gendered norms that contributed to women's being marginalized. This realization led to various efforts to identify and affirm the feminine (Irigaray) and to examine the specifically feminine sites of philosophy (Conley).

What we are now developing are reading strategies often motivated by our feminist commitments and our previous work in the history of philosophy that contribute to a deeper engagement with the texts of philosophy. These strategies emerge out of the earlier work on the gendering of the central concepts of philosophy and employ it and more recent attempts to reclaim the feminine as a basis for developing an enriched historiography that foregrounds forgotten elements of texts, as well as ignored authors, to advance new ways of thinking about reason, morality, and other philosophical concepts. Once we chronicled the denigration of feminine traits and the reasons for the forgetting of gender, we could begin to participate in new ways of reading historical texts that permitted or enacted unifications of emotion, intellect, and imagination. That is, we began to identify resources for engendering the central concepts of philosophy in ways not predicated on the forgetting of gender. These reading strategies are diverse and reflect the different positions and training of feminists themselves. Some, like Michèle Le Dœuff, Penelope Deutscher, Sara Kofman, and Luce Irigaray, bring decon-structive methods to bear on canonical texts. Others, like Annette Baier and Barbara Herman, read through the lens of contemporary feminist revaluing of the emotions. Yet others, like John Conley and Susan James, work to recover forgotten voices and themes.

Let me return to Descartes to provide an illustration of feminist reading strategies. Naomi Scheman in "Though This Be Method, Yet There Is Madness in It: Paranoia and Liberal Epistemology" (1992) argues that it was not so much Descartes himself but later readings and applications of his philosophy that are to blame for the denigration of the emotions. This insight led to a recovery of aspects of Descartes's philosophy that had been forgotten by many feminist and nonfeminist theorists[8] and a rereading of the potential of Cartesian views.

Linda Shapiro in "Princess Elisabeth and Descartes: The Union of Soul and Body and the Practice of Philosophy" (1999) provides an example of the type of reading strategy feminists are bringing to the history of philosophy. With the assistance of Elisabeth, Shapiro develops a method of rethinking the mind-body dualism that provides an alternative to dualism or materialism. She reminds us that it is at Elisabeth's request that Descartes undertakes his study of the passions. Struggling with the difficulties of figuring as a philosopher in her own right a woman whose work is always in dialogue with Descartes's philosophy, Shapiro attempts to delineate a line of thought proper to Elisabeth herself concerning the nature of the union of the body and the soul.

Shapiro argues that "Elisabeth traces out for us a unique philosophical position: she defends neither a reductionist materialism nor a substance dualism, but rather wants to find a way of respecting the autonomy of thought without denying that this faculty of reason is in some essential way dependent on our bodily condition" (1999, 505). Shapiro identifies in Elisabeth's writings an awareness of the interactions between the body and the mind that neither reduces the one to the other nor denies Descartes's intuition that thought is not determined by extension. Reminding Descartes that one can lose full use of her or his reason from an illness, Elisabeth critiques his dualism. Mind is autonomous in that it has its own proper activity, that is, thought, giving us control over what we think. But its ability to engage in thought is dependent on the condition of the body—whether it is ill or healthy, indeed whether it is male or female. Shapiro argues that Elisabeth "does not want to deny that her femaleness affects her thought…she is unwilling to deny that she is female and moreover that this fact of her embodiment figures in who she is and in her ability to reason. What she does deny is that her femaleness is in any way *debilitating* to her power of thought" (1999, 512).

Much of Shapiro's essay focuses on the development of Elisabeth's philosophy and thus could be seen as a chapter in the recovery of women philosophers or an argument for the importance of women's standpoint—indeed perhaps a version of Elisabeth's own position. However, woven into her discussion is the question of influence. As she traces the development of Elisabeth's perspective, she also notes lines of influence on Descartes. She notes that "it is interesting that in the *Passions of the Soul,* a work written at Elisabeth's request as a result of this portion of their correspondence, Descartes wants to distinguish the functions of the soul from those of the body, but he does not refer to them as two distinct substances" (1999, 516). Shapiro acknowledges that the Descartes of the *Passions* recognizes the role of embodiment on our passions and appears to have agreed with Elisabeth's insights concerning the mind's dependence on the health of the body.

As another example of a reading strategy, consider Susan James's *Passion and Action: The Emotions in Seventeenth-Century Philosophy*. James presents her work as a corrective not only to nonfeminist histories of 17th-century philosophy but also to feminist histories. She argues that contemporary philosophers "tend to forget that philosophers of this era worked within an intellectual milieu in which the passions were regarded as an overbearing and inescapable element of human nature, liable to disrupt any civilized order, philosophy included, unless they were tamed, outwitted, overruled, or seduced" (1997, 1). She identifies an inherent tension within the then dominant view of the emotions, seeing them on one hand as "functional characteristics essential to our survival and flourishing; on the other hand they are painful and destructive impulses which drive us to pursue the very ends liable to do us harm" (1997, 14).

James notes the partiality of contemporary histories of philosophy that are preoccupied with scientific and secular forms of inquiry that have ignored topics like the emotions, which are seen as tangential to the main aims of philosophy. Arguing that accounts of the passions were integral to 17th-century philosophy, James illustrates that contemporary histories miss crucial aspects of philosophical positions such as how the passions provided a resource for subtly theorizing the interconnections between thoughts and bodily states or how the emotions are important components of rational thought and action, leaving readers with an inaccurate image of a thoroughgoing dualism between mind and body and a dismissal of the role of the passions in rational thought. While noting this to be a flaw of feminist as well as nonfeminist histories, James reminds feminist philosophers of the gravity of reinforcing a division that casts asunder mind and body and allows for the gendering of the division. By rather seeing our own feminist-inspired desire to wed reason and emotion as continuous with past philosophies, we can both enrich our contemporary efforts to reinstate the emotions and recover forgotten strains of philosophy.

Another style of feminist reading can be found in the work of Luce Irigaray, who focuses on the contradictory movements and unstable logic of the exclusion of sexual difference in the history of philosophy. Irigaray argues that representation of the feminine as the "other" actually sustains the ideal identity of the masculine subject. But it is here that she detects an inherent instability. She argues that in order to shore up masculine identity, philosophers have had to "eradicate the difference between the sexes" (1985b, 74). But, she argues, this effort to reduce women to an economy of the same (A/–A) risks the realization that they exceed it. It is in this place of excess, in the realm of how women *cannot* be represented, that Irigaray finds a resource for recovering "sexual difference." She argues that this sexual difference is on the border of histories of the representation of femininity. It is not *within* those histories in that it has been excluded, yet it is not wholly *outside* them, for in the exclusion, it must be gestured toward. Her goal is based on her belief that "the recognition of a 'specific' female sexuality would challenge the monopoly on value held by the masculine sex alone" (1985b, 73). In such a rereading, we open the historical texts of philosophy to contemporary feminist concerns not simply to confront what has been repressed but to rethink it.

In the philosophical hands of Irigaray, Descartes's *Passions of the Soul* becomes a resource to attempt to speak that which has been rendered silent—namely, an ethics of sexual difference. Irigaray begins at the place of wonder, labeled by Descartes "the first of all the passions" (Descartes, 1995b, 358). She builds upon Descartes's view of the fundamental nature of this passion to argue that it is also the basis of the creation of an ethics—that is, an ethics of and through sexual difference that prohibits incorporation of the one into the other through assimilation and forgetting. Echoing and elaborating on the voice of Descartes, Irigaray explains:

> This other, male or female, should *surprise* us again and again, appear to us as *new, very different* from what we knew or what we thought he or she should be. Which means that we would look at the other, stop to look at him or her, ask ourselves, come close to ourselves through questioning. *Who art thou?* I *am* and I *become* thanks to this question. Wonder goes beyond that which is or is

not suitable for us. The other never suits us simply. We would in some way have reduced the other to ourselves if he or she suited us completely. An *excess* resists: the other's existence and becoming as a place that permits union and/through resistance to assimilation or reduction to sameness (1993, 74).

For Irigaray, wonder serves as a site for rethinking/reembodying the interaction and the attraction between those who differ, especially sexually. Rather than our current forgetting of difference through a logic of sameness and annihilation, a return to wonder, in the voice of Irigaray, echoing Descartes, constitutes a new potential for becoming ethical.

> Wonder would be the passion of the encounter between the most material and the most metaphysical, of their possible conception and fecundation one by the other. A third dimension. An intermediary. Neither the one nor the other. Which is not to say neutral or neuter. The forgotten ground of our condition between mortal and immortal, men and gods, creatures and creators. In us and among us (1993, 82).

While Irigaray is certainly a feminist philosopher noted for a reading style attentive to the history of the exclusion of women's experiences and concerns, it is important to see that her reading style does not end at the point of exclusion. Her attention to the absences and presences of women in the history of philosophy presents an opening for the possibility of true difference and enables her to discover in the texts of canonical philosophers like Descartes resources for an ethics of sexual difference.

My claim in this all-too-brief and admittedly partial overview of feminist reading strategies is that our efforts to refuse the forgetting of gender are making contributions to the history of philosophy that are too important to exclude from courses in the history of philosophy. I would also call attention to the fact that in attending to neglected aspects of historical texts, we are motivated by our own feminist wonder at the relation between reason and emotion in the play of the canon, a feminist-inspired desire to find a place in-between mind and body, a third way that is neither a reductionist materialism nor a substance dualism. In this sense, our desires are enacted in our reading strategies.

REREADING THE CANON

In her introduction to *Feminist Interpretations of René Descartes,* Susan Bordo reminds us of the difficulties and the value of feminist rereadings in the history of philosophy.

> The range of feminist thinking is wider, and the point of much feminist argument subtler and less polemical than is often represented (even, sometimes, by other feminists). These misrepresentations are, in part, the results of stereotypes circulating in *our* own cultural milieu, stereotypes that encourage readings of feminist thought as male hating and canon bashing. So, for example, when feminists criticize existing models of reason (engaging in a critical, reconstructive project that has occupied male philosophers from Aristotle and Hegel to James, Dewey, and Whitehead), it is sometimes read as an all-out attack on rationality or as an "assault on reason"—creating the image of Lorena Bobbit–like viragoes, heading at the canon with their sharpened steak knives. But in fact, with few exceptions, the point of feminist criticism has been to reveal what dominant models have *excluded* rather than to attack what they have *offered* (1999, 3).

My goal in this essay has been to demonstrate the multifaceted nature of feminist philosophies of history and to replace the steak-knife or labrys-wielding image of the feminist virago with an appreciation of both the complexity of feminist work in the history of philosophy and the value of feminist work to the (nonfeminist) classroom. Although I intend my outline to be informative, I would be the first to admit that it is not exhaustive of feminist approaches. I did not, for example, detail the work of those feminists who examine the historical and cultural impact of a canonical philosopher's thought on women's lives (both at the time of the writing and in later centuries). Nor did I attempt to outline the ways feminist philosophers have turned to the canon either to identify feminist foremothers or to find resources for contemporary feminist projects and concerns.

Feminist history of philosophy is a complex field of study offering numerous resources for those of us who wish to rethink the traditional history of philosophy course. Take this essay as an invitation to attend to the forgetting of gender so that we can transform not only our courses but also our very ways of being philosophical and becoming ethical. Think about how you would now teach Plato's dictum "Wonder is the feeling of the philosopher, and philosophy begins in wonder." (Theaetetus 155d)

Notes

1. For an excellent discussion of some of these issues, see Bruce Kuklick's "Seven Thinkers and How They Grew: Descartes, Spinoza, Leibniz, Locke, Berkeley, Hume, Kant."

2. See, for example, J. B. Schneewind's essay "Divine Corporation and the History of Ethics" for a discussion of why contemporary history courses emphasize metaphysical and epistemological concerns rather than the history of ethics.

3. Claims like this must always, of course, be modified to be accurate. First of all, it has never been the case that *men* was a generic term, and here I do not mean the issue of whether women were included. Men whose lives or bodies did not reflect privileged categories were never the subject of attention. Their bodies, their roles, while not always feminized, were devalued and "othered" in complex ways. Second, what constitutes masculine roles is not historically stable. Not only do these roles shift historically, but also there are often internal instabilities in how such roles are defined.

4. I am not here including the somewhat different activity of reclaiming the history of feminist philosophy, but this exclusion does not mean I do not think it is important. Indeed, a study of the work of those philosophers, often but not always women, whose work included efforts to identify and decry the exclusion or oppression of women is a valuable contribution. My point is only that it does not have a central role in a history of philosophy course.

5. I refer here, of course, to Elisabeth, Princess Palatine, Abbess of Herford, and Anne Finch, Viscountess Conway, respectively.

6. As soon as the subject becomes specific—a female person rather than a person—the door is opened for other differences to be examined for epistemic relevance: race, class, religion, sexuality, ethnicity, ability, etc. Which is why feminist approaches to the history of philosophy resonate with, stimulate, and often include axes of examination other than or in addition to gender.

7. Although some women philosophers were feminists and questioned the denigration of women, it would be an essentialist mistake to think that women philosophers would not replicate societal biases about gender.

8. I am well aware that the ranks of nonfeminist historians of philosophy are no more homogeneous than those of feminist historians of philosophy and that the statement I just made is far more true of analytic philosophers than of Continental ones.

Bibliography

Baier, Annette. *A Progress of Sentiments: Reflections on Hume's Treatise.*
Cambridge, Mass.: Harvard University Press, 1991.

Blom, John J. *Descartes: His Moral Philosophy and Psychology,* trans. John J.
Blom. Hassocks: Harvester Press,1978.

Bordo, Susan. *Feminist Interpretations of René Descartes.* University Park, Pa.:
Penn State Press, 1999.

Conley, John J. *The Suspicion of Virtue: Women Philosophers in Neoclassical
France.* Ithaca, N.Y., and London: Cornell University Press, 2002.

Descartes, René. "Discourse on the Method of Rightly Conducting the
Reason." In *The Philosophical Works of Descartes,* trans. E. Haldane and
G. Ross. New York: Dover, 1955a.

———. "Passions of the Soul." In *The Philosophical Works of Descartes,* trans.
E. Haldane and G. Ross. New York: Dover, 1955b.

———. "Meditations on First Philosophy." In *The Philosophical Works of
Descartes,* trans. E. Haldane and G. Ross. New York: Dover, 1955c.

Deutscher, Penelope. *Yielding Gender: Feminism, Deconstructionism, and the
History of Philosophy.* London and New York: Routledge, 1997.

Dykeman, Therese Boos, ed. *The Neglected Canon: Nine Women
Philosophers—First to the Twentieth Century.* Dordrecht/Boston/London:
Kluwer Academic Publishers, 1999.

Gardner, Catherine Villanueva. *Rediscovering Women Philosophers:
Philosophical Genre and the Boundaries of Philosophy.* Boulder, Colo.:
Westview Press, 2000.

Hegel, G. W. F. *The Philosophy of Right,* trans. T. M. Knox. New York:
Oxford University Press, 1973.

Herman, Barbara. *The Practice of Moral Judgment.* Cambridge, Mass.:
Harvard University Press, 1993.

Irigaray, Luce. *An Ethics of Sexual Difference,* trans. Carolyn Burke and
Gillian C. Gill. Ithaca, N.Y.: Cornell University Press, 1993.

———. *Speculum of the Other Woman,* trans. Gillian C. Gill. Ithaca, N.Y.:
Cornell University Press, 1985a.

———. *This Sex Which Is Not One,* trans. Catherine Porter. Ithaca, N.Y.:
Cornell University Press, 1985b.

James, Susan. *Passion and Action: The Emotions in Seventeenth-Century
Philosophy.* Oxford, England: Clarendon Press, 1997.

Kofman, Sarah. *The Enigma of Woman: Women in Freud's Writings,* trans.
Catherine Porter. Ithaca, N.Y.: Cornell University Press, 1985.

———. *Socrates: Fictions of a Philosopher,* trans. Catherine Porter. Ithaca,
N.Y.: Cornell University Press, 1998.

Kuklick, Bruce. "Seven Thinkers and How They Grew: Descartes, Spinoza, Leibniz, Locke, Berkeley, Hume, Kant." In *Philosophy in History: Essays on the Historiography of Philosophy,* ed. Richard Rorty, J. B. Schneewind, and Quentin Skinner. Cambridge, England: Cambridge University Press, 1984.

Le Dœuff, Michèle. *The Philosophical Imaginary,* trans. C. Gordon. Stanford, Calif.: Stanford University Press, 1989.

Lloyd, Genevieve. *Feminism and the History of Philosophy.* New York: Oxford University Press, 2002.

———. *The Man of Reason: "Male" and "Female" in Western Philosophy.* Minneapolis: University of Minnesota Press, 1984.

O'Neill, Eileen. "Disappearing Ink: Early Modern Women Philosophers and Their Fate in History." In *Philosophy in a Feminist Voice: Critiques and Reconstructions,* ed. Janet A Kourany. Princeton, N.J.: Princeton University Press, 1998.

Rorty, Richard, J. B. Schneewind, Quentin Skinner. *Philosophy in History: Essays on the Historiography of Philosophy.* Cambridge, England: Cambridge University Press, 1984.

Rousseau, Jean-Jacques. *Émile, or On Education,* trans. Allen Bloom. New York: Basic Books, 1979.

Scheman, Naomi. "Though This Be Method, Yet There Is Madness in It: Paranoia and Liberal Epistemology." In *A Mind of One's Own: Feminist Essays on Reason and Objectivity,* ed. Louise Antony and Charlotte Witt. Boulder, Colo.: Westview Press, 1992.

Schneewind, J. B. "Divine Corporation and the History of Ethics." *Philosophy in History: Essays on the Historiography of Philosophy,* ed. Richard Rorty, J. B. Schneewind, and Quentin Skinner. Cambridge, England: Cambridge University Press. 1984.

Shapiro, Linda. "Princess Elisabeth and Descartes: The Union of Soul and Body and the Practice of Philosophy." *British Journal for the History of Philosophy,* vol. 7, no. 3, 503–20, 1999.

Tougas, Cecile T., and Sara Ebenrick, eds. *Presenting Women Philosophers.* Philadelphia: Temple University Press, 2000.

Tuana, Nancy. *The Less Noble Sex: Scientific, Religious and Philosophical Conceptions of Woman's Nature.* Bloomington, Ind.: Indiana University Press, 1993.

———. *Woman and the History of Philosophy.* New York: Paragon Press, 1992.

Waithe, Mary Ellen, ed. *A History of Women Philosophers: Volume III, Modern Women Philosophers,* 1600–1900. Dordrecht/Boston/London: Kluwer Academic Publishers, 1991.

The Forgetting of Gender and the
New Histories of Philosophy:
A Response to Nancy Tuana

EILEEN O'NEILL

GENDER IN NEW AND OLD HISTORIES OF PHILOSOPHY

THE MERE INCLUSION of women philosophers in histories of early modern philosophy need not by itself give us genuinely "new" histories. Mary Warnock's book *Women Philosophers* (1996) is a case in point.[1] In the introduction to this anthology of philosophical selections by women from the 17th to 20th centuries, we are told that a philosopher claims "not only to seek the truth, but to seek a truth, or theory, that will explain the particular and the detailed and the everyday."[2] In addition, a philosopher is "concerned not merely with stating his views, but with arguing for them."[3] In short, general and explanatory arguments are the "hallmark" of philosophy. Warnock proudly notes that "in putting together the collection I have hardly widened the scope of what is generally thought to be covered by the concept of philosophy."[4]

Given these generally held views, Warnock finds for the 17th century only Anne Conway and Catharine Trotter Cockburn to include in her collection, and for the 18th century, only Mary Wollstonecraft. The bulk of the anthology (12 out of 17 authors) consists of 20th-century philosophers, and aside from Simone de Beauvoir, all of the women wrote in English. Warnock is surely deriving her list of women philosophers from criteria that go beyond the innocuous requirement that philosophers provide general and explanatory arguments, for there are a lot more women philosophers who meet Warnock's requirements than those whom she includes in her anthology. But which other factors are informing Warnock's selections?

Warnock claims that the generally held views about philosophy forced her to omit the writings of women who seemed to "rely more on dogma, revelation or mystical experience than on argument."[5] This might explain why St. Teresa of Avila and Antoinette Bourignon are omitted from her book. But why is Warnock excluding Mary Astell's arguments against occasionalism and her defense of dualistic interactionism in *Letters Concerning the Love of God*, as well as Astell's criticisms of Locke on thinking matter, and her defense of the "real distinction" argument in *The Christian Religion*? In Warnock's zeal to separate religion from philosophy proper, she eliminates genuine philosophical writings—at least, relative to her own criteria—simply because they deal with religious issues. Finally, Warnock notes that a great deal of feminist literature "satisfies my criteria of generality and of the hoped-for explanation of phenomena.... Yet, just as in the case of religion, there tends to be too much unexamined dogma in these writings, too much ill-concealed proselytizing, too little objective analysis, to allow them to qualify for inclusion among philosophical writings proper."[6] Well, no doubt there is a good deal of philosophy that is produced that is bad philosophy—and for precisely the reasons she gives. But why is feminist thought singled out as exemplary of this sort of illegitimate philosophy? Here is Warnock's answer: "[T]he great subjects of philosophy...must be concerned with 'us' in the sense in which 'we' are all humans. The truths which philosophers seek must aim to be not merely generally, but objectively, even universally true. Essentially they must be gender indifferent."[7] This is a very interesting and hefty modal claim. Not only has philosophy, as it has been practiced heretofore, been such that its claims are gender indifferent, but also there is a conceptual connection between philosophy and gender indifference. What are the arguments that Warnock offers for this thesis? She says only this: "Those who deny that any such [universal and gender-indifferent] truth is possible... are engaged, it seems to me, not in philosophy but in a species of anthropology."[8] In short, it is a conceptual truth, *which requires no argument*, that thought that is not gender indifferent lies outside the scope of philosophy. A strange way to proceed for one who eschews unexamined dogma and ill-concealed proselytizing.

Warnock's views about women philosophers and gender can serve as a foil against which we can see what is genuinely new and fresh about the various strategies feminist historians of philosophy have been employing. As Nancy Tuana's rich overview of their recent work demonstrates, feminist philosophers have challenged the generally held views that women have no place in the history of early modern philosophy and that philosophy is by its very nature gender indifferent.[9] With these challenges on the table, arguments now need to be produced in defense of the formerly unexamined dogmas. I think it is significant that each section of Tuana's paper is heavily interwoven with interrogative sentences—a mark of the opening up for critical interrogation of so much that was formerly taken as obvious. Of course, if feminist philosophy is to be more than just a series of skeptical challenges, if it is to proffer claims of its own, then it too will have to offer arguments. And Tuana has outlined quite a number of arguments and argumentational strategies. In what follows I want to comment on some of these that are relevant to the following three issues: Which early modern women deserve places in our histories of philosophy? Can gender be "epistemically significant"? And are Descartes's conceptions of mind and reason gender neutral?

WHICH EARLY MODERN WOMEN DESERVE PLACES IN OUR HISTORIES OF PHILOSOPHY?

Tuana reads the recovery of the work of Mary Astell, Sor Juana, Judith Sargent Murray, Marie de Gournay, and Anna Maria van Schurman in Therese Dykeman's *Neglected Canon* as "part of an effort to convey a more accurate picture of the chronicle of philosophers and their contributions to the fundamental philosophical questions of their time" (63). Let us consider three ways of deciding which issues are the philosophically central ones in a given period. The first method will take as central those issues deemed by the philosophers of the past to be the central ones, and it will take scholars to be philosophers of the past just in case they were so deemed by their contemporaries. Notice that given this method, the history of philosophy will not include most of the women in Dykeman's list, for Sor Juana, Gournay, Murray, and Schurman were important mainly for their contributions to the *querelle des femmes*. And those deemed to be philosophers by their contemporaries in the 17th century did not, for the most part, take "the woman question" to be a serious philosophical issue. So given our first method, only Astell—from Dykeman's list of neglected, canonical early modern female philosophers—emerges as someone dealing with central philosophical issues, for Astell discussed such topics as mind-body interaction and the contract theory of the state. But it is not at all clear that Astell's contemporaries perceived her fine work on these issues as reason to count her as a philosopher.

Consider a second method, according to which the issues in a past era that are philosophically central are those that most closely match our current philosophical concerns or that have led causally to our coming to have our current concerns. Tuana is surely right that, for a variety of reasons, the work of early modern female philosophers has had far less influence on subsequent generations of philosophers than the work of male philosophers has. But there is exciting work being done currently by historians of feminist philosophy that uncovers foreshadowings of contemporary feminist issues and arguments in the work of newly rediscovered female philosophers of the past. We are just beginning to see that in the 17th century there were lines of influence that tied together the protofeminist texts of Lucrezia Marinella, Marie de Gournay, Anna Maria van Schurman, and Bathsua Makin.[10] In 18th-century England, women were beginning to trace a history of feminist philosophy that linked Mary Hays, Mary Wollstonecraft, and Catharine Macaulay back one hundred years to Mary Astell.[11] Through Wollstonecraft, English feminist thought responded to the views of Mme de Staël and Mme de Genlis[12]; through Astell, it was influenced by Mme Dacier and Madeleine de Scudéry.[13] By 1790, the American Judith Sargent Murray was able to provide a minihistory of feminist philosophers, including Gournay, Scudéry, Dacier, Astell, Damaris Masham, Macaulay, Genlis, and Wollstonecraft, among others.[14] In the 20th century, Simone de Beauvoir explicitly tied her efforts to those of Christine de Pisan, Mary Wollstonecraft and Olympe de Gouges.[15] My point is that perhaps not all of the evidence is yet in. It may turn out that some of the figures in Dykeman's canon, such as Gournay or

Astell, will emerge as having a greater influence on current philosophy than, say, Kenelm Digby or Ralph Cudworth.

These two methods for deciding the issues and thinkers to be included in our histories of philosophy, which I have been discussing, are certainly not the only ones. If they were, it would be hard to see what place Margaret Cavendish, for example, could ever have in our histories. It is true that she wrote on topics considered by the 17th century to be central to philosophy: why mechanism fails as an explanatory theory, why materialism must be true, what the correct theory of perception is.[16] But despite the fact that she constructed an original, Stoic-influenced system of nature, the 17th century not only did not consider her to be a philosopher, but it also considered her posture as an ambitious natural philosopher to be literally "mad." Furthermore, Cavendish's views were not taken up by any of her successors, and it seems unlikely that metaphysicians or philosophers of science today would see in her work foreshadowings of views that they now find compelling. But there is a third method of historiography according to which Cavendish might be accorded a place in our histories of philosophy. Like the first method, this one would include in our histories those issues and figures deemed important by the past eras in which they were situated, but it would also include those figures and issues that *would* have been taken to be philosophically important in the past *had there not been systematic prejudice at work*. Given this method, it will not be difficult to make the case that Cavendish, Astell, Catharine Trotter Cockburn, Mme du Châtelet and a number of other early modern women philosophers deserve significant places in our histories of philosophy.

CAN GENDER BE "EPISTEMICALLY SIGNIFICANT"?

Tuana is careful to distinguish the thesis of "gender standpoint" from a "gender essentialist" thesis. According to the former, women do not have a nature distinct from that of men, in accordance with which they focus on certain issues, and use argumentational styles, which differ from those of men. Rather, the view is that certain concerns, methodologies, and styles of philosophizing can be identified as reflective of women's social roles and experience. In considering how "feminist standpoint" theory and "Marxist standpoint" theory work, I take it that *gender standpoint* might imply that because of their unique social location, women are in the position to know certain things that men's social positioning obscures for them. This could be held in a stronger or a weaker sense. The stronger view is that there are philosophical truths that only those who occupy women's social location can come to know. I do not know how to evaluate this claim. But the weaker view is that there are philosophical truths that those who occupy women's social location are more likely to discover.

In the 17th century, Sor Juana famously held the weaker view. She asked: "What is there for us women to know, if not bits of kitchen philosophy?... If Aristotle had been a cook, he would have written much more."[17] She gave examples of how one could learn a good deal about natural philosophy through the empirical investigation o f egg yolks, oil, and sugar. Her point was not that women are by nature better at understanding certain bits of chemistry but that our social and gendered roles make certain topics more accessible for philosophical scrutiny. But while Sor Juana thought that the topics and subject matter upon which we choose to focus are colored by gender, as are perhaps even the philosophical methods of exposition, she did not hold that reasoning itself was affected by gender. In the remainder of this section, I want to make some remarks about gender, style, and argumentational strategies. In the next section, I'll briefly raise some questions about gender and reason.

I do not think that I follow Tuana's summary of Catherine Gardner's main argument in the latter's book *Rediscovering Women Philosophers*. Gardner claims that the dominant, male model of moral theory "leaves little room for the emotions or the imagination in moral decision-making and demands an impersonal approach in moral activity" (70). Gardner argues that the form and the content of the writing of Christine de Pisan, Catharine Macaulay, Mary Wollstonecraft, and some other women philosophers challenge this dominant model of moral philosophy. For these women philosophers, "reason and sensibility mutually strengthen and support one another," and sensibility drawn out of the experience of women is not just a subject of these women's works; it is exemplified in their very style of writing.

I am not sure whether philosophical writing that exemplified sensibility was marked by the feminine gender at the time when Christine, Macaulay, and Wollstonecraft were writing. Christine de Pisan's blending of reason, feeling, and imagination in her *Book of the City of Ladies* is amply matched in the work to which she was in part responding: *The Romance of the Rose*. Jean de Meung poured emotion (some of it misogynist) and imaginative fancy into this work. Similarly, it seems to me that Rousseau's *Émile* surely intertwines sentiment with reason as much as do the works of Macaulay and Wollstonecraft, which attempted to respond to it. And Edmund Burke's *Reflections on the Revolution in France* is no less passionate than Wollstonecraft's response in *A Vindication of the Rights of Man*. Indeed, Wollstonecraft referred to Rousseau as "the true Prometheus of feeling," and she thought he was dangerous because, like Burke, he was "so powerful and emotional a writer."[18]

The other example that Tuana gives of the gender standpoint thesis is John Conley's work on the gender-specific moral methodology practiced by the women of the 17th-century Parisian salons. Conley claims that "gender analysis…explores sex-specific reasons why these authors…distance themselves from a distinctively male critique of virtue" (69). Conley offers as an example Mme de Sablé, whose position as a salon hostess required that she inculcate in herself qualities such as civility, diplomacy, and politeness. Precisely because she was a woman who fulfilled certain social roles, she found it impossible to engage in the "acerbic dissection of virtue" of her salon associate La Rochefoucauld. Thus, she invented an alternative type of moral maxim more moderate in tone and content, which nonetheless allowed her to unmask the hidden vices in the social world of the aristocracy.

Conley may well be correct about the gender-specific reason for Sablé's choice of her type of maxim as the method by which she would engage in moral psychology. But I would like to suggest that as historians of philosophy, we should not let the thesis of gender standpoint, which will lead us to external/social (explanatory) reasons for women's choices of philosophical position or method, block us from also searching for (justificatory) reasons "internal" to philosophy to explain these choices. (I have no reason to think

Conley is guilty of this; I am just voicing a general concern.) Consider this example: In the 1980s and 1990s, some scholars turned to gender standpoint in order to explain Margaret Cavendish's decision to embrace a form of vitalism.[19] They argued that her experience as a woman moved her toward a "more organic and nurturing view of nature" and away from the "male-dominated" and "masculinist" mechanical science. But these scholars left matters there. Had they more closely examined Cavendish's texts, they would have found philosophical arguments for her rejection of atomism and mechanism and on behalf of organicist materialism—for instance, those drawn from her criticisms of the causal model that underlies mechanism.

ARE DESCARTES'S CONCEPTIONS OF MIND AND REASON GENDER NEUTRAL?

This is a complicated issue about which I will make only two remarks in this context. First, I think that some recent literature that attempts to expose the "masculinity" of the Cartesian mind has rested on an incorrect understanding of Descartes's "real distinction" argument. It is sometimes argued that Descartes held that the mind is independent of the impediments of the body—including gendered bodily impediments—not only in the sense that the mind *can* be freed from these impediments but also in the sense that Descartes's thinking subject *is* drained of "all feeling and emotion connected to the body."[20] It is then claimed that for a woman to become this sort of thinking subject, she would have to "transcend her female characteristics and reject her female roles (maternal feelings, attachment to individuals, etc.)" (75). I think that Descartes does believe that the mind *can* exist separately from the body in the sense that there is nothing inconceivable about such a separation. And he thinks that the real distinction paves the way for the doctrine of the immortality of the soul. But I also think that his view is that while we are alive, our mind is in union with—that is, not separated from—the body. It is because of this union that the thinking subject *is not* drained of all feeling and emotion. Because of this union, the body can affect the mind in the many ways that Princess Elisabeth describes.[21]

Second, I would like to focus on Genevieve Lloyd's rather different strategy in her book *The Man of Reason,* which Tuana discusses. Lloyd argues that Descartes presents us with two notions of reason. In the first sort of reasoning, "the complex and obscure is reduced to simple, self-evident 'intuitions,' which the mind scrutinizes with 'steadfast, mental gaze,' then combines in orderly chains of deduction."[22] And it is this type of reason that "provides the foundations of science."[23] But Lloyd says that "this was not the only kind of thought which Descartes recognized as rational. In the Sixth Meditation he acknowledged that the inferior senses, once they have been set aside from the search for truth—where they can only mislead and distort—are reliable guides to our well-being. To trust them is not irrational."[24] Lloyd concludes that "the sharpness of [Descartes's] separation of the ultimate requirements of truth-seeking from the practical affairs of everyday life reinforced already existing distinctions between male and female roles, opening up the way to the idea of distinctive male and female consciousness."[25] This is an extremely interesting conclusion, but I do not think that in her book Lloyd has yet made the case for it.

Margaret Atherton has argued that for Lloyd's argument to work, "it must be possible to distinguish the Cartesian reason that constitutes the masculine from some other thought process that can be identified as feminine. Lloyd achieves such a distinction by identifying Cartesian reason with trained reason, with those thought processes that belong to someone who has acquired a certain abstract-reasoning skill. This way of thinking, she argues, came to be seen as stereotypically masculine."[26] But Atherton complains that Lloyd has not been able to identify in the untrained mind anything that links it to the stereotypically feminine, for "the untrained mind is just the mind that relies heavily and uncritically on sense experience and on less than fully rigorous connections between ideas. There does not seem to be anything about such a mind that recalls images of the feminine."[27]

I would like to suggest that Lloyd might be able to go some way toward meeting Atherton's complaint if Mme de Lambert's *New Reflections on Women* (1727) should turn out not to be an anomaly but rather part of a tradition. In that work, Lambert takes as her point of departure the remarks of the Cartesian Malebranche about the senses and faculty of imagination in women. On one hand, in *The Search after Truth* (Bk. 2, Pt. 2, Ch. 1), Malebranche had argued that because of the delicacy of the brain fibers found in most women, they have "great understanding of everything that strikes the senses." And so they have by and large "more knowledge, skill, and finesse" in matters of taste than men. On the other hand, they are normally "incapable of penetrating to truths that are slightly difficult to discover. Everything abstract is incomprehensible to them." In contrast to the soft and delicate brain fibers in women and children, the "strong and vigorous" brain fibers in grown men make them "capable of finding the truth." Mme de Lambert also attributes to Montaigne the view that women have an "impulsive mind"—a mind with a quick and intuitive grasp that "has nothing to do with reason." Lambert draws on Malebranche and Montaigne, as she understands them, to sketch a distinctively female consciousness that is rooted in sense and imagination. Lambert states: "In the case of women, ideas arise spontaneously and arrange themselves in a particular order intuitively, rather than as a result of reflection. Nature, in a word, does the reasoning for us and spares us the trouble of doing our own. In my opinion, feeling does not vitiate understanding. On the contrary, it produces different kinds of minds. ..." [28]

Lambert's text appears to provide some evidence for the view that, in the late 17th and early 18th centuries, a mind that relies uncritically on the presentations of sense and imagination and that consciously downplays its powers of abstraction and reflection was identified as "feminine." But it is significant that early modern authors such as Mary Astell and François Poullain de la Barre make explicit that they take the Cartesian conception of reason to be gender neutral. At best, then, Lloyd may be able to assemble evidence to show that *some* Cartesians (although neither Descartes himself nor Cartesians such as Astell) held that the search after truth, via reason's project of pure inquiry, is "masculine," while the intuition, feeling, and impulsiveness of sense that guide us in our practical life are "feminine." Further research will be needed, however, to determine how pervasive Lambert's gendered view of reason was in the early modern era.

NOTES

1. Mary Warnock, *Women Philosophers*. London: J. M. Dent, 1996.
2. Ibid., xxx.
3. Ibid.
4. Ibid., xxxi.
5. Ibid., xxxii.
6. Ibid., xxxiii.
7. Ibid., xxxiv.
8. Ibid.
9. All parenthetical references in the body of my paper are to Nancy Tuana's "Forgetting of Gender and the New Histories of Philosophy" in this volume.
10. Eileen O'Neill, "Disappearing Ink: Early Modern Women Philosophers and Their Fate in History." In *Philosophy in a Feminist Voice: Critiques and Reconstructions,* ed. J. Kourany. Princeton, N.J.: Princeton University Press, 1998, 21.
11. Ibid., 28.
12. Mary Wollstonecraft, *A Vindication of the Rights of Woman*, ed. C. Poston. New York/London.: W. W. Norton & Company, 1988, 103–5.
13. [Mary Astell], *A Serious Proposal to the Ladies for the Advancement of Their True and Greatest Interest,* Part I. London, 1701, 51.
14. Judith Sargent Murray, "Observations on Female Abilities." In *Selected Writings of Judith Sargent Murray,* ed. S. Harris. New York/Oxford, England: Oxford University Press, 1995, 32–38.
15. Simone de Beauvoir, *The Second Sex,* trans. H. M. Parshley. New York: Vintage Books, 1989, 128.
16. Margaret Cavendish, *Observations upon Experimental Philosophy,* ed. E. O'Neill. Cambridge, England: Cambridge University Press, 2001.
17. *A Sor Juana Anthology,* trans. A. Trueblood. Cambridge, Mass.: Harvard University Press, 1988, 226.
18. Moira Ferguson and Janet Todd, "Feminist Backgrounds and Argument of *A Vindication of the Rights of Woman."* In Mary Wollstonecraft, *A Vindication of the Rights of Woman,* 323.
19. Lisa Sarasohn, "A Science Turned Upside Down: Feminism and the Natural Philosophy of Margaret Cavendish." *Huntington Library Quarterly* 47, 4 (1984), 299-307. See also John Rogers, *The Matter of Revolution: Science, Poetry and Politics in the Age of Reason.* Ithaca, N.Y.: Cornell University Press, 1996.
20. Erica Harth, *Cartesian Women: Versions and Subversions of Rational Discourse in the Old Regime.* Ithaca, N.Y.: Cornell University Press, 1992, 81–82.

21. See my "Women Cartesians, 'Feminine Philosophy,' and Historical Exclusion." In *Feminist Interpretations of René Descartes*, ed. S. Bordo. University Park, Pa.: Pennsylvania State University Press, 1999, especially 240–41.

22. Genevieve Lloyd, *The Man of Reason: "Male" and "Female" in Western Philosophy*. Minneapolis: University of Minnesota Press, 1984, 44–45.

23. Ibid., 49.

24. Ibid.

25. Ibid., 49–50.

26. Margaret Atherton, "Cartesian Reason and Gendered Reason." In *A Mind of One's Own: Feminist Essays on Reason and Objectivity*, ed. L. Antony and C. Witt. Boulder, Colo./San Francisco/Oxford, England: Westview Press, 1993, 26.

27. Ibid.

28. *New Reflection on Women by the Marchioness de Lambert*, trans. E. McNiven Hine. New York: Peter Lang, 1995, 40.

The Idea of Early Modern Philosophy

KNUD HAAKONSSEN

As EDITOR of a history of 18th-century philosophy, I have had occasion to wonder in what sense such a work has an identifiable subject.[1] While there undoubtedly was a great deal of philosophy in the 18th century, it is less obvious whether there was something that usefully can be identified as 18th-century philosophy in other than a temporal sense. This question pertains to the idea of early modern philosophy more generally, and for the purposes of the present discussion, it is this wider concern with philosophy from the Renaissance and Reformation to the close of the 18th century that shall have my attention, though my emphasis is on the latter part of this period. My basic suggestion is that the issue of the identity of early modern philosophy is a philosophical and historical one in its own right. Those who do identify a distinctive early modern philosophy tend to work on the basis of specific assumptions about the nature of philosophy, and these assumptions have their own history. However, once we begin to apply historical considerations to the concept of philosophy that has identified the history of philosophy, we are leaving behind the idea of such history as rational reconstruction. We are then making—or attempting to make—the history of philosophy into an empirical study. Such an endeavor to subject ideas of intellectual coherence to empirical scrutiny makes tradition an object of investigation rather than a source of affirmation of a presupposed normative standpoint about what is "real" philosophy. In this perspective, it is not clear in what sense a philosophical canon can be identified and made the means of inculcation in the discipline.

In the first section, I outline the basic features of the conception of philosophy that have informed the writing of the history of early modern philosophy since the end of the 18th century. In the second section, I argue that this notion of philosophy itself is the outcome of late-18th-century philosophical debate. In the third section, I give a number of reasons for believing that the paradigm that has dominated our histories of the subject is seriously inadequate to capture the scope of early modern philosophy. In the fourth section, I speculate that this gulf is so wide that it questions the idea of a coherent philosophical tradition with a teachable canon.

From this, it will be clear that I do not think that the difference between "old histories of philosphy" and "new histories of philosophy" is simply a matter of procedures and intellectual tastes; it is also a difference in subject matter. Accordingly, I have to run the considerable risk inherent in saying what "old" histories of philosophy in general were about. I should enter the caveat that I am concerned primarily with the *general* history of early modern philosophy as reflected in survey works, as presupposed in a great deal of more specialized scholarship and as employed very widely in university curricula. I am well aware of the significant amount of scholarship, especially from recent times, that helps undermine the paradigm to which I am now turning. In fact, part of my purpose is to apply some of these new historical studies to my subversive purposes. However, my purposes remain subversive. I do not think that the "new histories" add up to a new, alternative canon and curriculum, and I think that is a great deal of their attraction.

ONE

The most basic of the ideas that have dominated the writing of the history of philosophy during the past two centuries is that the theory of knowledge is at the core of all sound philosophy, the true *prima philosophia.* Furthermore, the significance of early modern philosophy is commonly considered in this historiography to be that the roughly three centuries from the late Renaissance to 1800 constituted the period when philosophers increasingly came to understand this true nature of philosophy. The problem of knowledge that philosophy was supposed to deal with was the one posed by skepticism conceived as a denial of the possibility of justified beliefs or scientific explanations. The philosophical history of the period has therefore commonly been told as the story of an ever-deepening struggle with skepticism that culminated in a total rejection of the premises upon which the contest had taken place or, rather, in two such rejections: that by Immanuel Kant and that by Thomas Reid.

For these two thinkers, the central question of philosophy was not, How can we acquire true knowledge? It was, rather, Given that we do have knowledge (especially, science), how is this possible, or what are its presuppositions? This standpoint inspired subsequent generations to a view of the trajectory of early modern philosophy according to which traditional ontology was largely an encumbrance on epistemology, and the development from the 17th to the 18th century consisted in shedding this burden. It was the Hegelian transition from substance to subject, from the so-called great systems within which Descartes, Spinoza, Malebranche, and Leibniz had fought skepticism, to the theories of perception, ideas, and judgment with which Locke, Leibniz (again), Wolff, Berkeley, Condillac, Hume, and many others tried to found the new sciences. It was a development, in other words, that confirmed and underlined one of the most elementary assumptions of the historians who traced it—namely, that knowledge is to be understood in terms of the individual person's mind, an assumption that remained remarkably unshaken despite Hegel.

Integral to the view indicated here is that the epistemological approach divided post-Renaissance philosophy into two major schools or directions—namely, rationalism and empiricism. The former has commonly been seen as characteristic of the European continent, though one of the defining features of 18th-century philosophy, on this view, was that France gradually switched from Cartesian rationalism to Lockean empiricism, embodied in Condillac. Germany, however, was supposed to maintain a continuous development of rational system building through Leibniz, Wolff, and their followers and opponents. In contrast, the English-speaking world was seen to pursue the empiricist view in ever finer detail from Bacon and Hobbes, through Locke, Berkeley, and Hume.

This way of understanding the core of early modern philosophy I call the epistemological paradigm. It sees philosophy as concerned essentially with the justification of beliefs and judgments; it understands such justification in terms of events, whether perceptive or inferential, in the mind—or as if in the mind—of the individual person; and it tends to apply this idea of epistemological justification as the criterion for what is properly included in the discipline of philosophy.

This basic model is familiar to everyone who has looked into the general histories of early modern philosophy, both current and past, and to any teacher of the subject. Needless to say, there are a great many variations on this interpretative theme—often with acknowledgment of important exceptions and additions, such as the presence of an empiricist strain in German Enlightenment thought—but the general features have been remarkably pervasive. Furthermore, the paradigm has reigned for a long time. The emphasis on the struggle against skepticism was already a prominent feature of the philosophical historiography of the Kantians at the close of the 18th century, and it has inspired some of the most appreciated contemporary scholarship in the form given to the thesis by Richard Popkin. Similarly, the preeminence given to epistemology is comparable in the Kantian Wilhelm Gottfried Tennemann's 12-volume *Geschichte der Philosophie* (1798–1819) and Father Frederick Copleston's 9-volume *History of Philosophy* (1946–74). It is also noticeable that while morals, politics, law, and art have gained status as objects of past philosophical inquiry in some recent general histories of philosophy, they are more often treated in the same stepmotherly manner as they were in the great 19th-century works, such as those by Friedrich Ueberweg and Kuno Fischer. Often, they have been treated as separate disciplines with their own histories, obviously so in the case of the many histories of political thought but also in major histories of ethics from, for instance, Christian Garve's *Uebersicht der vornehmsten Principien der Sittenlehre, von dem Zeitalter des Aristoteles an bis auf die unsre Zeiten* (1798), through Sir James Mackintosh's *Dissertation on the Progress of Ethical Philosophy* (1830), and Friedrich Jodl's *Geschichte der Ethik als philosophischer Wissenschaft* (1882–89), to J. B. Schneewind's *Invention of Autonomy: A History of Modern Moral Philosophy* (1998).

TWO

The epistemological paradigm for the history of early modern philosophy has held sway so universally, at least until recently, that it may be surprising to suggest that it itself has a history—in fact, that it can be traced back to a particular episode or couple of episodes at the close of the 18th century. The paradigm became so widely accepted because it was propagated by two remarkably successful philosophical movements in which a useful past was an integral part—namely, as mentioned, the Scottish Common Sense philosophy formulated by Thomas Reid and Dugald Stewart and the critical philosophy of Immanuel Kant. As far as the latter is concerned, the way had been cleared in one fundamental respect by Johann Jakob Brucker's and the Wolffians' downgrading of practical philosophy relative to theoretical philosophy, as Tim Hochstrasser has shown.[2] However, it was the Kantians who had the decisive influence on the writing of the histories.[3]

The pattern of philosophical history laid down by Reid, Kant, and their followers became prescriptive far beyond their own heyday. One reason for this continuing impact seems to have been that the history of philosophy became the subject of more or less basic university courses on the European continent during the early and middle parts of the 19th century. It was during this period that it became widely accepted that the best introduction to the discipline of philosophy was through its history, and the textbooks for these courses were written under the influence of the views indicated here. Thus was created a teaching and textbook tradition that, as Ulrich Johannes Schneider has shown in great detail, swept through German- and French-dominated Europe.[4] It also crossed the English Channel, for although the English and Scottish universities were much slower to adopt systematic tuition in the history of philosophy, there was clearly an interest in the subject sufficient to sustain public lecture series, such as the early ones by Coleridge and Hazlitt; general texts, both domestic products such as Dugald Stewart's *Dissertation Exhibiting the Progress of Metaphysical, Ethical and Political Philosophy Since the Revival of Letters in Europe* (1815–21), George Henry Lewes's *Biographical History of Philosophy* (1845), Frederick Denison Maurice's several histories, and a large number of more specialized or limited histories; and imported works in the form of translations, such as Brucker, Tennemann, Hegel, Erdmann, Ueberweg, Windelband, Lefèvre, Alfred Weber, Cousin, Höffding, and many more. However, it is clear that the acceptance of the subject was much slower in England than on the Continent. The English long considered the history of philosophy a recent German invention, in a sense quite rightly. It may be a sign of the time it took for the epistemological paradigm to conquer Britain that Enfield's (i.e., Brucker's) distinctly pre-Kantian history—Brucker first published in 1742–44—remained acceptable so late in Britain: the fifth and last edition appeared in 1839.[5]

The epistemological paradigm has had a remarkable ability to transcend most major shifts in philosophy for nearly a couple of centuries. To take just one obvious example, often there was virtually no difference of view between the Neo-Kantians and the logical positivists when it came to the general shape of the history of early modern philosophy. Indeed, when a philosopher switched from the Kantian to the positivist camp, his idea of historical development might well remain unchanged (even though his *appraisals* changed). Similarly, the paradigm has been able to straddle the major confessional divides. There is not a whole lot of difference between, say, Karl Vorländer, Father Copleston, Bertrand Russell, and Anders Wedberg when it comes to deciding what is the mainstream of philosophy from Descartes to Kant.

The philosophical differences between the two founders of the modern concept of the history of philosophy, Reid and Kant, were, of course, profound, but there was a striking similarity in their reactions to the immediate philosophical past. Both of them considered that David Hume had brought the modern philosophical tradition to a skeptical crisis because he reduced knowledge to perceptually derived ideas whose representational warrant was impossible to establish. And both of them rejected this notion of knowledge as ideas in favor of a concept of knowledge as judgments that are warranted by features of undeniability on the part of any individual who wants to claim any beliefs at all. At the same time, while there is a gulf between Reid's establishment of the first principles of common sense and Kant's transcendental deduction of the pure forms of sensible intuition and of the categories, both of them retained a fundamental feature of what they took to be Hume's approach—namely, that knowledge is a matter of the activity of the individual mind. Both sides of this, the individualism and the mentalism, were to remain dominant assumptions in subsequent philosophy and, not least, in interpretations of the history of early modern philosophy.

Kant's and Reid's views of how modern philosophy had reached what they considered the impasse of Hume's skepticism were not the same, but they were compatible. Neither thinker wrote a history of philosophy, yet both developed their views in often intense dialogue with their predecessors. However, their discussions were generally conducted as if with contemporaries. Both of them were distinct "presentists" for whom the philosophy of the past had to be overcome by making it a moment in their own thought. In Kant's case, this meant that we should deal with the history of philosophy not as "historical and empirical" but as "rational, meaning, possible a priori"—a "philosophical archaeology" of "the nature of human reason" (Lose Blätter, F 3). When Kant does approach the history of philosophy as "historical and empirical" in his *Lectures on Logic,* his surveys are not dramatically different from those of his contemporaries, and his own promise of progress—namely, the critical establishment of metaphysics as "the real, true philosophy"—itself seems to be within empirical history.[6] However, when we turn to the treatment of the same history in the *Critique of Pure Reason,* we find the critical overcoming of dogmatism and skepticism and the stalemate, "indifferentism," to which they have fought each other to be inherent in reason itself. "The critical path alone is still open."[7] Of course, it was this well-known idea of an unavoidable dialectical opposition between, on one hand, Leibniz's and Wolff's rationalism and dogmatism and, on the other, Locke's empiricism tending to Hume's skepticism that became the prototype of the canonical philosophical histories mentioned earlier.

The foundational history in this vein was the already mentioned 12-volume work by Wilhelm Gottlieb Tennemann. Springing from Tennemann's own lectures in Marburg, the work was of central importance to the three remarkable lecture series on the history of philosophy that signaled the changing status of the subject at the opening of the 19th century—namely, Hegel's in Berlin in the 1820s (and perhaps earlier), Cousin's in Paris in 1815, and Coleridge's in London in 1818.[8] Of these, Hegel's were undoubtedly the most significant; they represented an important step in Hegel's philosophical development, and they helped establish the central role of the history of philosophy in the philosophical curriculum.[9] However, one cannot say that Hegel substantially changed the contours of early modern philosophy and its priorities as laid down by the Kantian revolution. Despite all he had to say about Kant, in his lectures he did not deal with the most recent period in general, and what he had to say on these topics elsewhere, while of obvious importance, does not amount to a real revision of the subject. Something similar may be said about Schelling's lectures called On the History of Modern Philosophy, probably from 1833–34. Despite their title, the lectures are devoted to the development of German idealism and its ancestry in Descartes, Spinoza, Leibniz, and Wolff, but they do devote a couple of pages to Bacon and Hume, mainly so as to invoke the formula that "From the beginning of modern philosophy…, rationalism and empiricism move parallel to each other, and they have remained parallel until now."[10]

True to his ardent empiricism, Reid made the history of philosophy a moment in his own philosophy by thinking of it as, in Kant's words, "historical and empirical" and, more particularly, as something that could be discarded in the discussion of mental philosophy once this had rid itself of silly metaphysical squabbles as natural philosophy had done. But until that day, Reid was sure that he had to "build with one hand, and hold a weapon with the other."[11] Reid's warfare was predominantly against the emergence of skepticism in modern thought.[12] From René Descartes via Nicholas Malebranche, John Locke, and George Berkeley to Reid's own time, philosophical views of how the human mind acquires knowledge of the world that enables people to conduct the business of life had become, as Reid saw it, more and more at variance with common understanding.

Philosophers had been misled by the triumph of natural sciences into drawing an analogy between matter and mind and thus to using the methods of these sciences to explain both the cognitive and the active faculties of the mind. The very language that was being used in talking of mental phenomena was "physicalistic," as we might say. The mental world was thus said to be composed of elements and ideas, and the composition was explained in spatial and mechanistic terms. Although few philosophers were materialists in the strict sense, most tended to understand the connection between ideas, passions, the will, and behavior in causal or quasi-causal terms. When driven to its final, absurd conclusions, which Reid found in the work of David Hume, modern philosophy had created a phantom world of so-called ideas that sprang from objects of observation; the self was a conglomeration of perceived ideas; and the will as the source of action was nothing but the balance of passionate impulses at any given moment.

This was Reid's understanding of modern philosophy, which he considered not only false but also dangerous.[13] It is well-known that Dugald Stewart elaborated considerably on this scheme in his influential introduction to the *Encyclopaedia Britannica,* the above-mentioned *Dissertation,* which Victor Cousin was instrumental in having published in French.[14] It is less well-known that a Reidian view of the history of philosophy was being propagated to the French-reading public already in the 1790s by the professor of philosophy at the Academy of Geneva, Pierre Prévost.[15]

The impact of Common Sense philosophy in France became significant, however, mainly through the efforts of Pierre-Paul Royer-Collard and, as far as the writing of the history of philosophy is concerned, through his pupil Victor Cousin.[16] Royer-Collard had used the idea of common sense as a means of going beyond any of the established schools of philosophy to an underlying general rationality, and Cousin in effect developed this idea into a philosophical eclecticism with explicit reference to the long German tradition of eclecticism (especially in Brucker). In such a scheme, all philosophizing was directly dependent upon the history of the various philosophical standpoints, and Cousin's preaching of the eclectic gospel gave a tremendous boost to the history of philosophy as a subject of teaching and scholarship in France. Soon he came under the influence of German idealism, especially Hegel and Schelling, and created his own less-than-perspicuous ego-philosophy as an amalgam of the Germans, the Scots and, first and last, Descartes. His idea of the shape of the philosophical past remained more or less stable—namely, that there were four fundamental forms of philosophy: sensualism (that is, what was commonly taken to be Condillac's sensationalism), idealism, common sense, and mysticism.[17] From these the eclectic philosopher could distill the appropriately knowing subject.

Although widely different, Kant's critical philosophy, Reid's Common Sense, and Cousin's eclecticism had similar views of the role that the history of philosophy should play. All three saw it as their mission to overcome and go beyond the problems that had made up the history of philosophy. But while the past was history, it served well to make their own philosophies intelligible, to show the point in their argument. Consequently, there was a *philosophical* justification, indeed, a philosophical need, for the "pedagogical" use of the history of philosophy. In shaping this history, the philosophical priorities of Kant and Reid constituted the fundamental factor. In their own ways, they shaped the epistemological paradigm for the history of early modern philosophy that has dominated the subject ever since they wrote. Our notion of the history of post-Renaissance philosophy is, in other words, itself the outcome of a particular episode in that history.

THREE

The epistemological paradigm for early modern philosophy is at considerable variance with the philosophical self-understanding common in that period. Without pretending to any magic formula for finding out *wie es eigentlich gewesen*, it is not too hard to see that, not only in the detail but also in the general lines, 17th- and 18th-century philosophy, as seen by its practitioners, is inadequately captured by this paradigm.

We may begin with a simple observation about the geographic comprehensiveness of modern (19th- and 20th-century) versus early modern history of philosophy—namely, that the former is overwhelmingly Euro-centric. It may not be surprising that the philosophy of the North American colonies and the early American republic generally has been treated as an extension of British thought, when noticed at all in general histories and university courses. But it is remarkable how suddenly all interest in non-European thought dropped out of the general histories of philosophy. Commonly the pre-Enlightenment histories as well as the major 18th-century works, such as Brucker's, as a matter of course were "universal" in their ambitions and included chapters not only on ancient "barbarian" thought but also on Near and Far Eastern thought of the Christian era. However, once the idea of the distinctiveness of "modern" philosophy took over, the non-European world disappeared from sight.[18] The epistemological paradigm may here have had support from retrograde steps in the philosophy of mind and the philosophy of language in both the idealist and the emerging positivist world. It is thus remarkable that, for example, both Kant and James Mill were of the opinion that "barbarians" could not have a philosophy because they thought concretely in images, not abstractly in concepts, a feat reserved for the Greeks and their European heirs.[19] Closely associated with such views was the linguistic racism that gained strength in the 19th century.[20]

A more complicated issue is the effect of gender bias on the writing of the history of philosophy during the past two centuries. Here feminist scholarship has gone to the roots of the epistemological paradigm. Through scrutiny of the standard idea of body-mind dualism and the associated masculinity of mind and reason, feminist scholars have questioned the tradition's emphasis on the solitary rational mind as the focus of knowledge.[21] This has happened especially through attention to early modern theories of the passions.[22] Such work has connected easily with the increasing attention to philosophical anthropology, which will be noted below. However, feminist scholarship has largely shadowed the canon by adding figures to be analyzed, and insofar as it has questioned the overall shape of early modern philosophy, this has not yet had a major impact on general histories and courses.[23]

Another general limitation in the common histories of philosophy is, as mentioned earlier, the treatment that ethics, politics, and aesthetics have been subject to. Until recently, ethics and aesthetics (when discussed at all) have been dealt with mostly to the extent that they could be seen to raise modern meta-ethical issues of relevance to the general theory of knowledge. This is clearly the consequence of the combined Kantian and Reidian legacy. Both thinkers in effect subsumed ethics and aesthetics under epistemology by making the former two disciplines centrally concerned with the justification of moral, respective aesthetic judgments (which is not to deny that such justification and philosophy as a whole ultimately had a moral purpose). However, as we will see later, it is a considerable simplification of early modern ethical and aesthetic concerns to reduce them to questions of justification. What is more, it has until recently been forgotten that moral philosophy very often had pedagogic priority as a "foundation course" in university studies. Partly because of this status, it had its own historiography, which has been subjected to careful analysis by Tim Hochstrasser and which shows a completely different idea of the shape of philosophy from the one assumed by later historians of ethics.[24] This finding is amply confirmed by Christian Garve's above-mentioned general history of ethics from the close of the 18th century.[25]

Political theory, in contrast, has either been excluded from general histories of philosophy or been treated as a separate subject—a tendency reinforced by the development of political science as an independent discipline with a need for its own canon and a useful past. The idea that a concern with the possibility of social living in general and its political implications could be *the* fundamental problem in philosophy and that metaphysics and epistemology were to be seen as esoteric learning without claim to primacy and universality has therefore been more or less incomprehensible. Those thinkers who pursued such a line of argument, notably Samuel Pufendorf and Christian Thomasius, have not only not been taken seriously as philosophers; they have simply been written out of the history of philosophy altogether—a process that began already with the Wolffian takeover of the German universities and that has continued ever since.[26] Only in recent years, and notably with the work of Hochstrasser and Ian Hunter, has this extraordinary distortion of the whole shape of German philosophical development in the 18th century begun to be rectified.

The narrowing effect of the histories of philosophy may be indicated by contrasting some of the structural features of early modern philosophy with those imposed on it subsequently. Of the four traditional disciplines into which philosophy continued to be divided—namely, logic, metaphysics, natural philosophy, and moral philosophy—none was a natural place for the epistemological endeavors that subsequently came to be seen as the hallmark of the period's thought. Right through the 18th century, many epistemological questions turn up in the context of metaphysics, while the rest are to be found in logic. However, this was a logic that had largely become a mental classification scheme. Of the two other disciplines, natural philosophy was wholly classificatory and explanatory, and moral philosophy was much more so than its modern heirs. The issues that are considered "philosophical" in our histories of philosophy, such as the epistemic adequacy of ideas or the normative warrant of obligation, have been picked out of these contexts. It is not at all clear in what sense we can be said to understand such pickings divorced from their explanatory framework, but it is clear that we have excluded a major part of what our forebears thought of as philosophy. It is equally clear that they did not have room for the subdisciplines of either epistemology or metaethics.

Natural philosophy has its own historiography in the form of what is now called the history of science. However, it is still rare to see general histories of philosophy making more than highly selective use of this discipline. The historical gains have made the subject awkward for the epistemological high road from Descartes to Kant. An equivalent history of moral philosophy, understood as the "science of morals," has been much slower to develop, but the intense study of Enlightenment anthropology in recent times has provided means to remedy the situation. It will be very difficult, however, to integrate much of this material into the standard history of ethics, for 18th-century moral science in general had a much wider scope than the issues that are at the core of contemporary ethics, especially the ground of normativity and obligation. Much of moral philosophy was as descriptive and explanatory in intent as natural philosophy, and the basic justificatory mode of argument was often the same in both branches—namely, teleological and, generally, providential. The major novelty of 18th-century moral thought prior to Kant's critical turn—namely, the idea that a law-governed ethics could be rejected by showing that morals were a matter of sentiment—was in itself an important element in the reinvigoration of the teleology of natural religion. When Hume pointed out to Hutcheson the fragility of this foundation, he was making it clear that such moral justification could not be part of the science of morals and that this science had to be part of a "true" skepticism. Much of early modern ethics was simply not concerned with the justification of moral beliefs and judgments in the way that Kant, Reid, and subsequent philosophers were. And insofar as the earlier thinkers were dealing with the moral faculties of the human mind, they were doing so as part of a wider science of morals—indeed, a general anthropology. The Copernican revolution Hume saw as necessary in the moral sciences was fundamentally different from the more famous one proclaimed by Kant. Hume wanted the mind explained by means of general principles similar to those applied elsewhere in nature. Kant wanted an epistemic certification that objects conform to knowledge.[27]

All this is not to say that early modern philosophers were not concerned with questions of how to lead the good life, but these questions have tended to lie outside the interests of contemporary histories of ethics, at least until very recently. We may approach the question of how early modern thinkers pursued normative concerns, as we would call it, by means other than the justification of belief through a consideration of early modern ideas of the practice of being a philosopher. The ancient idea that the value of a philosophy had to show itself in the life of its proponent retained great significance. While there is an established literature that approaches ancient philosophy in this light, it is only recently that something similar has been attempted with some aspects of early modern thought. As Matthew Jones and others have argued, even the more recondite parts of Descartes's philosophy, such as his geometry, are properly to be understood as a spiritual exercise in the service of self-cultivation.[28] At the other end of our period, the three sections of Kant's *Groundwork*, as interpreted by Ian Hunter, are to be seen as "stages in the spiritual grooming of a particular intellectual deportment—one that will regard true morality in terms of the commands of a pure rational being acceded to through the purifying discipline of metaphysics."[29] More broadly, Hunter has pursued the continued function of metaphysics as a spiritual exercise that has both personal and social aims.[30]

Closely associated with such ideas was the notion that the philosopher's proper role was to undergo such exercises so as to live an exemplary life. The depth of this understanding of the nature of philosophy can be illustrated in many ways. It is clearly shown through the reaction Pierre Bayle was able to provoke with his presentation of Spinoza's life as exemplary, a feat studiously repeated by Adam Smith nearly a century later in his "obituary" for David Hume, who himself was deeply concerned with properly presenting the sort of life his philosophy entailed.[31] Shaftesbury was ever in pursuit of the appropriately stoic stance, as he saw it, and Berkeley obviously considered it a particularly sore point to assail that stance as a sham.[32] It is telling also to notice the parallel between the philosopher's and the preacher's concern with the importance of conspicuously filling their roles. Francis Hutcheson was never unmindful of the dignity of his office, and the biography of him by his clerical colleague, William Leechman, reinforced the point.[33] The significance of the phenomenon is further underlined by the universal success of Fontenelle's invention of the *éloge*.[34] Considered in a wider perspective, the proper conduct of the philosophical life was just a special—and especially important—case of the general method of approaching normative, practical, "applied" ethics by delineating the ideal fulfillment of the offices of life.[35]

In view of this role of the life of the philosopher, three other structural features of early modern philosophy fall into place. First, the pervasive use of the ad hominem argument is significant. Wave after wave of undesirables—Epicureans, deists, Skeptics—was stemmed by the argument that they could not "live" their philosophy. Secondly, if philosophy is viewed as inherently connected with the conduct of life, it is not so strange that the ancient arrangement of the history of philosophy into "sects," or schools, should have remained influential through the 17th and 18th centuries. The pivot of a sect was the founding figure whose example in self-cultivation was what made the school cohere. Not only was this approach maintained in the writing of the history of ancient philosophy, but it was also a persistent concern in the period under consideration to see early modern philosophy in light of the traditional sect system. This is conspicuously the case in the histories of philosophy, such as Brucker's. It was clear to these historians, as to most people, that it was difficult to extend the ancient system unaltered to modern times, yet it remained the obvious classificatory system. This dilemma led them to a new development, and this is the third point I want to mention in this connection. I am thinking of the role of eclecticism. While this was a complex phenomenon, it is probably safe to say that the eclecticism that came to the fore in the late 17th and early 18th centuries, especially in Germany but with interesting features in common with English deism, was concerned basically with the possibility that a modern philosophy could be above the sects without itself being a sect if it could define the philosophical life as a nondogmatic (nonsectarian) utilization of all of the sects.[36]

There's a lot more to be said about these early modern ideas of the intimate connection between life and philosophy and the associated conception of the historical passage of philosophy. Undoubtedly, a lot more will be said in new scholarship. However, it seems quite clear already that the epistemological paradigm for early modern philosophy has little chance of capturing this feature of the history of philosophy. In the common perspective, the exemplary philosophical life and its historiographical significance are, at best, quaint details. Similarly, the practical ethics formulated through the notion of fulfilling one's offices is not going to be a concern for those who are in pursuit of early forms of deontology and consequentialism.

Perhaps the most deep-rooted element in the epistemological paradigm is what I referred to as its individualism and mentalism—the assumption that knowledge has to be accounted for in terms of the activity (or passivity) of the individual person's mind. This assumption has made it difficult to give satisfactory accounts of some of the debates that were absolutely central in early modern philosophy. First, there was the never-ending concern with history, sacred and profane, which demanded a theory of testimony or of knowledge as something shared interpersonally. This is the key to understanding the philosophical debates of such things as the status of miracles, the authority of Scripture, and the possibility of civic history.[37] In view of the difficulties of fitting these matters into the framework of traditional histories of philosophy, it is not so strange that even a figure of Vico's stature either is ignored or is treated without much connection to the rest of philosophical culture in the period. In connection with testimony and nonmentalistic ideas of knowledge, it would also repay to attend to what we may call the literary cultivation of memory in the form of the commonplace book, and the like, a combination of some relevance to Locke's idea of personal identity.[38]

Secondly, the late 17th and 18th centuries saw a revolution in the theory of language whose wider importance goes unacknowledged in the common history of philosophy. As Tim Hochstrasser has pointed out, already Samuel Pufendorf formulated the basic idea that reasoning is linguistic in nature, that language originates in social interaction, and that mental ratiocination as a consequence is derivative from social life.[39] Furthermore, as Hans Aarsleff has shown, even as Locke formulated the classic theory of language as, at core, labels of ideas, he admitted that some of the key elements in language could be accounted for only in functional, not referential, terms. However, it was, as Aarsleff has argued for many years, Étienne Condillac who worked out a sophisticated theory of language as performative behavior. In doing so, Condillac made it possible to make connections between language in the narrower sense and other forms of communicative behavior that had been studied intensely for both their cognitive and their practical significance, such as rhetoric, theater, dance, music, and art. What's more, it was this approach to linguistic behavior that helped philosophers in their attempts to understand folk culture and the "primitive" mind.[40]

In other words, it is necessary to set aside the epistemological paradigm in order to understand the philosophical discussions of "social" forms of knowledge ranging from revealed religion and scriptural criticism through secular history to language, the arts, and anthropology.

FOUR

It has been objected to me that tracing historical shifts in the notion of philosophy, including the shift to the currently dominant one(s), proves nothing about the true concept of philosophy, about the difference between sophists and philosophers. I need hardly point out that such objections beg the question by presupposing what is under debate—namely, whether there is a timelessly true concept of philosophy by means of which we can disqualify the sophists. By the same token, I obviously have no need of *denying* that there is such a concept. Still, in the realm of the obvious, what is offered here is not meant as an alternative paradigm to the one that has reigned for so long. Nor are the difficulties outlined earlier exhaustive of what is available in the many "new histories of philosophy," let alone the "new histories" of neighboring fields, such as theology, anthropology, science, and the arts. The point in promoting an empirical approach to the history of philosophy in opposition to the prevailing normative one is precisely to avoid the narrowing focus of paradigms and canons that tend to be institutionalized.

My aim has been the much simpler, if not entirely immodest, one of sketching enough difficulties that go to the heart of the epistemological paradigm. Enough, in the following sense. If early modern philosophy includes central strands that are so profoundly at variance with the common assumptions in our histories of philosophy, then we are far beyond a merely quantitative revolution in philosophical history. It is not simply a matter of adding items to the old agenda of scholarship, or new courses to the old syllabus. We have questioned the historical coherence of the concept of philosophy itself, as far as the standard history is concerned. Since this concept itself is a historical formation, we are in effect querying what traditional history of philosophy was a history of.

If we apply these considerations to the teaching of the history of philosophy, we see that we have put a large question mark at the use of this subject as a vehicle for the discipline's canon and, hence, as a foundation for the type of philosophy that is being taught in the rest of the curriculum, for the idea of the canon has been shaped to fit the philosophical type; it is not the case that the latter in any meaningful sense is the outcome of the former considered as a historical process. In both teaching and writing the history of philosophy in general and that of the early modern period in particular, we have a choice. We can begin with a more or less fixed notion of what philosophy is (persuaded, for example, by Kant or Reid) and proceed to find historical instantiations of and approximations to it. Or we can let the concept of philosophy itself be part of the object for historical investigation. In the former case, it is not clear in what sense the enterprise is history; in the latter case, it is an open question whether it has a more than locally identifiable object.

However, the latter choice—the way of history—does of course have its own philosophical rationale—namely, a form of what Hume called "true skepticism." The point of such history is to query the predominant concept of philosophical history and to make the historical coherence of the concept of philosophy itself into an object of historical investigation. It is not to deny the possibility of such coherence but to make it a fruitful question of empirical history. This mode of *philosophierende Geschichte der Philosophie* is certainly critique but historical critique. Within the framework of an undergraduate curriculum, this means that it is questionable practice to use a standard course called History of Modern Philosophy as a survey of *the* fundamental problems of philosophy and require all majors in a philosophy department to take it. Rather, courses in the history of the subject might be introductions to ways of thinking that are quite uncertainly related to our own contemporary ones, in and out of philosophy classes. This may make our students historical gadflies upon philosophy, but who is to say that is unphilosophical?

NOTES

1. This paper overlaps with my introduction to *The Cambridge History of Eighteenth-Century Philosophy*, edited by Knud Haakonssen (Cambridge, England: Cambridge University Press 2005). It is a pleasure to acknowledge the helpful discussions on these matters that I have had with Aaron Garrett, Charles Griswold, Ian Hunter, James Schmidt, Åsa Söderman, and M. A. Stewart.

2. T. J. Hochstrasser, *Natural Law Theories in the Early Enlightenment*. Cambridge, England: Cambridge University Press, 2000, 170–5.

3. While Karl Ameriks may well be right that the interpretation of Kant's own philosophy was distorted by Karl Leonhard Reinhold, Johann Gottlieb Fichte, and Georg Wilhelm Friedrich Hegel, I do not think that this was the case with the Kantian view of philosophical history; Ameriks, *Kant and the Fate of Autonomy*. Cambridge, England: Cambridge University Press, 2000.

4. Ulrich Johannes Schneider, *Philosophie und Universität. Historisierung der Vernunft im 19. Jahrhundert*. Hamburg, Germany: Felix Meiner Verlag, 1998.

5. See my introduction to William Enfield, *The History of Philosophy from the Earliest Periods: Drawn Up from Brucker's 'Historia critica philosophiæ'* [1837], 2 vols. Bristol, England: Thoemmes Press, 2001.

6. "Logik Jäsche," in Kant, *Gesammelte Schriften*, Akademieausgabe, vol. 9, Berlin, 1923, 32; translated in Kant, *Lectures on Logic*, trans. J. M. Young. Cambridge, England: Cambridge University Press, 1992. Kant gives three general overviews of the history of philosophy in the lectures as published, "Logik Blomberg," Ak 24: 31–7; "Wiener Logik," Ak 24: 800–804; and "Logik Jäsche," Ak 9: 27–33, all in *Lectures*. In the first and earliest of these, from around 1770, Kant divides modern philosophy into dogmatic and critical, the latter represented by Locke. While Kant clearly drew on Formey's *Kurzgefassete Historie der Philosophie* (Berlin, 1763; first in French, Amsterdam 1760), it is Kant's merit to bring Locke up to parity with Leibniz. Formey devotes only a few lines to Locke as a "logician" in a work that is heavily dependent upon Brucker, including the latter's perverse view that Wolff is the epitome of Eclecticism.

7. *Kritik der reinen Vernunft*, A855/B883, after *Critique of Pure Reason*, trans. P. Guyer and A. W. Wood. Cambridge, England: Cambridge University Press, 1998. See also and esp. Preface A.

8. Cf. Schneider, *Philosophie und Universität*, 213–14. For Coleridge, see *Lectures, 1818–19: On the History of Philosophy*, ed. J. R. de J. Jackson, *The Collected Works of Samuel Taylor Coleridge*, vol. 8, London: Routledge, and

Princeton, N.J.: Princeton University Press, 2000; lectures 11–13 are on early modern philosophy.

9. Hegel's manuscripts were compiled by Karl Ludwig Michelet and published as *Vorlesungen über die Geschichte der Philosophie* (1833–36), now vols. 18–20 of *Werke*, ed. E. Moldenhauer and K. L. Michelet, 20 vols. Frankfurt am Main, Germany, 1969–71. Translation in *Lectures on the History of Philosophy*, trans. E. S. Haldane and F. H. Simson, 3 vols. London, 1892–96. Reestablished texts in *Vorlesungen über die Geschichte der Philosophie*, vols. 7–9 of *Vorlesungen*, ed. P. Garniron and W. Jaeschke. Hamburg, Germany: Felix Meiner Verlag, 1986, 1989, 1996. Cf. Alfredo Ferrarin, *Hegel and Aristotle*. Cambridge, England: Cambridge University Press, 2001, 31–3.

10. Friedrich Wilhelm Joseph Schelling, *Zur Geschichte der neueren Philosophie. Münchener Vorlesungen*. Berlin: Verlag das Europäische Buch, 1986, 54; quoted from Schelling, *On the History of Modern Philosophy*, trans. A. Bowie. Cambridge, England: Cambridge University Press, 1994, 61. I am indebted to Alfredo Ferrarin for a conversation about Schelling in this context.

11. Thomas Reid to James Gregory, June 8, 1783. In *The Correspondence of Thomas Reid*, ed. P. Wood. Edinburgh, Scotland: Edinburgh University Press, 2002, 163.

12. Reid does not seem to have availed himself of any of the standard histories of philosophy. In *Essays on the Intellectual Powers of Man*, ed. D. Brookes and K. Haakonssen. Edinburgh, Scotland: Edinburgh University Press, 2002, 28, he refers to Brucker's first major work, *Historia philosophica doctrinae de ideis* (1723), but I know of no references to the *Historia Critica* or to Stanley's *History of Philosophy*.

13. Reid's engagement with the history of modern philosophy was so extensive that he toyed with James Gregory's suggestion that he should turn this material into a separate work. See the letter referred to in note 5 and my Introduction to Thomas Reid, *Essays on the Intellectual Powers of Man*.

14. *Histoire abrégée des sciences metaphysiques, morales et politiques depuis la renaissance des lettres*, trans. J. A. Buchon. Paris, 1820.

15. See Daniel Schulthess, "L'ecole ecossaise et la philosophie d'expression française: le rôle de Pierre Prevost (Geneva 1751–1839)," *Annales Benjamin Constant*, 18–19 (1996): 97–105; same, "L'impact de la philosophie écossaise sur la dialectique enseignée à Genève: Un cours latin inédit (1793–1794) de Pierre Prevost," in *Nomen Latinum. Mélanges de langue, de littérature et de civilisation latines offerts au professeur André Schneider...*, ed. D. Knoepfler. Geneva: Librairie Droz, 1997, 383–90. It is well-known that Common Sense philosophy also had an extraordinary

influence in the United States for several decades of the 19th century. For a general overview, see Benjamin W. Redekop, "Reid's Influence in Britain, Germany, France, and America," in *The Cambridge Companion to Reid*, ed. Terence Cuneo and René van Woudenberg. Cambridge, England: Cambridge University Press, 2004, 313–39.

16. *Les fragments philosophiques de Royer-Collard*, ed. A. Schimberg. Paris, 1913; first appended to Thomas Reid, *Œuvres complètes*, trans. T. Jouffroy. Paris, 1828. Cf. Schneider, *Philosophie und Universität*, 180–212; Donald R. Kelley, *The Descent of Ideas. The History of Intellectual History*. Aldershot, Hants, England: Ashgate Publishing, 2002, ch. 1.

17. Later he incorporated this into a world-historical scheme of cultural cycles.

18. Those, such as Hegel and Cousin, who made philosophy part of grand cycles of civilization would find room for an "Oriental" epoch some time in the gray past, and as the Middle Ages became established as an object for philosophical scholarship, the Arab contribution began to be noticed.

19. Kant, "Wiener Logik," Ak 24: 800, and "Logik Jäsche," Ak 9: 27; James Mill, *History of British India*, vols. in 4. New York: Chelsea House, 1968, I: 232, II: 240, 242; etc., and see *Selected Economic Writings*, ed. D. Winch. Edinburg/London: Oliver and Boyd; Chicago: Chicago University Press, 1966, ch. V.

20. See Hans Aarsleff, Introduction, in Wilhelm von Humboldt, *On Language: The Diversity of Human Language-Structure and Its Influence on the Mental Development of Mankind*, trans. P. Heath. Cambridge, England: Cambridge University Press, 1988, x and lxiii; same, Review Essay in *Anthropological Linguistics*, 43 (2001): 491–507; Ruth Römer, *Sprachwissenschaft und Rassenideologie in Deutschland*, 2nd edition. Munich: Fink, 1989.

21. See especially the pioneering study by Genevieve Lloyd, *The Man of Reason. "Male" and "Female" in Western Philosophy*. Minneapolis: University of Minnesota Press, 1993.

22. See Susan James's magisterial *Passion and Action: The Emotions in Seventeenth-Century Philosophy*. Oxford, England: Oxford University Press, 1997. Cf. also Annette Baier's interpretation of Hume, e.g., "Hume, the Women's Moral Theorist?" in *Moral Prejudices: Essays on Ethics*. Cambridge, Mass.: Harvard University Press, 1994, 51–75.

23. See the impressive body of work reviewed in Nancy Tuana's and Eileen O'Neill's papers in this volume.

24. Hochstrasser, *Natural Law Theories in the Early Enlightenment* (note 2).

25. Garve's *Uebersicht der vornehmsten Principien der Sittenlehre*.

26. Formey (see note 6) in the 1760s could still spare Grotius and Pufendorf

(not Thomasius) a couple of pages, but only as reformers of natural law; by the end of the 19th century, Ueberweg made do with less than a page each for Pufendorf and Thomasius—and identified them under the characteristic section heading "Zeitgenossen von Leibniz." In our own time, the following declaration by Lewis White Beck is probably representative of common opinion: "Had Kant not lived, German philosophy between the death of Leibniz in 1716 and the end of the 18th century would have little interest for us and would remain largely unknown." In *The Age of Reason,* ed. R. S. Solomon and K. M. Higgins, vol. 6 of *Routledge History of Philosophy.* London: Routledge, 1993, 5.

27. Hume, *Treatise of Human Nature,* II.1.3; Kant, *Critique of Pure Reason,* B xvi. I am indebted to Aaron Garrett for reminding me of this contrast.

28. Matthew L. Jones, "Descartes's Geometry as Spiritual Exercise," *Critical Inquiry* 28, 1 (Autumn 2001), 40–71.

29. Ian Hunter, "The Morals of Metaphysics: Kant's *Groundwork* as Intellectual *Paideia,*" *Critical Inquiry* 28, 4 (summer 2002), 908–29.

30. Ian Hunter, *Rival Enlightenments: Civil and Metaphysical Philosophy in Early Modern Germany.* Cambridge, England: Cambridge University Press, 2001.

31. Pierre Bayle, *The Dictionary Historical and Critical,* trans. Pierre Des Maizeux, 5 vols. London, 1734–38, art. "Spinoza," V:199–224; Adam Smith to William Strahan, November 9, 1776, in *The Correspondence of Adam Smith,* ed. E. C. Mossner and I. S. Ross. Oxford, England: Clarendon Press, 1977, 217–21.

32. George Berkeley, *Alciphron, or the Minute Philosopher,* Third Dialogue. In *The Works of George Berkeley,* ed. A. A. Luce and T. E. Jessop, 9 vols. Edinburgh, Scotland, 1948–57, III: 112–40.

33. William Leechman, "The Preface, giving some Account of the Life, Writings, and Character of the Author," in Francis Hutcheson, *A System of Moral Philosophy,* 2 vols. London 1755, e.g., at xxx–xxxii and xxxviii–xxxix.

34. See especially Charles B. Paul, *Science and Immortality: The Eloges of the Paris Academy of Sciences,* 1699–1791. Berkeley, Calif.; Los Angeles; and London: University of California Press, 1980.

35. It is telling that when Reid was performing his role as teacher, this traditional form of practical ethics was his organizing method; see the lectures reconstructed in Reid, *Practical Ethics: Being Lectures and Papers on Natural Religion, Self-Government, Natural Jurisprudence, and the Law of Nations,* ed. Knud Haakonssen. Princeton, N.J.: Princeton University Press, 1990. For the historical background, see, e.g., Paul Marshall, *A Kind of Life Imposed on Man: Vocation and Social Order from Tyndale to Locke.* Toronto: University of Toronto Press, 1996.

36. See Michael Albrecht, *Eklektik: Eine Begriffsgeschichte mit Hinweisen auf die Philosophie- und Wissenschaftsgeschichte*. Stuttgart-Bad Cannstatt: frommann-holzboog, 1994; Horst Dreitzel, "Zur Entwicklung und Eigenart der 'Eklektischen Philosophie,'" *Zeitschrift für Historische Forschung*, 18 (1991): 281–343; Tim Hochstrasser, *Natural Law Theories*, passim; Donald R. Kelley, The Descent of Ideas, esp. ch. 5.

37. For historically informed philosophical analysis of testimony in general, see C. A. J. Coady, *Testimony. A Philosophical Study*. Oxford, England: Clarendon Press, 1992. For the theological aspects, see M. A. Stewart, "Revealed Religion: The British Debate," ch.15 of *The Cambridge History of Eighteenth-Century Philosophy* (see note 1). For testimony and history, see Dario Perinetti, "Philosophical Reflection on History," ibid., ch. 27.

38. Cf. Richard Yeo's suggestion that Enlightenment efforts to organize knowledge, such as Ephraim Chambers's *Cyclopedia*, were closely connected to the commonplace book, "A Solution to the Multitude of Books: Ephraim Chalmers's *Cyclopedia* (1728) as 'the Best Book in the Universe,'" *Journal of the History of Ideas* 64, 1 (2003), 61–72.

39. T. Hochstrasser, *Natural Law Theories*, 83–95.

40. H. Aarsleff, *From Locke to Saussure: Essays on the Study of Language and Intellectual History* (Minneapolis: University of Minnesota Press, 1982, 146–224; Introduction to Étienne Bonnot de Condillac, *Essay on the Origin of Human Knowledge*, ed. H. Aarsleff. Cambridge, England: Cambridge University Press, 2002, xi–xxxviii; and "The Philosophy of Language," in *Cambridge History of Eighteenth-Century Philosophy*, ch. 10.

Response to Knud Haakonssen

JEFFREY EDWARDS

LET ME FIRST say something about the perspective from which I am commenting on Knud Haakonssen's paper. The perspective is determined by two practical tasks and a belief. The tasks are these: (1) teaching undergraduate survey courses in the history of modern philosophy and (2) advising doctoral students about how to teach these survey courses. The belief is this: although the results of, and the theoretical insights achieved by, the "new histories" of philosophy are generally compelling, we cannot afford (at least not in the North American context) simply to dissolve the structure of the now traditional historical survey courses at the undergraduate level. In view of this belief, I should perhaps clarify several further points right at the outset: First, most of what I am going to say applies to undergraduate teaching. (My teaching in doctoral seminars, especially on the history of ethics, has never relied on the epistemological paradigm that Haakonssen targets, so I cannot speak from experience about what it's like to be constrained by the paradigm in graduate teaching.) Second, experience has taught me to teach undergraduate history of modern moral philosophy separately from the institutionally standard courses on Descartes to Kant or on the "Rationalists" and the "Empiricists." Third, I agree emphatically with the position that no curricular priority should be given to the history of epistemology and metaphysics course over and above a course on modern moral philosophy that moves along various paths between Montaigne and Kant.[1]

In discussing the epistemological paradigm or approach that has long conditioned our understanding of modern philosophy's history, Haakonssen pays special attention to the restrictive, and hence historiographically distorting, features of the "Kantian and Reidian legacy." I will have time to discuss three of these features.

ONE

Haakonssen writes that the epistemological paradigm has obscured the basic systematic arrangement of early modern philosophy—namely, its division into natural and moral philosophy. If I understand him correctly, he is suggesting that the failure to respect this arrangement is due to the Kantian and Reidian legacy's reductive fixation on the justificatory concerns of modern philosophy, as distinguished from its broader explanatory and classificatory aims.

This criticism no doubt raises a number of issues about the distinction between justification and explanation as it applies to 17th- and 18th-century philosophy. But accepting (as I do) that the criticism is on target, I would suggest the following. The failure to do justice to the basic systematic arrangement of early modern philosophy stems from the Kantian and Reidian *legacy*, not from Kant and Reid. Indeed, rescuing Kant and Reid from their historiographic legacy may well be a highly significant task for contemporary work on the history of philosophy precisely because of the epistemological paradigm's historical dominance. Let me just indicate here several features of Kant's and Reid's ethics and metaphysics that might be of interest in this regard.

1. Take the various templates that Kant provides for making systematic sense of the history of ethics prior to his theory of morality as autonomy of the will. Consider, for example, the different types of nonautonomous ethics treated in the first chapter of the *Critique of Practical Reason*.[2] Kant's list there includes not just sentimentalist ethics and rationalist perfectionist ethics. It has a separate classification for theonomous ethics (as represented by Crusius, among others), and it makes room for the different types of approach represented by the figures of Montaigne and Mandeville.[3] If one is planning a course on modern ethics through Kant, then this kind of classificatory schema is at least worth thinking about. And it does not conform in any obvious way to the reductive impetus of the epistemological paradigm.

2. There are historically interpretive aspects of Reid's ethical theory that are relevant to teaching 17th- and 18th-century moral philosophy. Take, for example, chapter VI of essay III in the *Essays on*

the Active Powers of the Human Mind. There, Reid demonstrates the concern to overcome the standard divide separating intellectualist and intuitional theories, on one hand, and sentimentalist theories, on the other, by bringing to bear his conception that sense itself involves the power to judge. The historical interpretive line that Reid runs in this chapter clearly does fit in—perhaps a little too neatly—with key features of the epistemological paradigm. Yet it does not require one to disregard in any way the basic systematic arrangement of early modern philosophy. Moreover, it lends itself quite handily to structuring a course or seminar in 18th-century moral philosophy in Britain that culminates chronologically in Reid's ethics.

3. Consider, finally, Kant's efforts at working out a plan for understanding the main developmental strands of theoretical philosophy in terms of the opposition between enthusiasm (*Schwärmerei*) and metaphysical dogmatism.[4] This plan, which is already in evidence by the 1780s and which shapes the course of Kant's historicophilosophic reflections in the *Opus postumum*, goes well beyond the Locke/Berkeley/Hume versus Descartes/Leibniz/Wolff opposition that has tended to provide for the systematic substructure of the epistemological paradigm since the time of Kant's contemporaries and followers.[5] According to the alternative scheme at issue, Spinozism represents the culmination of, and the essential link between, *Schwärmerei* and dogmatic metaphysics. Kant purports to locate the origins of enthusiasm in the Platonic and Neoplatonic tradition(s). He also wants to locate the origin of dogmatism in the principle *Nihil est in intellectu quod non prius fuerit in sensu,* which he links to the name of Aristotle. The theories of knowledge that underlie the two streams of metaphysical thought converge in the Spinozistic theory of substance. Thus, what Kant regards as the two main streams of precritical metaphysics in Western philosophy come together in the reservoir of Spinozisitc thinking. And the figure of Spinoza represents the hypostasis of any non-critical metaphysical undertaking that asserts *either* that the objects of human rational cognition are purely intelligible *or* that the origins of our rational cognition are empirical. In effect, Kant maintains that the historically central Platonic and Aristotelian traditions in

metaphysics can, in the end, amount to nothing more than a form of Spinozism. The implication is that the history of theoretical philosophy must be understood in terms of an encompassing developmental scheme that includes the core elements of the epistemological paradigm—namely, the histories of modern empiricism and rationalism—but is not reducible to those elements.

I think that Kant's inclusive plan is rather interesting for a good many reasons, and one does not have to accept it at face value in order to put it to productive use. For example, it allows one to think about various ways of constructing a survey course framework in which early modern debates on enthusiasm and religious doctrine can be treated. It also gets one to thinking about what to do with Spinoza in that horrible-even-to-think-about course that is expected to line up and look at all the usual suspects between Descartes and Kant.

Two

I now come to Haakonssen's considerations on what he under-stands as the most deeply rooted element in the epistemological paradigm: its individualism and mentalism. The paradigm's exclusive focus on the activity and passivity of the individual person's mind does make it difficult even to address in a satisfactory manner many of the central themes in early modern philosophy, and Haakonssen discusses two of the themes that have been neglected: (1) the debates surrounding theories of testimony that were based on the supposition that knowledge is something shared interpersonally and (2) the revolutionary developments in the theory of language. In dealing with these themes, Haakonssen recommends that we set aside the epistemological paradigm in order to understand the contempora-neous discussion of the specifically social forms of knowledge in question—forms ranging from revealed religion and scriptural criticism to secular history and accounts of language.

I am not sure, though, why we should *set aside* the epistemological paradigm when attempting to understand how modern thinkers attempted to come to grips with the social forms of knowledge. A lot depends, of course, on what such setting aside involves. But we do need to be careful not to miss the epistemological (if "mentalistic") sides of various debates pertaining to those forms. Can one understand, for example, Hume's chapter on miracles in the first *Enquiry* by stepping aside from the epistemological approach? Can one understand, say, section XXIV of chapter 6 in Reid's *Inquiry into the Human Mind on the Principles of Common Sense* if we lose close *contact* with the standard paradigm? (The title of section XXIV is "Of the Analogy between Perception and the Credit We Give to Human Testimony.") To be sure, there are many highly significant dimensions of the discussions of social forms of knowledge that cannot be understood from an epistemological approach severely limited by what Haakonssen refers to as individualism and mentalism. At the same time, however, there are important dimensions of these discussions that cannot be adequately interpreted in abstraction from the recognizably epistemological concerns of modern thinkers. And as luck has it (or not), these are precisely the dimensions that have come to be of increasing interest to contemporary philosophy.

Generally speaking, my sense is that the epistemological paradigm is indeed subject to the limitations described by Haakonssen. Yet I think it makes sense to be cautious about setting aside that paradigm for teaching purposes—at least when we are talking about philosophy programs in which the standard undergraduate survey courses on Descartes to Kant and on the rationalists and the empiricists are for the most part still central requirements in the philosophy major. The paradigm can of course be *subverted* by operating from within its framework. It can also be subversively supplemented in a variety of ways—the most important way being, in my view, a broadly laid-out course (or courses) on the history of modern moral philosophy. But I doubt that it is practicable or even desirable to dissolve the paradigm, at least as it has been used in philosophy programs.[6] We need to bear in mind that the still standard undergraduate survey courses are, in the North American context, usually the only ones in which philosophy students get *any* kind of exposure to *some* kind of synthetic treatment of 17th- and 18th-century philosophy. This holds true even of many students—indeed most students, I suspect—who end up going on to graduate school in philosophy.

THREE

As Haakonssen points out, there has been the tendency in the past two centuries to assimilate ethics and aesthetics to epistemology by way of reduction of the ethical and aesthetic concerns of modern philosophy to questions of justification. He maintains that the epistemological fixation inherent in the dominant historiographic paradigm is responsible for this reductive tendency. For the most part, I can agree with these claims. Yet, again, I am not convinced that either of the source figures of the Kantian and Reidian legacy is responsible for this fixation (if I may call it that)—at least not in ethics. Obviously, Kant and Reid take general epistemological positions in working out their ethical theories, and both of them have recognizably metaethical concerns. But I do not understand the sense in which these theories can be said to boil down to accounts of justification, if that is what has been said. Haakonssen also points out that political theory, particularly the political dimension of natural law theory, either has been excluded from general histories of philosophy or else, at best, has had its history treated in isolation from the mainstreams of philosophic inquiry. He mentions in this vein that Pufendorf and Thomasius have been written out of philosophy altogether. Since much of my professional formation took place in Germany, I confess that I never really had the opportunity to be strongly struck by this fact. But I definitely agree with the general line of criticism, especially as it pertains to the philosophical devaluation of major figures like Pufendorf and Thomasius. It is unquestionably implausible to think that one could teach the history of modern natural law theory in relation to the broader history of ethics without taking Pufendorf and Thomasius as centrally important thinkers. (How *would* it be possible to give a historically well-founded account of obligation in modern philosophy without going into Pufendorf? How *can* one explain the historical import or even the conceptual significance of the separation of *ius* and *ethica* in Kant without saying something about Thomasius?) At any rate, the bad days *are* over. It simply is no longer a serious option to ignore such figures.

Still, a key question remains to be addressed. Just how is one to teach the natural lawyers? In the time remaining, I can try to explain only my own decision in this regard. I have decided *not* to treat modern natural law theory (starting with an account of the differences between Suarez and Grotius) as a *central* part of courses on the history of 17th- and 18th-century *ethics*. I hasten to add that I cannot imagine how to get by in a course on modern ethics without doing some explanatory work on subjective natural right(s), natural law conceptions of the grounds of obligation in general, the systematic distinctions between perfect and imperfect duties, and the like. But at this historical juncture, I think it is crucial to give fullest possible play to modern natural law theories of political obligation, sovereignty, and international law from the Grotians through Rousseau and Kant. In the North American context at least, one will tend to do this within a curricular framework that does not have an especially well-defined place for the theoretical discipline in question—namely, juridical philosophy (in the sense of classic *Rechtsphilosophie*). There are many reasons for this lack of commonly accepted disciplinary space, not the least of which stems from the fact that we do not work on theoretical terrain historically contoured by the subterranean drainage network, as it were, of Roman law: the water tends to collect in the hollows and remain on the surface, often to stagnate. (For the Scots, of course, things are rather different in this regard.) Yet despite the lack of standard disciplinary space, I think that it makes sense to treat the kind of theoretical undertaking in which the modern natural lawyers were engaged as something distinct from (though of course intimately connected with) ethics, political philosophy, or even what ordinarily qualifies as philosophy of law. Indeed, I would say that we *ought* to do this, given that we are now confronted by wielders of power who seem quite happily intent on dismantling the real secular achievements of the entire history of natural law thinking in the domains of international law and international political institutions. So how do we treat the various histories of natural law thought? Any way we can.

NOTES

1. By *history of [modern] epistemology and metaphysics* I mean, of course, the history of epistemology apart from moral epistemology and the history of metaphysics apart from the metaphysics of morals. As a Kant scholar, I take these distinctions seriously.

2. See 5:40; cf. also 4:441–43; 19:118 (Reflection 6631), 121–22 (Reflection 6637); 27:3–5, 107–110, 1404–06. (Kant is cited according to the volume and page numbers of *Kants gesammelte Schriften* [the "Academy Edition"].)

3. Kant names Hutcheson as the prime representative of the sentimentalist approach. Wolff and the Stoics are mentioned in connection with the perfectionist idea. "Crusius and other theological moralists" represent the voluntarist strain. I discuss the developmental background and some theoretical implications of Kant's classifications in "Egoism and Formalism in the Development of Kant's Moral Philosophy," *Kant-Studien* 91 (2000): 411–32.

4. See 18:434–438 (Reflections 6050 and 6051).

5. I discuss the implications of Kant's plan in relation to the *Opus postumum* in in ch. 9 of my *Substance, Force, and the Possibility of Knowledge: On Kant's Philosophy of Nature*. Berkeley, Calif; Los Angeles; and London: University of California Press, 2000.

6. I should point out that the Princeton conference on teaching the new histories of philosophy has made my conviction in this regard much less firm than it was when I wrote these comments.

Arguments over Obligation:
Teaching Time and Place in Moral Philosophy

Ian Hunter

THERE SEEMS to be a degree of agreement about what might count as the so-called new histories of philosophy.[1] In the epilogue to his monumental *Invention of Autonomy*, J. B. Schneewind provides a snapshot of the old and the new, pointing to the difference between histories of moral philosophy that assume a chain of thinkers all trying to solve the same problem and those newer histories that drop this assumption in favor of a "variable-aim approach." In accordance with the newer approaches: "We will not, in particular, suppose that everyone who thought about morality in a way we consider philosophical was trying to solve the same problem or answer the same questions. We will think instead that the aims of moral philosophy—the problems that moral philosophers thought required reflection—are at least as likely to have changed as to have remained constant through history." To approach past philosophers in terms of their own problems and arguments, instead of those we now deem essential, we must adopt a historical investigative attitude. "Here," Schneewind says, "only historical information, and not rational reconstruction of arguments in the best modern terms, will tell us what we need to know" (Schneewind, 1998: 550-1). Finally, if the historical course of moral philosophy is not governed by a single problem and its one true solution, then in order to take up the historical attitude, we must not assume that philosophy advances by coming closer to this truth or, presumably, that it "advances" in any particular direction at all.

> Failure to achieve coherence or to produce valid supporting arguments may explain the change in some cases. But the single-aim view leaves unexplained a great deal that the historian will

naturally wish to consider. Why do some theories emerge and flourish and then disappear, why do some recur, why is there so little convergence, what does moral philosophy as a practice or discipline do in and for the societies in which it is supported? It is more useful for the historian to turn away from the single-aim view and adopt a variable-aim approach instead (Schneewind, 1998, 553).

Schneewind thus offers some important pointers to histories of moral philosophy that are new in the sense of dropping the assumption that history advances (or regresses) along a single problem-path, requiring us instead to discover anew the problems over which philosophers struggled, the contexts driving these struggles, and the circumstances leading to always-contingent triumphs. History of philosophy written in this style may not be absolutely new, yet it feels novel because during the second half of the 20th century, the history of philosophy was overshadowed or colonized by dominating, systematic philosopies. In Germany, it was post-Kantian metaphysics in the form of Hegelian philosophical history and, especially, Husserlian transcendental phenomenology that dominated the *Geisteswissenschaften*, giving rise to a present-centered history of philosophy focused on the goal of a rational moral autonomy (Mommsen, 2001). Especially in the hands of Jürgen Habermas and the critical theorists, this led to a single-aim view in which the history of philosophy is seen as one long series of attempts to bring the transcendental moral law down to earth by embodying it in the process of discourse, understood as the intersubjective exercise of rational autonomy. (Habermas, 1992) In the American setting, those influenced by the towering figure of John Rawls have produced a similarly monocular history, albeit on different metaphysical premises (Ball, 2001, 121). On this view, the history of moral philosophy is a long chain of failed attempts to reconcile rationalism and voluntarism—or the light of transcendental reason and the obligating force of moral command—leading up to Kant's epochal recovery of the self-commanding rational will (Korsgaard, 1996b).

Given the commanding presence of these philosophies in today's humanities academy—itself testimony to the intensity of the contemporary moral cultures they embody—we should take a sober view of the obstacles faced by any attempt to teach a contextualist and pluralist history of philosophy. Some of these obstacles will be institutional, as in many universities the history of philosophy is taught in predominantly analytic philosophy departments, often in the form of service courses, or as preparation for the purely theoretical discussion of canonical philosophers or problems. Located thus in the curriculum, the new history of philosophy will be still-born, as it will lack the room to develop as an independent intellectual enterprise and will be smothered by those who wrap it too tightly in the problems of their philosophical heroes.

Despite its importance, however, I shall not be addressing the institutional question on this occasion. Instead, I shall concentrate on two prior questions: first, the question of how to introduce students to philosophical argument in a contextualized and pluralist manner and second, the question of what kinds of texts such a pedagogy requires at its disposal. The two questions are of course intimately related, as the dominance of the single-aim present-centered approach brings with it a highly selective publication of the archive, in editions typically suited to the aims of rational reconstruction rather than historical investigation. The influence of a secondary text such as Lewis Beck's *Early German Philosophy*—symptomatically subtitled *Kant and His Predecessors*—goes together with the fact that while Kant's texts are available in numerous modernized student editions, many of the so-called predecessors (Thomasius, Wolff, Crusius—the "popular philosophers") have not even been translated into English (Beck, 1969). This was the kind of deficit that the Cambridge green and blue series of Texts in the History of Philosophy was intended to address and, more recently, Knud Haakonssen's ambitious series of Natural Law and Enlightenment Classics.

In this paper I shall make use of an early modern text—newly reedited and published in Haakonssen's series—in order to show how the German moral philosopher and political historian Samuel Pufendorf—together with his critic Gottfried Leibniz and his apologist Jean Barbeyrac—may be introduced to students other than as one of Kant's predecessors. The text is the first English translation of Pufendorf's *De officio hominis et civis*—rendered as *The Whole Duty of Man according to the Law of Nature* by Andrew Tooke in 1691—which

I have reedited with David Saunders (Hunter and Saunders, 2003). This new edition also includes Saunders' translation of Barbeyrac's presentation of Leibniz's famous attack on Pufendorf, in addition to the Huguenot's two discourses on natural law.[2] It thus provides a simulacrum of Barbeyrac's own French translation of the *De officio*— the most influential in early modern Europe—whose fourth edition included these additional materials as appendixes, ostensibly to aid in the reception of Pufendorf's ideas (Barbeyrac and Pufendorf, 1718).

Deployed in an appropriate pedagogy, this reedited text would permit students to approach key early modern arguments— specifically those over moral and political obligation—not as fumbling approximations to later known truths but in an altogether more historical manner: as bitterly fought disputes invoking competing "known truths" and driven by wider cultural-political struggles, hence lacking the comfort of a universally acceptable resolution. Students would thus be asked not to reconstruct the conceptions of obligation advanced by Pufendorf, Leibniz, and Barbeyrac in the light of a later one presented to them as true but to assume a quite different attitude and undertake a different series of tasks. They would be asked to adopt a posture of descriptive inquiry oriented to an empirical historical investigation of the rival conceptions—first, in terms of the larger doctrines informing them and then in terms of the cultural and political issues that the participants themselves saw as at stake in their arguments. The present paper might thus be seen as providing the rationale, the structure, and some of the bibliographic materials for an extended case study on arguments over obligation in early modern Europe.

Pufendorf's Place in Kantian Historiography

In designing a curriculum oriented to historical study of the arguments over obligation clustered around Pufendorf's moral and political philosophy, it would not be necessary, and might not be advisable, to begin with a prophylactic discussion of noncontextual approaches of the Kantian present-centered kind. For our immediate purposes, however, some such discussion is necessary in order to clarify the orientation of such a curriculum and the conventional wisdom that it must challenge if it is to cross the threshold of historical inquiry.

In fact, Pufendorf's place in the Kantian history of philosophy was prepared during the late 18th century. At this point, Kantian philosophical theologians like Buhle, Tennemann, and Stäudlin erased Pufendorf's earlier position—in which he was regarded as one of the founders of a secular civil ethics—and repositioned him as one of a series of minor thinkers who had failed in the Kantian task of harmonizing voluntarist and rationalist conceptions of morality (Hochstrasser, 2000, 206–12). In more recent elaborations of this view, Pufendorf is routinely regarded as someone who takes an important step along the Kantian path, by developing a (deontological) command theory of moral obligation, but who fails to complete the journey, for lack of rational philosophical justification of the source of these commands.

The key text for these discussions is Pufendorf's construction of obligation, as it is given in the *De officio* or *Whole Duty*. Here Pufendorf stipulates that: "An *Obligation* is superinduced upon the Will of Men properly by a *Superior*; that is, not only by such a one as being *greater* or *stronger*, can punish Gainsayers: but by him who has *just Reasons* to have a Power to restrain the Liberty of our Will at his own pleasure." Neither coercion nor just reasons by themselves will create obligation because, in the absence of just reasons, coercion merely terrifies without responsibilizing, while, in the absence of coercive force, just reasons merely inform without conforming the will. Pufendorf clearly regards the key to this combination of coercion and just reasons as lying in the form of the just reasons (*justae causae*) themselves, which he characterizes thus:

> Now the *Reasons* upon which one man may *justly* exact *Subjection* from another, are; If he have been to the other the *Original* of some extraordinary *Good*; and if it be plain, that he designs the other's *Welfare*, and is *able* to provide better for him than 'tis possible for *himself* to do; and on the same account does actually lay *claim* to the Government of him: and lastly if any one does *voluntarily* surrender his Liberty to another, and subject *himself* to his Direction (*WDM*, 45).[3]

Modern Kantians are flatly dismissive of Pufendorf's construction of obligation as arising from legitimate superiority or subjection, itself understood in terms of the exchange of obedience for protection and care; for such an exchange or agreement does not count as a philosophical justification of the kind they require. In her commentary on Pufendorf's formula, Christine Korsgaard puts the point succinctly—in the form of a dilemma:

> If we try to derive the authority of morality from some natural source of power, it will evaporate in our hands. If we try to derive it from some supposedly normative consideration, such as gratitude or contract, we must in turn explain why that consideration is normative, or where its authority comes from. Either its authority comes from morality, in which case we have argued in a circle, or it comes from something else, in which case the question arises again, and we are faced with an infinite regress (Korsgaard 1996b, 30).

Given a certain set of background assumptions this knockdown argument is of course highly persuasive. One of the benefits of locating Pufendorf's obligation formula in its historical setting, however, is that we can see such arguments as strategic moves in a certain contestatory domain, and this shines a light on their underlying assumptions and the conditions of their persuasiveness. It is striking then that in his attack on Pufendorf, as presented by Barbeyrac, we find Leibniz mounting an argument almost identical to Korsgaard's:

> Perceptive though he was, the author [Pufendorf] fell into a contradiction for which I do not see how he could easily be excused. For he bases all legal obligation on the will of a superior.... Yet, shortly afterwards, he then says that a superior must have not only power sufficient to oblige us to obey him, but also just cause for claiming a certain power over us. (book I, chapter ii, part 5) Therefore the justice of the cause precedes the establishment of the superior. If to discover the source of the law a superior must be identified, and if, on the other hand, the authority of the superior must be founded in causes drawn from the law, then we have fallen into the most blatant circularity ever (*WDMJ*, 300).

It is immediately clear in the context, however, that this charge of circularity works only against the background of two metaphysical assumptions: namely, that humans are beings capable of inner rational self-governance, and that rationally binding norms must be self-grounding; otherwise, we could ask, for any putative source of norms, what makes *this* normative? Leibniz specifies this self-grounding source of normativity in his comment that "the rule of his [God's] actions, like the very nature of justice, depends not on a free decision of his will, but rather on the eternal truths which are the objects of the divine mind and which are established, so to speak, by his divine essence" (*WDMJ*, 289). Korsgaard shares both of these assumptions but differs from Leibniz in locating the self-grounding source of normativity not in a divine mind but in a totality of rational beings—Kant's "kingdom of ends"—whose collective willing constitutes a self-grounding moral law and an ultimate moral identity. (Korsgaard, 1996b, 98–105). It is this second assumption in particular that allows Leibniz and Korsgaard to argue the circularity of Pufendorf's derivation of legitimate superiority from just causes—that is, the exchange of obedience for protection—on the grounds that this exchange must itself either be moral (in the sense of being morally self-grounding) or not be (in which case it must derive its normativity from a higher self-grounding source).[4]

As we shall see, though, not only does Pufendorf not make these assumptions, but he rejects them in an explicit and highly self-conscious manner. He begins by rejecting the conception of man as a self-obligating rational being, treating this as wholly unsuited to an ethics oriented to the civil governance of a creature whose passions require externally imposed limits (*WDM*, 43–4). And he declares that the associated notion of morality, as arising from man's participation in the excellence of the divine intellect, is incapable of showing how such a creature might be placed under obligation. Pufendorf thus views the exchange of obedience for protection (the "just reasons") as neither essentially normative (legitimate in itself) nor as dependent on a higher truly moral source. Instead, he treats the civil pact as a profound convention or institution that determines what will count as just or right in the civil domain. When combined with coercive force, the pact gives rise to the legitimate superiority from which civil obligation flows. As we shall see in more detail later,

Pufendorf cites decisive religious and political reasons for refusing to treat civil authority as the expression of a distinct or higher normative source—as it is in Aristotelian conceptions of politics and Kantian conceptions of morality—because this would give rise to the dangerous view that citizens are already obligated by norms higher than those imposed by such authority. For the moment, then, we can say that Pufendorf is not compelled to (circularly) assume that the civil compact is itself normative or moral, for two reasons: first, because he regards it as instituting the *sui generis* moral domain consisting of civil authority and duties, and, second, because he self-consciously rejects the assumption that the personae of this domain (subjects and superior) are the bearers of some higher source of norms—whether Leibniz's divine ideas or, by extrapolation, Korsgaard's Kantian collective rational will.

The point of this exercise is not of course to show that Pufendorf's conception of obligation is right and Leibniz's and Korsgaard's wrong; rather, it is to show that it is unhelpful to seek to understand Pufendorf's conception by importing metaphysical assumptions and problems that he explicitly rejected. The problem Pufendorf felt compelled to confront was not Korsgaard's Kantian problem of deriving the "authority of morality" but the quite different one of constructing the morality of authority. Far from trying (and failing) to provide a source of obligating norms in a self-grounding rationality, Pufendorf self-consciously rejected all such attempts as contrary to the new model of civil obligation he was elaborating and as dangerous to the legitimacy of civil authority. Of course, he may well have been wrong about this too, but, again, that is beside the point. Our obligation as historians and teachers is not to comprehend Pufendorf's model on the basis of one that we take to be right; it is, rather, to understand it in terms of the concepts and doctrines actually used to elaborate it, and the cultural and political purposes driving this elaboration.

Once we have taken this turn, then we can begin to teach the history of philosophical arguments over obligation. Now we can ask our students to investigate how Pufendorf, Leibniz, and Barbeyrac constructed their conflicting models of obligation, and the larger cultural and political circumstances they sought to engage by doing so. How, then, might the reedited *Whole Duty of Man* be used in this pedagogical undertaking? In answering this question I shall not of course be outlining a concrete syllabus but sketching a set of core issues that might inform a lecture series, a group of related case studies, or the parameters for guided project work, and so on.

PUFENDORF'S CIVIL ETHICS

In introducing students to a contextual approach to Pufendorf's conception of obligation, one needs to begin by sketching some of the relevant features of the circumstances in which the *De officio* first appeared, the cultural and political problems that it sought to address, and the ways in which the text itself was shaped to engage these. In this initial phase, then, it would be helpful to point out that the *De officio* (1673) was written as a student abridgment of Pufendorf's massive *De jure naturae et gentium* (1672) and that this abridgment was initially intended for law and politics students in several northern European Protestant states (Sweden, Brandenburg, Prussia), even though it was fairly quickly translated into the major vernaculars of German (Weber's *Einleitung zur Sitten- und Stats-Lehre*, 1691), English (Tooke's *Whole Duty*, 1691), and French (Barbeyrac's *Les devoirs*, 1707). In clarifying the social disposition of its first intended audience—the future civil and religious officials of Protestant territorial states—one provides pointers to both the cultural role envisaged for the text and to the initial context in which this role was to be played out. In relation to the latter, early lectures and readings would need to offer orienting material on Pufendorf's publicistic career in the immediate aftermath of the Thirty Years' War and the Treaties of Westphalia (1648). Here, like other "civil philosophers," he was preoccupied by the problem of religious civil war and the various attempts to restructure the relations between church and state in response to this problem.[5] This setting—in which he regarded the emergent Protestant territorial states as threatened externally by a hostile transterritorial Catholicism and, internally, by fissile Protestant estates and churches—is the envisaged context that Pufendorf addressed in his attempt to reconfigure politics and ethics in the *De jure* and the *De officio*.

It was in this setting that Pufendorf deployed his quasi-Epicurean moral anthropology, positioning man as a being capable of free choice but dominated by destructive passions and incapable of rational self-governance. Here too he developed his Hobbesian reconstruction of obligation—as grounded in the exchange of obedience for protection—and also his conception of civil authority or legitimate subjection, as instituted by the civil pact and disconnected from higher moral sources. Taken together, these core elements of Pufendorf's thought offered a way of reconstructing politics and ethics in a manner that would free the civil authority of emergent territorial states from potentially dangerous forms of "higher" moral authority. Of particular concern to Pufendorf was the divine authority claimed by a hostile Catholic natural law and political theology, as well as the supracivil moral authority of conscience claimed by Protestant political theologians, secular metaphysicians, and inner-light sectarians.[6] This at least might form a framing hypothesis, offering a way into the *Whole Duty* and opening up a series of investigative topics.

An early issue to be tackled is that of the moral idiom in which the *De officio* was composed and that finds a ready reception in the moral lexicon employed by Tooke in the *Whole Duty*. This idiom is deeply indebted to the concept of office (*officium*), understood narrowly as duty and, more broadly, as the capacity in which an individual acts as the bearer of a delimited bundle of duties. In its broad sense, office is close to the notion of persona as the identity assumed in a capacity.[7] The first sentence of the *Whole Duty* contains a definition of duty—as "*That* Action *of a Man, which is regularly order'd according to some prescrib'd* Law, *which he is obliged to obey*"—which the editors of the fourth (1716) edition saw fit to explicate by adapting one of Barbeyrac's footnotes:

> The ancient *Stoicks* call'd Actions by the Greek Word καθηκον, and by the Latin OFFICIUM, and in English we use the Word *OFFICE* in the same Sense, when we say, *Friendly Offices*, &c. but then the Definition hereof given by the Philosophers, is too loose and general, since thereby they understood nothing but an *Action conformable to Reason*. As may appear from a Passage of *Cicero*...(*WDM*, 27).

But the clearest statement of why the Philosophers' conception of duty is insufficient comes at the beginning of chapter 1 of book II—

"Of the Natural State of Men"—where Tooke uses *state,* in the sense of condition or capacity, to translate Pufendorf's *status:*

> In the next Place, we are to inquire concerning those Duties which are incumbent upon a Man with Regard to that *particular State* wherein he finds himself ordained by Providence to live in the World. What we mean by such *State,* is in general, That *Condition* or *Degree* with all its Relatives, in which Men being placed, they are therefore supposed to be obliged to these or those Performances: And such *State,* whatever it be, has some peculiar Rights and Offices thereunto belonging (*WDM,* 166).

In fact, Pufendorf's original does not mention Providence, referring only to duties arising from the different statuses or capacities of social life (*ex diverso statu, in quo in vita communi degere deprehenditur*). Still, the basic message comes through: Pufendorf regards duties as a class of actions rendered normative through occupancy of a particular status, office, or persona. It is striking that he extends this understanding to the *status naturalis* itself—that is, the condition imposed on man by God and in which he finds himself prior to the existence of social institutions and civil authority. Pufendorf thus insists that man's nature must also be regarded as a status imposed for governing a certain class of actions, rather than as a substance or soul containing all duties.

From the outset then, Pufendorf discusses duties and obligation using the moral idiom of multiple offices and personae. It is thus quite anachronistic to approach his civil ethics from a post-Kantian standpoint, in which morality is constructed in terms of maxims willed by a totality of rational beings, membership of which determines an ultimate moral identity. The different ethical landscape in which Pufendorf operates is made strikingly clear in the preface, in which he invokes the multiplicity of moral ends and offices in order to demarcate the civil domain of natural law by differentiating it from moral theology and positive law. Natural law, says Pufendorf, pertains to man in his civil persona, or "Civil Deportment," as Tooke has it, which is restricted to "the Compass of this life only, and so thereby a Man is informed how he is to live in Society with the Rest of Mankind." Moral theology, though, deals with man in his persona as a Christian, whose end is salvation rather than sociability and whose duties are thus distinct from those of the citizen: "Hence it is that the Dictates of the *Law of Nature* are adapted only to *Human Judicature*, which does not extend it self beyond this Life; and it would be absurd in many respects to apply them to the *Divine Forum*, which concerns itself only about Theology" (*WDM*, 19–20). The idiom of multiple moral personae thus allows Pufendorf to carve out a distinctive and delimited space of duties for natural law, now understood as civil ethics. In this *sui generis* moral domain, whose architecture is provided by the *Whole Duty*, the deepest and most divisive questions regarding access to an ultimate moral identity are deliberately nullified, while all references to God and our duties to him are subordinated to the overarching end of civil peace and the duties of sociability. To approach Pufendorf's civil ethics from a post-Kantian perspective—in terms of an ultimate moral personality formed through membership of a community of rational beings— is thus worse than anachronistic; it actually traduces Pufendorf's desacralizing pluralization of ethics by retrospectively imposing just the kind of ethical culture that he was intent on avoiding.

Once students have grasped the twin themes of the multiplicity of offices and the civil demarcation of natural law, it becomes possible to introduce a range of other topics for the *Whole Duty*, of which I shall mention just a few of the more significant. One set of issues is clustered around the separation of religious and civil morality and its role in relation to conflicts and controversies associated with the place of religion in the civil polity. The language of office-specific duties offers Pufendorf a flexible and powerful means for reconfiguring the relation between religious and civil identities by treating these as separate personae, each with its own normative horizon and neither one reducible to the other. Having begun by tying the persona of the Christian to the domain of theology and the end of salvation, Pufendorf is free to construct a civil persona in terms of duties derived from the end of social peace. This construction applies not only to duties to one's neighbors and oneself but also to religious duties, insofar as these are known by natural reason rather than revelation. Pufendorf thus elaborates his "natural religion" in terms of the acknowledgment of a few basic propositions regarding the existence of God and his providential care of the world. These are regarded as distinct from salvational religion and required solely by their role fostering civil sociability (*WDM*, 60–9).[8]

Students wishing to do further work on this question might be encouraged to read *Of the Nature and Qualification of Religion in Reference to Civil Society* (Zurbuchen, 2002). Here Pufendorf establishes mutually exclusive yet complementary relations between the twin personae of the church—the teacher and learner bound together by relations of love and care exclusive of all coercive power—and those of the state, whereby sovereign and citizen are bound together by the relations of subjection and coercion needed to maintain civil peace. In denying the church any access to civil power while simultaneously insisting that, under normal circumstances, the sovereign can be only a teacher or learner in the church, this work again shows the immediacy with which Pufendorf sought to address the pressing questions of confessional conflict, religious persecution, and the confessional state.

A further cluster of issues that may be approached in this way concerns the ethical basis of the state, which the *Whole Duty* formulates in terms of the transition from the natural to the civil "status." Here students can be prepared to investigate the consequences of Pufendorf's distinctive treatment of man's "nature," as a status gratuitously imposed by God rather than as a rational substance or soul shared with God and capable of participating in divine reason. These consequences might be brought out through comparisons with Locke's version of the transition from the natural to the civil state. In conceiving of the natural condition as an imposed status bereft of faculties and rights, and giving rise only to the duty to cultivate sociability, Pufendorf allows no room for (Lockean) natural rights. He thus attempts to preclude the possibility of natural rights and duties' being carried into the civil state, where they might be invoked by rebellious religious or moral communities as supracivil limits to the sovereign's legitimate authority. As a result, Pufendorf formulates "resistance" wholly in terms of the ruler's failure to fulfill the duties of the sovereign office, which betokens not a limit or sharing of civil sovereignty but its dissolution and a return to the natural condition (Seidler, 1996, 91–98). Similar consequences follow for the construction of criminal law and punishment, which Pufendorf views as wholly internal to the civil state whose security it serves, hence as disconnected from all notions of crime as immorality and punishment as restitution of natural morality within the civil order (*WDM*, 225–32). This is one of several key places where Barbeyrac sides with Locke against Pufendorf, arguing that crime and punishment are possible in man's natural state, which means that the sovereign of the civil state is only the executor rather than the source of legal norms and criminal sanctions.

To understand Pufendorf's views here one must return to his conception of offices and their institution, for only against this backdrop will students be able to grasp the distinctive character of Pufendorf's treatment of the political pact and entrance into the civil state. Pufendorf views the pact not as the expression or civil transmission of a preexisting moral nature, but as the institution of a new status or persona (the sovereign/subject) on top of the natural one instituted by God. Given that in his *status naturalis* man is characterized by his uncontrolled passions and an unfulfilled need for sociability—rather than by a rational nature or soul—then the personae of sovereign and subject, instituted by the exchange of protection for obedience, indicate the creation of a new moral state of affairs: civil subjection, independent of any higher moral nature or source of norms. Students should be able to understand this independence non-anachronistically, in terms of Pufendorf's goal of providing an ethical bulwark for the civil state against its religious delegitimation, rather than as an anticipation of modern totalitarianism, although this latter comparison might well serve a useful pedagogical purpose.

By approaching Pufendorf's construction of obligation via this itinerary of topics and issues, students will be better placed to understand it in terms of the intellectual instruments used to shape it, and the cultural and political circumstances to which Pufendorf was responding. They will, for example, be able to pay proper attention to the fact that this construction concerns not a universal obligation or ultimate moral identity, but that it pertains only to man's "Civil Deportment" insofar as "he is to live in Society with the Rest of Mankind." They will also be in a position to acquire a properly historical understanding of the "just reasons" informing the legitimate authority that imposes civil obligation. These reasons will appear not as faulty approximations of the laws of Aristotelian sociality or the Kantian moral law but as indications of the exchange of obedience for protection that institutes the sui generis personae of superior and subject. Finally, in gaining some insight into the larger cultural and political conflicts driving Pufendorf's construction—his attempt to protect the emergent civil state against its religious and moral subversion—students will have begun to grasp its essentially contested character. To further develop this understanding, it would be helpful to introduce Leibniz's attack into the historical mix, as this helps to illuminate not only the specific cultural-political circumstances driving Pufendorf's model but also those fueling Leibniz's ostensibly universal rebuttal.

LEIBNIZ'S MORAL UNIVERSE

Students can learn a good deal about the immediate circumstances prompting Leibniz's attack on the *De officio* from the opening paragraphs of Barbeyrac's presentation and commentary (*WDMJ*, 267–69). Among other things, Barbeyrac records that Leibniz wrote his *monita*, or admonition, at the request of Gerhardt Walter van den Muelen (Molanus), abbot of Locum and director of Brunswick-Lüneburg's Lutheran Consistory, and hence a significant figure at the Hanoverian court. Barbeyrac does not mention that this request was made in 1701, when Leibniz was court historian and adviser to the Dukes of Brunswick-Lüneburg or that Molanus explicitly asked Leibniz to comment on the suitability of Pufendorf's work as a teaching text for university students.[9] An introductory lecture, though, would also need to supplement Barbeyrac's account with a sketch of the broader circumstances in which Molanus's request was made and satisfied.

In fact, this was only the latest in a series of exchanges between the two men, dating back to the 1680s and driven by Leibniz's visionary project to reunify the divided faiths of Christendom into a new version of the universal church. Unlike Pufendorf's desacralizing program, Leibniz's reunion project was at a tangent to the Westphalian settlement, which had enshrined the separate existence of the three main confessions in Imperial public law while otherwise recognizing the sovereignty of territorial states in religious matters. Leibniz viewed the division of the churches not as an irreversible political reality but as a mistake that might be corrected if the faiths could be made to cohere around a properly rational theology. A reunified church would in turn contribute to a rejuvenated Holy Roman Empire, whose variegated sovereignty Leibniz refused to view as a sign of sickness or monstrosity—as Pufendorf had in his *De statu imperii Germanici* (1667)—but as a means by which the Hobbesian territorial states might be reincorporated in a virtuous *Respublica Christiana* (Riley, 1972, 26–33, 111–20). Despite their utopian complexion, these proposals made a degree of religious and political sense in the Hanoverian context of the 1680s, when the dukes were bidding for Imperial Electoral status, for this required that they remain open to Imperial and papal claims regarding the primacy of the "universal" (Catholic) church (Utermöhlen, 1995). Certainly this religious and political context can be strongly contrasted with Pufendorf's at the Swedish and Brandenburg courts, where he was preoccupied with defending frontline Protestant territorial states, threatened externally by ultramontane Catholicism and internally by the unruly religious estates of the Empire (Seidler, 2002a).

Leibniz's attack on Pufendorf's conception of obligation and on Pufendorf's civil philosophy, more broadly, was also informed by a crucial difference in intellectual formation and outlook. In this regard students will need to be provided with a basic orientation to Leibniz's metaphysics and to the philosophical theology and natural law doctrines that he extrapolated from this metaphysics. Here again, the standard Kantian accounts will not do the job, as they view Leibniz either in terms of his supposed failure to tame his epistemic rationalism through the addition of a Kantian sensibility (Beck, 1969, 196–240), or in terms of his failure to modify his moral intellectualism by acknowledging the need for a commanding Kantian moral law (Korsgaard, 1996a, 5–18). As Patrick Riley has argued, such accounts obscure Leibniz's profile as an early modern Platonistic metaphysician by retrospectively imposing a Kantian silhouette (Riley, 1996), even if this imposition does less damage to Leibniz—in whose footsteps Kant will follow—than to Pufendorf. In addition to Riley's own study, therefore, it might be necessary for lecturers to mediate some German studies that approach Leibniz's metaphysics as a Platonistic improvisation on scholastic metaphysics, deeply embedded in late-17th-century religious-cultural conflicts (Jasinowski, 1972; Sparn, 1986; Döring, 1993).

Such studies provide an overview of Leibniz's doctrine of the substances or intelligibles, which he views as products of divine intellection and as attaining consciousness in the "spiritual monads," or souls, whose unfolding in space and time constitutes the phenomenal world. More importantly, however, they allow students to approach Leibniz's metaphysics as a culture or worldview. Through the core doctrines, the metaphysician learns to view himself as participating in divine intellection—hence to view the empirical world and its sciences as mere manifestations of pure concepts or intelligibles whose disclosure is dependent on the purified intellect of the metaphysical personage (Hunter, 2001, 95–147). In this regard it is important to convey that Leibniz's ethics and metaphysics are inseparable. He understands the *summum bonum* in terms of the purification or perfection of the intellect that occurs through transcendence of sensuous (*sinnliches*) perception and desire, and that issues in immediate intuition of the divine truths or perfections. To view Leibniz's pursuit of intellectual intuition in Kantian terms, as a theoretical error, is to misunderstand its role as the telos of a specific way of relating to and shaping a self—a culture—that, like Kant's notion of membership in the noumenal community, can be neither true nor false. This culture informs Leibniz's natural law doctrine in which the metaphysical sage, transcending merely empirical conceptions of law as the sovereign's command, is rewarded with participation in the divine intellection of justice (Riley, 1996, 156–69, 182–89). But it is no less central to his philosophical theology. Here Leibniz presumed that his self-purifying insight into the transcendent substances gave him the spiritual prestige to propose definitive metaphysical explications for such bitterly contested doctrines as transubstantiation, and to canvass a new unity for Christianity on the basis of his own metaphysics (Sparn, 1986).

Students will thus have been introduced to what Detlef Döring has characterized as the basic difference in intellectual culture separating Leibniz from Pufendorf (Döring, 1992, 138-39). If Leibniz viewed reason itself as normative and the human as a being capable of rational self-governance, that is because he was the inheritor of a metaphysical culture configured in terms of the metaphysician's self-transformative participation in divine intellectual intuition. In rejecting this culture, Pufendorf not only discarded the notion of normative reason and a higher rational self, he also turned his back on the whole metaphysical outlook, in which all the spheres of life and their various sciences are to be viewed from a single transcendental vantage point.

The most immediate symptom of this difference can be seen in their opposed attitudes to the relation between theology and "philosophy"—that is, non-revealed knowledge—that lies at the heart of metaphysics itself. Leibniz continued the long-standing pursuit of a metaphysical reconciliation of theology and philosophy that, he hoped, would provide theology with the kind of rational unifying grounds capable of restoring the universal church and the imperial *Respublica Christiana*. Pufendorf, however, begins the *De officio* by declaring that revealed and natural knowledge should not be mixed, and that the Christian and the political subject constitute diverse moral personae, governed by the discrete ends of salvation and sociability. Drawing on the centripetal language of divine intuition, Leibniz was intent on maintaining an integral moral and ethical viewpoint from which a unified religious-moral culture might be projected onto a world order. Deploying the centrifugal language of offices and personae, however, Pufendorf's aim was to disarticulate religion and politics—the duties of the Christian from those of the political subject—with a view to relocating civil ethics within the confines of the nonconfessional territorial state whose legitimation was his paramount concern.

Having mastered this introduction to Leibniz's intellectual culture and his religious and political objectives, students will be in a position to undertake a historical interpretation of his attack on Pufendorf. They will, for example, be able to engage with the historical significance of Leibniz's criticisms of Pufendorf's separation of natural law from moral theology—or of civil peace from salvation—where they will find the following passage:

> For it could not be doubted that the supreme ruler of the universe, most wise and most powerful, has resolved to reward the good and punish the wicked, and that He will execute His plan in the life to come, since in this life as we manifestly observe He

leaves most crimes unpunished and most good actions unrewarded. Thus here and now to neglect consideration of the next life, inseparably linked as it is to divine providence, and to rest content with a lower degree of natural law valid even for an atheist…would be to deprive this legal science of its finest part and, at the same time, to destroy many of this life's duties (*WDMJ*, 275).

Far from being a cultural throwback, Leibniz's insistence that providential rewards and punishments remain part of civil ethics was integral to his conception of a Christian republic, for the extension of natural law into the Christian afterlife is the condition of maintaining the presence of a salvational morality in the civil domain. Conversely, in confining natural law to the maintenance of sociability within "the Compass of this life only," Pufendorf was indeed establishing an ethics "valid even for an atheist," for he regarded this as unavoidable when states had to govern religious communities locked in violent conflict over the true path to salvation or moral regeneration.

A further opportunity for historical contextualization is provided by Leibniz's criticism of Pufendorf's argument that a civil ethics should concern itself only with man's external actions, eschewing all interest in his purity of will. In rejecting Pufendorf's restriction of moral philosophy (natural law) to external civil actions and his reciprocal restriction of moral theology to the domain of inner purity, Leibniz comments: "Yet we see that not only Christian philosophers, but also the ancient pagans, made this [inner purity] the subject of their precepts, such that even pagan philosophy is in this regard more wise, more severe and more sublime than the philosophy of our author" (*WDMJ*, 280). Leibniz continues by saying, "It is dangerous, or at best unrealistic, for our author to imagine a corrupt heart, the external actions of which are entirely innocent," and that "internal actions" must be central to natural law because "it cannot be denied that law and obligations, sins committed against God and good deeds done in his sight alone, by their nature involve internal actions" (*WDMJ*, 284).

Again, students will grasp that they are not dealing with a superseded argument but with an unfinished contest over the moral depth appropriate for civil ethics. Leibniz's insistence that inner purity remain central to civil ethics, together with his claim that moral philosophers should be instrumental in determining this purity, indicates his rejection of moves that would restrict civil delinquency to disturbances of civil order and helps explain his resistance to the decriminalization of heresy.[10] One only has to consider Kant's restoration of purity of will to the very center of moral philosophy to see that this was anything but a lost cause. Conversely, "dangerous" and "unrealistic" or not, Pufendorf's demarcation did indeed involve accepting that innocent actions might arise from a heart considered corrupt—at least when judged according to religious or metaphysical models of purity—as this was the condition for (among other things) removing crimes such as heresy from the law books and establishing religious toleration in the civil sphere. It also meant, of course, that purity of will would be off-limits to moral philosophers, who would be required to leave this as a matter between an individual and his confessor, restricting their attention instead to the individual's deportment in civil life. Lying behind this argument over the opacity of conduct was a fundamental schism between the Christian conception of morality as requiring moral transparency between the members of a spiritual or rational community and the Hobbesian rejection of this requirement in favor of an externally imposed order.

Finally, having traveled this route, students will be in a position to grasp the historical import of Leibniz's attribution of circularity to Pufendorf's construction of obligation in terms of the command of a superior. Leibniz, we recall, argues that by invoking the superior's "just reasons" for command, Pufendorf is appealing to the very concept—justice—that he is purporting to explain. This argument is based on the assumption that justice cannot be grounded in a decision or pact, because we must be able to apply the concept of justice to this decision or pact itself, and for this to be possible there must be an essential or self-grounding conception of justice, which Leibniz locates in divine intuition.

> I insist, we need to recognise that God is praised because He is just, and thus there is justice in God, or rather a supreme justice, no matter that He recognises no superior, and that by propensity of His excellent nature ... He acts always as He must, such that none can with reason object. And the rule of His actions, like the

very nature of justice, depends not on a free decision of His will, but rather on the eternal truths which are the objects of the divine mind and which are established, so to speak, by His divine essence (*WDMJ*, 289).

At this point students will be able to situate this pursuit of absolute grounds for morality in the historical culture of metaphysics itself. We have seen that metaphysics seeks self-grounding universal moral concepts ("perfections") by lodging these in an unsurpassable moment of pure intellection—the divine mind that creates what it intelligizes—and by treating human participation in this intellection as a contemplation of the pure ideas that immediately conforms the will. Despite his criticism of Leibniz's rationalistic failure to acknowledge the recalcitrance of the desires, Kant too maintained a version of this absolute contemplative conception of morality, in his teaching that the mere thought or representation (*Vorstellung*) of the moral law should be enough to conform the will to it, thereby bringing the search for grounds to an end in self-grounding "pure practical reason."[11] From Pufendorf's viewpoint, however, it is precisely this metaphysical culture—this conception of a self that is capable of purifying its will through secular philosophical participation in pure reason—that had to be rejected; for, in blurring the boundary between philosophy and theology, it tempts metaphysicians to imagine a source of civil norms higher than the exchange of obedience for protection that institutes civil authority, thereby opening the latter to subversion. Again from Pufendorf's perspective, there is nothing circular in his construction of obligation because he rejects the whole idea that morality should be founded in a self-grounding universal reason. Pufendorf would thus have been at ease with Wittgenstein's blank dictum that, "Giving grounds, though, justifying the evidence, comes to an end…not in certain propositions immediately striking us as true, i.e., as a kind of *seeing* on our part, but in our *acting*, which lies at the bottom of the language-game" (Wittgenstein, 1969, 28). So, for Pufendorf, civil duties should be regarded as anchored no more deeply than in the personae of sovereign and subject, instituted to achieve a civil peace regarded not so much as self-grounding as not worth questioning.

In approaching the conflict between Pufendorf's and Leibniz's conceptions of obligation in this way—as symptomatic of radically different moral cultures driven by divergent religious and political commitments—students can explore the question of whether any kind of philosophical argument could demonstrate the logical superiority of either conception. This would open a pedagogical door to Schneewind's theme that philosophical positions may triumph (or may not) other than via the validity of their supporting arguments. In fact, in this case it starts to look as if the arguments deployed are integral to the divergent intellectual cultures, where their central role is to fashion a certain kind of intellectual deportment, reminding us again that Leibniz's attack on the *De officio* was prompted by Molanus's anxiety about its suitablity as a "topic of instruction for the young" (Riley, 1972, 65). If this is so, then it's less surprising that there appears to be no philosophical resolution to these arguments, which continue today despite Leibniz's ostensible knockout blow. Jean Barbeyrac's attempt to mediate and adjudicate the conflict between Leibniz and Pufendorf offers students plenty of material relevant to this theme.

BARBEYRAC'S CONSCIENCE

Barbeyrac's presentation of and commentary on Leibniz's attack was appended to the fourth edition of his French translation of the *De officio, Les Devoirs de l'Homme et du Citoien*, published in Amsterdam in 1718. This formed part of his prodigious publicistic work on Protestant natural law. In addition to the *De officio* (trans. 1707), Barbeyrac produced translations of Pufendorf's massive *De jure naturae et gentium* (trans. 1706) and Grotius's *De jure belli ac pacis* (trans. 1724), which he embedded in a continuously expanding apparatus of notes and appendixes. Barbeyrac's Pufendorf editions may thus be regarded as a specific kind of reception text, making the works available to non-Latinate audiences (generally those in training for public office) and surrounding them with auxiliary materials designed to ensure that they would be read in a particular way.[12] What kind of mediation, though, was Barbeyrac performing for Pufendorf? For students to explore this question—thence the larger one of fathoming the kind of future that Barbeyrac sought to secure for Pufendorf's doctrines—it would be necessary to outline his religious and political context in a manner permitting comparison with Pufendorf's and Leibniz's.

Students would thus need to learn that Barbeyrac was a religious refugee, his Calvinist family having fled Catholic France for Switzerland thence Berlin (where Barbeyrac settled in 1697), following Louis XIV's revocation of the Edict of Nantes (1685), and that he commenced his translations while teaching at Berlin's French Collège, which served the sizable Huguenot community. As the beneficiary of the Brandenburg court's policy of regulated religious toleration, Barbeyrac had reason to endorse Pufendorf's basic positions. Not only did Pufendorf's works provide an intellectual rationale for a state containing multiple and potentially conflicting religious communities, but from 1688 until his death in 1694, Pufendorf personally played an important role in shaping and administering Brandenburg's *Religionspolitik*.[13] It is not surprising then that Barbeyrac sought to disseminate Pufendorf's desacralized ethics and politics, initially to the Huguenot diaspora (Hochstrasser, 1999, 383). Neither will students be surprised to learn that the refugee was hostile to Leibniz's arguments for a metaphysically grounded civil authority, which might well turn out to be less pluralistic than Pufendorf's version of a civil authority restricted to the maintenance of "external" civil peace.

Nonetheless, Barbeyrac's religious and political circumstances, no less than his religious and intellectual formation, were very different from Pufendorf's. In the first place, Barbeyrac was the servant not of a real state but of a metaphorical one, the republic of letters, to which he was connected via his participation in Étienne Chauvin's *Nouveau Journal des Scavants*. Through this journal, which had been based in Rotterdam and then Berlin (1696–98), Barbeyrac would have encountered freethinking and heterodox religious and political discussion, particularly on such vital topics as heresy, toleration, church-state relations, and natural law (Othmer, 1970). At the same time, though, Barbeyrac remained a member of a diasporic Calvinist community whose identity was determined almost wholly by religion, and in which he expected to find a place as a teacher or minister. Suspicious of Pufendorfian natural law and deeply concerned by the spread of the Socinian heresy among its younger community members, the Berlin Huguenot Consistory asserted orthodox Calvinist articles of faith that all candidates for clerical office were required to sign, including Barbeyrac, who was studying for the ministry while teaching at the French Collège. This was the trigger for charges of heresy to be brought against him in 1699, an episode that tells us much about both the development of heterodoxy in the Reformed Refuge and the character of Brandenburg *Religionspolitik*.

Barbeyrac had encountered and evidently been attracted to Socinian heterodoxy during his time at the University of Frankfurt/ Oder in the early 1690s and later through his participation in the milieu surrounding the *Nouveau Journal*. Focused in the denial of the trinity and its treatment of Christ as a moral teacher rather than a divine mediator—and seeking to ground these innovations in a "rational" reinterpretation of the Bible—Socinianism has been regarded as the natural "rational religious" complement to Pufendorfian natural law.[14] This interpretation is not very plausible, however, as Socinianism seeks to make religion more rational— in the "advanced" Calvinist sense of more like a nonsacramental ethicotheology—and thereby to maintain it as the rational religious basis of a civil ethics. (Hochstrasser, 1999) Pufendorf's natural law, though, seeks to remove moral theology from civil ethics—by deriving the latter from social peace—while leaving revealed sacramental religion untouched in its own sphere, where the goal is salvation rather than civility.[15]

This helps to explain the fact that Pufendorf viewed Socinianism as a kind of sect rather than as part of a broad rationalist enlightenment, himself sitting on the tribunal assembled in 1693 to judge the heterodoxy of Friedrich Wilhelm Stosch, a Spinozist Socinian (Döring, 1995). In a typical instance of Brandenburg *Religionspolitik*, Stosch was found guilty of heterodoxy, was required to desist from theological publication, and was then quietly restored to his former civil rank and entitlements. Similarly, while confirming the French Consistory's finding that Barbeyrac was indeed guilty of teaching Socinian heterodoxy, and requiring that he cease lecturing in theology at the Collège, in 1700 a commission of the Brandenburg Privy Council refused to countenance Barbeyrac's excommunication and declared that he could continue to teach philological subjects as a learned and worthy man (Othmer, 1970, 72–74). The commission thus separated the duties of the Christian from those of the citizen in a manner in keeping with Pufendorf's cultural-political program and, of course, with the Privy Council's interest in governing a multiconfessional state.

Taking shape in these circumstances, Barbeyrac's religious and political thought differed significantly from both Leibniz's and Pufendorf's—this observation dictating a degree of skepticism regarding the long-standing view of Barbeyrac as Pufendorf's faithful mediator and publicist. If Leibniz's updated Protestant scholasticism provoked Barbeyrac's alarm at the prospect of a new (metaphysical) version of the confessional state, then his own commitment to an ethicotheological civil order remained quietly subversive of Pufendorf's fundamental desacralization of civil authority. When working on Barbeyrac's "defense" of Pufendorf against Leibniz's criticisms, students can thus be asked to explore the Huguenot's covert transposition of Pufendorf's central doctrines, no less than his overt opposition to Leibniz's.

A good source for approaching this challenging task can be found in the two other Barbeyrac texts appended to the 1718 edition of *Les Devoirs* and included in the reedited version of the *Whole Duty*. In his *Discourse on What Is Permitted by the Laws* and his *Discourse on Benefits Conferred by Laws*, Barbcyrac cssays his own views on the relation between positive civil law and natural law, the latter understood as a divine institution accessed via individual conscience. While incorporating Pufendorf's central theme of the restricted character of laws oriented to maintaining civil order, Barbeyrac's emphasis falls in a different place: on the ultimate insufficiency of conduct satisfying such laws, in comparison with the more comprehensive demands of conscience. A similar shift of emphasis occurs in Barbeyrac's comments on Leibniz's attack on Pufendorf for restricting natural law to external actions while consigning inner purity to the domain of moral theology; for Barbeyrac's strategy here is not to defend Pufendorf's separation but to argue that he did not intend it to be as sharp as Leibniz implies (*WDMJ*, 280–1). In fact, Barbeyrac walks a fine line, rejecting Leibniz's attempt to make inner purity an object of natural law and civil authority but seeking to soften Pufendorf's apparent expulsion of conscience from the political domain. Barbeyrac thus has no hesitation in rejecting Leibniz's proposal, arguing that external actions are often unreliable signs of inner purity and observing that "the greatest number" of natural laws concern perfect or juridical right that "does not extend beyond the external act." Leibniz's worrying plan must therefore be rejected because "Once one has done in this regard all that one was required to do, whether the internal act was as vicious as you please, nobody can ask any more of us, nor, finally, must they do so, even though the internal principle of the action by which one has acquitted oneself of what was required had something about it that the divine tribunal and our own conscience would condemn" (*WDMJ*, 281). At the same time, he refuses to exclude conscience and the divine tribunal from the civil sphere.

Covertly contradicting Pufendorf, Barbeyrac requires that the condition of the soul should play a role in civil ethics, although not in positive law—a view he then ascribes to Pufendorf. Against Leibniz, he insists that this condition not be judged by a potentially intolerant doctrinal theology, whether philosophical or confessional. Barbeyrac thus opens a space in which lawful external conduct might still be subject to a further level of inner moral judgment, although not one capable of doctrinal codification or legal enforcement. This is the space of conscience (Hochstrasser, 1995; Hochstrasser, 1999). Barbeyrac agrees with Pufendorf that natural law arises from God's will rather than divine reason, but he diverges from Pufendorf in his Socinian-Lockean insistence that human reason is capable of knowing and internalizing this law in the form of conscience.

> For from the moment that one has a just idea of God, one cannot but recognise His right to set whatever limits He pleases to the faculties He has granted us. Nor could one prevent oneself thinking that He surely wishes men to follow the light of their reason, as that which is best in them, and which alone can lead them to the destiny of their nature (*WDMJ*, 294).

This appeal to rational conscience as the singular source of norms is no closer to Pufendorf's doctrine of instituted moral personae than is Leibniz's appeal to participation in divine intellection. Moreover, like Leibniz, Barbeyrac wishes away Pufendorf's central themes. He thus ignores Pufendorf's view that, far from being able to access the divine will, man has just enough reason to know that sociability requires a superior. Further, he betrays no awareness of Pufendorf's argument that the institution of the superior via the civil pact is not the realization of man's nature or the expression of God's, but represents instead the historical institution of a new moral persona whose commands establish the normative horizon of civil life. By retaining the notion of an ultimate moral identity capable of accessing divine law, Barbeyrac subordinates the sphere of permitted civil conduct to a higher inner morality, albeit one incapable of immediate civil enforcement. In doing so, he departs fundamentally from Pufendorf's program for desacralizing the civil sphere. In fact he transforms Pufendorf's permanent cleavage of civil ethics from religious morality—the persona of the citizen from that of the Christian—into a temporary caesura, across which an agile conscience might reconnect the "civil kingdom" to the "kingdom of truth."

Armed with a knowledge of this array of positions, students will be in a position to make sense of the otherwise puzzling strategy that governs Barbeyrac's commentary. This sees him loudly attacking Leibniz while quietly assimilating Pufendorf to a Lockean-Socinian political theology subversive of Pufendorf's cultural-political program. When approaching the crux of Pufendorf's conception of obligation, students might notice that this strategy actually permits Barbeyrac to invert the accounts of the source of obligation given by Leibniz and Pufendorf. Disingenuously treating Pufendorf's deliberate exclusion of divine rewards and punishments as a "slight omission," Barbeyrac argues that Pufendorf was led to this by his noble conception of obligation as arising from "the impressions surely made by the mere sight of law on the heart of any reasonable person" (*WDMJ*, 277). At the same time, he ascribes to Leibniz the view that men are incapable of being motivated by mere knowledge of the law, necessitating ignoble rewards and punishments. We have seen, though, that Pufendorf's construction of obligation begins by rejecting the possibility that men might be obligated through mere contemplation of a higher moral law or nature, even God's. As he puts it in the *De jure*, given the waywardness of man's will, "contemplation of an essence so noble can, indeed, excite admiration, but it cannot create obligation," for which external compulsion is required (Pufendorf, 1934, 100). Conversely, flying in the face of Barbeyrac's imputations, Leibniz insists that "when one does good for the love of God or one's neighbor, one finds pleasure in the act itself (such being the nature of love); one needs no other stimulant, nor the command of a superior" (*WDMJ*, 295).

Why then, students might be asked, does Barbeyrac praise Pufendorf for a doctrine he explicitly rejects—the doctrine of the contemplative self-conformation of the rational will—while attacking Leibniz for failing to embrace this doctrine, which is actually central to Leibniz's metaphysical morality? In fact, Barbeyrac is well aware that Leibniz advocates a version of this doctrine, because one of his central aims in the commentary is to relegate Leibniz's intellectualist metaphysical version in favor of his own, based in the rational conscience. Against Leibniz's claim that the wise man accedes to his duties through intellectual participation in the divine mind, Barbeyrac advances his ethicotheological assertion that it is individual conscience rather than academic metaphysics that gives access to God, whom we experience via divine commands rather than divine ideas (*WDMJ*, 291–5). Despite the Kantian view of this as another version of the philosophical dispute between rationalism and voluntarism, it is clear that Barbeyrac's objection to Leibniz's rationalism is to a rival religious-moral deportment rather than to a false theory. Not only does Leibniz's version of rational self-governance underestimate the countervailing force of man's passions and his consequent need for direction by a higher will, but also it fails to capture (what is for Barbeyrac) the most noble way of acceding to obligation: namely, unconditional submission to the divine will as the will of a perfect being.

> Whoever has a true idea of God knows that he is good, as well as great, and that his will necessarily conforms with his perfections; wise and holy, he can will nothing that is not just and which, moreover, is not for our good.... To conform to this wholly good and sacred will, on which we recognize that we depend, is to act according to duty; this is what imposes moral necessity on all men, regardless of any other consideration. Hope or fear are only motives to encourage us to practice duty, to overcome the resistance we may find within us, and to sustain us in the midst of strong temptations (*WDMJ*, 296).

With this wholly un-Pufendorfian theistic conception of the superior in place, Barbeyrac concludes by rebutting Leibniz's allegations of circularity against Pufendorf's construction of obligation. For Barbeyrac, there is no need for Pufendorf to (circularly) posit a conception of justice independent of the superior's will, because justice is immanent to the divine will—in the sense that by willing in accordance with his perfect nature, God, the ultimate superior, can do nothing unjust.

In so willing, however, it is God who creates the natural right from which all earthly superiors derive the justification of their laws.

> Every superior, below God, bears an authority founded on reasons, the justice of which derives from a certain law of natural right, being related to the rules of that justice whose obligation truly emanates from the will of a superior, or from the will of the king of kings and the lord of lords. But this supreme being's right of command is founded in reasons whose justice is immanent, such that they do not need to draw their force from elsewhere (*WDMJ*, 302).

While this might provide a coherent theological response to Leibniz's political theology—relegating justice as a transcendent idea governing God's will in favor of justice as the consequence of God's perfect willing—it neither elucidates nor supports Pufendorf's reconstruction of civil authority. On the contrary, Barbeyrac's "defense" subverts this reconstruction by returning earthly superiors to a subordinate position in relation to transcendent moral right, thereby threatening civil authority with the religious and moral subversion that Pufendorf had sought to neutralize.

For Barbeyrac, the "just reasons" underpinning civil authority or the earthly superior are expressions of a Lockean natural right, instituted by a morally self-grounding divine superior and acceded to by rational conscience. They are thus quite unlike Pufendorf's just cause for civil authority—the exchange of obedience for protection—which gives rise to a superior whose commands institute civil norms. Yet Pufendorf's refusal to distinguish his superior as divine or human, coupled with his post facto treatment of natural law as imposed by God, has led some scholars to treat Pufendorf as sharing with Barbeyrac a "genuine divine command theory of morality"

(Saastamoinen, 1995, 107). It has led others back to the quasi-Leibnizian view that without a properly transcendent conception of the superior, Pufendorf's conception of the just superior must (circularly) assume the concept of justice that it is purporting to derive (Palladini, 1990, 22–23).

It needs to be kept in mind, however, that Pufendorf's construction of legitimate superiority comes after the demarcation arguments of the preface, in which he deliberately excludes from the domain of civil ethics all revealed knowledge of God and all conceptions of duties and right attached to the end of salvation. Not only does this show why Barbeyrac's salvational conception of natural right is precluded by Pufendorf's construction, it also reminds us of what it is in this construction that preempts the charge of circularity: namely, Pufendorf's explicit rejection of the metaphysical demand for a self-grounding moral principle and his treatment of civil obligation as internal to the personae created by the civil pact. Having excluded metaphysical reason as the higher source of civil obligation, Pufendorf was in no mood to admit Lockean right and Calvinist conscience in its place. For Pufendorf, the pact that creates the superior is not a luminous moment in which a higher reason or a higher will delegates its justice to the civil sovereign via a community bearing natural rights. Rather, this event takes place on the flat plains of history, where men, cut off from transcendent insight and fearful of mutual predation, institute a superior to whom they have transferred their will for social peace.

The justice of Pufendorf's superior is thus indeed immanent to his commands, but in a manner quite unlike Barbeyrac's "lord of lords and king of kings." For Barbeyrac, justice is immanent to the divine superior's commands because these declare the will of a morally perfect creator to his imperfect creatures, imbuing them with the rights on which civil authority is founded. For Pufendorf, however, civil morality is immanent to the superior's commands not because he is moral and not because the exchange of obedience for protection itself is moral. Rather, this pact, driven by exigency and fear, not reason and conscience, opens a new region of moral space— the one that emerges when individuals place their reason and conscience in matters pertaining to social peace at the disposal of a civil superior—inside which individuals come to occupy the new persona of the political subject. Pufendorf's superior thus also presides over an autonomous moral universe, but one invented or instituted by men intent on resetting the norms of civil ethics within the horizon of civil peace, in order to defend civil authority against the schoolmen and the man of conscience.[16]

CONCLUSION

One can imagine concluding this extended study or, more likely, inaugurating a new one, by giving students some sense of the fortunes of the intellectual cultures represented in Barbeyrac's presentation of the conflict between Leibniz and Pufendorf. Students might explore, for example, the progressive Barbeyracian transformation of Tooke's 1691 translation, with the reedited fourth edition of 1716 containing not just the Lockean footnotes from Barbeyrac's 1707 edition but also Barbeyrac's unauthorized interpolations designed to produce a more Lockean text.[17] Leibniz's attack, which was not added to Tooke's translation until 2002, thus probably had little impact on the English reception of Pufendorf, whereas Barbeyrac's stealthy Lockean transposition of Pufendorf's arguments may well have found its mark, particularly in the Whig circles for which it was probably intended. Leibniz's metaphysical critique of Pufendorf's central doctrines seems, however, to have had greater success in the Scottish environment. Here, in the *Supplements and Observations* to his 1724 Latin edition of the *De officio*, Gershom Carmichael warned his Glaswegian students against Pufendorf's separation of natural law from moral theology, endorsing Leibniz's account of their harmony in terms of the divinity's perfection and providence as known by natural reason (Moore and Silverthorne, 2002, 17).

Students might conjecture then that in Glasgow it would have been possible to teach Leibniz's demonstration of Pufendorf's circularity as a philosophical truth, whereas in London it is likely that Pufendorf's construction of obligation would have been assimilated to Barbeyrac's, so the question of circularity would remain mute or moot. In neither city, though, would Leibniz and Pufendorf have been regarded as the reciprocally deficient (rationalist and voluntarist) predecessors of a Königsberg metaphysician hovering in the wings of history. That view would have to wait until a modified version of Leibniz's metaphysical ethics took root in the Protestant universities of 18th-century Germany from whence, having been transformed by Kant, it would pass to America during the 19th century and impose itself retrospectively during the 20th. It would be a significant contribution to their intellectual equanimity were our students able to understand this latter development in terms of the local triumph of a certain kind of intellectual culture, circumscribed by particular national religious, political, and academic circumstances and coexisting with the flourishing of rival cultures in other institutional settings and moral worlds. But that would take more than a single course.

NOTES

1. Thanks to Knud Haakonssen, Fiammetta Palladini, and David Saunders for helping me avoid several errors and to Tim Hochstrasser for his careful and illuminating respondent's remarks.

2. Barbeyrac transformed Leibniz's continuous discourse by interpolating his own counterarguments and commentary and by retitling it *Jugement d'un Anonyme sur l'original de cet Abrégé*, or *Judgment of an Anonymous Writer on the Original of this Abridgement*, which I shall cite as *WDMJ*.

3. In this instance I am quoting from Tooke's original 1691 translation, 28–9, in order to avoid the unauthorized interpolations, made by Barbeyrac, and introduced into Tooke's translation by the editors of the 1716 edition. For more, see footnote 6 in the Hunter and Saunders edition, 45. The reader should also compare, in this and other instances, with Michael Silverthorne's accurate, modern English translation. (Pufendorf, 1991)

4. There is no need to discuss here the difference between "realist" (Leibnizian) and "constructivist" (Kantian) versions of the foundations of morality, as this difference was moot for those involved in the historical debate.

5. Student-friendly overviews are provided by Tully 1991, Seidler 2002b, and Hunter and Saunders 2003. There is no standard biography of Pufendorf, but important materials toward one can be found in Döring 1992.

6. For a discussion in these terms that situates Pufendorf in the broader context of Protestant natural law, see the important essay by Haakonssen 2003. For a broad overview of natural law thought, see Hunter 2002b, and for more detailed treatments, see Tuck 1987, Haakonssen 1996, and Hochstrasser 2000.

7. Conal Condren recently completed a major study of the idiom of office—*Of Oaths and Offices: The Presuppositions of Political and Moral Argument in Early-Modern England*—which I have been fortunate to see in draft form. For earlier published studies on this theme, see Condren 1997; 2001.

8. Pufendorf's natural religion thus contrasts sharply with the natural theologies elaborated by Leibniz, Wolff, and Kant, which were understood as philosophical reconstructions of salvational religious doctrine designed to make the promise of moral regeneration available in a secular register.

9. One can, however, gather this from Patrick Riley's edition and translation, which should be used in tandem with Barbeyrac's version as given in the appendix to the *Whole Duty* (Riley, 1972, 64–75).

10. This resistance is manifest in his circa 1698 rejection of Thomasius's Pufendorfian argument that heresy should not be treated as a crime (Leibniz 1948). Thomasius had argued that heresy was often just unpopular religious belief and was at worst a form of spiritual corruption with no direct bearing on civil duties or actions. For further discussion, see Hunter, (2001, 146–47).

11. Consider this passage from Kant's *Groundwork of the Metaphysics of Morals:*

> Everything in nature works in accordance with laws. Only a rational being has the capacity to act *in accordance with the representation* of laws—that is, in accordance with principles—or has a *will.* Since reason is required for the derivation of actions from laws, the will is nothing other than practical reason. If reason infallibly determines the will, then the actions of such a being that are cognized as objectively necessary are also subjectively necessary; that is, the will is a capacity to choose *only that* which reason independently of inclination cognizes as practically necessary—that is, as good (Kant 1996, 66, original emphasis).

For further discussion, see Hunter (2002a).

12. For an overview of Barbeyrac's role in this regard, Sieglinde Othmer's study contains much that would be of use for introductory contextualizing lectures. (Othmer 1970)

13. We obtain an excellent snapshot of Pufendorf's role in this regard from Döring's account of his part in the Stosch affair (Döring 1995).

14. For this interpretation, see Oestreich (1979) and Othmer (1970, 54–59, 68–81).

15. Pufendorf's separation of church from state did not hinge on denying Christ's divinity—hence the church's role as Christ's mystical body on earth—but operated much more directly, by giving church and state discrete ends, salvation, and social peace. In the event, Pufendorf's proved to be the more far-reaching desacralization of politics, as, unlike Socinian-Lockean radicalism, it excluded even Christ the moral teacher from the political sphere, thereby confining the teaching office to the religious domain and denying that the prince could rule in the name of moral truth.

16. For a compelling discussion of the completely conventional character of Pufendorf's construction, see Haakonssen (2003).

17. These interpolations, and excisions, are recorded in the notes to the Hunter and Saunders edition.

BIBLIOGRAPHY

Ball, T. "American Histories of Political Thought." In *The History of Political Thought in National Context*, ed. D. Castiglione and I. Hampsher-Monk. Cambridge, England: Cambridge University Press, 2001,107–33.

Barbeyrac, J. (S. Pufendorf). *Les devoirs de l'homme et du citoien, tels qu'ils lui sont préscrits par la loi naturelle (quatrième édition, augmentée d'un grand nombre de notes du traducteur, de ses discourses sur la permission et le bénéfice des loix, et du jugement de M. de Leibniz sur cet ouvrage, avec des réflexions du traducteur)*, trans. Jean Barbeyrac. Amsterdam: Pierre de Coup, 1718.

Beck, L. W. *Early German Philosophy: Kant and His Predecessors*. Cambridge, Mass.: Harvard University Press, 1969.

Condren, C. "Liberty of Office and Its Defence in Seventeenth-Century Political Argument." *History of Political Thought* 18, 1997, 460–82.

———. "The Problem of Audience, Office and the Language of Political Action in Lawson's *Politica* and Hobbes's *Leviathan*." *Zeitschrift für Historische Forschung* 26, 2001, 287–303.

Döring, D. *Pufendorf-Studien. Beitrage zur Biographie Samuel von Pufendorfs und zu seiner Entwicklung als Historiker und theologischer Schriftsteller.* Berlin: Duncker & Humblot, 1992.

———. "Leibniz als Verfasser der 'Epistola ad amicum super exercitationes posthumas Samuelis Puffendorfii de consensu et dissensu protestantium.'" *Zeitschrift für Kirchengeschichte* 104, 1993, 176–97.

———. *Frühaufklärung und obrigkeitliche Zensur in Brandenburg: Friedrich Wilhelm Stosch und das Verfahren gegen sein Buch "Concordia rationis et fidei."* Berlin: Duncker & Humblot, 1995.

Haakonssen, K. *Natural Law and Moral Philosophy: From Grotius to the Scottish Enlightenment.* Cambridge, England: Cambridge University Press, 1996.

———. "Protestant Natural-Law Theory: A General Interpretation." In *New Essays on the History of Autonomy*, ed. N. Brender and L. Krasnoff. Cambridge, England: Cambridge University Press, 2003.

Habermas, J. *Postmetaphysical Thinking: Philosophical Essays*, trans. W. M. Hohengarten. Cambridge, England: Polity Press, 1992.

Hochstrasser, T. J. "The Claims of Conscience: Natural Law Theory, Obligation, and Resistance in the Huguenot Diaspora." In *New Essays on the Political Thought of the Huguenots of the Refuge.* J. C. Laursen, ed. E. Leiden and J. Brill, 1995, 15–51.

————. "Conscience and Reason: The Natural Law Theory of Jean Barbeyrac." *Grotius, Pufendorf and Modern Natural Law*, ed. K. Haakonssen. Aldershot, England: Ashgate, 1999, 381–402.

————. *Natural Law Theories in the Early Enlightenment.* Cambridge, England: Cambridge University Press, 2000.

Hunter, I. *Rival Enlightenments: Civil and Metaphysical Philosophy in Early Modern Germany.* Cambridge, England: Cambridge University Press, 2001.

————. "The Morals of Metaphysics: Kant's Groundwork as Intellectual Paideia." *Critical Inquiry* 28: 2002a 908–29.

————. "Natural Law." *Encyclopedia of the Enlightenment,* ed. A. C. Kors, New York,: Oxford University Press, 2002b.

Hunter, I., and D. Saunders, eds. *Samuel Pufendorf: The Whole Duty of Man According to the Law of Nature (Together with Two Discourses and a Commentary by Jean Barbeyrac),* trans. Andrew Tooke, 1691. Natural Law and Enlightenment Classics. Indianapolis, Ind.: Liberty Fund. Cited in text as *WDM,* 2003.

Jasinowski, B. "Leibniz und der Übergang der mittelalterlichen in die moderne Philosophie." *Studia Leibnitiana:* 4, 1972, 251–63.

Kant, I. "Groundwork of the Metaphysics of Morals." *Immanuel Kant: Practical Philosophy,* ed. M. J. Gregor. Cambridge, England: Cambridge University Press, 1996, 37–108.

Korsgaard, C. M. *Creating the Kingdom of Ends.* Cambridge, England: Cambridge University Press, 1996a.

————. *The Sources of Normativity,* Cambridge, England: Cambridge University Press, 1996b.

Leibniz, G. W. Sur Thomasius, *Utrum haeresis sit crimen. G. W. Leibniz: Textes Inédits,* ed. G. Grua. Paris: Presses Universitaires de France, 1948, I: 210–12 (orig. pub. ca. 1698).

Leibniz, G. W. and J. Barbeyrac. "The Judgment of an Anonymous Writer on the Original of This Abridgment," ed. Hunter and Saunders, 2003, 267–306, orig. pub. 1718. Cited in text as *WDMJ.*

Mommsen, W. J. "History of Political Theory in the Federal Republic of Germany: Strange Death and Slow Recovery," ed. Castiglione and Hampsher-Monk, 2001, 40–57.

Moore, J., and M. Silverthorne, ed. *Natural Rights on the Threshold of the Scottish Enlightenment: The Writings of Gershom Carmichael.* Natural Law and Englightenment Classics. Indianapolis: Liberty Fund, 2002.

Oestreich, G. "Die Bedeutung des niederländischen Späthumanismus für Brandenburg-Preußen." *Humanismus und Naturrecht in Berlin-Brandenburg-Preussen,* ed. H. Thieme. Berlin: Walter de Gruyter, 1979, 16–28.

Othmer, S. C. *Berlin und die Verbreitung des Naturrechts in Europa. Kultur-und sozialgeschichtliche Studien zu Jean Barbeyracs Pufendorf-Übersetzung und eine Analyse seiner Leserschaft.* Berlin: Walter de Gruyter, 1970.

Palladini, F. Di una critica di Leibniz a Pufendorf. *Percorsi della ricerca filosofica: filosofie tra storia, linguaggio e politica.* AAVV. Rome, Italy: Gangemi Editore, 1990.

Pufendorf, S. *The Law of Nature and of Nations in Eight Books,* trans. C. H. and W. A. Oldfather. Oxford, England: Clarendon Press, 1934.

———. *On the Duty of Man and Citizen according to Natural Law,* trans. Michael Silverthorne. Cambridge, Mass.: Cambridge University Press, 1991.

Riley, P., ed. *Leibniz: Political Writings.* Cambridge, Mass.: Cambridge University Press, 1972.

———. *Leibniz' Universal Jurisprudence: Justice as the Charity of the Wise* Cambridge, Mass.: Harvard University Press, 1996.

Saastamoinen, K. T*he Morality of Fallen Man: Samuel Pufendorf on Natural Law.* Helsinki: Finnish Historical Society, 1995.

Schneewind, J. B. *The Invention of Autonomy: A History of Modern Moral Philosophy.* Cambridge, Mass.: Cambridge University Press, 1998.

Seidler, M. J. "Turkish Judgment and the English Revolution. Pufendorf on the Right of Resistance. *Samuel Pufendorf und die europäische Frühaufklärung. Werk und Einfluß eines deutschen Bürgers der Gelehrtenrepublik nach 300 Jahren (1694–1994),* ed. F. Palladini and G. Hartung. Berlin: Akademie Verlag, 1996, 83–104.

———. "Pufendorf and the Politics of Recognition." *Natural Law and Civil Sovereignty: Moral Right and State Authority in Early Modern Political Thought,* ed. I. Hunter and D. Saunders. Basingstoke, England: Palgrave, 2002a, 235–51.

———. "Samuel Pufendorf." *Encyclopedia of the Enlightenment,* ed. A. C. Kors. New York: Oxford University Press, 2002b.

Sparn, W. "Das Bekenntnis des Philosophen. Gottfried Wilhelm Leibniz als Philosoph und Theologe." *Neue Zeitschrift für Systematische Theologie* 28, 1986, 139–78.

Tuck, R. "The 'Modern' Theory of Natural Law." *The Languages of Political Theory in Early-Modern Europe,* ed. A. Pagden, Cambridge, England: Cambridge University Press, 1987, 99–122.

Tully, J. Editor's Introduction. *Samuel Pufendorf: On the Duty of Man and Citizen according to Natural Law,* ed. J. Tully. Cambridge, England: Cambridge University Press, 1991, xiv–xl.

Utermöhlen, G. "Die irenische Politik der Welfenhöfe und Leibniz'
    Schlichtungsversuch der Kontroverse um den papstliche Primat."
    Religion und Religiosität im Zeitalter des Barock, ed. D. Breuer. Wiesbaden,
    Germany: Harrossowitz Verlag, 1995, I, 191–200.
Wittgenstein, L. *Ueber Gewissheit/On Certainty*, trans. Denis Paul and G. E.
    M. Anscombe. Oxford, England: Blackwell, 1969.
Zurbuchen, S., ed. *Samuel Pufendorf: Of the Nature and Qualification of
    Religion in Reference to Civil Society*. Natural Law and Englightenment
    Classics. Indianapolis: Liberty Fund, 2002.

Response to Ian Hunter

T. J. Hochstrasser

In response to Ian Hunter's fine exposition, I offer a brief commentary that falls into two parts. In the first, I shall provide a number of comments upon some of the theoretical perspectives with which he opened his paper, and in the second, I shall present a short, parallel examination of how the Kantian reading of 17th-century natural law theories as a stand-off between inadequate voluntarist and rationalist accounts itself became an established orthodoxy, especially through the interventions of Carl Friedrich Stäudlin. The purpose of this case study is simply to provide some further information to shape our discussion and also to focus attention on the important role that second-rank and second-generation philosophers, such as Barbeyrac and Stäudlin, played in establishing a historiographical orthodoxy which reflected *their* priorities as much as the stated and often different intentions of their intellectual mentors—in this case, Pufendorf and Kant.

In our present conference sessions, we are concentrating our attention on how new research in the history of philosophy may be incorporated within our own present-day curricula. But at several points in his presentation, Ian Hunter rightly draws attention as well to the inescapable contemporary *institutional* context within which the various key stages in this episode in early modern moral philosophy take place: Leibniz's comments on Pufendorf occur in response to Molanus's request for an assessment of the suitability of Pufendorf's compendium as a university textbook; that textbook itself is conceived as a concise and accessible survey of Pufendorf's doctrines, as a tool in their dissemination; and Barbeyrac's editions of Grotius, Pufendorf, and Cumberland are envisaged as explications of the full implications of those texts for a Francophone cultural community that shared some but by no means all of the political and social assumptions of the natural law school. Finally, we should note that the Kantian rewriting of the 17th-century history of philosophy was also a matter of institutional politics, in the so-called Conflict of the Faculties, which embodied the promotion of philosophy not simply above the other recognized traditional faculties of law, medicine, and theology but also—potentially—beyond the control and regulation of the state itself. So it is not only our agenda but also the evolving historiography of the subject itself that is framed and directed by educational questions: how the achievements and controversies of modern philosophy may best be explained and articulated to students who will themselves go on to provide a graduate pool of scholars, bureaucrats, lawyers, doctors, and pastors within the contemporary "society of orders" and enlightened absolutist state.

In this context it is perhaps helpful for us to reflect on how *contemporaries* thought the history of philosophy might best be taught within their own curricula and how that contrasts with our own practice.

Ian rightly notes that courses that address the history of philosophy today are often service courses in analytic philosophy that seek simply to link a number of major philosophers in heroic, if not teleological, sequence. The institutional practice in the German Protestant universities at both ends of the 18th century was somewhat different. The leading pedagogue and disciple of Pufendorf, Christian Thomasius, shared one principle in common with Kant and that was the importance of placing the history of philosophy *first* in the student's educational program. Kant describes philosophy's role as that of a gatekeeper, and Thomasius insists that all students *irrespective of discipline* should take a course in the history of morality, or the history of moral philosophy, as we would now call it. The importance of this measure for Thomasius was twofold: first, it ensured a common starting point in ethics for all students whatever their later specializations, and second, it provided an example in practice of the philosophical method—eclecticism—that he believed should characterize the practice of modern philosophy: the new historiography was in a real sense constitutive of the practice of critical reevaluation of schools and doctrine that he wished to recommend. In a similar, but not identical, fashion Kant's various sketches of the previous history of metaphysics before his own time were intended not simply as educational tools but also as programmatic encapsulations of why the need for the Critical Theory was so pressing, and the form of its revolution so necessary. A new history of philosophy was an essential prolegomenon to the enactment of the Kantian era itself.

From these 18th-century examples we can, I think, derive a number of important lessons for how we might incorporate more recent revisions of method and practice in the history of philosophy into our teaching practices. One point that emerges, I think, with great clarity, is the need to place any course on the history of philosophy *first* rather than last in pedagogy. This obviously makes sense as a way of overcoming ingrained historiographical assumptions, but more significantly, it would bring students into contact with exactly the kind of many-layered examples of practical rewriting of the history of philosophy that Ian highlights in his focus on the Barbeyrac-Leibniz-Pufendorf engagement. Such examples provide a window of access not only to the embedded institutional aspect of most philosophical discussion—certainly in the early-modern era—but also to the way in which methodological and historiographical shifts of gear are often deeply implicated with one another. Such confrontations were often battles for authority as much as disembodied disagreements over conceptual formation, and so far from derogating from the novelty or originality of system building by Pufendorf or Kant, a full knowledge of the contemporary circumstances enchances our sense of the complexity of the speech acts involved here.

Such a focus within our teaching may also be of benefit to us in recovering a more nuanced sense of the social function of moral philosophy at a given period, which as Ian's quotation from J. B. Schneewind illustrates, has too often been restricted to the boundaries of academe. For beyond the dry detritus of long-abandoned curricular arrangements, we may be able to reach out into the mind-set of the officials, clergy, lawyers, and doctors—the professional elites of given states—who passed through that educational system and were shaped as much by courses in philosophy as by more vocational options. In so doing, we may be able to reunite ourselves with the work of general social and cultural historians of the 18th century, who have in recent years had a tendency to adopt into their approaches many of the insights associated with Habermas's account of the the transition from representational culture of the Baroque through to the growth of the public sphere by the 1790s. As Ian points out, the Habermas thesis is one that is best described as a single-aim thesis, which perhaps fits uneasily with a history of philosophy that seeks to incorporate a variable-aim approach. Yet careful study of episodes in which the canon formation of 18th-century philosophy collides with the regulatory role of the state and public opinion can be informative on both levels. One example that suggests itself in this connection is the collision between Kant's religious views and the Wöllner decrees of the 1790s. Kant's anguished and convoluted sets of distinctions between the private and the public would ironically not have existed under the Pufendorfian separation of the civil and religious spheres, which meshed much more effectively with the society of orders of its day. It was the intervening period of the disenchantment of the world—a key aspect of the Enlightenment era in both practical cultural history and intellectual history—that made it suddenly much more difficult in the 1790s to integrate a true separability of offices with a continuing close relationship between university culture and the goals of the state. It was ironic indeed that Kant—who had been so much the beneficiary of state sponsorship himself under Frederick the Great—should find himself caught in the crosshairs of this dilemma in the following decade.

In the process of canon creation, the early reception of texts is often crucial, and it is surely helpful therefore for students to be given some insight into this process through the study of examples, such as those of Barbeyrac and Stäudlin, wherein the critical changes of tone and weighting are still discernible in the texts themselves. In each case, the protagonists are responsible for setting up dominant images of Pufendorf and Kant to the immediate successor generation of students. Yet this is not simply a passive, unmediated transcription but also an adaptation designed to suit the priorities of the junior partner in the enterprise. For Barbeyrac, as Ian has indicated, the doctrines of Pufendorf on respective duties needed to be modified in a direction that took account of the predicament of those who did not belong to any particular state—namely, the Huguenots. This involved him in considerable incorporation of Lockean ideas that imported into the notes to his editions of Pufendorf many of the notions that Pufendorf had himself striven hard to exclude. The agenda that he imposes on Pufendorf implicitly is in fact *his own*—that of the stateless rather than the determinate citizen. Similarly, the histories of philosophy that Stäudlin compiled laboriously in the 1790s were driven not simply by admiration for Kant but also by Stäudlin's acknowledged need to find a philosophical antidote to the skeptical notions that he had encountered in his reading of contemporary British philosophy, not merely Hume. It is to that example that I now wish to turn briefly.

Far from being the inevitable or the only reading of Kant available in the later 18th century, Stäudlin's reading was a direct product of its historical setting. Kant's own brief and preliminary ventures into the relationship between his ethics and his predecessors indicated that any Kantian history of ethics would have to separate out those previous theories that took human nature as their starting point from those grounded on an objective, higher principle; it would also have to situate itself roughly athwart a tripartite conflict between skepticism, empiricism, and systematic rationalist philosophy in which Kant's own rationalism supersedes them all; finally, as Ian has remarked, it would build on Kant's conceptual reunification of access to moral truth with duty to place in question other systems of moral obligation that sought to separate out ethics from moral theology. Stäudlin was well equipped to perform all of these roles in his multiple histories of philosophy, but he did so from the perspective of a theologian who felt threatened by the full range of 18th-century British philosophy, and this inevitably took his history away from the actual circumstances of the birth of the Critical Theory.

Stäudlin's primary objective all along—which is clear from his first published reactions to the Kantian system—was to argue that the Critical Theory was compatible theologically with supernatural revelation as a mutually reinforcing basis for Christian belief. For him it was essential, more so than for Kant, that moral theology and practical ethics be reunited and that Christ's teachings be recognized as the highest expression of positive law. Any separation of offices of the kind argued for by Pufendorf was quite unacceptable to him. As he makes clear in numerous critiques of Pufendorf in his historical works, a failure—as he sees it—to distinguish between empirical and rational concepts produced no more than counsels of prudence in Pufendorf's ethics. For Stäudlin, more clearly than for Kant, this was a clear *wrong* turning in the history of moral philosophy that simply should be rejected and passed over.

Much more interesting from Stäudlin's perspective was the last hundred years of British philosophy in its empiricism and its skepticism: *here* were the real, positive challenges that Kant responded to, and the importance of Stäudlin to us here is in the care and skill with which he reassembles thinkers as various as Bacon, Hobbes, Locke, Shaftesbury, Cudworth, Price, Hutcheson, and Hume into a seamless sequence that Kant then perfects. This is directly parallel to the way in which Barbeyrac in his history of morality (prefacing his major edition of Pufendorf in 1706) had assembled an apostolic succession of philosophers vindicating Pufendorf's culminating synthesis and casting into the shade the contemporary German orthodoxy of post-Melanchthonian Aristotelianism. But I would stress that Barbeyrac and Stäudlin *needed* this synthesis rather more than either Pufendorf or Kant did. Moreover, though this ancestry was one that the latter authors would have recognized as plausible, it would by no means have registered a comprehensive account of the derivation of their thought.

Thus Stäudlin's history, as much if not more than Kant's Critical Theory, serves to relegate Pufendorfian ethics to a subordinate position within the history of moral philosophy in Germany. Predictably, in what he does say of pre-Kantian German debates, Stäudlin sides with Leibniz and Wolff on the question of moral obligation, finding the rationalism of the monadology and Wolff's concept of perfection far preferable to Pufendorf's voluntarism. Moreover, with the exception of Crusius, the majority of later-18th-century German moral philosophy is seen to take its bearings from British sources, especially through those authors, such as Ferguson, who had been mediated through Göttingen. Kant's originality on this basis lay in his proclaiming his *a priori* framework as the "free and individual product of human reason itself" and not merely a transfer of divine ideas to the human mind. By presenting the categorical imperative as the formal presupposition of ethics, he successfully got behind and transcended all of those other first principles of ethics, which could in essence be reduced to self-love and which in turn could not be the basis for any ethical system. In this insight lay his refutation of modern skepticism and corresponding vindication of reason's role as its own lawgiver.

A final—and unrelated—point is simply to note a further area of the historiography of moral philosophy that arguably experiences a profound change in this period. So far, we have been discussing debates that focused on the offices that involved individuals and their relations to God and/or the state. But of course another area of great concern for all of the philosophers discussed in Ian's paper involves the relationships that should obtain between states. Hobbes, Pufendorf, Leibniz, Barbeyrac, Wolff, and Vattel—to just name a few—are important players in this discourse whose focus of attention lies precisely on whether international law derives by direct analogy from the principles of natural law or should be regarded as a state of nature itself, to which separate categories have to be applied. If one focuses on the influential tradition of thought that originated in Leibniz and was then mediated through Wolff and Vattel before depositing its own residue in Kant's own *Perpetual Peace*, one might wish to argue that in this area it is Leibniz and not Pufendorf who has the last laugh. Leibniz's notion that there are shared rational truths that govern the conduct of international affairs that supervene over the particular offices of the state and church may be said to be a further expression of the contest for moral authority with Pufendorf that Ian has described for us so compellingly. We may well wish to expand our discussion to include it.

(Note: For further discussion of the role and contribution of Carl-Friedrich Stäudlin within the historiography of moral philosophy, see my study *Natural Law Theories in the Early Enlightenment* [Cambridge, 2000], pages 207–12, and the further references listed there on page 207.)

Teaching the History of Moral Philosophy

J. B. SCHNEEWIND

UNDERGRADUATE COURSES called History of Modern Philosophy in most American and British philosophy curricula are generally courses on the history of epistemology and metaphysics from Descartes through Kant. They rarely cover the ethical thought of the philosophers they study, and the curriculum almost never includes an introductory course on the history of ethics that parallels the course on the history of epistemology and metaphysics. There may be courses on the history of ethics at a more advanced level. But the Descartes-to-Kant course is usually required for majors, and comparable historical coverage of moral philosophy is not.[1] In this paper I first raise some questions about the rationale for giving such curricular priority to the history of epistemology and metaphysics. I go on to offer some suggestions for one-term undergraduate courses that might serve both as introductions to the history of ethics and to satisfy the history requirement in philosophy departments. The courses I outline sometimes involve texts not usually studied these days. And they all involve contextualizing the philosophy by relating it to the social, religious, and political situations in which philosophers understood themselves to work. I discuss briefly some reasons for teaching the history in this fashion. And I end with some remarks on the significance of teaching moral philosophy and its history in the undergraduate curriculum as a whole.

ONE

The standard Descartes-to-Kant course reflects the histories of their subject that philosophers have written. In these histories, the history of moral philosophy has typically received little if any coverage. Aristotle studied the metaphysics of his predecessors historically but not their ethics. Brucker wrote far less about the history of ethics than about the history of the religious, metaphysical, and epistemological aspects of philosophy.[2] Dugald Stewart's *Dissertation exhibiting the Progress of...Philosophy* (1815) falls into the same pattern, as do more recent histories of philosophy. There are 17th-century histories of natural law theories, of which Tim Hochstrasser has written an important study, but it was not until the 19th century that separate histories of moral philosophy began to appear.[3]

One possible rationale for this state of affairs lies in the religious heritage of the West. If morality contains God's instructions to us, then it might make sense to precede our study of it by asking what we know of God and how we know it.[4] If the questions here are not purely theological, they would fall to philosophical metaphysics and epistemology. More generally, if we supposed that morality must be rooted in metaphysical aspects of the universe, it would again seem to make sense to study these before moving to the ethics dependent on them.

This is the vision suggested by Descartes's famous tree of knowledge. "The roots [of knowledge] are metaphysics, the trunk is physics, and the branches emerging from the trunk are all the other sciences...medicine, mechanics, and morals," he says.[5] If moral knowledge is dependent on knowledge about the metaphysical and physical nature of the world, including human nature, then morality and its philosophy will be comprehensible only once we understand their foundations and our ability to know them. On this view it may be reasonable to suppose that histories of philosophy should reflect the dependence of moral philosophy on what analytic philosophers view as the core disciplines: metaphysics and epistemology.

It may be possible to revive the view that all sound thinking must begin by acknowledging God and the limits of human abilities to understand him.[6] But secular thinkers would hardly appeal to such claims to justify the subordination of ethics to epistemology and metaphysics. And general foundationalist views of a Cartesian kind have been widely criticized and rejected in recent years. If we abandon foundationalism, we also give up the assumption that there is a natural order of knowledge, in which some disciplines are essentially more basic than others. Then it is hard to see on what a priori grounds we could insist that the history of epistemology or metaphysics must be studied before getting on to the history of other parts of philosophy.

Whatever we think of foundationalism, when we are teaching history it is not very useful to presuppose that modern moral philosophy is best understood as an offshoot of views about more general or allegedly more fundamental theories in epistemology and metaphysics. Such foundationalist views may blind us to possibilities about the history that interests us. We need to be ready to examine the thought that just as changes in scientific belief may have stimulated new philosophizing about knowledge, so changes that upset accepted moral belief may have been the occasion for philosophical rethinking of morality. We will then want to explore the possibility that moral philosophy has a history of its own, which may have exerted its influence on other developments in philosophy and not merely been dependent on them.

Our thinking about the history of moral philosophy is constricted not just by religious or philosophical preconceptions of the proper order of knowledge but also by certain views about what moral philosophy is or does. Philosophers often write as if moral philosophy has always had a single aim or function, but for teaching the history of the subject, this is not a helpful assumption. Aristotle thought that "a knowledge of the Good is of great importance for the conduct of our lives," since we all aim at the good and are more likely to get it if we have the kind of clear knowledge of our target that philosophy can give.[7] Sidgwick urged us to reject Aristotle by making the improvement of knowledge, not of practice, our philosophical aim. In Sidgwick's opinion, "The predominance in the minds of moralists of a desire to edify has impeded the real progress of ethical science." We should instead approach the issues with "the same disinterested curiosity to which we chiefly owe the great discoveries of physics."[8] Sidgwick's view was reinforced by logical positivism. In 1930 Moritz Schlick said that moral philosophy "is a system of *knowledge* and nothing else...the questions of ethics...are purely theoretical problems." The philosopher, he urged, "must forget that he has a human interest as well as a cognitive interest" in morality. Moral philosophy is "in essence, theory or knowledge," and therefore "its task cannot be to produce morality, or to establish it, or to call it to life."[9] Schlick here assumes both that moral philosophy has only one aim or purpose and that the purpose is simply to obtain knowledge about morality. Twentieth-century metaethics even after positivism worked on the same assumption.

We need not accept Sidgwick's suggestion that the sole alternative to treating moral philosophy as a search for theoretical under-standing is to treat it as an effort to edify. Pierre Hadot, Michel Foucault, and Alexander Nehamas have argued that in antiquity, moral philosophy was treated as the source of a "way of life."[10] More recently, Ian Hunter has argued that at least some of the major contributors to early modern moral philosophy also had highly practical aims in publishing their theories and that their aims were as diverse as their theories.[11] John Stuart Mill agreed with Auguste Comte that most people take their opinions from experts and that "the moral and intellectual ascendancy, once exercised by priests, must in time pass into the hands of philosophers and will naturally do so when they become sufficiently unanimous, and in other respects worthy to possess it."[12] American moral philosophy from the early decades of the 19th century until the end of the Civil War was supposed to provide a system of values and goals that all citizens ought to pursue.[13] All of this goes beyond an effort at edification, with its suggestion of individual religious uplift and encouragement.

An open mind about foundationalism and a natural hierarchy of knowledge suggests that philosophy departments have no compelling philosophical grounds for refusing to give the history of moral philosophy equal weight in the curriculum with the history of epistemology and metaphysics. Awareness that some of the moral philosophers took their task to be practical and not solely or even centrally theoretical leads to the thought that even an introductory survey of the history of modern moral philosophy should present the philosophical writings in relation to the varying practical problems about morality and social life that different philosophers may have aimed to address. I begin by sketching some of the ways one might structure a one-semester course on the history of 17th- and 18th-century moral philosophy, keeping these points in mind.

TWO

Any good undergraduate course in the history of philosophy needs a story line—a narrative with beginning and end. Both will be to some extent arbitrary, dictated by current interests as well as by our understanding of the sources. For an undergraduate offering that can serve as an alternative to the Descartes-to-Kant course, I suggest a history of moral philosophy from Montaigne to Kant.[14]

Montaigne makes a good beginning. It is not the least of his merits that students like to read him. To the instructor he gives an excellent reason to present a brief review of both ancient and Christian ethics before launching into early modern efforts to rethink the whole subject. Montaigne himself looks to classical moral philosophy to provide a way of life, but he gives up that effort. "Men are diverse in inclination and strength," he says. "They must be led to their own good according to their nature and by diverse ways."[15] He stresses the importance of the goods of this life, including the bodily pleasures. He expresses extreme distaste for enthusiastic otherworldliness, whether it comes as Socrates's appeal to his daimon or as extreme religious devotion. He says that although many thinkers assert that there are universal moral laws of nature accepted everywhere, he has never been able to find one. And he claims that each of us can discover a ruling pattern within which suffices as a guide. Well before Descartes asked each of us to make a clean sweep of the clutter of our inherited beliefs about the world, Montaigne gave an example of someone doing just that with the main positions on morality that were then available. In doing so, he opened up leitmotifs that run through much of modern moral philosophy.

Why end with Kant? It is not necessary to do so. It would be more fun to end the course with the Marquis de Sade's critique of modern moral philosophy. But he was not influential in the respectable and increasingly academic circles that produced later moral philosophy.[16] Those who mattered were Reid, Bentham, and Kant. They superseded or overshadowed the work of their early modern predecessors. And it was their work that became the starting points of moral philosophy after the French Revolution. If departments sponsored a second course, covering the history of moral philosophy from Kant to Rawls, instructors could avoid the anguish of trying to cover Kant in a short time at the end of a term. (They would exchange it for the perhaps worse anguish of having to do so at the beginning of a term.) But Kant introduced some utterly new ideas into ethics, as neither Reid nor Bentham did.

So it is worth trying to include him in the one-term survey, as we do in the counterpart history of epistemology and metaphysics, which could also end with Reid.

Even when we have decided on a beginning and an end, we can shape the narrative in different ways. We might treat it as a story of progressive enlightenment, showing morality's breaking free from subordination to religious belief and ending with three paths that independent ethics took in the 19th century. We could go further in this direction and allow our own preferences to let us endorse one of the three, declaring Benthamism, say, the triumphant outcome of our story. But we need not be progressivist. We could see the history of moral philosophy as a falling away from insights once possessed. MacIntyre, explaining how a Thomist might account for Nietzsche's genealogical attempts to unmask morality as a front for the will to power, suggests that the Thomist would begin with what Aquinas says about the roots of intellectual blindness in moral error, with the misdirection of the intellect by the will, and with the corruption of the will by the sin of pride—both that pride that is an inordinate desire to be superior and that pride that is an inclination to contempt for God. Where Nietzsche saw the individual will as a fiction that conceals from view the impersonal will to power, the Thomist can elaborate out of the materials provided in the *Summa* an account of the will to power as an intellectual fiction disguising the corruption of the will.[17]

If we choose to work out the history of moral philosophy in terms like these, we would be in line with a criticism of Locke published in 1697.

> [God has] imprinted all natural truths in created beings...from whence, by the vehicles of our senses, they are copy'd and transcribed into our minds...Thus was mankind put into a plain roadway of gaining clear intellectual light [by developing logic] ...But...the crooked bias of men's wills perverted their reason and made them disregard this well-grounded and regular method, given them by the Author of Nature.[18]

THREE

The way we teach the history of ethics is almost unavoidably affected by our assessments of modernity and the current state of morality. Those with strong convictions on the matter may well decide to make their views explicit and embed them in their historical narrative. But that is not inevitable. Narratives of progress or of decline in moral thought suppose that the narrator knows the truth. So too does a Weberian position that reserves for natural science the categories of progress and the obsolescence of old theories and that views philosophy as more like art. But the historian does not have to be sitting in some assured judgment seat. We can avoid this, I suggest, by treating past moral philosophers as responding to large-scale practical problems that were urgent in their time. We do not need to decide on the truth or falsity of the views we discuss. We can teach the critical skills the students need by showing them how to assess the philosophers' arguments and positions in the light of the questions that actually concerned them.[19] It takes historical work to unearth those questions and to avoid substituting for them the issues that we consider central now. But this can be done, and the students need to learn how to do it. We can also use the criticisms later philosophers made of their predecessors to get students to discuss the merits of positions. Butler's objections to egoism, Hume's to cognitivism, and Reid's to Hume's sentimentalism all provide important introductions to major disputes in ethics and are excellent exercises for students.

Setting moral philosophy in the context of the issues disturbing the philosopher's culture allows us to be on the watch for the kinds of discontinuity or rupture that Kuhn and Foucault stressed. Nearly a century ago, Dewey put a similar point quite forcibly.

> Intellectual progress usually occurs through sheer abandon-ment of questions together with both of the alternatives they assume—an abandonment that results from their decreasing vitality and a change of urgent interest. We do not solve them: we get over them.[20]

The history of moral philosophy is a good place to go to observe philosophers abandoning old questions.

What then might a course on the history of moral philosophy from Montaigne to Kant look like? Here's a start, organized for three sessions per week in a 13-week semester.

HISTORY OF MORAL PHILOSOPHY: MONTAIGNE TO KANT

I.	1. Introduction; 2. Montaigne; 3. Montaigne
II.	1. Modern natural law: Grotius; 2. Hobbes; 3. Hobbes
III.	1. Hobbes; 2. Hobbes; 3. Hobbes
IV.	1. Pufendorf; 2. Pufendorf; 3. Pufendorf
V.	1. Intellectualism: Leibniz; 2. Leibniz; 3. Leibniz [Wolff]
VI.	1. Self-interest and morality: Nicole; 2. Mandeville; 3. Gay
VII	1. Moral sense: Hutcheson; 2. Hutcheson; 3. Butler
VIII.	1. Butler; 2. Butler; 3. Hume
IX.	1. Hume; 2. Hume; 3. Hume
X.	1. Common sense intuitionism: Reid; 2. Reid; 3. Reid
XI.	1. Utilitarianism: Bentham; 2. Bentham; 3. Bentham
XII.	1. Kantianism: [Crusius]; 2. Kant; 3. Kant
XIII.	1. Kant; 2. Kant; 3. Kant

What carries the students through these authors is a narrative nicely opened by Montaigne's ambivalence about human beings. At the end of the essay on Sebond, Montaigne uses Seneca and Plutarch to say that man is a "vile and abject thing" if he does not "raise himself above humanity" and that he cannot do this unless he renounces his own means and relies on God to lend him a hand: only Christian faith can help. But in "On Repentance" he rejects the thought that he ought to regret being human. His conscience is "content with itself," he says, "not as the conscience of an angel or horse but as the conscience of a man." The judgment comes from his own "court and laws," and he does not look elsewhere. The *Essays* thus move from a view of man as lowly and needing external control to a much higher estimate of our capacities, particularly our ability to govern ourselves. I take this movement to be central to the development of modern moral philosophy. Not surprisingly, Kant provides a fitting end to the story.

To introduce the course, I discuss the Reformation and the religious wars tied to the ideological splits it introduced or exacerbated. Religious controversy is a leitmotif throughout. Even after the worst of the wars were over, confessional controversy remained. And with it there remained the need—desperate, for those who remembered the horrors of war—to find a morality that could be widely accepted despite confessional differences. Most people could not live a morality to which God was irrelevant, but at the risk of renewed bloodshed, God, whose will naturally had to be passed on by his official ministers, could not play an active role in it. This forms a large part of the context in which I try to explain the history of moral philosophy.

It is important not to overdo the amount of departure from religion that occurred in the 17th and 18th centuries. If Bentham gives us a wholly secular morality, neither Reid nor Kant do. One function of the course, therefore, is to correct misleading views of "the enlightenment and secularization" that are still current. Another is to explore the different ways in which religion has been taken to be of importance for morality and to raise questions about what morality might be without it. The rise of science was of course important, as was religion. I do not make much of it in this course, but the Newtonianism that gave Hume the model for his naturalism and the rhetoric in which he explained his philosophical ambitions deserves brief mention.

As general background, and to be helpful for understanding Montaigne, then, I say something about St. Thomas's views on natural law and about the strong positions of Luther and Calvin on our sinful condition. A lecture, with or without brief selections, suffices for Grotius, but it is important to bring in at the start his views on human sociability and the difficulties put in its way by our tendency to overreach ourselves. Hobbes goes further than Grotius in his estimate of the difficulty we have in living together. Comparing his view of the state of nature with St. Augustine's, visible in *The City of God*, highlights his Montaignian refusal to call us sinful. And his view of how we give effect to the dictates that become morality is a step on the path toward showing how we can construct our own governance. Pufendorf brings out the voluntarism that Hobbes himself espouses more overtly and fully than Hobbes does, and argues—against Montaignian skepticism—that international and not just national law is a possibility.

I pick Leibniz to speak for intellectualistic perfectionism partly because Spinoza is harder to understand and partly because Leibniz's criticisms of Pufendorfian voluntarism exemplify a major theme in the development of modern moral philosophy. (One could use Cudworth's critique of Cartesian voluntarism for this purpose as well, but his own positive views are hard to extract and present briefly.) The disagreements between Pufendorf and Leibniz raise serious questions about what sort of foundation, if any, a moral outlook should have. Pufendorf himself might have offered reasons for not being convinced by Leibniz's critique. Leibniz is useful also because his views, mediated and somewhat transformed by Wolff, were important in Kant's development. It is, however, quite possible to teach Spinoza instead, using material from the *Theological-Political Treatise* and the *Ethics*. When I do teach him, I confess that I do not expect the students to master the arguments for the propositions in the latter work. I aim at most to give them an overview of the position. Either Leibniz or Spinoza will introduce the students to the view that moral improvement comes only from clarified and increased knowledge.

I put three mischief makers next—Nicole, Mandeville, and Gay—partly because the students get a kick out of them. And of course most of those who wrote later tried to come to terms with them. Hutcheson is direct in doing so and is easier to read than Shaftesbury. Butler, though students find him difficult, is vital. More clearly than many other thinkers, he uses the major alternative to voluntarism or divine command theory for keeping God essential to morality. God, for Butler, is the supervisor of the universe who makes sure that if each of us does our duty, as it is made evident to us through conscience, all will be for the best. Thus God is a utilitarian though we cannot be. In addition, Butler's arguments against egoism, his claims about the superior authority of conscience as distinct from its strength, and his pluralistic critique of Hutcheson's view that benevolence is the whole of virtue raised issues that have not yet disappeared from moral philosophy.

Hume's distinction between natural and artificial virtues builds from Pufendorf's distinction between imperfect and perfect duties, and his conventionalist theory of justice is a response to Butler's objections to Hutcheson's quasi-utilitarianism. His insistence that approval is directed primarily at motives, not at acts, is a direct disavowal of the severe protestant position that in order to show us our need for grace, God could command us to act in ways that we are unable to act. Putting Hume in this context helps students see his originality. And it gives them a good sense of how his sentimentalism goes far beyond the thought of his predecessors in developing a way to understand ourselves as capable of self-governance. In connection with Hume's theory of justice, it is worth pointing out that Hume wrote on economics and was concerned about the severe under-development of his native Scotland.

Reid presents a different picture of self-governance as well as a host of arguments against Hume. And Bentham fires a huge battery of objections at all of his natural law, intuitionist, and sentimentalist predecessors. When he is done with them, utilitarianism seems to be the only show in town. But of course he did not know Kant. Like Bentham, Kant hoped to eliminate the views of all of his own predecessors, many of them the same as those of Bentham. I sometimes try to talk a little about Crusius to help the students see that Kant did not come just out of the blue and that he was using as well as criticizing earlier work. But time presses at the end of term, and there is enough to do in getting the students to have some understanding of morality as autonomy as it is spelled out in the first two sections of the *Groundwork*. I do not try to get them through the third section, though I summarize it for them.

There are several themes that keep coming up in the authors I have proposed for study. Montaigne abandons the search for a highest good that will be the same for all human beings, and Grotius follows him. Hobbes vehemently denies that there is any such thing. Even Bentham does not claim that there is, as his "pleasure" is merely a placeholder for preferences, and his defense of homosexuality makes it clear that he knew how varied those could be. Kant insists that we each be allowed to pursue the good as we ourselves see it—within limits, of course. The problem of finding a common morality without relying on a highest good is thus one central issue.

Here is another: Montaigne does not deny the authority of the Catholic Church in moral matters but sets it aside; Hobbes subordinates religious teaching to the secular ruler. This provides a reason to bring in the emergence of moral philosophy as a discipline independent of moral theology.[21] It is worthwhile occasionally to point out that moral philosophy—as our curriculum conceives of it—is itself a discipline that emerged during the debates the course is covering. For the natural law theorists, morality was just a part of law. It was separated out by thinkers I have usually not tried to include: Malebranche and Thomasius. But one can't cover everything in one semester.

Is this a course on the rise of enlightenment moral philosophy? Yes, indeed, but it is an open question how useful it would be, while teaching it, to make enlightenment a major theme. To do so, one has to give an account of what enlightenment was. Using Kant's account in a semester ending with his ethics makes the voyage all too obviously destined for that goal from the start. If we take pure opposition to religion as the dominant focus of enlightenment, we will have a skewed approach to the moral philosophers who insisted on somehow keeping God involved in morality but who still must be considered enlightened. It is worth playing the enlightenment motif from time to time, but to do it full justice would pull the course away from its central subjects.

Another way of presenting the history of moral philosophy would be to offer alternating courses: one on the 17th century (roughly) and one on the 18th. They could be taught in alternate years and allowed to satisfy the same requirements. A 17th-century semester, starting with the religious controversies and Montaigne, could give more time to the natural lawyers and to the rationalist theorists than the course already outlined. Stoicism could get a little time, with some Lipsius or DuVair as text, and Spinoza can be presented partly in this light. Students are quite intrigued by Malebranche, but one can avoid his metaphysical oddities and teach Clarke instead as a sort of finale. For the 18th century Shaftesbury, Mandeville, and Butler make a good beginning; Hume and Reid show the kinds of position against which Bentham specified his view; and Rousseau can be enjoyed for a week or two before landing at Kant's doorstep.

A rather different kind of course on the history of moral philosophy could begin with Machiavelli by using material on the classical republic from the *Discourses* as well as a little on unscrupulousness from *The Prince*. The absence of Christianity from his treatment of social life provides a view of human self-governance against which to teach some Aquinas, Luther, and Calvin. I would then move to Hobbes's rejection of republicanism together with his subordination of religion to the ruler. Pufendorf might come next, raising questions about the importance of religion in society, to be followed by Mandeville, whose cynical take on morality as political manipulation links him more to Machiavelli than to Hobbes. Shaftesbury asked questions about what sort of moral psychology is presupposed in the citizens of a modern classical republic. Butler can be fitted into this narrative, though not, I think, as interested in the political bearing of his moral psychology. Hume rejected republicanism; Rousseau revived it; and Kant gave it a new shape. Here the religious themes would be less prominent, and questions about politics, moral psychology and the relation of individual and community would be more prominent than they would be in the other courses I have suggested.

Another approach to the history of moral philosophy would be to concentrate on modern views about virtue.[22] Here Machiavelli might be a good starting point, since he uses a term translated as *virtue* but does not use it to mean quite what the ancients meant by it. The development in modern times away from Machiavelli's understanding of *virtù* is a good story—one that can be set in the frame of the decline of admiration for the nobility and their warrior virtues, the rise of new views of courtesy independent of courts, and the admission of shopkeepers and other ordinary folk into the ranks of those who might possess all the important virtues. Montaigne is again important, since he comments on many ancient views of the virtues and is highly critical of the preeminence accorded to the character of the ruthless soldier or military leader.[23] Grotius's critique of Aristotle on virtue could be the focus for a brief discussion of his thought, followed by Hobbes's concerns about virtue in connection with republicanism and his attempt to create a law-centered alternative. Pufendorf's category of imperfect duties is best explained as his way of making room for something like the virtues of concern for others. In Shaftesbury, Hutcheson, Butler, and Hume, virtue takes center stage, and Rousseau deserves an important place in this narrative, bringing back Machiavelli's admiration for the classical republic but with a distinctly different twist. In ending with Kant, one would need to give the students some pages from his *Doctrine of Virtue* to supplement the usual reading in the *Groundwork*.

FOUR

Any of these courses would give students a good idea of the richness of the traditions of modern moral philosophy. My suggestions show that I am not favorably disposed to the sometimes popular course on "the British moralists" as a first survey of the history of modern ethics. That has long been a standard offering, partly because anthologies of 17th- and 18th-century English-language ethics have been available for over a century. Moreover, the British writings are accessible to beginners, and it is easy to link the main authors in a narrative going from Hobbes to Bentham and Reid. Nonetheless, to teach the history of modern moral philosophy in this way is to leave out as much of what shaped its course as we would omit if we tried to teach only British thinkers in the other introductory history class.

To put it another way, British moral philosophers were deeply involved with many Continental thinkers. Including them in the introductory history course is one way of broadening the context in which we locate the philosophers. I have suggested also some of the nonphilosophical contexts in which I would try to situate the moral philosophy. A comment is now in order about why I propose to give so much emphasis to the broader cultural issues with which modern moral philosophy has been involved. Why, in a word, do we need the new histories of moral philosophy that I have been proposing?

Quentin Skinner and John Pocock have done more than anyone else during the past several decades to bring us to recognize the importance of situating philosophical thought in relation to historically local issues to which the philosophers were responding.[24] In working on the history of moral philosophy in the 17th and 18th centuries, I have been influenced by their writings. But I must make two comments about their views in connection with undergraduate teaching.

First, their complex rationales for contextualizing the works we study do not need to be explained in any detail in a beginning course on the history of moral philosophy. It suffices, I think, to make a comment now and again about the need a writer has to be understood by the people he wishes to affect and about the ways in which this need requires us to understand his language as he and his readers would have understood it.

Second, I have found that the history of moral philosophy requires a somewhat different approach to contexts than those that Skinner and Pocock take when they discuss the history of political thought. To put it briefly, I cannot always find specific cultural or political events to which philosophers were responding when they worked out what we now take to be their moral philosophy. And even when specific needs for rethinking ethics can be located, the philosophical inquiries go beyond what initially occasioned the work. Hobbes was indeed concerned about the English civil wars spurred by religious controversies, and Spinoza and Pufendorf were responding to different religious controversies in different social and political settings. But all of them were aware that the issues went beyond the local controversies that provoked their theories. Their concerns extended to the more general issues that were made specific in different ways in England or the Netherlands or Germany. Those issues, as well as the particular embodiments of them, changed over time. We can bring out the pastness of past moral philosophy by relating it to the large-scale issues prominent at the time. They will frequently not be the same as the questions that concern us now.

Context is indeed vital if we are to be historically careful about the meanings of the assertions of past philosophers. For undergraduates, context has an additional kind of importance. Explaining the different sorts of practical problems in which philosophers hoped to make a difference helps students see that what they are reading was not intended to be of merely academic interest. Philosophy nowadays does not have a large appeal to the public, not even to the undergraduate public. If we are to make the history of moral philosophy significant now for students, we need to show them that it mattered in its own time for reasons that went beyond the classroom. What that suggests is that moral philosophy might be as important now as it was then.

FIVE

A basic one-semester course in history of moral philosophy could have a role in the curriculum like that of the course on the history of epistemology and metaphysics that has been standard for nearly a century. For many students the history course is an introduction to the problems of philosophy as well as to its history. Any of the history courses I have outlined introduces central problems of ethical theory and allows as much scope for their discussion as the Descartes-to-Kant course allows for its problems. At least as many students are interested in moral issues as are concerned about problems of knowledge. And the writers treated in the courses I have outlined are basic for the moral philosophy that follows. Aside from preconceptions about what is basic and what is derivative, a course on the history of moral philosophy seems as well suited as the traditional one to serve the purposes of a basic history course.

To allow such a course to satisfy the departmental history requirement would not, however, be a minor change. The standard history course serves, among other things, to prepare students for more advanced work in the subjects whose history it covers. There is more in the standard curriculum on epistemology and metaphysics than on ethics. Even advanced historical courses on rationalism or empiricism are not mainly, if at all, about the moral thought linked to these orientations. Giving history of moral philosophy a weight equal to the weight that has been given to epistemology and metaphysics might necessitate changes in the advanced offerings that have presupposed participation in the standard history course: less metaphysics, more ethics. Curricula are not easy to change in any case. And in this case, the curricular pattern displays some deep, or anyway old, currents in philosophy and in higher education that call for rethinking.

During much of the 19th century, American college education, like its British counterpart, was designed to prepare a leadership elite for positions of responsibility in the ministry, government, or business. In the United States, the capstone course during the senior year, often given by the college president, was a course on ethics. It provided an orientation to life in the form of a comprehensive overview of Christian morality. It criticized philosophical positions believed to be inimical to that morality and provided at least a rudimentary rationale for what the young men who took it were supposed to be assured of otherwise through revelation.[25] College presidents do not teach that course any more, and neither do philosophy departments. Colleges and universities on the whole no longer present themselves as preparing their students for leadership roles. Many students think that the idea that they might go into politics is bizarre or foolish. And the thought that philosophy courses might help prepare them for such a career would seem equally if not more bizarre.

Philosophy's own contribution to this situation is complex. In ancient times, as I suggested earlier, philosophers were looked on as sources of wisdom about the overall care of the self, about how to conduct oneself in matters familial and sexual, about how to use power and how to lose it, and about how to sustain either success or misery with dignity.[26] We do not now expect philosophers to be wiser about practical matters than other people are: indeed, probably the contrary. Christianity took over the guidance of life from pagan philosophy, and modern moral philosophy never took it back.

For this failure or refusal there were several reasons. One was that the Reformation ensured that it would be at least as hard for moderns to achieve agreement about the good life as it had been for the ancients. Moreover, there were urgent public problems about morality and politics, about which philosophers hoped to have more useful things to say than they could about the good life. Priests and ministers might continue to claim the authority to direct the private lives of individuals, but the universities in which philosophers came to be at home did not confer any such authority on them. And the academicization of philosophy also played a part in moving philosophers away from the kind of claim that John Stuart Mill made in the last third of his century: that philosophers should shape public morals. To sustain funding for the work of philosophy in 20th-century universities dominated by science, it seemed necessary to make the subject look like the sciences. Analytic philosophy seemed just the right way to go for this purpose. It enabled Anglophone moral philosophy to present itself as a tough-minded discipline with an agenda of difficult and purely theoretical problems. But the civil rights movement, the Vietnam war protests, the women's movement, and developments in biology and medicine have moved different questions to the front. Rawls's moral and political thought and the rise of applied ethics have brought about remarkable changes in what can now count as serious work within the discipline.

What might justify allowing the history of moral philosophy to share the place traditionally accorded the history of epistemology and metaphysics? I have claimed that moral philosophy itself has had different aims and purposes over its long history. Study of the history of the subject has had a much shorter life span, and we have no good examination of it.[27] But insofar as the history has been taught, its teaching has also had varying aims. For Sidgwick, one point of the function of the historiography of ethics was to show that there really was—that there always had been—the discipline of moral philosophy; it therefore should have a secure place in the curriculum. Today, I think, we need a different service from study of the history of moral philosophy. We need it to show us how moral philosophy at different times has served different practical purposes. Historicizing the past of the discipline raises questions about what is being done now. Is the debate about deontology, consequentialism, and now virtue ethics still worth continuing? Or are there other issues that might well be addressed? Can moral philosophy address the larger issues of the time? Or is it at best part of the training for the new casuistry of applied ethics?

Moral philosophy no longer needs to present itself as the spectator sport it was in the heyday of analytic ethics. Philosophy departments have not completely caught up with this development. If our universities and colleges were more interested in preparing students for leadership positions than they now seem to be, they might ask more of ethics courses and of courses on the history of moral philosophy than they now do. Philosophy departments themselves might even take the lead in bringing back this ancient and honorable function of their institutions. If they do, they will find that courses on the history of moral philosophy will need to occupy a far more central place than they do now.

NOTES

1. Mr. Todd Beattie of Princeton University examined 200 college catalogs and found that almost all philosophy departments require a course in the history of modern philosophy for the major. In most cases, this is a course on the history of epistemology and metaphysics. Only about eight schools allowed a course on the history of moral philosophy to count. I am grateful to Princeton High School for permission to use its collection of college catalogs and to Mr. Beattie for his assistance.

2. See the explanation of this in T. J. Hochstrassser, *Natural Law Theories in the Early Enlightenment,* Cambridge University Press, 2000, 174.

3. The first, to my knowledge, was C. F. Stäudlin's *Geschichte der Moralphilosophie* of 1822. The only 19th-century history still in use is Henry Sidgwick's *Short History of Ethics,* 1886.

4. But well before Kant, both Lord Herbert of Cherbury and Pierre Bayle held that we must use moral knowledge to determine whether an alleged divine command really comes from God or not.

5. Preface to *Principles of Philosophy,* in *Philosophical Writings* I, trans. Cottingham et al. Cambridge, England: Cambridge University Press, 1985, 186.

6. See, e.g., Nicholas P. Wolterstorff, "What New Haven and Grand Rapids Have to Say to Each Other." In *Seeking Understanding.* Grand Rapids, Mich.: William B. Eerdmans Publishing Co., 2001.

7. Aristotle, *Nicomachean Ethics,* I.i.

8. Henry Sidgwick, *The Methods of Ethics,* London, 1874, vi–vii. Hegel, in the Preface to the *Phenomenology of Mind,* trans. A. V. Miller, says, "Philosophy must beware of the wish to be edifying." Oxford, England: 1979, 6.

9. Moritz Schlick, *Problems of Ethics,* trans. David Rynin. New York: 1939 (original in German, 1930).

10. Pierre Hadot, *Philosophy as a Way of Life,* ed. Davidson. Oxford, England: 1995; Michel Foucault, *The Care of the Self,* trans. Robert Hurley, New York: 1986; Alexander Nehamas, *The Art of Living,* Berkeley, Calif.: 1998.

11. Ian Hunter, *Rival Enlightenments.* Cambridge, England: Cambridge University Press, 2001.

12. John Stuart Mill, *Autobiography,* ch.VI, ed. Stillinger, 126–27.

13. See D. H. Meyer, *The Instructed Conscience.* Philadelphia: 1972.

14. My view of the history of moral philosophy is set out at length in *The Invention of Autonomy,* Cambridge University Press, 1998. My anthology, *Moral Philosophy from Montaigne to Kant,* Cambridge University Press,

1990, now reissued in a single volume, contains sufficient excerpts to keep students busy for more than a term, but the selections are not long enough to make possible the detailed study of any of the authors included.

15. Montaigne, *Essays*, trans. Donald Frame. "Of Physiognomy." Stanford, Calif.: Stanford University Press, 1958, 805.

16. For de Sade as precursor of nihilism, see Winfried Schröder, *Moralischer Nihilismus*. Stuttgart-Bad Cannstatt: 2002, ch. V.

17. Alasdair MacIntyre, *Three Rival Versions of Genealogy*, Notre Dame, 147.

18. John Sargent, *Solid Philosophy Asserted against the Fancies of the Deists*, 1697, A2–A3.

19. We will show what we consider to be important or unimportant as much by the practical issues we choose to highlight as by the philosophers we read and those we skip.

20. John Dewey, "The Influence of Darwinism on Philosophy," 1909, *Middle Works* vol. 4, Carbondale, Ill.: 1977, 14.

21. On this, see Wilhelm Schmitt-Biggeman, "New Structures of Knowledge," in *A History of the University in Europe*, ed. Hilde de Ridder-Symoens, Cambridge, England: Cambridge University Press, 1996, 489–529. And note Ian Hunter's objections to his views, *Rival Enlightenments*, Cambridge University Press, 2001, 20–21, 37–38.

22. For an argument against those who claim that modern moral philosophy ignored virtue, see my "Misfortunes of Virtue," *Ethics* 101.1, Oct. 1990, 42–63.

23. See David Quint, *Montaigne and the Quality of Mercy*, Princeton, N.J.: Princeton University Press, 1998.

24. See Quentin Skinner, *Visions of Politics*, vol. I. Cambridge, England: Cambridge University Press, 2002, for Skinner's papers, and *Meaning and Context*, ed. James Tully, Princeton, N.J.: Princeton University Press, 1988, for discussion. See John Pocock, *Virtue, Commerce, and History*, Cambridge, England: Cambridge University Press, 1985, ch. 1, for one of Pocock's several accounts of his approach.

25. See Meyer, referred to in note 13.

26. See the work of Hadot, Foucault, and Nehamas referred to in note 10.

27. See Norman Fiering, *Moral Philosophy at Seventeenth Century Harvard*. Chapel Hill, N.C.: 1981, and *Jonathan Edwards's Moral Thought and Its British Context*, Chapel Hill, N.C.: 1981.

Historicism, Moral Judgment, and the Good Life: A Response to J. B. Schneewind [1]

JENNIFER A. HERDT

OVER THE COURSE of his career, Jerry Schneewind has worked tirelessly and with great success to advance the discipline of the history of moral philosophy and to define *modern* moral philosophy in particular as shaped by a distinctive problematic. This conference and the rich and suggestive paper he has offered us today grow quite naturally from this sustained endeavor. My own thought, like that of many of our conference participants, has been shaped in lasting ways by Jerry's thought. It will come as no surprise, then, if I register my hearty agreement that the time is ripe for dethroning courses in the history of epistemology that masquerade as "the history of philosophy" and that students should be exposed to the history of ethics. I should, though, note from the outset that my comments come from the margins, for I speak from outside the discipline of philosophy, as one trained within a program in religious studies— here at Princeton—that can be seen as studying ethics and its history in a way already informed by the historicist, postfoundationalist, postanalytical insights proffered by Schneewind, and as one now teaching within a department of theology—at the University of Notre Dame—that can be regarded as a site where the divide between theory and practice has already been bridged. My hope is that a perspective coming from this oblique angle can prove fruitful for our common reflections.

Schneewind rightly suggests that "the way we teach the history of ethics is almost unavoidably affected by our assessments of modernity and the current state of morality."[2] Yet he still seems to want to cling to a posture of neutrality. Thus, his preference is to avoid grand narratives of progress and regress in favor of an approach that eschews claiming "some assured judgment seat." We can, he argues, treat "past moral philosophers as responding to large-scale practical problems that were urgent in their time. We do not need to decide on the truth or falsity of the views we discuss."[3] Such an approach, Schneewind stresses, teaches important critical skills that students need. It also, he implies, embodies the moral virtue of humility. Myself a product of a liberal college education, I have considerable appreciation for a pedagogical approach that avoids didacticism and understands itself as teaching critical thinking skills. Given contemporary college students' almost total lack of historical awareness, surely it is right that one of our primary responsibilities as educators is to engender in students a sense of how foreign the past is to us. However, contra Quentin Skinner's classic essay "Meaning and Understanding in the History of Ideas," there is more to the value of studying the history of ideas than the discovery of "the essential variety of viable moral assumptions and political commitments."[4] If we stop with this, we are likely simply to encourage relativism—another vice to which contemporary students are particularly prone. Students may conclude either that a moral philosophy is arbitrarily to be chosen or that we are, given our particular historical situation, simply fated to a particular under-standing of moral philosophy. Moreover, it is not clear that we can even adequately articulate the foreignness of the past without a sense of how we and our commitments are situated with respect to that past. But to orient ourselves to the past is just to occupy some sort of judgment seat, even if one that is more fallibilist than self-assured.

Constructing narratives of progress and regress need not involve assuming that there are certain timeless philosophical questions whose true answers are either gradually discovered or lost over time. On Schneewind's own approach, one of the most important things we learn from studying the history of moral philosophy is that old questions are often abandoned and new questions taken up; within the history of philosophy, there are Kuhnian paradigm shifts, to which grand narratives do not do justice. This, I take it, undermines in Schneewind's eyes the notion of a tradition of moral reflection stretching back from our own time to, say, Socrates or to the Hebrew prophets. It is not clear to me, though, that the fact that old questions are abandoned and new ones formed undermines the viability of tradition. To see this shifting of questions as undermining the category of tradition would be to treat tradition as requiring some sort of static substance, a "deposit" that underlies historical change. If a tradition is instead a relationship to the past constantly constructed by the current generation, then it is compatible with the recognition of dramatic shifts within the narrative. Questions may have been wrongly abandoned, and recognizing this may stimulate us to take them up again. Or questions may have been appropriately abandoned, recognized as stemming from problematic assumptions or a social context that has dramatically changed. So, for instance, a great deal of energy may have been devoted to reflecting on the conditions of moral agency that would make it just for God to punish human beings eternally for their sins, but such questions may lose their urgency if hell is understood no longer as punishment but simply—as the current *Catechism of the Catholic Church* now has it— as "definitive self-exclusion from communion with God."[5] Historicism may make us suspicious of overly neat narratives of progress or decline and may incline us to more complex and differentiated accounts of change, but it does not preclude us from identifying traditions of moral reflection. To do so is just to acknowledge, with Gadamer, that we ask our questions not only of our contemporaries but also of our predecessors, even as we recognize that they are properly our own questions.

In his closing reflections, Schneewind comes closest to acknowledging the inevitability—and the fruitfulness—of occupying a judgment seat, of assuming a stance from which to narrate. Here he recognizes that historicizing the discipline of moral philosophy, showing how different questions have been asked at different times, is valuable precisely because of how it "raises questions about what is being done now. Is the debate about deontology, consequentialism, and now virtue ethics still worth continuing," he asks. "Or are there other issues that might well be addressed? Can moral philosophy address the larger issues of the time? Or is it at best part of the training for the new casuistry of applied ethics?"[6] This strikes me as just the right sort of question to be asking. Insofar as it involves judging certain questions as irrelevant and wrongheaded, it also means that the dropping of them will be regarded as progress. There is, then, I would argue, no sharp methodological differentiation—

though there are many substantive differences—between MacIntyre's story of decline in *After Virtue* and Schneewind's own account of the invention of autonomy.

In his conclusion, Schneewind tentatively answers some of the questions that the history of modern moral philosophy raises concerning the practice of moral philosophy today. Moral philosophy, he argues, thanks in large part to Rawls and the rise of applied ethics, need no longer present itself as a spectator sport; it might seek to prepare students for leadership positions and address issues of public concern. This Schneewind depicts as a recovery of the "ancient and honorable function" of the discipline of philosophy. And yet, he does not call on philosophers to offer wisdom on the highest good, the good life as such, or moral perfection. His call for moral philosophy to return to practice is governed by the assumption of a private/public divide: moral philosophy should address public issues of common morality, not private issues of self-cultivation and moral perfection. Christianity, he suggests, "took over the guidance of life from pagan philosophy, and modern moral philosophy never took it back."[7] This, though, leaps too quickly from the Patristic to the modern eras, as I'm sure Schneewind himself would acknowledge. In fact, as Knud Haakonssen notes in his paper for our conference, even early modern philosophy continued to be understood as a form of spiritual exercise directed toward exemplifying the good life.[8]

The appearance of and the sense of a continuing need for a sharp distinction between public ethics and private perfection itself arises out of a certain narration of the history of modern moral philosophy: that it was engendered by the experience—in the early modern period—of irresolvable religious conflict and the need for a shared moral vocabulary that prescinds from confessional controversies. Real as religious differences and thus the need for cooperation across confessional boundaries are, though, it is not clear that a sharp division between public and private ethics can or should be maintained. In multiple senses, visions of the good life are not individual but social. First, our visions of the good are communally shaped and transmitted, even if they are also continually transformed through the actions and reflections of individuals. Second, the good life is rarely envisioned as something attainable by an individual in isolation from others. Of course, what is social need not be fully public; it need not be offered as encompassing all members of a society. But we can hope to address public moral and political problems and shape public leaders only if we have some substantive vision of the good life and of the place *within* this life of politics and of cooperation with those whose visions of the good life differ substantially from our own. Otherwise, moral philosophy is reduced to training in conflict mediation. It is as if we were to create a new kind of umpire trained to help opposing teams determine what rules to play by while remaining agnostic about what game is being played or even what might constitute a scoring point.

Although Rawls insisted on the priority of right, he also granted that justice as fairness itself embodies an idea of the good. He hoped that an overlapping consensus among various comprehensive doctrines could be forged in support of justice as fairness, and he granted that "just institutions and the political virtues would serve no purpose— would have no point—unless those institutions and virtues not only permitted but also sustained conceptions of the good (associated with comprehensive doctrines) that citizens can affirm as worthy of their full allegiance… In a phrase, the just draws the limit, the good shows the point." [9] Yet there are times when Rawls seems to hope that justice as fairness might be attractive enough without support from any comprehensive doctrine. This suggests that justice as fairness would show its own point. But this in turn implies that justice as fairness is itself already a substantive moral commitment, a conception of the good, even if a modest one that declines to be fully comprehensive. In fact, it is only insofar as it is a substantive moral commitment that it can serve to constrain what other such moral commitments are admissible. Ultimately, then, even for a Rawlsian, it is difficult to draw a sharp dividing line between the right and the good, public and private.

If we acknowledge the radical historicity of moral philosophy, abandon the illusion of neutral theoretical analysis as its task, and recognize the parasitic and always incomplete nature of public ethics, then moral philosophy will begin to look more and more like moral theology or religious ethics. Moral theology has, of course, never sought to be a neutral descriptive or analytical enterprise. Questions of practical ethics are studied historically, through the lens of tradition, rather than as marching grounds for the deployment of theories. Theory and practice as well as reflection and embodiment are seen as interpenetrating. And while questions of public ethics or common morality are indeed addressed, they are addressed within the broader context of questions about the good life and indeed about the nature of reality as such. It is this broader context, in fact, that motivates dialogue and seeks productive cooperation with those who are drawn by differing visions of the good. I do not want to exaggerate this convergence. Moral philosophy will, of course, remain a space for serious moral reflection on the part of thinkers who do not comfortably rest within any theological tradition or whose vision of the good is not regarded, whether by others or by themselves, as religious or theological. But we can, I hope, at least recognize theological and philosophical narratives of the history of moral philosophy as inhabiting the same playing field and therefore as capable of fruitful dialogue.

Schneewind's paper sketches a potential course, or rather several, in the history of modern moral philosophy. I don't have time to comment fully on these proposals, except to note that a theological approach might resist treating the history of modern moral philosophy as comprehensible on its own, given that the dominant theological options represented within this period—that of voluntarism on one hand and providentialism on the other—both were theologically problematic. There will be good reason for a theological approach to spend more time discussing St. Thomas, the late-medieval voluntarists, and Reformation thought in order to understand why voluntarism and providentialism came to seem to exhaust the possibilities.[10] The result may be a narrative that moves not, as Schneewind's does, from "a view of man as lowly and needing external control to a much higher estimate of our capacities, particularly our ability to govern ourselves" but rather from an understanding of human beings as created in the image of God and capable, through the renewal of grace, of self-government by virtue of participating in divine reason to a view of human freedom as competing with divine freedom and thus of human self-government as necessarily a rejection of divine government.[11] This may not, in fact, be a higher estimate of human capacities after all.

NOTES

1. I regret that I was not able to be present in person to deliver my comment and would like to thank Mark Larrimore for graciously agreeing to read my remarks at the conference.
2. J. B. Schneewind. "Teaching the History of Moral Philosophy," 177.
3. Schneewind, 183.
4. Quentin Skinner. "Meaning and Understanding in the History of Ideas." *History and Theory* 8 (1969): 52.
5. *Catechism of the Catholic Church.* Rome: Libreria Editrice Vaticana, 1994, para. 1033.
6. Schneewind, 194.
7. Schneewind, 193.
8. Knud Haakonssen, "The Idea of Early Modern Philosophy," 112.
9. John Rawls, *Justice as Fairness: A Restatement,* ed. Erin Kelly. Cambridge, Mass.: Belknap Press of Harvard University Press, 2001, 141.
10. Thomas A. Lewis points out that, particularly given what I say earlier about how the identities of moral philosophy and moral theology merge together, there is no reason to expect Aquinas to be any less significant for a philosophical than for a theological account of the history of moral thought. He is correct; it is not because it is theological rather than philosophical that the alternative I hint at would spend more time with Aquinas. Rather, it is because of its particular, substantive theological-cum-philosophical commitments that it would do so.
11. Schneewind, 184.

Integrating History of Philosophy with History of Science after Kant

Michael Friedman

ONE

I SHALL BEGIN by saying a few words, as background, about my own approach to integrating history of philosophy with history of science in my research. The idea that the history of early modern philosophy should give a central place to the contemporary context provided by early modern science has now become widespread and well established, thanks to the work of Margaret Wilson, Daniel Garber, and others.[1] My own work in the history of modern philosophy concerns primarily Kant, and here, unfortunately, the idea that the contemporary (18th-century) scientific context is centrally important to Kant's philosophy in general is not yet so widely accepted. Building on the work of Gerd Buchdahl and others,[2] I have tried to give this scientific context a central place in Kant-interpretation as well. I have focused, in particular, on Kant's philosophy of mathematics and mathematical physics—wherein the primary paradigm in mathematics was of course Euclid's Elements and the primary paradigm in mathematical physics was of course Newton's *Principia*. In connection with the latter, more specifically, I have tried to show how Newton's argument for universal gravitation in book III of the *Principia* provides Kant with his model for how laws of nature—and therefore causal connections—are grounded in and made possible by the necessary principles of the human understanding. And this same procedure provides Kant with a model, as well, for how the objectivity of scientific knowledge is grounded in universally intersubjective principles common to all rational human beings. The universality and necessity of this conception are then threatened by later developments within the sciences—principally, the development of non-Euclidean geometries and non-Newtonian foundations for physics—and these developments have their origins in the early years of the 19th century. Indeed, it is possible to show that Kant's own struggles with late-18th-century scientific innovations—primarily Lavoisier's new chemistry—already led him, in the so-called *Opus postumum*, to undertake a profound reconsideration of the basic principles of his critical philosophy.[3]

The second main focus of my historical research is on the development of logical empiricism in the early years of the 20th century. Here, once again, the contemporary scientific context is of central importance—especially the development of Einstein's theories of relativity and parallel developments in the foundations of modern mathematics and modern logic. It was precisely these developments, of course, that seemed to cause the biggest problems for Kant's original conception of scientific knowledge, and it was precisely this situation, in particular, that provided the logical empiricists with their most important philosophical motivation. Indeed, it is not too much to say that logical empiricist philosophers such as Moritz Schlick, Rudolf Carnap, and Hans Reichenbach took as their primary philosophical mission to do for modern mathematics and modern physics what Kant had done for the mathematics and physics bequeathed to the 18th century by the work of Newton. In this way, they hoped, one could fashion a parallel revolution in "scientific philosophy" appropriate to the revolution in the foundations of mathematics and mathematical physics associated with Einstein's work—wherein the relevant developments in mathematics especially involved revolutionary changes in the foundations of geometry due to the articulation and development of non-Euclidean systems throughout the 19th century.[4]

The logical empiricists, not surprisingly, took substantial philosophical inspiration from these 19th-century developments. Indeed, they explicitly appealed to earlier work in "scientific philosophy" by such 19th-century thinkers as Hermann von Helmholtz, Ernst Mach, and Henri Poincaré—where these thinkers, of course, were primarily professional scientists rather than professional philosophers. Indeed, in the cases of Helmholtz and Poincaré, in particular, the work we now take as important contributions to scientific epistemology was intimately connected with their own more properly scientific contributions concerning the foundations of the new non-Euclidean geometries. This work had already led them to attempt to modify Kant's original conception of the necessary character of specifically Euclidean geometry as grounded in the fundamental form of our human sensibility (our perception of space), so as to provide a more general conception adequate to the new non-Euclidean geometries to which they themselves were then making important mathematical contributions. This led, both for the 19th-century thinkers in question and for the logical empiricist philosophers who were inspired by them, to a new view of scientific epistemology capable of competing with, and eventually replacing, the Kantian system. The fact that Einstein himself, in developing his theories of relativity, also took inspiration from the thought of precisely these 19th-century thinkers, provided further confirmation for this new philosophical ambition.[5]

A third focus of my historical research, accordingly, concerns the developments in 19th-century "scientific philosophy" that formed the bridge, as it were, between Kant's original philosophical synthesis in the late 18th century and the philosophical revolution wrought by logical empiricism at the beginning of the 20th. What we see here, I want to suggest, is really a continuously evolving sequence of interactions between successively revolutionary philosophical innovations and a parallel set of revolutionary developments within the sciences. The 19th-century scientific innovations in question include the developments in the foundations of geometry indicated earlier, but they also include a complex web of related developments in such sciences as chemistry, the theory of heat, thermodynamics, electricity and magnetism, and psychophysics—together with evolutionary and developmental biology. Indeed, in some of my most recent work, I have attempted to articulate the very beginnings of these post-Kantian scientific and philosophical developments in the first modifications of Kant's so-called dynamical theory of matter by Friedrich Schelling—which were undertaken in the course of Schelling's deep immersion in the new discoveries in electro-chemistry at the turn of the century. These discoveries led Schelling to introduce an essentially developmental and dialectical dimension into Kant's original theory of matter, and this essential feature of Schelling's *Naturphilosophie* proved decisive in both the further development of German philosophy within the tradition of post-

Kantian idealism and the further development of German science in such areas as chemistry, electricity and magnetism, and evolutionary and developmental biology.[6]

My picture of how the history of philosophy and the history of science relate to one another, therefore, is one of thoroughgoing developmental interaction. It is not just that contemporary science, in any given period, provides an important part of the background to whatever is happening within philosophy during that same period. It is, rather, that both the scientific context and the philosophical context are continuously evolving, and a continual interaction between the two is a primary stimulus for both developmental processes. Kant's original synthesis is a reflection of 18th-century Newtonianism, of course, but Kant also attempts to adapt his ongoing philosophical thinking to post-Newtonian scientific developments. Moreover, certain post-Newtonian developments, like those in the foundations of geometry or electricity and magnetism, for example, explicitly take their starting points from Kant's original conception, while simultaneously attempting to transform this conception in a way Kant himself never envisioned.[7] These developments then led 19th-century scientific thinkers like Helmholtz, Mach, and Poincaré—with one foot in science and one in philosophy—to undertake parallel reconceptualizations in both fields. Their work, in turn, influenced both Einstein and the philosophy of logical empiricism; Einstein and the logical empiricists interacted with one another against this common background; and so on.

One final point before I turn to teaching: This interaction between the history of philosophy and the history of science is important, in my view, not only for properly historical research into the evolution of philosophy as a discipline (and, by implication, into the evolution of the sciences as well); it is also centrally important for contemporary work in the philosophy of science. For one of the central intellectual developments framing contemporary philosophy of science is of course Thomas Kuhn's theory of scientific revolutions, and this theory, as is well known, gives overriding importance to the history of science in fashioning an adequate philosophical understanding of the nature of science. Moreover, some of Kuhn's main examples of revolutionary scientific change are drawn from precisely the developments sketched earlier: Einstein's theory of relativity, Lavoisier's chemical revolution, the articulation of thermodynamics in the context of the discovery of the conservation of energy, and so on. But Kuhn, in my view, gives insufficient attention to the contemporaneous philosophical developments associated with these revolutionary changes, and he is thereby led to both an inadequate understanding of the true philosophical sources of the challenges to scientific objectivity that have resulted from his historiographical work and a fundamental inability to adequately respond to these challenges. The true philosophical sources, in my view, derive from the way in which Kant's original conception of the necessary intersubjectivity of scientific reason has been successively challenged by subsequent developments within both philosophy and the sciences. And an adequate response to these developments involves both a full appreciation of the "relativized a priori" exhibited by successively articulated mathematical-physical conceptual frameworks (or Kuhnian "paradigms") and an understanding of how such successively articulated conceptual frameworks are nevertheless continuously—and rationally—connected with one another through precisely the *interaction* between philosophy and the sciences I am emphasizing here.[8]

With this general viewpoint on the relationship between the history of philosophy and the history of science as background, I shall now describe two of the courses I have been teaching recently: a course on Kant's theoretical philosophy and a course on the development of the philosophy of science "from Kant to Carnap." The first is primarily a graduate course; the second is for both graduate and undergraduate students. Since philosophy after Kant is our primary focus here, I shall give only a brief description of the first course and devote more space, accordingly, to the second. The first course does contain some of the essential background for the second, however.

In teaching Kant's theoretical philosophy, I give special emphasis, of course, to his philosophy of mathematics and physical science. In connection with the latter, in particular, I discuss in some detail a relatively less well-known work of Kant's—his *Metaphysical Foundations of Natural Science*—which appeared in 1786, between the first (1781) and second (1787) editions of the *Critique of Pure Reason* (the *Prolegomena* appeared in 1783).[9] It is in this work that the dynamical theory of matter mentioned earlier is developed, where this theory portrays matter as constituted out of the two "fundamental forces" of attraction and repulsion rather than as a primitively hard and absolutely impenetrable solid. Thus, the fundamental force of repulsion is responsible for relative solidity or resistance to compression, whereas the fundamental force of attraction is responsible for universal gravitation. On my reading, moreover, the fundamental force of attraction, in the guise of Newtonian universal gravitation, involves Kant in a profound reconceptualization of Newtonian absolute space and time. Kant understands them, specifically, not as great empty "containers" existing prior to matter and motion but, rather, as concepts we successively construct as we apply the Newtonian laws of motion to the observed "phenomena" or planetary motions with which Newton himself begins the argument of book III of the *Principia*. We thereby obtain both the law of universal gravitation (as noted earlier) and a privileged frame of reference—determined by the center of mass of the solar system— for defining the "true" or "absolute" motions in this system. And, in this way, Kant's critical dynamical theory of matter essentially involves Kant's more global views on the nature of space and time, as well as his more local views on the structure of material substance and its causal interactions.

In the first part of the course, therefore, we discuss the *Metaphysical Foundations* in the context of both Kant's more general critical philosophy expounded in the *Critique of Pure Reason* and the *Prolegomena* and in the context of contemporary scientific works— principally, Newton's *Principia*, but also the *Opticks*, parts of the *Leibniz-Clarke Correspondence*, and some of the works of Euler, Lambert, and others. We also pay attention to some of Kant's earlier precritical scientific works, such as the *Physical Monadology* (1756) and *Theory of the Heavens* (1755). In the second part of the course, we then read the main theoretical argument of the *Critique of Pure Reason*, as expounded in the transcendental analytic—including the metaphysical and transcendental deductions of the categories—and the chapter on the corresponding principles of pure understanding. The main strategy of this approach is to read the transcendental analytic backward: starting with the picture of material or physical nature presented in the *Metaphysical Foundations*, we view the discussion in the analytic in terms of successively more abstract conceptions of nature read from the end of the analytic to the beginning—from the more concrete picture of nature in general presented in the principles of pure understanding to the highly abstract discussion of the pure concepts of the understanding found in the metaphysical and transcendental deductions. The leading idea is to view the procedure by which Newton derives both the law of universal gravitation and a privileged frame of reference or absolute space for describing the true motions in the solar system as a model for Kant's more general conception, central to the analytic, of how phenomena or perceptions are successively transformed into what he calls objective experience.

The hope is that this way of presenting the main argument of the *Critique of Pure Reason* helps clarify and make more concrete the excessively abstract and abstruse argumentation of the earlier parts of the analytic by reference to a much more specific realization or application of this argumentation provided by the scientific context Kant has prominently in mind. We are also able to shed light, I believe, on Kant's specific place as a philosopher of modern science against the background of such early modern thinkers as Descartes, Locke, Leibniz, and Hume: Kant's specific contribution is fully to assimilate the depth of Newton's mathematical and physical innovations against the background of a broadly Leibnizean approach to fundamental metaphysical concepts or categories such as substance, causality, and interaction.

The guiding idea of the second course, on the development of the philosophy of science from Kant to Carnap, is to introduce students to 20th-century philosophy of science by looking in detail at its historical background. I take the development of logical empiricism in the early years of the century (that is, before the migration to the United States occasioned by the Nazi seizure of power and World War II) to be the pivotal event in the development of 20th-century philosophy of science. My primary goal, accordingly, is to depict the Vienna Circle period—primarily, the 1920s—as the high point of logical empiricism and to examine the 19th-century background to the formation of the Vienna Circle from this point of view. In this way, in particular, we are able to transcend conventional stereotypical characterizations of logical empiricism by concentrating on its actual historical context and background. The phrase *from Kant to Carnap* is taken from a now classic treatment by Alberto Coffa that functions as one of the main recommended secondary sources for the course.[10] My own aim is to cover roughly the same body of material as does Coffa, although from a rather different (and more Kantian) point of view. The full syllabus for the course, which goes under the more prosaic title of The Development of Modern Philosophy of Science, is reproduced in the Appendix.

The main primary sources for the course are drawn from five key figures in the development of scientific philosophy: Hermann von Helmholtz, Ernst Mach, Henri Poincaré, Moritz Schlick (founder of the Vienna Circle and first "professional philosopher of science"), and Rudolf Carnap. The culmination of the course is a reading of Carnap's *Der logische Aufbau der Welt*, one of the twin testaments, along with Wittgenstein's *Tractatus Logico-Philosophicus*, of the philosophy of the Vienna Circle. The aim, throughout, is to depict a continuous series of transformations of the philosophical perspective on fundamentally Newtonian science originally articulated by Kant—stimulated by, and interacting with, 19th-century scientific developments such as the discovery of non-Euclidean geometries; innovations in the sciences of heat, light, and matter; and (with reference to Schlick and Carnap) Einstein's theories of relativity and related developments in modern mathematics and mathematical logic. We begin with a couple of weeks on Kant, Newton, and some main post-Newtonian scientific developments from the early years of the 19th century. This background is provided by secondary literature and lectures rather than primary sources. We then proceed to a more detailed and more focused reading of our five primary scientific philosophers.

In discussing Helmholtz, we focus on his early work on the conservation of energy, his work on the foundations and philosophy of non-Euclidean geometries, and his work in the psychophysiology of perception. The last topic includes his main contribution to scientific epistemology, "The Facts of Perception," which concludes our treatment of Helmholtz. Our aim is to exhibit the complex interactions among all of these different facets of Helmholtz's thought and to show how they all contributed, in particular, to his reformulation of some basic Kantian themes. Thus, his early work on the conservation of energy was associated with a kind of atomism of point centers of force, which Helmholtz himself explicitly linked to Kant's dynamical theory of matter in the *Metaphysical Foundations* and Kant's more general views on the principle of causality. In his later work, connected more explicitly with psychophysiology, Helmholtz gradually transformed this initial point of view so that the principle of causality, in particular, had more to do with lawlike relations among phenomena than with an underlying atomism of substantial causes. Moreover, this work in psychophysiology prominently concerned space perception, which led him, in turn, to an interest in the new foundations for non-Euclidean geometries recently provided by Bernhard Riemann in the context (for Helmholtz) of a reconsideration of Kant's basic doctrine that space is a "necessary form of our (outer) sensible intuition." In "The Facts of Perception" Helmholtz then puts these pieces together in his celebrated sign theory of perception—according to which both external physical bodies in space, and this (three-dimensional) space itself, are generated or constructed from lawlike relations among our sensations.

When we turn to Mach, our main emphasis is on his *Analysis of Sensations*, which, as in the case of Helmholtz, presents a new scientific epistemology in intimate connection with recent work in the psychophysiology of perception. We also discuss, in this context, Mach's opposition to mechanism and atomism in the philosophy of physical science and his historicocritical expository method for demystifying such physical concepts. The basic line of thought we pursue is that Mach's fundamental concern is with what he calls the unity of science rather than the philosophical-epistemological obsessions (with skepticism, certainty, etc.) stereotypically associated with the empiricist tradition. In particular, Mach wants a point of view suitable for a unified presentation of both the physical and the life sciences (including psychology), and he finds this point of view in a neutral monism of sensations or elements rather than in mechanistic atomism. Moreover, Mach's perspective on the psychophysiology of perception, under the explicit influence of Ewald Hering, has a decidedly evolutionary dimension missing from the work of Helmholtz: whereas, according to Helmholtz's sign theory of perception, the acquisition of our representations of space and of the external world is an *individual* adaptation made in response to the lawlike patterns in the sensations of a single organism, Mach and Hering view it as an evolutionary adaptation extending over many generations that then becomes wired in to individual organisms.[11] This gives Mach's scientific epistemology a parallel evolutionary dimension in the guise of his notorious principle of economy. We conclude by looking at the famous exchange between Mach and Planck at the beginning of the 20th century from this point of view.

Our treatment of Poincaré emphasizes his celebrated geometrical conventionalism, of course, and also his closely related work on electrodynamics and the foundations of what we now call the special theory of relativity. Our primary reading is *Science and Hypothesis*, and we pay special attention to the sequence or hierarchy of sciences he presents there: arithmetic, the theory of continuous magnitude, geometry, mechanics, and properly physical theories of force (such as gravity and electromagnetism). We use Poincaré's work in the foundations of arithmetic and geometry to introduce the characteristically modern conception of mathematics as dealing with what we would now call abstract structures (the number series, groups of transformations, and so on). (This conception is entirely missing from Mach, for example, who has a much more empirical conception of mathematics essentially tied to calculation and measurement.) We then look at Poincaré's geometrical conventionalism against the background of Helmholtz's earlier work on what we now call the Helmholtz-Lie theorem characterizing the geometry of space in terms of groups of transformations or bodily motions subject to a condition of free mobility. In particular, whereas Poincaré follows Helmholtz's basic ideas about how the representation of space is acquired (with a bit of an evolutionary twist derived from later work in the tradition of Hering and Mach), he takes the Helmholtz-Lie theorem, in this context, to indicate a fundamental freedom left over in the choice between Euclidean and non-Euclidean representations of the same empirical facts. We conclude by embedding Poincaré's work on special relativity within this same point of view, and we attempt to depict the differences between Poincaré and Einstein against this general background.

The discussion of Schlick, the first 20th-century *philosopher* of science, concentrates on his first major work, *General Theory of Knowledge,* published in 1918—and thus before he moved to Vienna in 1922 and founded the Vienna Circle. Here Schlick is deeply influenced by the three 19th-century thinkers we have been discussing so far, although he is here more negative toward Mach's subjectivism or sensationism than he is during the period of the Vienna Circle. But Schlick is also working against the background of two decisive new influences: David Hilbert's axiomatization of (Euclidean) geometry first published in 1899 and Einstein's creation of the general theory of relativity in 1915–16.[12] Hilbert's axiomatization solidified the modern conception of geometry as dealing with an abstract formal structure having no intrinsic connection with space perception or any other intuitive experiences. (This contrasts sharply with the view of Poincaré, for example, who still worked in the earlier group-theoretical conception due to Felix Klein, on which geometry retains an essential link with spatial intuition.) Moreover, Einstein's creation of the general theory of relativity contributed important confirmation of this idea—since it uses a geometry of variable curvature to represent gravitational phenomena and thus breaks away from the framework of the classical non-Euclidean geometries of constant curvature that formed the background for Helmholtz's and Poincaré's work. The space(-time) of Einstein's general theory, therefore, is an entirely abstract and nonintuitive representation in the same spirit as Hilbert's conception of the axiomatic foundations of (Euclidean) geometry. Schlick then generalizes this conception of axiomatic or implicit definitions to embrace all of the concepts of mathematical-physical science, which are now viewed in terms of purely formal systems of logical relationships as described in one or another Hilbert-style axiomatic system.

Our final work, Carnap's *Aufbau,* represents the high point of Vienna Circle logical empiricism, and it is viewed as taking its starting point from Schlick's conception of purely formal implicit definitions presented in *General Theory of Knowledge.* However, whereas Schlick himself has a fundamental problem in explaining how purely formal axiomatic systems can apply to or designate empirical physical reality,

Carnap obviates this entire problematic by beginning his logical constitution of the world from a Machian subjective starting point in the elementary experiences of a single (representative) cognitive subject. Carnap employs "purely structural definite descriptions," using the language and logical resources of Whitehead's and Russell's *Principia Mathematica* (1910–13), to constitute or construct all of the concepts of empirical science step by step: first, the autopsychological realm of the full subjective experiential world (as described, ideally, by Gestalt psychology); then the physical realm of the external world (as given to commonsense perception and as described by modern abstract mathematical physics); and, finally, the heteropsychological realm of the totality of cognitive subjects (including the "cultural sciences" of sociology, history, political theory, and so on). Carnap thereby hopes to embrace *all* of empirical science while simultaneously doing justice to Schlick's emphasis on the importance of purely formal logical structure and the complementary emphasis of Machian positivism on the necessary subjective starting point of all human knowledge, no matter how refined. Here, at last, we have the characteristic conception of logical empiricism, according to which modern science is represented, at its best, as a combination or synthesis of a priori rational form (now captured entirely within the new mathematical logic) with uncontroversially empirical content. Indeed, in the preface to the second (1961) edition of the *Aufbau*, Carnap himself explains this view, clearly echoing Kant, as a synthesis of rationalism and empiricism. It is also clear in the context of the historical developments we have been studying that Carnap conceives this new synthesis of rationalism and empiricism as the final replacement for Kant's original conception of scientific objectivity based on the *synthetic* (and therefore nonlogical) a priori.

As the conclusion of the course, we look at one of Carnap's applications of the new type of philosophy he dubs "constitutional theory" to a central traditional problem of philosophy at the time Carnap calls "the problem of reality." This involves a debate between realism, idealism (both transcendental and subjective), and what was then termed phenomenalism—that is, Kant's version of transcendental idealism retaining unknowable things-in-themselves behind the phenomena. Carnap's aims are twofold. In the first place, he distinguishes constitutional and metaphysical versions of the problem of reality, where the first rises within rational science as the question of which entities, according to this science, actually exist, and the second arises outside rational science as the question of which entities, already recognized by this science, are "really real" in some extrascientific or distinctively philosophical sense. So here the materialist, for example, contends that only physical objects are real, whereas the subjective idealist contends that only psychic objects are real. Both are wrong from the point of view of constitutional theory, because both types of objects in fact occur in the constitutional system. Moreover, it is perfectly possible to take psychological (or even autopsychological) objects as basic and define everything else (including physical objects) from them, and it is equally possible to take physical objects as basic and define everything else (including psychological objects) from them. Indeed, according to Carnap, this extra, metaphysical problem of reality cannot be rationally stated or answered at all, because the metaphysical concept of reality cannot itself be constituted or defined in any legitimate constitutional system.

In the second place, however, Carnap is also concerned to show that the traditional debate between the various epistemological schools can be dissolved by showing that they all agree in the domain of constitutional theory: for example, there is no issue from the point of view of constitutional theory between realism and subjective idealism. Indeed, each of the traditional schools has a perfectly legitimate part of the truth, and they disagree, as Carnap puts it, only by transgressing their proper boundaries—by going beyond the properly epistemological question of how cognition in fact proceeds to irresoluble metaphysical questions about which objects of cognition are "really real." Constitutional theory, as Carnap puts it, represents the "neutral foundation [*neutrale Fundament*]" which all of the traditional schools share in common. We therefore see, finally, that Carnap's antimetaphysical stance is not fueled primarily by a commitment to verificationism or radical empiricism—although what is correct in positivism or radical empiricism is in fact represented in the constitutional system. It is fueled, rather, by an overarching commitment to place the discipline of philosophy itself on a scientific or metaphysically neutral path, on which, at the same time, the traditional problems of philosophy are not so much militantly rejected as radically reconceived in a true scientific spirit.

And the model for this new spirit is precisely the distinctively logically structural conception of the objectivity of scientific knowledge that gradually evolved, throughout the 19th and early 20th centuries, against the background of Kant's original conception.[13]

APPENDIX: THE DEVELOPMENT OF MODERN PHILOSOPHY OF SCIENCE

This course traces the historical development of the philosophy of science from approximately 1800 to the early 20th century, beginning with the philosophy of Newtonian science developed by Immanuel Kant and ending with Rudolf Carnap's *Der logische Aufbau der Welt* (1928). It is in these years that the philosophy of science begins to take shape as a specialized discipline within philosophy more generally; and the problems, in the first place, are stimulated and framed by revolutionary developments in 19th-century science: the discovery of non-Euclidean geometries, the wave theory of light and electrodynamics, thermodynamics and the conservation of energy, and molecular-atomic theory. Accordingly, the initial work in what we now call philosophy of science is undertaken by professional scientists attempting to come to terms with these new developments—in particular, by Hermann von Helmholtz, Ernst Mach, and Henri Poincaré. Then, about the turn of the century, philosophy of science is stimulated once again by revolutionary developments: Einsteinian relativity theory, on one hand, and new work in logic and the foundations of mathematics by Gottlob Frege, Bertrand Russell, and David Hilbert on the other. Now philosophy of science is pursued more by professional philosophers—and, in particular, by the so-called Vienna Circle of logical positivists represented especially by Moritz Schlick and Rudolf Carnap. The work of these philosophers then sets the stage for most of 20th-century philosophy of science.

Required Reading
(Volume numbers refer to photocopied course readers.)

Boltzmann, "The Recent Development of Method in Theoretical Physics," 1900, vol. 2, 63–78.

Boltzmann, "On the Necessity of Atomic Theories in Physics," 1901, vol. 2, 79–86.

Carnap, *The Logical Structure of the World* [*Aufbau*], 1928, vol. 4.

Einstein, "Geometry and Experience," 1921, vol. 2, 187–202.

Helmholtz, "The Aim and Progress of Physical Science," 1869, vol. 1, 87–98.

Helmholtz, "The Conservation of Force," 1847, vol. 1, 1–27.

Helmholtz, "The Facts in Perception," 1878, vol. 1, 51–86.

Helmholtz, "Introduction to the Lectures on Theoretical Physics," 1894, vol. 1, 99–107.

Helmholtz, "On the Origin and Significance of the Axioms of Geometry," 1870, vol. 1, 31–49.

Mach, *The Analysis of Sensations,* 1886, vol. 3.

Mach, "The Guiding Principles of My Scientific Theory of Knowledge", 1910, vol. 2, 128–35.

Mach, "Newton's Views of Time, Space, and Motion," 1883, vol. 2, 39–52.

Mach, "The Relations of Mechanics to Other Departments of Knowledge," 1883, vol. 2, 53–62.

Mach, *Space and Geometry,* 1906.

Planck, "On Mach's Theory of Physical Knowledge," 1911, vol. 2, 136–40.

Planck, "The Unity of the Physical World-Picture," 1909, vol. 2, 114–27.

Riemann, "On the Hypotheses which Lie at the Foundations of Geometry," 1854, vol. 2, 31–38.

Poincaré, *Science and Hypothesis,* 1902.

Poincaré, "Space and Time," 1912, vol. 2, 145–50.

Schlick, "Critical or Empiricist Interpretation of Modern Physics?" 921, vol. 2, 159–65.

Schlick, *General Theory of Knowledge,* 1918/25.

Recommended Reading

Bellone, *A World on Paper*

Bonola, *Non-Euclidean Geometry*

Brush, "Mach and Atomism," vol. 2, 87–98.

Buchdahl, *Metaphysics and the Philosophy of Science*

Carnap, "The Structure of Space," vol. 2, 21–30T.

Coffa, *The Semantic Tradition from Kant to Carnap: To the Vienna Station*

Friedman, *Kant and the Exact Sciences*

Friedman, "Logical Positivism, Philosophy of" (handout)

Friedman, "Poincaré's Conventionalism and the Logical Positivists," vol. 2, 151–57.

Greenberg, "The Poincaré Models," vol. 2, 141–44.

Hankins, *Science and the Enlightenment*

Harman, *Energy, Force, and Matter*

Kant, *Philosophy of Material Nature (Metaphysical Foundations, Prolegomena)*

Klein, "Planck, Entropy, and Quanta, 1901–1906," vol. 2, 99–113.

Kuhn, "Energy Conservation as an Example of Simultaneous Discovery," vol. 2, 1–20.

Miller, "Why did Poincaré not formulate Special Relativity in 1905?" vol. 2, 244–60.

Poincaré, "On the Foundations of Geometry," 1898, vol. 2, 203–24.

Schlick, "The Philosophical Significance of the Principle of Relativity," 1915, vol. 2, 167–85.

Torretti, "The 'Relativity Theory of Poincaré and Lorentz,'" vol. 2, 225–29.

Zahar, "Poincaré's Independent Discovery of the Relativity Principle," vol. 2, 230–43.

Unit I: Introduction

Kant and Newton
Kant; Friedman, *Kant*, Part One; Coffa, 1
Newtonianism and the Nineteenth Century
Hankins; Harman, I, II

Unit II: Helmholtz

Energy and Atomism "Conservation," "Aim and Progress," "Introduction"; Kuhn; Harman, III, IV
Geometry and Intuition
"Axioms," "Facts"; Carnap, "Space," 125–43, 177–83; Bonola; Riemann; Coffa, 2, 3

Unit III: Mach

Phenomenology and Phenomenalism
Analysis, I–V, XIV, XV, "Relations"; Boltzmann; Brush; Harman, V–VI; Bellone, 1–4, 7; Planck-Mach, 1909–11; Klein
Concept Formation
Analysis, VI–X, XIV, XV, *Geometry*, "Newton's Views"

Unit IV: Poincaré

Arithmetic and Geometry
Science, Parts I–III, "Foundations"; Greenberg; Coffa, 3, 4, 7
The Structure of Physical Theory (Electrodynamics and Relativity)
Science, Parts IV, V, "Space and Time"; Bellone, 5, 6; Miller;
Torretti; Zahar

Unit V: Schlick

Geometry and Relativity
"Critical or Empiricist," "Principle of Relativity"; Einstein;
Friedman, "Conventionalism"; Carnap, "Space," 144–76;
Coffa, 9, 10; *Knowledge,* Part I
Concepts and Reality
Knowledge, Parts II, III

Unit VI: Carnap

Logic, Mathematics, and Sense-Experience
Aufbau, Parts I–III, §107; Coffa, 4–6
The Logical Construction of the World
Aufbau, Parts IV, V; Coffa, 11, 12

Notes

1. See M. Wilson, *Ideas and Mechanisms,* Princeton, N.J.: Princeton University Press, 1999; D. Garber, *Descartes' Metaphysical Physics,* Chicago: University of Chicago Press, 1992; and (for example) the essays collected in S. Voss, ed. *Essays on the Philosophy and Science of René Descartes,* Oxford, England: Oxford University Press, 1993.

2. See G. Buchdahl, *Metaphysics and the Philosophy of Science,* Oxford, England: Basil Blackwell,1969, and (for example) the essays collected in E. Watkins, ed. *Kant and the Sciences.* Oxford, England: Oxford University Press, 2001.

3. See M. Friedman, *Kant and the Exact Sciences,* Cambridge, Mass.: Harvard University Press, 1992.

4. See M. Friedman, *Reconsidering Logical Positivism,* Cambridge, England: Cambridge University Press, 1999.

5. For more on Helmholtz and Poincaré see M. Friedman, "Helmholtz's *Zeichentheorie* and Schlick's *Allgemeine Erkenntnislehre,*" *Philosophical Topics* 5, 1997, 19–50, and "Geometry, Construction, and Intuition in Kant and His Successors," in G. Scher and R. Tieszen, ed. *Between Logic and Intuition,* Cambridge, England: Cambridge University Press, 2000. For Einstein and the logical empiricists, see my "Geometry as a Branch of Physics," in D. Malament, ed. *Reading Natural Philosophy,* Chicago: Open Court, 2002.

6. See my "Kant—*Naturphilosophie*—Electromagnetism," in M. Friedman and A. Nordmann, ed. *Kant's Scientific Legacy in the Nineteenth Century,* Cambridge, Mass.: MIT Press, forthcoming. To see the connection between these developments and the foundations of geometry, for example, note that Helmholtz's work in this subject was a part of his larger project in the psychophysiology of perception, which, for him, was intimately connected with his work in thermodynamics and electricity and magnetism—and his work in these latter sciences, in particular, was in part a reaction against Schelling, but it also built on Kant's original dynamical theory of matter to which Schelling had recently given scientific prominence.

7. A further example of this phenomenon, discussed in the reference cited in note 6, is H. C. Oersted's work in electrochemistry and electromagnetism, which is explicitly framed under the influence of both Kant's original theory of matter and Schelling's radical revision thereof.

8. For a first attempt to develop this point of view, see my *Dynamics of Reason,* Stanford, Calif.: CSLI, 2001. For a discussion of Kuhnian

historiography in this context, see my "Kuhn and Logical Empiricism," in T. Nickles, ed. *Thomas Kuhn*, Cambridge, England: Cambridge University Press, 2003.

9. For my translation of this work (together with an introduction and notes) see I. Kant, *Metaphysical Foundations of Natural Science*, Cambridge, England: Cambridge University Press, 2004.

10. See J. A. Coffa, *The Semantic Tradition from Kant to Carnap*, Cambridge, England: Cambridge University Press, 1991.

11. For Helmholtz and the dispute between nativism and empiricism, see G. Hatfield, *The Natural and the Normative*, Cambridge, Mass.: MIT Press, 1990. For the more general debate, including the position of Hering, in particular, see R. Turner, *In the Eye's Mind*, Princeton, N.J.: Princeton University Press, 1994.

12. Immediately before *General Theory of Knowledge* Schlick published an extremely influential semipopular philosophical explanation and defense of Einstein's new theory, *Space and Time in Contemporary Physics*, which went through four editions from 1917 to 1922, and which secured Schlick—most likely with help from Einstein himself—the chair in the philosophy of inductive sciences at the University of Vienna previously occupied by Ernst Mach and Ludwig Boltzmann.

13. Carnap's mature antimetaphysical position is articulated in "Empiricism, Semantics, and Ontology," *Revue Internationale de Philosophie* 11 1950: 20–40; reprinted in the second edition of *Meaning and Necessity*, Chicago: University of Chicago Press, 1956. Here, too, Carnap's position owes less to traditional empiricism and verificationism and more to the idea that the distinctive task of philosophy lies in the formulation and logical investigation of alternative "linguistic frameworks" in which the language of science may be formally represented.

Response to Michael Friedman

JULIET FLOYD

As SOMEONE interested in tracing Kant's philosophical effects and fate through the 19th and 20th centuries or back from a 20th-century perspective, I am grateful for the breadth and rigor of Michael's stimulating work. In am genuinely curious about the extent to which a neo-Kantian framework will be able to fit an overarching account of 20th-century philosophy as a whole, even if we focus on the history and philosophy of science—and especially if we don't. I myself think that the development of early-20th-century philosophy as a whole, including analytic philosophy, is not all that well understood in historical terms, partly because it's barely conceived of as history—epistemologically centered or otherwise. Michael's work has done a great deal along a certain axis to begin to make historical and philosophical sense of it.

When I was an undergraduate studying history and philosophy of science in England in the early 1980s, an aging obsession with methodology still dominated the scene. There were some who tried to convey a sense of the historical development of modern science, and of course Kuhn and Feyerabend were read, but it was difficult to understand how these studies were to impact constructively on one's overall conception of either philosophy or its history. One could welcome skepticism about the notion of something called scientific method, resist the full reduction of philosophy to the logical syntax of the language of science, and appreciate the importance of knowing some genuine (as opposed to rationally reconstructed) history of science without in any way seeing how one might integrate these insights into constructive *philosophical* work. The fall of methodology left a kind of vacuum. Few seemed interested in looking at the history of 20th-century philosophy as part of the history of philosophy. But in order to see how the contingently given intellectual world of my contemporaries had been constructed, I at least wanted to understand how it might be questioned and changed. The history of recent philosophy is difficult to understand historically, partly because we are too close to it in time and partly because of our understandable tendency to impose our own preferred philosophical commitments and local ideological needs upon its taxonomy and structure. There are also more texts and more philosophers to be read—an increase in the amount written.

Michael's dynamical neo-Kantianism has the great advantage of offering a unified, articulated, and wide-ranging account of the roots of present-day analytic philosophy. What binds it together is an overarching narrative in which philosophy is in constant and fruitful mutual interaction with scientific developments, especially those in physics, logic, and mathematics. Michael takes philosophers to have been continuously seeking to construct a unified set of general metaphysical principles in the light of the best available contemporary science. This Kantianism is post-Carnapian in that it relativizes the a priori to a localized structure within particular problem contexts rather than invoking the idea of a universal, timeless set of principles. Indeed, Michael's interpretations of logical positivists like Schlick and Carnap show in great detail how important and difficult it was for the neo-Kantian tradition to see how to surrender the image of a universally applicable, a priori structure of thought while at the same time retaining an epistemology that would emphasize the humanly conditioned nature of knowledge without falling into skepticism, subjectivistic psychologism, or simple-minded relativism and/or conventionalism. Michael's account casts crucial light on the roles of mathematics and logic, showing how their notions and techniques provided throughout the modern period a framing, evolving language within which to pose both empirical and philosophical questions. He tells a story about early modern philosophy that is not underpinned by the claim of any single a priori philosophical principle but invokes the Kantian (or Carnapian) framework idea when it seems scientifically defensible. This allows him to argue against the direct reduction of philosophy to science precisely through a detailed analysis of the historical development of each. His picture is appealing because it comforts us with the thought of a fairly continuous philosophical tradition— unbroken since Kant's time—that we may hope to project into the future indefinitely: a quest for as universal a set of scientific principles as we can find. On Michael's view there is no grand error or illusion to be unearthed or unmasked in looking at the past 300 years of philosophy. Metaphysics is not necessarily a bad thing. Instead, there remains primarily the work of history, which, when properly done, is a history of ever-more-complex, ever-more-fruitful scientific and mathematical work, interacting in significant measure with the efforts of philosophers to try to pull together what we know into a coherent scheme of general principles.

The richness of Michael's dynamical neo-Kantian framework brings out just how obsessed with the rise and fall of method the most widely read historians of 20th-century philosophy have been. From Michael's point of view, Rorty's neopragmatist account is a fiction, for it imputes to modern philosophy the single overarching error of trying to find an autonomous epistemological basis for science, of questing too fervently after certainty in sense experience. This story does not contemplate the possibility that philosophy and science have continuously shaped and interacted with one another in complex and surprising ways that are nearly impossible to summarize in terms of this scheme. An account like Rorty's does not admit that a quest for certainty has been largely lacking in most philosophers who contributed substantially to the development of science in the past 200 years, or at least, it has not trumped the search for general structural, mathematically articulate principles with which to describe nature. An important application of Michael's work is its persuasive rejection of any strong program of sociological or institutional reductionism in doing the history of science: Michael retains the hope that philosophy will not be asked to surrender its distinctive ambition of aiming at a broad vision of nature that comes to terms with the best science we have by offering us general principles and frameworks for thought. He has learned from Kuhn—but not reacted with the same kind of hostility as many of Kuhn's followers to the idea that philosophy is autonomous (to a degree) and cognitively fruitful. Furthermore, while his historical method keeps the focus on individual philosophers, it does so without emphasizing biography over philosophy reductively and without becoming too static in its understanding of any one problem. Thus, while he believes philosophy has something distinctive to contribute, Michael is neither a general revisionist nor an antirevisionist when it comes to philosophy's interplay with mathematics, logic, and the empirical sciences.

I especially admire the rigor and detail of Michael's pedagogical approach: the way in which his syllabi do not kowtow to popular generalities about scientific heroes but force students to dig in and delve into an analysis of abstract structure. These are difficult courses, however, as Michael says, and it is not easy to ask every undergraduate in philosophy or history of science to enjoy them. The primary advantage of Michael's approach will be to help history of science students appreciate the importance of the history of philosophy to their work and to help history of philosophy students appreciate the importance of knowledge of the history of modern science to their work. This kind of course is crucially needed especially now. Without a detailed understanding of this projection of the Kantian tradition, the development of 20th-century analytic philosophy—and with it, contemporary philosophy of science—will remain misunderstood. So, in particular, will Kant's philosophy.

None of this implies that Michael's sophisticated form of Kantianism is ultimately defensible, either as the best position available for understanding or explicating Kant's most important philosophical contributions, the development of early modern philosophy, or the development of early analytic philosophy. Nor does it imply that for an introductory course on the philosophy of science and technology, this is the best way to get every kind of student interested in the subject. Michael does not claim these implications for his view. So it remains to me, as commentator, to sketch some alternatives and raise some questions.

My own experience in doing history of philosophy, especially philosophy of the past hundred years or so, has been that the pressure of increased complexity, density, and articulation in the sciences and in technology during this period have changed human beings' lives drastically enough to have changed the kinds of philosophical questions that most grip them. This is especially true of the period after World War II. Balanced, informed, and inspiring teaching of philosophy—especially philosophy of science—has become increasingly difficult. In Kant's day, there were a few really great scientific treatises to be read, and virtually every student could read these works and profit from them. Of course, the possible philosophical extrapolations from Newton were and still remain various: Susan Neiman has reminded us of Kant's having called Rousseau the "Newton of the mind," and Reni Daston has explored ways in which our moral language about what is natural only partly and ambivalently came to reflect the Newtonian ideal of nature as governed by a small number of universally applicable principles. But at least the perceived fact of this intellectual situation remained in place for a long time. At some point beginning in the 19th century, science began to change—in style, content, and practice. It took a while for philosophy to catch up, partly because it took a while for the impact of science to make itself overwhelmingly felt in the culture at large. And I believe that the present-day situation—in which complexity, heterogenity, technology, and applications dominate the culture's attitude toward and interest in science—began to have a central impact on philosophy only in the 20th century. I believe historians of 20th-century philosophy have to keep hold of the variety of reactions to this situation if we are to properly (and historically) understand the place of philosophy and science in our culture today.

Students nowadays are, I think—and perhaps rightly—far more skeptical than earlier generations were about finding the time to learn enough technical details in any branch of science to be in a position to contribute something philosophically interesting and synthetic to the foundations of science itself. For one thing, there is too much mathematics to be learned by any one person. Furthermore, the concept of *science* seems almost too well understood; it is instead the philosophical (often ethical and political) questions related to the *applications* of science, engineering, and technology that take up far more of the foreground of the terrain. We have new, mathematically articulated branches of science that have emerged in their own right to impinge on our attention: molecular biology, evolutionary theory, economics, neurochemistry, and computer science spring to mind. The contributions of philosophy to basic conceptual revolutions in these kinds of science have become, I think by now, less direct, more heterogeneous, sometimes largely metaphorical, morally laden in an obvious sense, sometimes less intersubjective and more attenuated—more truly Kuhnian, if you will. Philosophy's foundational role with respect to these sciences has often been more that of a critic than of a participant: we can expect a philosopher frequently to be engaged, for example, in pointing out implausible or ambiguous presuppositions of idealizations, or in resisting extrapolation and direct applications of the models to too wide a range of phenomena, or in questioning the ethical implications of an emerging technology. Of course sometimes such critique is coupled with constructive scientific suggestions for foundational research. But philosophy is more diffuse in its reactions and when synthetic, is either quite speculative or anecdotal rather than principled.

I am asking whether or to what extent philosophy of science may no longer in its essence or center be a matter of philosophical system building or construction. It may be, at its best, much more like it was in, say, Plato's day: a matter of creative analogical leaps, unexpected conceptual connections, apologies, and criticisms, forging ties with the everyday lives of its readers and practitioners. If that is so, then in its institutional and pedagogical form, philosophy of science will be in large part a matter of exploring with students the cultural, historical, technological, biographical, and social impacts of science on their lives and their culture. That is why sociobiology, genetic food alteration, engineering ethics, ecology, psychiatry, medicine and neuroscience, feminism, the theory of meaning, and anthropology raise a far more easily motivated set of questions for the teacher of philosophy of science than do the fundamental, abstract structural questions—however exciting—that are currently being raised in cosmology, theoretical physics, and the foundations of mathematics. Of course, these abstract foundational studies are beautiful and of ultimate intellectual and scientific importance: it is to them that science will owe truly revolutionary progress on its theoretical side in the future. A large responsibility rests with teachers of philosophy of science to offer vivid summaries of the historical and philosophical roots of present-day scientific research, analyzing trends and their significance. But the latter activity, pedagogically, will tend to be of primary use in furthering research at the theoretical frontier, helping advanced undergraduates and graduate students formulate research programs that will aid in the production of further knowledge. It will not resolve the general problem of how to motivate for the undergraduate or the lay person an interest in the philosophy of science more broadly conceived.

The fact is that Michael's Cassirerian hope of unifying through history a narrative about the articulation of frameworks for thought, a kind of mixed, empirically fruitful dynamic of reason, may not and has not yet won out as a vision speaking to the *philosophical* need to understand the place of science and technology in the contemporary world. To pick up a thought from Michael's fine book on the Davos conference: the neo-Kantian tradition emanating from Cassirer has found far fewer adherents in the past 50 years than either the tradition emanating from Carnap or the tradition emerging from Heidegger. If Michael has his way, that missing tradition will be recovered. But I am skeptical that it will prove ultimately satisfying to students in the next generation, a kind of template from which one may leap off into a terrain already comfortably charted. This is because I do not believe that the position of philosophy relative to science has remained quite as constant as Michael's account would have us hope over the past 200 years. And this affects and shapes philosophical content, the available range of plausible philosophical positions, and the manner and style in which they are plausibly canvassed.

I can put this challenge in Humean terms. Part of the appeal of so-called naturalism, as the term came to be understood after Quine, is its shunning, at least in certain of its forms, of any principled or preconceived picture of what science should be. The naturalist lets science grow as it will, and describes. Of course, this has seemed to many to close off any hope of philosophy's making a recognizably distinctive contribution. It raises doubts about reductionism. But at least it has the advantage of not trying to *define* philosophy's aims, methods, and subject mater too sharply in advance, and it allows a place in philosophy for letting the sciences speak on their own terms before they are subjected to critical scrutiny. The primary philosophical and pedagogical challenge that remains—as in a way, ironically, the logical positivists saw—is the task of conceiving a *distinctive* role for philosophy to play in helping human beings orient themselves in the context of modern life.

Perhaps a few pedagogical anecdotes from the field will help make the point more clearly. The Boston University Colloquium for the Philosophy of Science has greatly expanded the kind of colloquia that we now run. Under the guidance of Alfred Tauber—himself an oncologist with a strong interest in philosophy and medicine—the colloquium includes a far larger technology- and ethics-oriented component than it used to. It retains a kind of mix of focused foundational, purely theoretical symposia and the applied, historical, and interdisciplinary symposia. This plurality has broadened the audience considerably and kept the colloquium alive to multiple kinds of philosophical change. It has not made the colloquium a place where a particular vision of philosophy is articulated; instead, it is a place where many different conceptions of philosophy are explored and brought into contact with emerging areas of historical, ethical, political, and scientific research. My colleague Alisa Bokulich is currently teaching a beginning undergraduate course called Science, Technology and Values—essentially, a kind of applied ethics course focusing on the societal role of engineering and technology. While the amount of science proper that can be effectively taught in such a course is perhaps minimal, student interest is high: questions about governmental, personal, and corporate levels of responsibility for technology and its effects interact in obvious ways with the world around the students and more easily motivate an interest in philosophy of science at the undergraduate level.

In the particular fields I have been teaching in our department—early analytic philosophy, philosophy of mathematics, language and logic—the problem of how to balance the purely foundational, mathematically articulated, structural approach against the applied, pluralistic approach is raised with a vengeance. In the wake of the explosive mathematical articulation of logic in the past 125 years, logic is really not one subject any longer. It is becoming less and less plausible to think that we will comfortably settle on an answer to the question, What is logic? The philosophical aspects of logic remain fundamental to all of philosophy, historically and rationally. As a branch of mathematics, logic becomes more and more difficult to survey as a whole; its mathematized parts become ever more fascinating and powerful, both abstractly (in the development of emerging foundational work) and concretely (in the applications of recursive function theory and complexity theory in computer science, cognitive science, cryptography, linguistics, optics, and neurobiology). I would say that the rigorization of the notion of *computation* and differing philosophical attitudes toward the notion of the *mechanical* in philosophy effected a central conceptual and historical shift in 20th-century thought. But a really good, philosophically sensitive and informed survey of these issues has not yet been written. Add to this the traditionally perceived mission of logic in the undergraduate curriculum—to foster the ability of students to write well and think more clearly—and the teacher of logic and philosophy has a very difficult series of pedagogical tasks to manage, especially if that teacher is interested in history. First-order quantification theory is a kind of formal core around which we can build connections to certain ongoing developments in cognitive science, epistemology, complexity theory, and the foundations of mathematics. But a new series of courses needs to be devised in philosophy of mathematics that will bring out how and why. My guess is that a historical approach is needed here, but perhaps allowing applications to guide course content—rather than foundational, principled questions—will be the best way to accomplish this.

Like Michael I believe that one way to motivate an interest on students' part in the philosophy of mathematics and logic is to tie the two in with history. But I have tended more than Michael to try to fit this historical development into an account of the various incompatible images of human reason we have inherited from ancient times. For this reason I have found it most helpful, pedagogically speaking, to emphasize with my students that very old and long-accepted notions—for example, logical notions like *concept, judgment, extension, form, object,* and *truth*—have been cast over the past hundred years in a new, very powerful, and extremely complex light. I would emphasize, I think more than Michael, that this complexity has impacted upon philosophy in general and philosophy of science in particular in a way that is difficult to summarize in terms of the Kantian epistemological project. In general, there has emerged very little consensus on whether these apparently most fundamental or simple philosophical notions can or should survive with anything like a systematic, settled usage. So far, they have not, either in theory or in practice. That does not mean that they might not receive a clearer, persuasive systematization in the future. But it is difficult to insist that students have faith in such a thing as we attempt to acquaint them with results, structures, and programs of a kind that require years of work to fully understand.

I can put my point in Kantian terms. Michael's reading of Kant has so far been selective and partial in terms of the philosophical problems it emphasizes. The framing roles of mathematics and physics for Kant's doctrine of the a priori and its descendants have been treated beautifully—but largely in abstraction from Kant's wider theological and moral concerns about the place of the human being in nature. In this respect, Michael's historical work in philosophy of science inherits a significant strand from his logical positivist forebears and departs, I think significantly, from the work of earlier Kantians to whom his work is explicitly indebted, such as Gerd Buchdahl and, perhaps to a lesser extent, Cassirer. Can one really understand the appeal of a Kantian approach without emphasizing Kant's concerns with problems of ethics, with the possibility of freedom, with the ineliminable need for human judgment, with the presence of evil, and with the difficulty of integrating our thought about these issues with our images of nature? Kant was engaged in picturing human life against the background of the world in which it unfolds, and his interest in a general philosophy of nature was always pervaded with his ethical concerns. His picture schematized the ways in which the individual and society are forced to struggle with their own ideals, morally and intellectually, in order to hope to become reconciled to the realities of and imperfection in the world. Kant took it to be an intrinsic feature of human reason that it could educate itself to see how to let go of certain insistent, ever-present intellectual questions about the ultimate nature of reality. An emphasis on this part of Kant's philosophy has been lacking in Michael's neo-Kantian efforts to integrate the philosophy of science with the history of modern philosophy. And to this extent, Kant's true metaphysics, his fascination with teleology and value, has so far been left out of the core of Michael's account. Of course, as Michael turns in his future research toward philosophical problems raised in biology and psychology, these metaphysical problems in the philosophy of science—problems Kant began to face in his *Critique of Judgment*—will press themselves upon him with increased force. The results—both philosophical and pedagogical—will be exciting and instructive, and I urge Michael to turn in this direction in his teaching and research.

Thought versus History:
Reflections on a French Problem

DENIS KAMBOUCHNER

IF YOU WILL allow me, I shall take with this discussion two kinds of liberties.

First, as a historian of philosophy accustomed to working with texts from the early modern period rather than those of the post-Kantian period, I will of course tend to refer, even in some detail, to certain modern or contemporary representations of the history of philosophy; however, concerning the approach and the treatment of the texts, I prefer to take the few examples in my study from the field that is the most familiar to me.

Second, neither the terms nor the urgency of the pedagogical problem posed by the history of philosophy in the lower levels of the curriculum are quite the same in France and the Anglophone world. I will begin, then, by discussing the French pedagogical context and the sort of intellectual tradition that one may associate with it. From this point of departure, I will strive to tackle what seems to be the most fundamental problem that we share: that of knowing whether, at least in the basic principles of teaching, there is a consistent distinction to be made, and a real opposition or notable tension, between the analysis of philosophical works and the teaching of a history of ideas and doctrines, with its cultural content.

ONE

A first and uncomfortable point is perhaps that the question of knowing how to teach new histories of philosophy—in other words, the question of what place to allocate to teaching the new forms and data of this history—does not seem to be raised in France at all. And if this is the case or if this risks being the case, it is because the history of philosophy is taught in France, at the introductory university levels, in a way that can be described in general as unproblematic. The first indication of this unproblematic status is that no one would think of establishing an advanced course of study in philosophy in which the history of philosophy would not have a large place. But the second and most alarming indication is that the manner of organizing related courses—whether it's a question of their details or their general distribution—does not appear to provoke any collective inquiry. Inasmuch as this education is organized, and of course it is, to a certain extent, this organization is left to personal initiative and—if a question arises—to negotiations that are just as personal, based on a culture and habits that are widely shared.

The lack of problematization in question here certainly does not exist to the point that everyone views history of philosophy teaching in France as satisfactory and in good order. For one thing, it has happened in France that the usual manner of treating texts be subjected to systematic critique (an example of which we will examine shortly); for another, a significant minority of philosophy professors—generally specialists in the philosophies of science, logic, or cognition—now frequently declare that history of philosophy's place in the program of study is excessively large and that it turns our students (including some of the best) away from authentically contemporary forms of inquiry and culture. Let's suppose, however, that this minority is bound to gain support in the near future (which is not at all improbable) and that it will then be in a position to significantly influence the evolution of the program. Will the question of knowing which history of philosophy to teach then be on the agenda? Not necessarily, precisely because the type of reform in question would not be a result of any internal evolution within the discipline. Why is a question that the evolution of research would naturally seem to lead us to raise so foreign to us? This is the enigma that I hope to touch on here.

The legitimacy granted to the history of philosophy in French universities, at least in the eyes of those who are in charge of it, is of course a function of its traditional nature. This tradition goes back to the first half of the 19th century and was strongly influenced in this first century of its existence by the works and institutional actions of figures like Victor Cousin, Jules Lachelier, Renouvier, Ravaisson,

Émile Boutroux, and, above all, in the first decades of the 20th century, Léon Brunschvicg. It is not at all evident, however, that the legitimacy in question can be traced to determinate principles formulated by specific authors or that it must thus be attributed to the authority of a certain doctrine that would have fashioned what some of us—rather immodestly—call the *philosophical institution.* Most likely, this legitimacy, on the contrary, subsisted, and was even constituted, over and above the introduction, reception, and criticism of determinate doctrines concerning the nature and practice of this history. And in fact, it is very difficult to describe it in anything other than extremely general terms, in the form of a few elementary convictions: the first being that a philosopher's library, as far as concerns past works, is organized according to an undoubtedly complex but relatively rigid hierarchy articulated around three cardinal authors—namely, Plato, Descartes, and Kant. These cardinal authors are not necessarily those who teach us the most decisive truths; in this respect one might prefer Epicurus, Pascal, Spinoza, Hegel, Kierkegaard, Marx, Nietzsche, or Heidegger. Yet it is in these three authors (each of whom has numerous, prestigious satellites) and more precisely in certain works of theirs, works reputedly more canonical than others, that one can truly learn what philosophy is. A familiarity with these authors and works is not only a constitutive part of philosophical culture but also a familiarity that makes the true philosopher. He who has examined the successive arguments in favor of the immortality of the soul in *Phaedo,* or who has mastered the demonstrative architecture of the *Meditations,* or who has followed in its two versions the Kantian deduction of the pure concepts of understanding, or who has meditated on the transcendental solution of the antinomies of pure reason is incontestably a philosopher. And the fact that this suffices to make that one a philosopher does not mean that the one will be a philosopher, even if he gets absolutely nothing out of knowing these texts; rather, the fact is that it is impossible that nothing philosophical follow from knowing these texts. Thus, the philosophical institution is in part the institution of these authors and works, which means that introducing students to them is unconditionally a task of the agents or representatives of this institution (or at least a delegated number of them assigned to such a task). This introduction, effectuated in the form of an explanation (*explication*) of part or all of these texts, has no specific larger goal than to verify the acquisition of some familiarity with these texts and the doctrinal elements articulated in them.

Just as it is not particularly difficult to define in this summary manner this spirit of history of philosophy teaching, neither is it difficult to list the elements of criticism that can be grouped together with respect to its institution. Criticism essentially becomes attached to the sort of sacredness that surrounds great authors and great texts and to the manner in which one presumes to make their meaning available. In the first place, one can emphasize the rigid nature of a hierarchy that, privileging a priori and rather overwhelmingly certain authors at the expense of others (and similarly, a number of these authors' texts at the expense of others), cannot but lead to serious lapses in the accuracy and precision of the analysis and even the description of these texts, whose content is not infrequently reduced to a vulgate disseminated by innumerable textbooks. In the second place, the study of these texts remains marked by a sort of devotion that is conducive neither to sophisticated philosophical interrogation (pointing out certain flaws in reasoning where need be) nor, generally, to encouraging students to take a strong position regarding their content. The deficit linked to such a study is therefore at least twofold: it is a matter of historical knowledge, since the study of canonical texts is generally frugal in its consideration of context and leaves to the shadows the textual or traditional mediations that perhaps existed between the considered authors or treats them in general, imprecise terms; it is also a matter of philosophical consciousness, since the relative atemporality that characterizes the approach to these texts is at the same time destined to inhibit a first-person type of interrogation[1] that would highlight the relation, or the gap, between the content of these texts and a contemporary questioning. Because of its indifference to the use students might make of the texts and the dogmatic character of its dispensation, teaching, thus defined, hardly seems to have broken ties with dubious pedagogical traditions of the 16th century, in which commentary and memorization were valued over the spirit of *disputatio*. This type of teaching gives rise as well to a wide sociological type of critical debate accentuating at once the large role of routine in the forms and content of teaching and, with respect to its recipients, a pressure to conform that goes without any sufficient explanation of the obligation to do so. In sum, numerous examples of Pierre Bourdieu's *reproduction* are to be found in this type of teaching, which was one of the first objects of his assessment.

My own intention in the following pages is neither to emphasize this critique in order to seek an alternative model for teaching the history of philosophy in France nor to defend this teaching against the reproaches it has received. It is all too clear that this teaching is not functioning efficiently due to the absence of a global program defining the objects of courses for each year of study (which means that an author as important as Aristotle, Leibniz, or Hume may not have been studied by the end of the third year[2]); the lack of library resources available to students, who rarely benefit from adequate infrastructures; the almost total (and correlative) absence of reading syllabi accompanying and supporting lectures; and, finally, the stereo-typical nature of assignments and exams that allow students to remain at a superficial and conventional level of comprehension of the texts treated. It is all too clear as well that the French habit of restricting history of philosophy education to great authors and great books produces a strong backlash in scientific production, which generally remains confined to the monograph genre at the expense of wide-range and synthetic historical inquiries. The paradoxical result of this state of things is that since World War II, the most notable studies of 17th-century French intellectual history have come from Anglophone authors (some of whom are among us now).

On the other hand, it is important not to paint too bleak a picture of this situation. As concentrated around certain canonical texts as history of philosophy teaching at the university level may seem, it is also true as a general rule that this teaching comes from professors who have accomplished genuine work in the history of philosophy and who are concerned with this history as such. It is not unusual therefore that undergraduate courses at least implicitly retain the results of the most recent research. Moreover, the kind of textual analysis that is academically practiced in France—*l'explication de texte*—is not an artificial exercise; provided that one sees to it that the rhetorical aspects are eliminated or limited, we're talking about an authentic conceptual examination likely to identify sophisticated structures and to ensure their assimilation on the basis of an acquired consciousness of the complexity of the intellectual material under consideration. Even a certain degree of suspension of judgment with respect to the thought studied—a suspension that is not at all obligatory—is not without some positive aspects. Nevertheless, with respect to a teaching centered on the prolonged explication (usually lasting a whole year) of a few major works, one cannot easily speak of a history of philosophy teaching in itself. And in this respect, to say that history of philosophy is taught among us in an unproblematic manner is to say that the task itself of teaching (that of history of philosophy as such) is highly problematic. The question is knowing whether it is problematic exclusively for bad reasons and, if some of these reasons are good, how to envisage relaxing the genre in a way similar to that which, for reasons just as good, is practiced elsewhere in the world.

Two

If we distinguish, within history of philosophy teaching, between a monographic style and a more narrative, synthetic style (let's call it historiographic, at least for the sake of balance), how do we then explain the (apparently quite specific) French predilection for the first at the expense of the second? If we agree to set aside sociological determinations, and, in a general fashion, the bad or negative reasons, there remains, it seems to me, the task of considering two specific and in fact indissociable factors that give rise to a sort of intellectual tradition: the distrust of putting thought into a narrative—or in other words, a sort of epistemological perplexity centered on historiography—and the sharp awareness of the indefinitely enigmatic quality of a great work or philosophical accomplishment. I must immediately add that this awareness and perplexity are manifested unequally depending on the genre of the works considered: they have much less affected works of natural philosophy, political theories, moral treatises, essays on art, or scientific theories than works whose explicit thrust or perceived scope permits us to describe them as metaphysical. The problem of the history of philosophy is thus essentially—and, moreover, predictably—that of the history of metaphysics. Regarding the particular persistence of this problem in France during the past century, which continues to weigh on our teaching today, I would like to cite three accounts from three great figures—all of them very different both in their period and by the nature of their work: Henri Bergson, Martial Gueroult, and Jacques Derrida (in his discussion with Michel Foucault).

Concerning Bergson, who, of these three authors, is the most venerable and the most remote from us, it is useful to at least mention the lecture on philosophical intuition given at the International Congress of Bologna in 1911 and taken up again in *The Creative Mind*. I am not aware of the reputation or basic influence that this text had in the United States. In France, this is a famous text, still frequently cited today, that takes the form of a meditation on what constitutes the ultimate unity of a body of thought. On a first encounter, Bergson stresses, a philosophical work, considered in its entirety, appears characterized by a high degree of complexity that is first of all a high degree of composition; the historian of philosophy, whose experience is in question, is not the person who, seeing before him an architecture of relatively enigmatic utterances, sets out on a quest for precedents. He is, rather, one who recognizes themes, schema problems, principles, and theoretical motifs, reorganized or reworked with a superior degree of ingenuity, that he has already encountered elsewhere. Yet, Bergson insists, this recognitive activity— which at once divides a philosophical enterprise, as a system, into distinct parts, and which studies each of these parts through a method of comparison with other, notably earlier, systems, and which is a form of exercising critical intelligence—does not constitute the only way that the historian of philosophy may experience a work. On the contrary, it constitutes only the beginning of a process of going deeper, which, paradoxically, tends toward simplification at the same time as, or because, it concentrates on a certain core matrix of the work. "As we seek to penetrate more fully the philosopher's thought instead of circulating around its exterior, his doctrine is transformed for us. In the first place its complication diminishes. Then the various parts fit into one another. Finally the whole is brought together into a single point."[3] Only this single point is something we have "no hope of reaching completely": we can only "ever more closely approach" it. And if this is the case, it is because this point—around which the whole work turns, since the philosopher has always focused on it— this central point is not of a nature such that it can be expressed in words: at most, one could form a certain image about it, a schema that would constitute the mediating element between pure intuition and the articulation of the discourse, an articulation that can continue infinitely precisely because of the incommensurability between the thing to be expressed and the means of expression. Now, for the historian, approaching ever closer to this point does not simply amount to retrieving a mediating image comparable to the one that the philosopher may have formed in his mind through his own expressive or creative effort; it neither simply nor precisely means taking the opposite path of the philosopher through this same effort; it means, at the same time and first of all, going beyond the level of correlation and succession of ideas at which he was first located. "Let us get rid of this complication [of the doctrine with its tortuous elements] and get back to the simple intuition, or at least to the image which translates it: in doing so we see the doctrine freed of those conditions of time and place upon which it seemed to depend" (110). "A philosopher worthy of the name has never said more than a single thing: and even then it is something he has tried to say, rather than actually said" (112), but "a thought which brings something new into the world is of course obliged to manifest itself through the ready-made ideas it comes across and draws into its movement" (112), and thus, "The philosopher might have come several centuries earlier; he would have had to deal with another philosophy and another science; he would have given himself other problems; he would have expressed himself by other formulas; not one chapter perhaps of the books he wrote would have been what it is; and nevertheless he would have said the same thing" (112).

Articulated through two examples—one treated rather briefly (that of Spinoza, with the image or the "feeling of a coincidence between the act by which our mind knows truth perfectly, and the operation by which God engenders it" [113]) and the other more fully so (that of Berkeley, with the double aspect of matter, "a thin transparent film situated between man and God" but also "a language which God speaks to us" [119]), the Bergsonian theory of philosophical intuition struck people's minds and of course, on an equal scale, provoked criticism with its triple affirmation of the ineffable character of this intuition, its absolute simplicity, and its constitutive ahistoricity. In his *History of the History of Philosophy*, published posthumously from 1984 to 1988, Martial Gueroult notably subjected this theory to a severe critique—on one hand, by questioning the compatibility between this vision of philosophical activity and the history of philosophy roughly sketched out by Bergson 15 years earlier in the last chapter of *Creative Evolution*, and on the other hand, by easily pointing out the inanity of a philosophy reduced to an absolutely decontextualized vision. "The spirit of simplification comes to destroy entirely the profound meaning of philosophy. In what can this ahistorical thought of Berkeley's consist, a thought that could have been the same ten centuries earlier or three centuries later? Considered in what remains of its philosophical content, it evaporates in an expression of vague panentheism.... The object proper to the history of philosophy, the accomplished work, in its suggestive complexity, has in the end evaporated."[4]

The question of the coherence of the Bergsonian theory of philosophy as it is expressed in diverse texts is not one that I can treat in depth here; this whole question is linked to the relation between metaphysical thought and scientific thinking, a relation that *Creative Evolution* tends to present as one of solidarity, whereas the Bologna conference emphasizes a heterogeneity that does not exclude affinity [*sympathie*] but, on the contrary, establishes it. As far as the heart of the matter is concerned, it is all too clear that Bergson subjects philosophical thought to a neo-Platonic sort of unifying model: the object of philosophical intuition is precisely the One from which intelligence descends toward a multiple given, all the while proving capable of an inverse movement of conversion and return. The neo-Platonic schema, studied by Bergson during a course on Plotinus, overdetermines the interpretation of Spinoza here, like that of Berkeley as well; it manifestly corresponds to a tradition in which Bergson recognizes and places himself. It is easy to debate it, as Gueroult does, or its pertinence to the case of Berkeley itself, or of course to point out contradicting cases to which it does not seem at all applicable precisely because the thought of these authors does not really accept any central metaphysical object, and, consequently, metaphysical vision—even if one distinguishes it from mystical ecstasy—has no teleological status in their works.

The Bergsonian view is therefore easy to contest with respect to its general validity—and yet, it has for systems, doctrines, or philosophical enterprises a particular sort of interest, in that it articulates a sort of inquiry and perhaps primarily a sort of experience that must be seen as relatively independent from Bergsonian philosophy itself. On one hand, since we never think without images, it is true that we can only with difficulty study a philosophical text— at least those that are relatively abstract or speculative—without imagining certain hard-to-describe schemata. It is not absolutely evident that these schemata are, as Husserl insists in the *First Logical Investigation*, simple "accompanying images" stripped of any constitutive function with respect to the process of reflection itself. And it is interesting that when we ask about the unity of a philosophical enterprise—a question that is still legitimate when we consider the integrality of an oeuvre, eventually including works very diverse in style and purpose—this question involves not just finding a definition but also articulating a perspective on the imaginative-schematic mode in question. In this respect, Gueroult can certainly assert against Bergson the dimension of philosophical activity that consists in confronting determined, contextualized, and relatively dated problems; he can also assert the multiplicity of the questions to be confronted—or the Cartesian plurality of battles to wage—against the simple expression of an intuition that is by nature evanescent: it is not certain that there is such a discontinuity between the interest in this central intuition—which Bergson does not say the historian of philosophy must strive to retrieve—and the interest in the system in itself. (One question is maintained: that of the realized form.)

The paradox to confront, in French history of the history of philosophy, would therefore be that of the absence of a total intellectual rupture between the spiritualist intuitionism that Bergson represents and the completely positive study of philosophical systems that has marked postwar historiography, of which Martial Gueroult was the greatest representative. In reality, it is not difficult to find a negative principle in this sort of continuity: if the Bergsonian theory of philosophical intuition represents in Bergson's work a superior degree of reflection in comparison to a historical vision in which the metaphysical tradition appears above all in the service of scientific thinking, then the textual approach of which Martial Gueroult made himself the representative starkly opposes the vision of the history of philosophy developed by Léon Brunschvicg, a vision at once evolutionist and critical that strives to identify in each philosophical work that by which the work corresponds to the progress of a reason essentially incarnated in mathematical form and that by which it remains within or breaks away from it. To this effort to separate the wheat from the chaff in each philosophical work Gueroult opposes— in his *Philosophy of the History of Philosophy*,[5] intended to be the second volume, after *The History of the History of Philosophy*, of a *Dianoématique* and written as early as the 1930s, that is, before Gueroult had conceived any of the great commentaries for which he is still known—the radical affirmation of the unity of spirit in each philosophical body of thought, associated with this thought's production of a specific objectivity or reality. Obviously, for Gueroult it is a matter of taking a most speculative sort of position, inspired largely by the study of Fichte and which he himself terms radical idealism. His theory can be summed up by a few propositions.

1. Every great philosophical work, defined in broad terms as the ensemble of texts or principal texts of an author, possesses and delivers by a process that Gueroult characterizes as explicative intellection—an absolutely peculiar content that one can describe as metaphysical. With respect to this intellective function, which we must consider as essentially disinterested, or in other words, as taking itself as its own end (cf. pp. 85–89), any practical or pragmatic dimension of philosophical reflection must be considered secondary. At heart, philosophical activity is the constitution of an Idea of the real. But the expression *Idea of the real* absolutely does not mean an image of a reality exterior to thought and accessible as such to all thinking subjects. Philosophical thought does not just produce here the Idea, but the real itself, or, more precisely, it gives a determinate form to a common real that remains indeterminable in itself and amounts to a transcendental function.

2. The Idea in question here being one, every great philosophical work, whatever the particular style of its texts or the physiognomy of their corpus, constitutes in its way a system, whose form or nature remains to be defined, with the specification of its particular mode of development. Such is therefore the essential task of the historian of philosophy: to clarify this Idea as such; to give prominence to the

content of each great philosophical work as a specific, consistent reality; and to specify the manner in which each system unfolds. This task can be accomplished only as a philosophical task, identifying or treating a philosophical objectivity by definition completely different from historical objectivity, which can be taken into consideration here only contingently.

3. The philosophical matter we are dealing with here can be distinguished a priori from a scientific matter that possesses its own form of historicity; it is precisely in opposition with the historical nature specific to this scientific matter that the philosophical matter offered by each great work is eternally instructive. There is therefore no evolutionist history of philosophical reason to be constructed, which would still amount to organizing the productivity of each body of thought according to a reality that is supposedly accessible independently of it. Each philosophical system, although developing according to a certain internal necessity, is based, as it is in Bergson, on an absolutely free initiative. The succession and deployment of several philosophical systems around the same time is absolutely impossible to anticipate and without any a priori determinable form. The history of philosophy must therefore renounce the rational form imposed, for example, by a Hegel, in order to make itself—under the name *dianoématique*—the pure exploration and experience of these contents in their diversity. Only in this way can it secure its objects and raise itself to their level, to the point of merging with its object, since it is philosophy itself that "only exists in the form of an indefinitely renewed experience". (*Ph. Hist. Ph.*, 28) However, in doing so, perhaps it strays less from its own historian's vocation than it would seem, if one keeps in mind a concept of history that likens it to pure inquiry and that radically removes it from its own disappearance in a unitary and doctrinally oriented narrative.

In its main affirmations, this doctrine, set out in the manuscript of *Philosophy of the History of Philosophy* in a vigorous but extremely abstract manner—even more abstract than the philosophical Intuition in Bergson—evidently includes something frightening. For one thing, the three monumental works that Gueroult was to consecrate subsequently to Descartes, Malebranche, and Spinoza evidently retreat from this radicality, their author revealing himself to be far too much of a historian, far too erudite to dispense with inscribing the systems studied in a space that puts them in dialogue with each other and authorizes a number of comparisons and contextualizations. Besides the irreducible concession made to the standard style of history of philosophy and other sciences, we must note, particularly in the three volumes on Malebranche, the over-accumulation of conceptual/technical-type problems, which provides evidence not only of the specificity of the internal constraints of each system but also of the difficulty of attaining the coherence or systematicity required while considering all of the details. As a result, the Idea of the real as presented in the *Dianoématique* seems to converge with Bergsonian intuition with respect to the unrealizable or the inexpressible, and the Gueroultian analysis of philosophical systems incessantly returns to a history of the failures of dogmatic rationalism.[6]

However, and although Gueroult's analyses have given rise from the outset to sharp debates,[7] one can cite a large impression produced in France by these vast systematic reconstructions—an impression that has notably benefited from a near conflation of his enterprise with the structuralist nebula that is not completely accidental. And this stamp or influence particularly concerned two of the directing principles of the *dianoématique:* on one hand, the fact that the commentator in principle should not allow any experience or "real" to play a role in his interrogation besides those that the texts themselves indicate or constitute; on the other hand, the low interest or even the intrinsic intellectual impossibility of a general or partial history of philosophy, which would attempt to identify in the successive production of systems (one can note in all this the disdain for the *minores*) a somewhat constraining logic, or only a minimum of overall intelligibility. I repeat: It is not a question of pretending that such principles have ever been observed to the letter. The important point is only that an interest in the formal aspect of philosophical investigation, or equally in the details of speculative invention, seems, in the field that interests us, to fit neither easily with a definition of the positions or the contributions of each thinker in a constituted or developing intellectual field nor in general with a consideration of the pragmatic inscription of philosophical thought in an empirical universe constituted independently of it.

One of the last notable controversies in French philosophy—that which more than 30 years ago set Michel Foucault and Jacques Derrida against each other with respect to the so-called madness argument in Descartes's *Meditations*—still bears the traces of this difficulty: that one can reduce to the apparent antinomy between an internalist and strictly monographic approach to philosophical works and an externalist, transversal, and pragmatic approach. Let me briefly recall the object of debate.

Everyone remembers that in the beginning of the *First Meditation*, in the context of the initial movement of doubting the information given by the senses, the possibility that the closest and most evident sensory facts be negated comes into question itself: "But on what grounds could [I] deny... Unless perhaps I were to liken myself to the insane, whose brains are impaired by such an unrelenting vapor of black bile that they steadfastly insist that they are kings when they are... naked."[8] The movement of repulsion that determines this reference to madness is immediately followed, however, by a return to doubt, with one new argument: that everyone who dreams imagines "the very same things... as these insane people do when they are awake"—the question becoming then how to know how we know we are not dreaming and that the things we believe we feel actually exist. In a few pages of his *Madness and Civilisation*, published in 1961,[9] Michel Foucault saw in these lines from Descartes the evidence or even the event of an historic turn in the comprehension of madness, a turn that becomes more noticeable in comparison with one of Pierre Charron's texts (*De la Sagesse* [*Of Wisdom*], 1601, I, XIV): "It is easy to see how temeritous and dangerous is the human mind, even if it is quick and vigorous ... it is a miracle to find a great, quick mind that is well-regulated and moderate ... wisdom and folly are close neighbors. They are two sides of the same thing ... What else is subtle folly made of but the most subtle wisdom?" Breaking with this representation of a constitutive proximity between wisdom and madness, the *Meditations* seems to announce the exclusion of the risk of madness from the rational universe and the reduction of madness to silence in what Foucault called the great confinement [*le grand renfermement*]. With this simple passage—"But what? These are mad people, and I would not be less extravagant if I enjoyed myself after their example"—madness, writes Foucault, "is excluded (excluded from himself) by the doubting subject, as it is excluded shortly after that he does not think, and does not exist."[10]

It is against this representation of a Cartesian forceful coup that Derrida rises up in his 1963 lecture entitled *Cogito and the History of Madness*[11] with the following argument: if madness is indeed at first distanced in the Cartesian text, it is because the floor is given here "to the nonphilosopher, to the novice in philosophy who is frightened by doubt and protests" (50), but it is precisely the difference between reason and madness, of which the nonphilosopher feels assured, that will be put into question again in the following paragraph: praeclare sane ("this would all be well and good"), "were I not a man who is accustomed to sleeping at night and to experiencing in my dreams the very same things...that the insane do while they're awake." (Descartes, 14) The dream that anyone might have is no less crazy and is often crazier than the thoughts of the crazy man. Thus, in the Cartesian text's methodical order, the reference to dreams represents not the exclusion of the madness hypothesis but on the contrary, its "hyperbolic exasperation" (51). And far from needing to speak here of an "impossibility of being crazy essential to the thinking subject," this exasperation of the madness hypothesis is perhaps only in its first phase, if that of the Evil genius, introduced shortly after, "the possibility of *total madness*" (52), madness "bring[ing] subversion to pure thought" (53) and no longer in the solitary perceptive consciousness that "will spare nothing" (53). Far from throwing out madness, Descartes "installs its possible menace at the very heart of the intelligible" (55) without "let[ting] any determined knowledge escape from madness" (55), and this is why the Cogito is posited against a background of possible madness—as an act that remains valid "even if I am mad, even if my thoughts are completely mad" (55). The Cogito is assuredly the moment in which philosophizing thought can again begin to insure itself against the risk of madness, but for this, the Cogito itself and the hyperbolic project out of which it arises must rest on a "mad audacity" (56) that one risks misunderstanding and reducing, not without violence, in striving "to enclose it within a determined historical structure" (57) or in "a determined history" (58). Derrida's transcendental truth is that, effectively, philosophy cannot not distinguish itself from madness— a distinction assuredly effectuated, in Descartes, with the whole reflection to which the Cogito itself is subjected after the fact—but that there is at the same time no meaningful philosophy, or philosophy in action, except "at the point of greatest proximity to madness" (59), at once liberating in itself the resource of hyperbole and an extravagance irreducible to any finite historical structure and "reassur[ing] itself against being annihilated or wrecked in madness or in death" (61). This relation, in which Derrida sees what he names a structure of deferral (*structure de différance*) (62), is impossible to inscribe in a history; it is, rather, the condition of historicity: "the historicity proper to philosophy" (60)—without which historicity in general would be impossible—"is located and constituted in...the dialogue between hyperbole and the finite structure" (60) (a finite structure that is the product of reason). This same relation is not therefore classical in the literal sense of an era of Occidental history: it is classical "in the sense of eternal and essential classicism" (62).

To this critique, it is noteworthy that nine years later (in 1972, with the second edition of *Madness and Civilization*), Foucault offers an extremely harsh response,[12] centered on two essential points.

1. Everything in the Cartesian text shows that to legitimize the doubt undermining the totality of sensory appearances, the dream is assumed by Descartes to be the best position of reference, whereas at no time is the place of the mad expressly assumed or taken up again by the meditating subject; on the contrary, madness, like amentia or dementia is the object here of a significant objectivizing distanciation—of a juridical or medical type—and it is only at the price of several "derivations around Descartes's text" (25) that the Cartesian meditation can be presented as a confrontation with madness. The "but what, these are mad people!" does not simply follow from the naive exclamation of the nonphilosopher scared by the doubt that is proposed to him; it marks an effective rejection, on the part of a subject from the outset completely master of himself, who "never lets himself be surprised" and assumes, from one end of the meditation to another, until the confrontation with the evil genius, a gesture all the more absolutely devised in that it concerns in this case a fiction.

2. In his refusal to relate the Cartesian decision to a historical structure that transcends it, Derrida perpetuates an "old old tradition" (26), incidentally transposable into a "small-minded pedagogy" (27) that reserves for philosophical discourse itself a "limitless sovereignty" (27), names it the sole producer of its statements, and as such takes away from it any sort of naïveté. "How," writes Foucault in a different version of this response, "how could a philosophy so preoccupied with remaining inside philosophy recognize this external event, this limit-event, this initial division by which the resolution to be a philosopher and to attain truth excludes madness?"

Thirty years later, this controversy between two minds of exceptional breadth has perhaps lost part of its topicality, notably inasmuch as philosophical thought, in France and elsewhere, is today much less fascinated than it was before by the question of madness. On the philological level, the question of the place and meaning of the "argument of madness" in the *Meditations,* studied during the same period by Harry Frankfurt, has been illuminated by J. M. Beyssade and F. Alquié. We remain, however, attentive, not only to the high tension of this controversy but also to its significant topical character and exceptional complexity. One part of its complexity is manifested in the triplicity of the levels on which the respective positions and styles of these two authors can be evaluated.

At first sight, nothing is more striking in these two authors than the opposition of their interests and the genres they use. *Madness and Civilization* addressed, occasionally and in fact a bit thoughtlessly, a known but neglected text of the *First Meditation,* in order to concern itself, for about 600 or 700 pages, with two or three centuries of transformation of discourses and practices. In contrast, Derrida's text, like many others, presents itself in fact as an extremely erudite and tight meditation on how to interpret a few sentences. On one side, we are dealing with an enterprise based essentially—with reservations about the complications tied to its specific definition—on the history of ideas, especially scientific ideas, and on the history of institutions, an enterprise that thus takes as its particular task to identify the function and operation of such and such a statement or collection of statements, produced at such a date, in a context or field that exceeds them. On the other side, we are dealing with a critical reflection and an interpretive exercise that, in the textual objects they choose (always objects slightly less canonical than some, but not by far), have always attempted to exhibit the highest degree of complication: complication in terms of the paradoxical difficulty of the approach—in other words, of the constitutive adventure of interpretation, grappling with singular situations and an always idiomatic given—but also the complication of intellectual, expressive, or scriptural gestures corresponding to several functions, participating in tortuous strategies in the relation of thought or, rather, of the signatory instantiation of these textual traces, to its objects, themes, and its own definition. In Foucault's enterprise, the categorizations studied are evolutionary: the task is precisely to study within them the correlations and transformations in given historical sequences; in Derrida's approach, it is meaning itself that is in motion, differing from itself, and the identification of this difference or constitutive trembling of meaning in several exemplary texts defines by itself not a program but a form of interest and a productivity. The type of complexity that is thus subject to study has of course no equivalent in either Gueroult or Bergson; in contrast it owes a lot to the Heideggerian manner of staging and reconstituting the "said" of each great text or thinker in the history of metaphysics. And yet, as in Bergson or Gueroult, it seems that it is a matter of approaching a sui generis given in its singularity, a given that in one way or another—although, for Derrida, not without notable complications—takes the appearance of *metaphysics as such*.

On a first reading, then, they have little in common, but on a second reading, one notices at least this common interest in madness, this idea of a constitutive relation between true thought and madness that is precisely at the heart of the disagreement and opposition of the two authors regarding the Cartesian method: Foucault sees in Cartesian doubt an intellectual strategy, while Derrida sees in it a limit-experience; for the first, Descartes distances philosophical thought from the experience and the understanding of madness in a lasting way, and it must now recapture the lost proximity; for the second, this proximity has never ceased and must as such have manifested itself—in a perhaps tenuous and always paradoxical way—throughout the history of philosophy. As a result, in two authors equally devoted to maximizing reflexive clarity and justifying their positions, there are more questions effectively or virtually in common—on philosophical thought, metaphysics, the transcendental, rationality, historicity, alterity, and the outside—than would first appear—more questions in common, but also, on a third reading, some notable reversals in concerns or emphasis that I must briefly mention because they permit us to return to our initial question.

The reversals in question are expressed in two ways.

1. The Foucault who responds to Derrida after 10 years' distance is—necessarily—much more sensitive than the author of the *Madness and Civilization* to the order and the form of the *Meditations*. The wording of the 1961 work—to begin with the first sentences: "On the path of doubt, Descartes meets madness *next to* dreams and all the forms of error. Doesn't this possibility of being mad risk depossessing him of his own body, like the world outside can slip into error or consciousness drift into sleep?"—revealed at best a certain penchant for shortcuts, at worst a certain casualness with respect to the norms of Cartesian commentary. The Foucault of 1972 has reread Descartes and meditated on the form and strategy of the *Meditations* in a way that allows him not only to point out certain inaccuracies and hyperboles in Derrida's reading but also to compare the thematization of madness with that of dreams and, generally, to define the organization of the Cartesian meditation with a precision, rigor, and virtuosity that have few equals. By force of circumstance, it is therefore with a meticulous description of the Cartesian text and according to a purely internal exploration that the Cartesian exclusion of madness is now demonstrated again—in a manner on the whole as clear as the first but less adamant in its formulation. At the same time, the historical meaning of the Cartesian text—the "initial division by which the resolution to be a philosopher and to attain truth excludes madness"[13]—ceases to be a fact (*donnée*) manifestly *anterior* to the Cartesian text and becomes a textual act (*fait*) and an operation ascribable to Cartesian thought itself. The empirical or historical exteriority to which the *Madness and Civilization* thought it could refer directly is rendered more uncertain in its status and its form of causality. This is not because the principle

of this causality is suspended but because one of the problems that Foucault had resolved to confront in *The Archeology of Knowledge* and the texts of the same period therefore presents itself. In the lecture *What Is an Author?* (1969), in which the controversy with Derrida is already notable, one thus sees the inventory and analysis of the conventions constituting the notion of the author return to a meditation on the founding act and on the sense of the "return to..." that takes such acts as its objects.[14] Foucault may have indeed intended "to free the history of thought from its subjection to transcendence..., to analyse this history, in the discontinuity that no teleology would reduce in advance..., to allow it to be deployed in anonymity on which no transcendental constitution would impose the form of the subject"[15]: yet the question of the relation between the anonymous deployment of discourses and mechanisms and certain subjective *acts* (unless it was a question of the fact of subjectivity itself) could no longer cease to preoccupy him.

2. In his critique of *Madness and Civilization*, Derrida for his part hadn't wanted to deny the accomplishment of a certain distancing of madness in the *Meditations* by philosophizing reason. He had only displaced and delayed this action from the supposedly pre-philosophical exclamation of the *First Meditation* ("But what? These are mad people...") until the reflexive apprehension of the Cogito by an *ego cogitans*, itself defined as a *ratio*. All the while refusing to see in an authentically Cartesian utterance the simple mark of a mutation exterior to the philosophical order, he had therefore admitted the reality of a certain event stemming as such from a certain historicity ("the historical enunciation through which philosophy tranquilizes itself and excludes madness" [62]—a madness about which, in addition, Derrida reproaches Foucault for having formulated a metaphysical and unduly unified concept). Rather than being understood as the negation of its historicity, the attribution of an "eternal and essential" (62) classicism to the Cartesian gesture results from the complication of the concept of historicity itself, a complication that takes up—together with the criticism of the *idea* of a "history of madness" without a reference to the problem of the *First Meditation*—the whole first half of Derrida's lecture, which for the rest responds to the directing inquiries of his early research (on the Husserlian notion of historicity) and to which Foucault barely

returns in his response. Just as the problem raised, *volens nolens*, by the passage that *Madness and Civilization* consecrates to Descartes is that of the relation between intellectual (and textual) eventiality and a much more general history, the problem of the historical inscription or dimension of philosophical gestures, and thus historiography as such, is reopened here rather than closed. This problem poses itself not only for each of the textual or thematic constructions to which Derrida turns his attention but also for deconstruction itself. And if the Derridean statements concerning this historical inscription have in general an aporetic, suspensive, or deliberately evasive appearance,[16] what one can call a transcendental skepticism with respect to the possibility of historiography has been associated, in putting texts in relation to one another—and not only to each other but also to events and given facts—with the highest degree of meticulousness and precaution. In general, beyond the provocative declarations ("there is no outside the text" [*"il n'y a pas de hors-texte"*]), it is of course inaccurate to say that Derridean deconstruction took only texts as its objects or that it developed in only a purely internalist style. The gestures considered by Derridean analysis, always with the same radical distrust of fixed structures and preestablished categories, are in no way purely discursive or purely intellectual acts: from the outset, they belonged to a historicopragmatic space that it is undoubtedly as impossible to describe as to totalize, yet which was nothing but that of the history of institutions, intersubjective factuality, and, to use its least incorrect denomination, the political and all of its dimensions.

THREE

If we must, then, note, between the two contemporary authors I spoke of, the principle of a certain convergence of preoccupations, verified and perhaps accentuated by a background of controversy, then the convergence is of course subject to historical interpretation: it is, in Foucaultian terms, a question of *épistémé* and results from the unity of an intellectual period. Yet one can give as well a philosophical and, if the case arises, a pedagogical interpretation of it, concluding that there exists a real unity in the complex of problems that the historian of philosophy (and undoubtedly not only the historian of philosophy) must confront in a way that perhaps varies according to the period and the object but that is fundamentally mutual and indissoluble. The bitterness of the controversy between Foucault and Derrida over the "argument of madness," the disagreement that subsisted between them even after new, more subtle analyses should have sufficiently demonstrated to whoever wishes to resist the Sirens of subjectivism that we still do not know precisely enough what was carried out, or is carried out, in the *First Meditation* and that in spite of the overaccumulation of commentaries and critiques, the singular *type* of the Cartesian process has not yet been apprehended with sufficient precision—with the risk that the task be specifically to define its constitutive ambiguity. On this level, between the fully mastered process and the limit-experience, the problem is precisely to conceive of a *nonexcluded third*, and in the present case less a median modality than a synthesis, with questions like, How can an intellectual vertigo (that of hyperbolic doubt) be organized? and How can this organized vertigo be tested?

We are thus, with respect to a certain textual matter, summoned to a superior degree of reflection that should coincide with what a great French historian of philosophy and reader of all of the authors I just mentioned, Gérard Lebrun, deceased in 1999, called the optimal adjustment [*réglage*] of interpretation.[17] In the case that interests us, this reflection brings into play at once the form of the *Meditations*, the definition of the project or the philosophical operation, the nature of a heroically founding intellectual experience, and the statuses assigned to *reason, madness,* and their variants in a designated historicocultural totality. One can cite the example of relatively less complex enigmas that, however, call for a deliberation on the nature of philosophical operations, the hierarchy of registers and intentions, the degree of constitution of theories, the directing intentions, and the pertinent categorizations: thus, for example—an example close to Descartes, well-known to several of us and that I would have liked to develop—the question of what Antoine Arnauld meant exactly in *Des Vraies et des fausses idées* (*Of True and False Ideas*) (1683) in affirming the possibility of our minds' immediately recognizing material things, "without there being any middle between our perceptions and the object."[18] Whatever the case, the adjustment of which Lebrun speaks constitutively rests on several sorts of resources or virtues: a superior attention to texts' form (with, if needed, a consideration of pertaining uncertainties), an extension of the field of comparison, an inventiveness in identifying pertinent themes (namely, in Lebrun's terms, the "refinement of the topic" and the "refinement of interest"[19]), a concern for the precision of technical language, an interest for the elements of cultural history, and a meditation on a certain number of fundamental problems, relative, notably, to historicity and the philosophical genre as such.

Along with the necessity and constitutive pluridimensionality of this adjustment, it is first of all, the unity of our discipline that will certainly be confirmed, with a strong relativization of the antinomy discussed at length here. In reality, the commentator the most inclined to an internalist monography never deals of course with a single object but always with a complex and undetermined collection of textual or intellectual traces, most of which are constitutively dated and therefore to be compared with each other, with the necessary mention of and inquiry into the mediations. Whether this is done through explicit references to one another within the texts, their heuristic comparison, or the use it makes of a necessarily dated metalanguage, the matter of his research is saturated with historicity. Conversely, the historian the most concerned with drawing up a complete picture of the intellectual evolutions of a period must be aware that this picture cannot be valid because of the rigor of its construction alone but that it must be informed by as meticulous and complete a reexploration of the texts and documents involved as possible. In no case, as we well know, does the diversity of the genres practiced imply the rigorous dissociability of the requisites.

I would like to insist on only two more points. The first point is that the unity of our discipline will precisely never be confirmed except through a persevering practice of the adjustment in question—thus in the form of a thoroughly *reflective* history of philosophy. This activity is, of course, dependent on the availability of a considerable number of solidly established textual and factual data; but far from being able to define itself only as a production of new data, it must just as necessarily define itself as an exploration of the limits of this given that are not only factual bounds; in this respect, we are historians of philosophy not only insofar as we *know* in a very extensive way what such and such authors have written and how it has been interpreted, but insofar as we know *that we do not yet know well enough* what such and such an author did or even wanted to do, what role such and such a text has played, and what, in sum, the global physiognomy of all that concerns us can be. The reflective character of this history is linked to weighing the interpretation of details, to the consciousness of the overabundance of virtually pertinent correlations, and equally to the awareness of the current lacunae in our information, but it is also linked to the consciousness of the fact that the philosophical works we are treating, whether they are major or even minor texts, are objects that *as such* are enigmatic to the highest degree, between which we can discern infinite differences but about which, in the final analysis, we are again reduced to *seeking* the adequate language or conceptuality; the same thing could be said of the history of philosophy as a process, whose detail we know very well, but whose interpretation, or even simply the representation as a whole remains, we must admit, unavailable.

The second and last point I would like to underscore is the following: the problem of the philosophical work as such, this problem of the history of philosophy as such, and the necessity of a related reflection are, in my opinion, things that, in principle, we should be taking the greatest care to render intelligible to our students. I am not saying this should be our first task, which remains in this case the organization of their familiarization with a fundamental philosophical library and verifying and facilitating the assimilation of its content. But neither is it the last of our tasks, in the sense that we would need to teach them a relatively schematic subject matter in the first place in order to elevate them only later to an awareness of certain complications. Certain complications—not all of them, but some of the ones we experience or have experienced, chosen by our care—must be presented and recorded early on, either through a thorough study of a text, or by testing a comparison between different texts, or by direct instruction of the history of notions and the complexity of historical relations. This means, perhaps, that the program of yearly courses of the kind called From Descartes to Kant, whose conception concerns the participants of the present colloquium, could be reconsidered in favor of a more segmented approach that would concentrate on either an author or a small group of authors, or on a text or a small number of texts, or on a problem or a small number of problems by putting at students' disposal a more global historical knowledge. But this means, of course, that the themes, texts, and authors to be studied are assumed to be defined; the essential element of intellectual communication to ensure stems from the commentary to which each teacher matches a study of the object of the day. In any case, whether we're talking about the first or last years of the curriculum, the type of interrogating consciousness that it is a question of cultivating can only ever be presented or actualized by samples or on samples of textual matter. But the idea of the work of thought; the ideas of instauration, tradition, periods, institutions, and intellectual revolution; the ideas of the plurality of genres, styles, modes of enunciation, and intellectual interests; and the idea of the immense complexity we are addressing and that of our own task with respect to it: how could constituting them from the outset as ultimate objects of discussion not be essential to teaching the new history of philosophy?

Translated by Nicole Simek and Zahi Zalloua

NOTES

1. I once suggested as a paper topic to *license* (third-year) students, with whom I was working on the *Meditations,* to write "Eight Objections" to these *Meditations.* The exercise was judged exciting but completely unusual. It produced only disappointing results, with the exception of one paper written in Latin whose main quality was its language.
2. Roughly equivalent to the master's level in the American system. (Trans. note)
3. *An Introduction to Metaphysics. The Creative Mind.* Totowa, N.J.: Littlefield, Adams, 108.
4. Op. cit., Aubier, 1988, t. III, p. 866.
5. *Philosophie de l'histoire de la philosophie.* Paris: Aubier, 1979.
6. Cf. Michaud (Y.), "The End of the History of Philosophy," *Social Research,* Summer 1982, vol. 49, n. 2, 467–80, which gives a stimulating comparison of Gueroult and Hume and contains a sharp critique of the French method of teaching history of philosophy. ("In short, it would often be necessary to reverse Gueroult's position by showing in what way a philosophy is in its principle a ruined monument," 478.)
7. Especially with F. Alquié and H. Gouhier. One must name Gouhiers's critical work as achieving an exceptional and unequaled equilibrium or combination of historiographic care and philosophical empathy.
8. Descartes, *Meditations on First Philosophy in Which the Existence of God and the Distinction of the Soul from the Body Are Demonstrated,* 3rd edition, trans. Donald A. Cress. Indianapolis: Hackett Publishing, 1993, 14.
9. Cf. the beginning of ch. 2, *Histoire de la folie à l'âge classique,* 2nd edition, Gallimard, 1972, 56–58.
10. Ibid., 57.
11. First published in the *Revue de Métaphysique et de Morale,* 1964, n. 3 and 4; quoted here in *Writing and Difference,* trans. A. Bass, Chicago: Chicago University Press, 1978.
12. "My Body, This Paper, This Fire," trans. Geoff Bennington, in *Oxford Literary Review* 4, n. 1, 1979, 9–28.
13. *Réponse à Derrida,* loc. cit., 1163.
14. "I wonder whether this notion of 'writing,' sometimes reduced to common usage, does not transpose, in a transcendental anonymity, the author's empirical characters....Isn't lending to writing an originary status a way of retranslating, in transcendental terms, the theological affirmation of its sacred nature on the one hand, and the critical affirmation of its creative nature on the other?" (*Dits et écrits,* 823).
15. *The Archaeology of Knowledge,* trans. A. M. Sheridan Smith. New York: Pantheon Books, 203.

16. Cf., for example, "A 'Madness' Must Watch Over Thinking," an interview with F. Ewald, 1991, in *Points…Interviews, 1974–1994*, ed. Elisabeth Weber and trans. Peggy Kamuf. Stanford, Calif.: Stanford University Press, 1995, 358: "Can one say that we are in an age of deconstruction? Let's say the age of certain *thematics* of deconstruction, which in fact receives a certain name and can formalize itself up to a certain point in methods and modes of reproduction. But deconstructions do not begin or end there. It is certainly necessary but still very difficult to account for this intensification and this passing into the theme and the name, into this beginning of formalization. What would be the appropriate historical marker? I don't know. To be sure, one should never give up on the historical recognition of such signposts, but I wonder whether something can take the form here of a sole 'historical marker,' whether even the question can be posed in this fashion without implying precisely a historiographical axiomatics that ought perhaps to be suspended, since it is too bound up with deconstructible philosophemes. The things we are talking about ('deconstructions,' if you will) do not happen within what would be recognizably called 'history,' an orientable history with periods, ages, or revolutions, mutations, emerging phenomena, ruptures, breaks, *episteme*, paradigms, *themata* (to answer according to the most diverse and familiar historiographic codes). Every 'deconstructive,' reading proposes another one of these multiple 'markers,' but I do not know around which great axis they are to be oriented."

17. Cf. G. Lebrun, "Devenir de la philosophie," in D. Kambouchner, ed., *Notions de philosophie.* Paris: Folio-Gallimard, 1995, t. III, 615 sq.

18. *Des Vraies et des fausses idées*, ch. VI, in fine; re-ed. Fayard, 1986, 60. See E. J. Kremer's English translation, Mellen Press, 1990.

19. Op. cit., 601.

Response to Denis Kambouchner

BÉATRICE LONGUENESSE

DENIS KAMBOUCHNER'S paper brings to our attention an aspect of the history of philosophy and its teaching that is specifically related to the French philosophical tradition. He addresses this tradition by considering four examples: Henri Bergson, Martial Gueroult, Michel Foucault, and Jacques Derrida. In my comments I will focus on what I take to be the most important points in Kambouchner's diagnosis, and I will offer a few friendly amendments to it. I will then offer some thoughts about what the relation may be between the tradition in history of philosophy described by Kambouchner and the "New Histories of Philosophy" whose teaching Jerry Schneewind invited us to think about.

Both of Kambouchner's first two examples (Bergson and Gueroult) present, albeit in very different ways, a conception according to which the main task of the historian of philosophy is to grasp the peculiar unity of a philosopher's thought. (1) According to Bergson, understanding a philosopher is grasping, or at least approaching, however imperfectly, his fundamental intuition. Kambouchner cites Bergson's famous declaration, in the 1911 lecture L'Intuition Philosophique (Philosophical Intuition): "A philosopher worthy of the name has said only one thing. Or rather, he endeavored to say it, rather than actually said it." (2) According to Gueroult, understanding a philosopher's thought, or even a particular philosophical text, is bringing to light the systematic unity of its fundamental concepts and leading arguments. Gueroult himself gave magisterial examples of such a method in his own studies of Spinoza (the two-volume study of books 1 and 2 of the *Ethics*), of Descartes's *Meditations* (*Descartes selon l'Ordre des Raisons*, 1953; English translation: *Descartes's Philosophy Interpreted according to the Order of Reasons*, 1984), of Malebranche (*Étendue et Psychologie chez Malebranche*, 1939, *Malebranche*, 1955), and of Fichte (*L'Évolution et la Structure de la Doctrine de la Science chez Fichte*, 1930; *Étude sur Fichte*, 1977). In contrast, the last two authors cited by Kambouchner (Foucault and Derrida) offer two examples of the ways in which traditional views of the internal unity of a philosophical work have been challenged.

Now if I understand him correctly, Kambouchner's intention in analyzing these four examples is to show that when all is said and done, the antinomy between an internalist approach and an externalist approach to the history of philosophy is not as stringent as one might initially think. He calls internalist (or monographic) an approach that treats the production of a particular philosopher, or even one particular text, as an independent entity having its own internal logic and motivations. He calls externalist (or historiographic) an approach that is sensitive to external influences, whether these influences have to be identified in earlier philosophical developments, in other fields of thought (scientific, religious, or political), or even in the institutional, social, or political context of the time. Kambouchner points out that in texts that preceded the 1911 lecture Philosophical Intuition, Bergson expressed a more flexible view of the relation between philosophy and the sciences— especially physics, evolutionary biology, and psychology. Similarly, however internalist and, to borrow Kambouchner's words, sometimes "frighteningly" ahistorical Gueroult's expressed theory of the history of philosophy sometimes seems, his own practice as a historian of philosophy is generally more open to externalist considerations. There are probably differences to be made here: Gueroult's extraordinary volumes on Spinoza are less dogmatically bound to a quest for systematicity than his *Descartes selon l'Ordre des Raisons*. His *Leibniz: Dynamique et Métaphysique* is a pioneering externalist approach, wherein Leibniz's metaphysics is studied in relation to his physics and his debates with such scientific figures as Bernoulli and Huyghens as well as Descartes. The encouraging fact here is that in the case of Bergson as well as Gueroult, what they do as philosophers and historians of philosophy is often better than what they say they do, or ought to do. This would confirm Kambouchner's suggestion that when it comes to the actual practice of the history of philosophy, any historian worthy of the name combines, to varying degrees, both internalist and externalist approaches.

Where do Derrida and Foucault respectively fall in this debate?

As Kambouchner reminds us, in chapter 2 of his *Histoire de la Folie à l'Âge Classique* (1st ed. 1961; 2nd ed. 1972; English translation: *Madness and Civilization: A History of Insanity in the Age of Reason*, 1965), Foucault argued that the "argument from madness" in Descartes's *First Meditation* was emblematic of a division between reason and unreason that is a grounding feature of the classical age, as opposed to the greater awareness and acceptance of the proximity between madness and reason that was characteristic of the Renaissance. Foucault's interpretation of this passage is of course characteristic of his radical questioning of the modern models of rationality, a questioning he will pursue, most notably, in *The Order of Things* and in *Discipline and Punish*. As Kambouchner notes, when Foucault opens chapter 2 of *L'Histoire de la Folie à l'Âge Classique* with his controversial interpretation of Descartes's argument from madness, what is of concern to him is not the argumentative strategy of Descartes's *Meditations*, but rather the place Descartes thus earns in the 17th-century enterprise to constitute reason by a gesture of exclusion that is not only intellectual or philosophical but also, and mainly, institutional.

Derrida's rebuttal of Foucault's analysis may seem at first to call us back to a more internalist approach: in his 1963 lecture Cogito et Histoire de la Folie, Derrida gives Foucault a stern lesson in reading texts. He reminds him that the madness argument is followed, in Descartes's *First Meditation*, by the dream argument, which wreaks havoc in any attempt to protect oneself from the threat of the former. You think you are free of the illusions of the madman, but how different is your own situation when you dream? Worse even, how much more radical is the unraveling of your reason if you have to admit the possibility that you think under the spell of an evil genius! As Kambouchner notes, Derrida's rebuttal is not just methodological (telling Foucault: "read the text, nothing but the text, but the whole text!"). The rebuttal is also doctrinal. Foucault interpreted Descartes's text as originating the division, characteristic of the classical age, between reason and unreason, or madness. Derrida objects that this passage, if read together with the dream argument and the evil genius argument that follow it, manifests an acute consciousness of the proximity between what Kambouchner calls the vertigo of philosophical doubt—or philosophical skepticism—and madness. This, according to Derrida, is not proper to a particular time; it is the very condition of philosophical thinking as such.

As Kambouchner notes, despite the typically Franco-French sharpness of the confrontation, even here the alternative between internal analysis of the text and reference to external influences and motivations is not a sharp divide. In his 1972 reply to Derrida, Foucault essentially endeavored to outdo him in providing a more precise textual analysis of the dream argument and its place in the overall strategy of the *Meditations*. Derrida, for his part, never denied the importance of what he called the political—namely, the field of social, national/cultural, and political forces at work in the production of a philosophical text. As Kambouchner reminds us, Derrida even turned against Foucault the reproach of ahistoricism when he accused him of having a metaphysical view of madness as the expression of some undifferentiated dark force by the exclusion of which, or by resistance to which, modern reason constitutes itself.

An additional remark is worth making where Foucault is concerned. In the English edition of *L'Histoire de la Folie*—*Madness and Civilization*, 1965—the discussion of the madness argument has disappeared. That's not the only passage that is cut from the English edition: the latter has been considerably shortened compared with the French. Nevertheless, one may ask, why has this particular passage disappeared? It is maintained in the second edition of the book in French (1972), and Foucault's reply to Derrida is added as an appendix. Maybe Foucault so well recognized that his earlier analysis could not stand as it was that he cut it in the shorter, English version rather than maintaining it without the further clarification he was able to give in the longer, French version. But it is also possible that really he was more interested in analyzing the institutional division between reason and madness in the modern period than in analyzing a philosophical text by an author as canonical as Descartes, even if that text had in his eyes the merit of being generally neglected. A few years later, in *Les Mots et les Choses* (1966, English edition, *The Order of Things*, 1973), Foucault provocatively declared that the *épistémé*—namely, the structure of what we might call the conceptual space characteristic of the modern period—was better represented in lesser-known studies in grammar, natural history, and the analysis of wealth than in the so-called great texts of the philosophical canon. This being so, the alternative for him was not between internalist or externalist method in analyzing philosophical texts. Rather, it was between continuing to do history of philosophy as it was traditionally done or doing something else altogether. This "something else" itself came under heavy fire from historians, who had some grounds for objecting that Foucault's ambitious program was simply too broad to satisfy the canons of rigorous historical inquiry. Paradoxically, one way of reading Foucault's project is to say that it extends to history as a whole the kind of unitary approach that his more traditional predecessors (Bergson and Gueroult, in Kambouchner's examples) reserved for the history of philosophy. The result is that the very same problems that Kambouchner points out in the case of Bergson's or Gueroult's theoretical views of what history of philosophy ought to be apply even more in the case of Foucault's generalized project of analyzing the discontinuous épistémé of the Renaissance, the classical age, and modern times.

It remains, nevertheless, that in his uniquely flamboyant and provocative way, Foucault belonged to, and benefited from, a lively and active tradition in the history of philosophy in France, where both internalist and externalist requisites were, in varying proportions, taken into account. I cited some of Gueroult's own works as representative of these twofold concerns. One might cite Alexandre Koyré, known for his work both in the history of science *and* in the history of philosophy in relation to the scientific revolutions of the 17th and 18th centuries. (Koyré had a direct influence on Kuhn's own work on the nature of scientific revolutions.) Or Georges Canguilhem on the history of biology and its relation to the history of philosophy from the 18th century to present times. Or, finally, Jules Vuillemin, especially in his two books on Kant: *Physique et Métaphysique Kantiennes,* and *L'Héritage Kantien et la Révolution Copernicienne.* The first is a study of Kant's critical philosophy in light of Kant's philosophy of physics, very much in the neo-Kantian spirit of Hermann Cohen that also inspires, today, Michael Friedman's work. The second is an analysis of the posterity of Kant's critical philosophy in the 19th and early 20th centuries, a posterity Vuillemin reads as a succession of interpretations of Kant's

Critique of Pure Reason wherein pride of place is given to its three main parts, as it were in backward order. First comes Fichte, who gave primacy to the Transcendental Dialectic and its relation to Kant's practical philosophy. Then comes Cohen, who gave primacy to the Transcendental Analytic and its relation to Kant's philosophy of physics. Finally—in Vuillemin's book—comes Heidegger, who gave primacy to the Transcendental Aesthetic and Kant's emphasis on the temporality of human intuition and experience.

In mentioning these few examples (many others could be given) my purpose is to concur with a point Kambouchner emphasizes at the end of his paper. One of the problems we encounter in dealing with philosophical texts of the past is the overabundance of connections and sources of meaning, both internal and external. There is no way any single plan for a course, or even a systematically organized series of such plans in a curriculum, will do justice to the richness of the material we have to deal with. Whatever we choose to emphasize in one area of the methodological or textual spectrum will be paid for by a sacrifice in some other area. It is of course important to keep in mind some canon of basic introductory texts and some working pattern of fundamental notions that will help our students make sense of this canon. But both canon and notions will benefit from their repeated questioning by faculty and students alike.

The examples I have given also lead me to express some measure of disagreement with Kambouchner's diagnosis of the situation of history of philosophy in France in the past half century. I think it is not quite fair to say, as he does, that since World War II, the most notable studies of 17th-century French intellectual history have come from Anglophone authors. The examples I cited show that there have been (and there still are) in France studies in the history of modern philosophy that do compare with the best of what is produced in the Anglophone world. (Maybe he speaks out of excessive modesty here: in more recent times, I would include Kambouchner's own work in the bunch.) However, it is true that what Jerry Schneewind calls the new histories of philosophy bring something more than what the French or, for that matter, the European Continental tradition could bring. This is what I would like to focus on briefly in what little time I have left.

I think it is fair to say that the New Histories of Philosophy have in common a reaction against a way of conceiving and doing history of philosophy that has been more or less prevalent in analytic departments of philosophy throughout the past century. According to this conception, philosophers of the past, especially in the early modern and modern periods, were evaluated according to the conceptual, methodological, and argumentative standards developed in the context of post-Fregean, post-Russellian logical analysis. Early modern philosophy thus became all too often a catalog of errors interspersed with bright premonitions that "we," with our modern analytic tools, were finally able to sort out. We all have in mind examples of exciting and provocative studies that proceeded essentially along these lines. In reacting against this trend, to someone like me coming from the French tradition Kambouchner described, the New Histories are not so new. They're, in a way, a return to a kind of history that was done in the tradition I come from. But as I said, they are also more, precisely because they are nourished by the fairly iconoclastic approach to history that they oppose. Namely, they're nourished by a tradition wherein evaluating an argument is more important than understanding a historical context. I suggest that the New Histories will keep their bite if they do not lose that side of their ancestry—the side they react against, as any bright child should react against a parent. Not having benefited from such a parent, that side is what I have most enjoyed and benefited from since I have been in America. It is what has made it worthwhile for me to teach history of philosophy—and to teach what I had learned from reading Kant, Hegel, and the recent Continental tradition—in a primarily analytic department.

Let me now say a few words about that teaching.

My own work on Kant has focused on Kant's theory of judgment, its role in determining the argument and architectonic of the first Critique (the *Critique of Pure Reason*), and the relation between the First and the Third Critiques (the *Critique of Judgment*), wherein Kant considers the particular cases of aesthetic and teleological judgments). In teaching Kant's philosophy, whether to undergraduates or to graduate students, I am particularly concerned to help students overcome the obscurities and misunderstandings stemming from the fact that Kant's logical and epistemological vocabulary is so vastly different from the vocabulary of the contemporary logic and epistemology they may be more familiar with or, for that matter, different from any other vocabulary they may be familiar with.

I have no general recipe to propose on how best to do justice to the Kantian project as a whole in a mere 12- or 15-week course. In fact, in the 10 years I've spent at Princeton, during which I have offered an upper-level undergraduate course on Kant's philosophy every other year, I have not taught the course twice in the same way. What I can say is that one concern I've had in all versions of the course has been to introduce students to selections from the whole *Critique of Pure Reason*, including the Transcendental Dialectic (Kant's criticism of the Cartesian and Leibnizian doctrines of the soul, of early modern representations of the universe after the Galilean and Newtonian revolutions, and finally of classical attempts to prove the existence of God), rather than just the Transcendental Aesthetic and Analytic. This is important both because the issues considered in the Dialectic are what initially motivated Kant's critical endeavor and because these issues make Kant's place in the history of philosophy and Kant's relation to the history of scientific, religious, and moral thought clearer than would the sole consideration of the arguments of the Aesthetic and Analytic.

Even so, such a plan still essentially leaves out, of course, Kant's practical philosophy. This raises the same worry as the one Jerry Schneewind voiced with respect to introductions to early modern philosophy: Why always give precedence, in an introduction to Kant's critical system, to his theoretical over his practical philosophy, even though an essential aspect of his solution to the problem of metaphysics consists precisely in the new relation and contrast he establishes between the two uses of reason: theoretical and practical? And how can one understand later developments of German Idealism, or, more generally, 19th-century German (or German-influenced) philosophy (including the Danish Kierkegaard as well as Schopenhauer or Nietzsche, to name only a few) without having given its full due to practical reason in the overall unity of Kant's critical system? Because of this worry, one version of my course on Kant's critical philosophy started with the second preface to the

Critique of Pure Reason and then continued directly with the *Groundworks of the Metaphysics of Morals*, followed by selections from the *Critique of Practical Reason, Religion within the Limits of Reason Alone*, and, finally, *Metaphysics of Morals*.

The problem of selecting manageable material is even greater where German Idealism is concerned. I have found it helpful to organize the course around a guiding theme. I have offered two versions of the course. The first centered on Hegel's moral, religious, and political thought and its influence in 19th-century political and social thought. We started with Hegel's Early Theological Writings, continued with excerpts from the *Phenomenology of Spirit*, devoted almost half the course to the *Philosophy of Right*, and finished with selections from the young Marx. Another version of the course was organized around the notion of self-consciousness. It started with selections from the second preface to Kant's *Critique of Pure Reason* and from *Groundworks of the Metaphysics of Morals*. It continued with the introduction to Fichte's *Wissenschaftslehre* (stressing the primacy of the practical "I"). The bulk of the course was then devoted to selections from the *Phenomenology of Spirit*, especially the Lordship and Bondage dialectic, together with selections from the numerous discussions it elicited in 20th-century philosophy.

I have also offered courses in recent Continental philosophy (focusing, again, on issues related to self-consciousness, with selections from Husserl, Heidegger, Sartre, Merleau-Ponty, and Foucault, in varying proportions). In addition, I have started developing a new course in which I try to follow the history of notions of self-consciousness and personal identity—from early modern philosophy to present time in both the analytic and the Continental traditions. So far, I have experimented with this course only in the more flexible form of a junior seminar. But I hope to develop it soon as a lecture course as well. It seems to me that such topical courses, in which one follows a notion over a long period of time and in very different traditions, are important means for giving the students a sense of the transformations of philosophical problems, concepts, and arguments. This is one of the important ways in which doing history of philosophy is an essential component of doing philosophy.

BIBLIOGRAPHY

Bergson, Henri. "L'Intuition Philosophique, Conférence faite au Congrès de philosophie de Bologne le 10 avril 1911," in *La Pensée et le Mouvant.* Paris: Presses Universitaires de France, 1st edition, 1938, 92nd edition, 1985. Engl. trans., Mabelle L. Andison, *The Creative Mind.* New York: Philosophical Library, 1946.

Canguilhem, Georges. *Études d'Histoire et de Philosophie des Sciences.* Paris: Vrin, 1968.

———. *Idéologie et Rationalité dans l'Histoire des Sciences de la Vie: Nouvelles Études d'Histoire et de Philosophie des Sciences.* Paris: Vrin, 1977. Engl. trans., Arthur Goldhammer, *Ideology and Rationality in the History of the Life Sciences.* Cambridge, Mass.: MIT Press, 1988.

———. *Le Normal et le Pathologique.* Paris: Presses Universitaires de France, 1975. Engl. trans. Carolyn R. Fawcett, with editorial collaboration of Robert S. Cohen and with Introduction by Michel Foucault: "On the Normal and the Pathological." Dortrecht, Holland/Boston: D. Reidel Publishing, 1978.

Derrida, Jacques. "Cogito et Histoire de la Folie," *Revue de Métaphysique et de Morale,* 1963; repr. in *L'Écriture et la différence.* Paris: Seuil, 1967. Engl. trans. with Introduction and Notes, Alan Bass, *Writing and Difference.* London: Routledge.

Foucault, Michel. *Folie et Déraison: Histoire de la Folie à l'Âge Classique.* Paris: Plon, 1961; 2nd edition, *Histoire de la Folie à l'Âge Classique.* Paris: Gallimard, 1972. Engl. trans., Richard Howard, *Madness and Civilization: A History of Insanity in the Age of Reason.* New York: Vintage Books, 1965.

———. *Les Mots et les choses: une Archéologie des sciences humaines.* Paris: Gallimard, 1966. Engl. trans., *The Order of Things. An Archeology of the Human Sciences.* New York: Pantheon Books, 1971; repr. New York: Vintage Books, 1973.

———. *Surveiller et Punir: Naissance de la Prison.* Paris: Gallimard, 1975. Engl. trans., Alan Sheridan, *Discipline and Punish: The Birth of Prison.* New York: Vintage, 1955.

Gueroult, Martial. *L'Évolution et la Structure de la Doctrine de la Science chez Fichte.* Paris: Les Belles Lettres, 1930.

———. *Étendue et Psychologie chez Malebranche.* Paris: Les Belles Lettres, 1939.

———. *Descartes selon l'Ordre des Raisons,* Tome 1: *L'Âme et Dieu;* Tome 2: *L'Âme et le Corps.* Paris: Aubier-Montaigne, 1953. Engl. trans., *Descartes's Philosophy Interpreted according to the Order of Reasons.* Chicago: University of Chicago Press, 1984.

————. *Malebranche*. Paris: Aubier, 1955–59 (3 vol.).

————. *Études sur Fichte*. Paris: Aubier-Montaigne, 1977.

————. *Leibniz. Dynamique et Métaphysique*, suivi de *Note sur le Principe de la Moindre Action chez Maupertuis*. Paris: Aubier-Montaigne, 1967.

————. *Spinoza*—Tome I, *Dieu*; Tome II, *L'Âme et le Corps*. Paris: Aubier-Montaigne, 1968–74.

Kambouchner, Denis. *L'Homme des Passions. Commentaire sur Descartes.* Tome I: *Analytique*; Tome II: *Canonique*. Paris: Albin-Michel, 1995.

Koyré, Alexandre. *Du Monde clos à l'univers infini*. Paris: Gallimard, 1955. Engl. trans., *From the Closed World to the Infinite Universe*. New York: Harper, 1958.

————. *Études Newtoniennes*. Paris: Gallimard, 1961. Engl. trans., *Newtonian Studies*. Cambridge, Mass.: Harvard University Press, 1965.

Vuillemin, Jules. *L'Héritage Kantien et la Révolution Copernicienne. Fichte, Cohen, Heidegger*. Paris: Presses Universitaires de France, 1954.

————. *Physique et Métaphysique Kantiennes*. Paris: Presses Universitaires de France, 1955.

Teaching the History of Philosophy in 19th-Century Germany

ULRICH JOHANNES SCHNEIDER

WHEN WE TAKE an interest in philosophy, we are not, by definition, asking for historical information about philosophy. Our study of philosophy, however, makes us consider past philosophers and this, I think, also by definition. Philosophizing has become, ever since the 19th century, an activity deeply devoted to reading older texts. Even those who openly deny this fact do so despite having themselves received an education almost entirely historicizing philosophy. This is not to say that philosophy is of no concern to the present or that it has turned into scholarship. The relation between historiographical work and philosophical interest is not easily explained, not least of all because a well-established legend has made history look irreconcilably different from philosophy—even hostile to it. This legend was produced by historians of philosophy, presenting philosophy foremost as a theoretical activity. We have inherited two traditions from the 19th century, when the history of philosophy was shaped into the preferred way of studying philosophy, when it became the way to do philosophy, but when also the legend was spread that philosophy had its own history, a history of arguments, ideas, and systems.

What does it mean to *do philosophy historically,* and when does the legend of philosophy begin? When Hegel tried to give a logical explanation of philosophy's history, was he doing the same thing as Eduard Zeller in his account of Greek thought, or Kuno Fischer in his narrative of modern philosophy? I do not believe so, and I shall suggest in the following that we should carefully differentiate between the different activities commonly referred to as the history of philosophy.[1] I will point out the enormous productivity of the 19th century in terms of printed books devoted to the history of philosophy. I will also point to the context in which these were produced and used rather than examining individual works or authors. There is an entirely new context in the 19th century, which is the study of philosophy. A proper culture developed around the historical interest in philosophy, and it is this culture I want to sketch here.

PRODUCTIVITY OF THE 19TH CENTURY

The 19th century is prodigiously rich in historical studies, and studies devoted to the history of philosophy prove no exception. Quoting statistics I undertook several years ago, I can provide impressive numbers for the linguistic areas of German, English, and French. There were 120 German, 37 English, and 86 French authors writing book-length texts on the history of philosophy from 1810 to 1899. Even more telling is the number of works they produced: 155 titles in German, 56 in English, and 108 in French. Many German and French works, few in English, comprised more than one volume, and so we get 248 volumes in German, 77 volumes in English, and 165 volumes in French on the history of philosophy, and those were only first editions. (Überweg, with 8 editions before 1900, and Schwegler, with 15, have not been counted.)[2]

The history of philosophy was in demand mainly because of teaching necessities; the authors were, in their majority, professors: the German authors at a university or a *Gymnasium*, the English-writing authors and translators as college or university professors in England, Scotland, or Ireland. The French authors were mostly teachers at a *collège* or at a university. What in the 18th century still was an exception—the history of philosophy being a proper part of the *historia literaria* tradition and the historian of philosophy being a scholar before anything else[3]—became a rule in the 19th century. Even if in France, like in the English-speaking countries, new universities were created later than in Germany, there was an obvious connection between writing a book on the history of philosophy and teaching philosophy.

However, the overall picture is not detailed enough to tell us about the driving forces behind all of this historiographical frenzy. Nietzsche in one of his diagnoses of his time spoke of "the historical man" and made him responsible also for the "erudite appearance of philosophy."[4] This does not lead to detailed observation either. In retrospect, we clearly have to acknowledge different types of the history of philosophy. There is the *general history*, encompassing the whole time span from ancient Greek philosophy to the present time. After Tennemann started his 11-volume account in 1798 and finished it in 1819, in Germany there were Hegel and Heinrich Ritter with several volumes each and in addition, a great many one-volume handbooks, as, for instance, Schwegler, Stöckl, or Windelband, to name but the successful ones. In England, George Henry Lewes and Frederick Denison Maurice were most productive authors; in France it was Pierre-Marie Brin; and, translated from the Spanish, González represented the history of philosophy in several volumes. The greater part again was handbook style and sometimes rather short, but still general in scope. So we find with notable exceptions that general histories of philosophy were often produced according to teaching needs.

As a second genre, *histories of ancient Greek and Roman philosophy* required comparatively more philological skills and were written with scholarly ambition too. The success of Zeller's *Philosophie der Griechen*, first published in four volumes 1844–1852 and translated into four English volumes and three French volumes, can probably not be explained solely by pedagogical requirements, even if the study of Greek and Roman literature was the common means of higher education. The history of Greek and Roman philosophy was at any rate closely linked to a long-standing tradition of scholarship and erudition, whatever extension the so-called classical education had beyond schools and universities. Ancient history was also the field of religious arguments, as witness in France the works on the school of Alexandria by Jacques Matter, Jean-Marie Prat, Jules Simon, Jules Barthélemy-Saint-Hilaire, and Étienne Vacherot.[5]

Yet another feature characterized *histories of modern philosophy*, accounting for the philosophy since Bacon, Descartes, or Kant and aiming at the actual situation of 19th-century philosophical thought. These works were written not as presentations of different thinkers or schools, as in the case of ancient philosophers, but mostly as histories of arguments, discoveries, and progress in psychology, logic, and science in general. This type of philosophical history came closest to the type of narrative commonly used in the history of science. Prominent authors who stuck only to modern philosophy were, for example, in German, Heinrich Moritz Chalybäus, Ludwig Feuerbach, and Karl Ludwig Michelet; in English, Dugald Stewart and John Daniel Morell; and in French, Jean-Philippe Damiron and Adolphe Franck.[6]

Other than these three distinct types of philosophical histories, more specific studies existed on the history of moral, mystic, religious, or other philosophy; of logic or parts thereof; of the philosophy of right; of aesthetics; and so on. There were obviously different historical interests at work and different types of history written about. If there was something like a "powerful urge to appropriate everything," as Prof. Ignaz Döllinger of the University of Munich, wrote in 1867 with respect to historical studies in general,[7] the histories of philosophy show different types with specific narratives.

Yet there is indeed one fact evident in the overall picture of the production of histories of philosophies during the 19th century, and that is the tendency toward reproduction. In the second half of the century there were more historical works reprinted than written.[8] There was no need for originality, but there was need for reliability. This tendency toward reproduction changed the character of philosophical historiography. When the young philosopher Schelling complained in 1798 that philosophy had become "a business of the learned,"[9] he was prematurely and out of philosophical disdain denouncing a phenomenon that manifested itself later much more visibly. Schelling lived long enough to witness his fear come true. By the beginning of the 1850s, shortly before Schelling's death, scholarship had overtaken philosophy to such a degree that the Prussian minister Schulze complained in a private letter that nothing much seemed of philosophical interest anymore, except logic and the history of philosophy.[10] As if to certify the new spirit of the time, Friedrich Adolf Trendelenburg, professor at the University of Berlin, published in the same year, 1852, a collection of essays under the title *Historical Contributions to Philosophy*, remarrying verbatim philology and philosophy with no problem at all.[11] Considering the historiographical activities in the field of philosophy, this title was emblematic of his age, the age of "historical contributions" to philosophy.

My thesis is that whatever the nature or the type of history written of whatever kind or period of philosophy, the historical interest can be separated from the philosophical interest not as being totally independent but as being an interest in its own right, with proper motives, aims, and methods.[12] However, the story goes that philosophy itself turned historical during the 19th century and that it was somewhat unsurprising that *historical* contributions to philosophy could indeed be contributions *to philosophy*. The influence of Hegelianism was thought to be important, even if Wilhelm Wundt, anti-Hegelian par excellence, also defended the history of philosophy as a philosophically important field of exercise. Wundt confessed in his autobiography to have lectured with much enthusiasm on the history of philosophy for mostly systematic reasons.[13] Two questions arise: Is the history of philosophy part of philosophy? and Is "doing the history of philosophy" a task of the philosopher, and in what way?

I will try to answer these questions in two parts. Starting with the observation that neither Hegel nor Wundt *wrote* about the history of philosophy but *lectured* on it, I will first shortly depict the history of philosophy teaching in 19th-century Germany and show that the history of philosophy was indeed part of philosophy—philosophy understood as an academic discipline. Second, I will consider the task of the philosopher confronting the history of philosophy in teaching, which will show the extent to which historical knowledge played a role in the shaping of the discipline.

PHILOSOPHY TEACHING

The following remarks concern 19th-century Germany, where I studied closely the structure and changes of the philosophical curriculum during the 19th century.[14] I start with three quotations: In 1799 the poet Jean Paul wrote about the study of philosophy that any young teacher would begin by trading the goods of others but will surely sell "his own stuff" after having made progress in his discipline. In 1854 Prof. Karl von Raumer of the University of Erlangen found it not suitable for a philosophy teacher to wear "other people's gowns" and counseled against the use of compendiums in lecture courses. Reflecting on his lifelong academic career, Ernst Troeltsch resigned in 1921, saying, "All we do is maybe not entirely useless, but epigonic anyway."[15]

Three voices framing the 19th century from its beginning, middle, and end. Three voices coinciding in the acknowledgment that philosophy teaching is endangered by historical knowledge. These are thoughtful voices filled with the hope that it could be otherwise, warning against the perils of historicizing, reflecting on the means to do so, meditating self-criticism. Schopenhauer and Nietzsche in their well-known attacks on university philosophy were unforgiving and apodictic by comparison[16]; they left no hope for originality or independent judgment in a discipline that was, this much is true, not bound in a proper sense to any meaningful purpose. In Germany, philosophy was officially unrestricted, since it was not taught in school; it was in no way directly influenced by any concrete demand outside the university. There were of course academic philosophers who lost their jobs for political or religious reasons, as was true for Bruno Bauer, Ernst Ruge, Kuno Fischer, and others.[17] The university was not a place exempt from politics, yet as a scientific discipline, philosophy was unregulated with regard to contents and form.

At the time, however, no student would ever have guessed the freedom the professors had in arranging the curriculum, because it would appear pretty much set at any given semester during the 19th century. There were courses on encyclopedia and logic, serving mostly as introductory courses. In addition, there were courses on psychology and anthropology, on ethics and the philosophy of law, on pedagogy, on the philosophy of religion, and on aesthetics.[18] Throughout the century these courses formed a canon of philosophical subjects offered at all 19 German universities,[19] whatever their size, and taught in intervals by pretty much every professor.[20] The canon mirrored a somewhat encyclopedic conception of philosophy, which was also propagated in books but for which no explicit agreement can be found. It was the whole structure of the university that was considered some sort of enacted encyclopedia, at least in the first half of the century. In 1898, university historian Friedrich Paulsen stressed the fact that German universities exchanged students and professors on a regular basis. Paulsen compared this coming and going to a "bloodstream" that was uniting the German institutes of higher learning into one body.[21] It is most likely due to this commerce of teachers and students that German universities developed in much the same direction, especially concerning the curriculum.

The canon of subjects regularly taught within the discipline of philosophy would have been incomplete without lecture courses on the history of philosophy and seminar courses on individual philosophers or single philosophical texts. These two "historical" courses taken together accounted for 10 percent of all of the philosophy courses of all 19 German universities at about 1810. At the end of the 19th century, they accounted for 50 percent of all courses. Their increase came steadily, regularly, everywhere in the same undramatic rhythm. Throughout the century, the number of philosophy teachers (professors and Privatdozents) at the university level was 80 to 100; it did not change much. Teaching interests did, however, and philosophy professors taught considerably more historical courses at about 1880 than they did at about 1820. For any student late in the century, philosophy became a historicized discipline. When in 1865 the University of Berlin rearranged its lecture course program and put the lecture on the history of philosophy first—before all other courses in philosophy—this was a fine expression of what was going on everywhere: The historical approach replaced the systematic or encyclopedic one. As Prof. Albert Peip of Göttingen University put it in his inaugural lecture in 1863, the history of philosophy had become the introduction into philosophy itself.[22]

Throughout the 19th century, the canon did not disappear, and the systematic appearance of philosophy was upheld, yet at the same time the focus implicitly shifted, and the philosophy teacher became professionalized as a historically learned individual. What this means in terms of intellectual activities is complex again. Outstandingly clear is the fact that historical knowledge required new methods of teaching and learning: the seminar was an entirely new instrument. At the beginning of the century, practically all philosophy teaching was done by lecture courses, although some private lecturing took place and allowed for more intimate didactics. The seminar course became altogether frequent only in the second half of the century, but here again its steady increase shows a slow but unhindered general acceptance of this new form of teaching. These courses were not announced by the title of any subdiscipline but simply by the name of a philosopher or of a text. So Plato and Aristotle, Kant and Hegel were studied with some of their books, as were Descartes, Spinoza, and Schelling, to give the most frequent names.

Seminar teaching was not necessarily bound to an institutionalized seminar. At the end of the 19th century, only 5 German universities (out of 20) had official so-called philosophical seminars—*seminar* here meaning a room, a library, and scholarships for selected students. But the teaching practice was more widespread, and seminar-style courses were offered everywhere. They were devoted to "source study," as the young *Gymnasium* professor Julius Deuschle wrote in an article on university teaching in 1855. Deuschle was with those who urged to "expand this principle of teaching to the teaching of philosophy in general."[23] Twenty years later, Jürgen Bona Meyer, university professor in Bonn, witnessed the success of seminar teaching and called it "one of the two pillars of academic teaching"— the other being the traditional lecture course.[24]

Seminar teaching consisted really of collective reading, discussing texts, and summarizing them in one's own words, which meant, also, in the students' own words. The professor stood back behind the "source" of philosophy, which offered itself to everyone prepared and intelligent.[25] If reading Plato under the guidance of a teacher and in the presence of a few chosen fellow students meant doing philosophy historically, it also meant, by way of interpretation, doing it hermeneutically. Bound to an authoritative text, philosophy was received as a strict way of formulating ideas that nevertheless needed translation. This translation went two ways: Every reader had to translate forward his problems into the language of the philosopher under study, only to translate backward whatever "answer" there was in those texts. Seminar teaching meant engaging in historical dialogue—and in the end it meant exchanging the authority of the teacher with the authority of an examiner. Historical knowledge had already become proof of qualification in the 19th century. The doctoral dissertation as the first demonstration of the scholarly expertise of a student had its origin in the seminars. French reports on German universities, written in the '70s and '80s of the 19th century—for instance, by Gabriel Séailles, Louis Léger, and Edmond Dreyfus-Brissac—underlined seminar teaching as a modern way to overcome frontal lecturing and praised them as a specific richness of German academic teaching.[26]

So we have arrived at the answer to the first question: Was the history of philosophy part of philosophy itself? It was indeed part of it as an academic discipline, as a newly developed structure of *the study of philosophy*. However, this fact of European cultural history did not and still does not go undisputed. Nineteenth-century lecture courses on the history of philosophy as well as seminar courses slowly built up a canon of great philosophers who were in turn linked to a canon of important philosophical topics. To study these topics historically meant getting to know them and thereby entering into philosophy itself. To know the history of philosophy in detail was seen as a prerequisite for philosophizing. This was a widespread belief in the 19th century. We can turn to a critic of university philosophy as fervent as Eduard von Hartmann to see it confirmed. Hartmann wrote in 1889, "In order to go your own way in philosophy, you have to have at least studied in detail one period of the history of philosophy in someone else's view and at least one system in its original language."[27] This seems to have been common opinion among philosophy professors in Hartmann's time. They saw an immediate passage from historical studies to philosophy itself, and so we get a different answer to the question of whether the history of philosophy was part of philosophy itself. Philosophy professors believed the history of philosophy was a part of philosophy in much the same way they presented it in their lecture—that is, as dealing with identical problems and topics.

Our previous answer must be modified accordingly. The history of philosophy is not only an integral part of the study of philosophy— which did not exist prior to the 19th century; it is also ideologically part of it. The very practice of teaching philosophy historically involved spreading the legend of philosophy as something theoretical and even timeless in nature. The 19th century produced this legend along with the system of philosophical study; it linked the history of philosophy not only practically to philosophy as a discipline but also ideologically to it as an idea.

Many things have been said about the connection between philosophy and its history. It has been a topic of serious debate ever since historical knowledge played a role in the education of philosophers, meaning, since the 19th century. Different approaches are still much discussed, ranging from historical or historicist understanding to rational or systematic reconstruction. At any rate, philosophers have accepted to cope with the history of philosophy and to find out on their own whatever significance lies in it. This precisely is the outcome of *the study of philosophy*, which has been in place since the 19th century. The history of philosophy is made to contain philosophically interesting material and nothing much else, especially not the teaching system or the disciplinary structure that demands such a restriction in the first place. So the legend works. But how does it work exactly? This is the second question mentioned before: Is "doing the history of philosophy" a task of the philosopher, and in what way?

There is probably no better example than Hegel if one wants to check what Harold Bloom would call "a strong reading"—in this case, of the history of philosophy. Heidegger was certainly right and expressed the opinion of many when he wrote that no one since Hegel had been able to muster the whole of the history of philosophy in a similarly convincing way.[28] Moreover, Hegel actually believed in the idea that the history of philosophy can be read philosophically.[29] Kant had asked himself whether an a priori history of philosophy was at all possible.[30] Hegel plainly wrote it down in his introduction to his lecture courses on the history of philosophy. He turned the reading of the history of philosophy into a legend in the proper sense of the word—a *legenda historiae philosophiae*.

THE LEGEND OF PHILOSOPHY

Hegel lectured several times on the history of philosophy. He was one of the first philosophy professors to do so. His lecture courses were put out in print a couple of years after his death in 1831, and the edition was based partly on his own manuscripts, which were, however, detailed only in the introduction (*Einleitung*). Here Hegel presented his listeners with the concept of a "living spirit," which would give a second birth to principles laid out in old texts. History represents, Hegel said, "the coming into being of our science [that is, philosophy]." And he borrowed from Schelling the expression *system in development* as another name for the history of philosophy. This is rather well-known and much discussed, ever since Feuerbach and Marx doubted Hegel's logicohistorical parallelism.[31] What is less well-known and yet patently apparent to any reader of the published lecture course—of which we have now also several earlier versions based on students' notes—is the fact that his philosophy of the all-understanding spirit *played no role at all* in his actual lecturing. Hegel's introduction and his lecture course had little in common except the belief that it was principles that characterize and differentiate philosophies one from the other.[32]

Hegel was a rather merciless lecturer, dismissing harshly the work of historians of philosophy—on which he nevertheless relied heavily, like Brucker and Tennemann. He openly disliked the idea of attributing insights to past philosophers, since it was a matter of thinking reasonably to have insights, not any individual achievement. So many past philosophers were to him so many "structures of thought" (*Gedankengebäude*), and this is why he wanted to cut short all biographical detail. Hegel cut short, but in the way of a commentary. He selected from available sources only what was, for instance, "pertinent to Plato's philosophy." He was always looking for the main principle, which he also called "the philosophical" (*das Philosophische*), "standpoint" (*Standpunkt*), "the general" (*das Allgemeine*), "the main question" (*die Hauptfrage*), "the main point of view" (*der Hauptgesichtspunkt*), "the main interest" (*das Hauptinteresse*), "fundamental interest" (*Grundinteresse*), "main determination" (*Hauptbestimmung*), and "main maxim" (*Hauptgrundsatz*).[33] Hegel's pupil and friend Karl Rosenkranz, also one of the editors of his works, pointed to the effect of this hermeneutics of principles: "For Hegel philosophy could associate concepts and names like any other science. Thus the Eleatic standpoint and the concept of immutable being, Plato and the concept of true affirmative dialectics, Aristotle and the concept of teleology were identical and so forth."[34] What Hegel did in his lecture course was to give the information provided by historians of philosophy and to strip it down to what he considered essential. He did not adopt the structure of his *phenomenology of spirit* in narrating the story of the living spirit. It is very plain that he just commented on historical knowledge.

One could look for similar undertakings and choose, for example, Samuel Taylor Coleridge and his lecture course on the history of philosophy in 1819 in London or Victor Cousin and his lectures in

Paris in 1828. Both based their comments on Tennemann's history, much like Hegel himself. Although completely different in address and in method, between those two and Hegel there are possible areas of comparison. Coleridge talked as much of great men as Hegel did, and he also used his lecture course to dwell on the relation between religion, mysticism, and philosophy.[35] Coleridge had no concept of spirit reading itself into history, which in turn Cousin had, although he did not characterize his spirit hermeneutically. Cousin saw the former one-sidedness of philosophy exemplified by competing systems in the 18th century come to an end in his own eclectic philosophy, which he considered a force of the future.[36] Hegel never dared to go that far and maintained to the contrary that "a living spirit" residing in any past philosophy needed a "kindred spirit" to be reborn.[37]

Hegel was less a prophet than a critic. Faithful to his criteria of the philosophical essential, he dismissed as "philosophically not interesting" the mythical form of truth in Plato, the Roman Stoics, Epicur's metaphysics, the whole of Arab and Jewish philosophy in the Middle Ages, scholasticism, the religious and political writings of Hobbes and Locke, and the popular writings of Fichte, to give a few examples. It is not at all astonishing to hear these verdicts: it is just another mark of the typical, and not extraordinary, character of Hegel's lecture course that those verdicts were *spoken*. In front of his Berlin audience, Hegel was fighting the philosophical past; he wanted to revive and bring to life what he thought was actual thinking. He did a great job, considering the extent to which he was willing to go: he almost never finished his course properly, even when lecturing more than four times a week. He also spent more than half of his time on Greek philosophy and later jumped whole centuries and many systems, because they would not bring new principles. Whatever Hegel was doing while lecturing, he was not putting forward any convincing philosophy that would absorb, so to speak, the history of philosophy and make it part of the system. This is just what he pretended in his introduction. In lecturing, Hegel did what most other philosophy professors would do: he commented on what was known about past philosophies.

Two consequences follow, it seems to me, from this observation. First, the philosophy of history cannot really digest historical knowledge. This knowledge can be cut, rearranged, narrated otherwise, and so on. It cannot be justified or accounted for, as Hegel claimed in his introduction.[38] Historical knowledge cannot be deduced from anywhere else—not even historical knowledge about philosophy from the idea of philosophy. What existing links there are among past philosophies is material enough to deal with: philosophers relate mostly one to another by criticism or adherence. And Hegel was right in demanding that the present must know what kind of history it produces. In the end, a truly philosophical history of philosophy is possible only if the term *history* is replaced by the term *development*. That much we can learn from Hegel.

So the positive insight we gain from the observation of Hegel's lecturing technique is that during the 19th century, the history of philosophy acquired pedagocial importance. Historical work was not primarily scholarship exercised in private, as was the case in the 18th century, but it is scholarship exercised in public. The success story of lecture courses on the history of philosophy during the 19th century made for an entirely new context for historiographical activities: historical narrative became an intellectual challenge for the lecturer who had to struggle for coherence in his presentation of past philosophies.

A last remark on Hegel and the mark he left on the 19th century. It is still widely believed that it was due to him and his immediate pupils that the interest in historical studies grew considerably, roughly around the middle of the century. However, with regard to the increase in lecture courses on the history of philosophy, this view does not hold. Johann Eduard Erdmann, a true Hegelian and a professor at Halle University, lectured there with fellow Hegelians Julius Schaller and Hermann Hinrichs, but they did not contribute more to historicizing philosophy than their non-Hegelian colleagues Rudolf Haym and Johann Gottfried Gruber. When Erdmann wrote in 1870 that many contemporary works in philosophy were read intensely in their historical parts, "whereas the speculative part is not cut at all," this applied to many more than just Hegelians, who by then were declining in numbers anyway.[39] We have to switch from the history of ideas—where Hegelianism is a factor—to the history of institutions—where it is the disciplinary status of philosophy and its respective academic practice that accounts for the historicization of philosophy.

CONCLUSION: ACTIVITY AND PRACTICE

Writing a history of philosophy was, before the 19th century, something quite remarkable as a literary activity, exercised mostly by private scholars and historians. It is only in the 19th century that philosophy professors started to take greater interest in this kind of literature. This is true on the whole for the English, the French, and the German production of histories of philosophy. Those histories played a role in the teaching of philosophy—most of all in Germany, where the university system was pretty stable after the closure of smaller institutions following the Napoleonic wars and the subsequent foundation of the Prussian universities at Berlin (1810), Breslau (1811), and Bonn (1818). Since in Germany the number of philosophy teachers did not vary much during the 19th century, we have reliable statistical material to prove the gradual but steady increase in lecture courses on the history of philosophy as well as in seminar courses. This process determined a new context for the literary production of works treating philosophy historically.

Most authors of historical works were then also professors of philosophy, and historical knowledge played an ever-more-important role in the curriculum. A legend arose at the same time, making the history of philosophy an introduction to or a part of philosophy itself. The legend implied that philosophy had "a special relation to intellectual history" or even that it "owned its history." However, the legend could not account for the new discipline that was created during the 19th century: *the study of philosophy* as a field of regular activity on both the teachers' and the students' sides. This new discipline was called philosophy by those who worked in it, and university philosophy by its critics like Schopenhauer and Nietzsche. The study of philosophy reframed historical knowledge about philosophy within the seminar through collective reading and interpreting, and within the lecture course through renarrating and commenting.

When Victor Cousin adressed his audience in 1828, he opened his lecture on the history of philosophy as follows: "We should first clarify, gentlemen, why we are here. Are you driven by vain curiosity and I myself by simple habit, or should we unite our forces to satisfy a higher need?"[40] Unfortunately, Cousin neither gave an answer nor specified what he meant by *higher need*. It has become clear, I hope, that the manifold activities that constituted *the study of philosophy* and that made the history of philosophy an important factor in the education of students—who aimed at philosophy and were confronted with the historical approach—can be summarized as activities of teaching and of commenting on historical knowledge, not producing it. But teaching and commentary became the new condition under which the production of histories of philosophy continued. Ever since, there has been no way to conceive of the history of philosophy as being the task of only the historian. And this is the condition we still work in. In going back to the 19th century, we follow the traces of our own discipline. We discover there no "distant" or "foreign" past, but our very own ways of reconstructing it.

NOTES

1. Research in the history of the history of philosophy was started by Martial Gueroult (*Histoire de l'histoire de la philosophie* [Dianoématique I], vol. 1: *En occident, des origines jusqu'à Condillac*, vol. 2: *En Allemagne, de Leibniz à nos jours*, vol. 3: *En France, de Condorcet à nos jours*, Paris 1984 and 1988; see also his *Philosophie de l'histoire de la philosophie* [Dianoématique II], Paris, 1979) and Lucien Braun (*Histoire de l'histoire de la philosophie*, Paris, 1974; see also his *La théorie de l'histoire de la philosophie*, Strassburg, 1985) and much elaborated by Italian researchers led by Giovanni Santinello (*Storia delle storie generali della filosofia*, ed. G. Santinello, 1979 sqq., vol. 1: *Dalle origini rinascimentali alla "historia philosophica,"* Brescia, 1981; vol. 2: *Dall'età cartesiana a Brucker*, Brescia, 1979; vol. 3 (in two parts): *Il secondo illuminismo e l'età kantiana*, Padova, 1988; vol. 4, part 1: *L'età hegeliana. La storiografia filosofica nell'area tedesca*, Padova, 1995; part 2: *L'età hegeliana. La storiografia filosofica nell'area neolatina, danubia e russa*, Padova, 2004; vol. 5: *Il secondo ottocento*, Padova, 2004.

2. Friedrich Karl Albert Schwegler's *Geschichte der Philosophie im Umriss* (first published 1848) went through 15 editions within five decades, and Friedrich Überweg's *Grundriss der Geschichte der Philosophie* (first published in 2 vols., 1862–64) was constantly revised and enlarged and appeared in 1897 in 4 vols. in its eighth edition.

3. U. J. Schneider, *Die Vergangenheit des Geistes. Eine Archäologie der Philosophiegeschichte*, Frankfurt am Main, Germany: Suhrkamp, 1990.

4. F. Nietzsche, *Unzeitgemäße Betrachtungen*, Zweites Stück: *Vom Nutzen und Nachteil der Historie für das Leben*, in Kritische Studienausgabe, ed. Giorgio Colli and Mazzino Montinari, vol. 1, 2nd edition. Berlin, 1988, repr. Munich, 1999, 255, 282.

5. Jacques Matter, *Essai historique sur l'école d'Alexandrie*, 2 vols. Paris, 1820; 2nd edition entitled *Histoire de l'école d'Alexandrie, comparée aux principales écoles contemporaines*, 2 vols. Paris, 1840–44; Jean-Marie Prat, *Histoire de l'éclectisme alexandrin, considéré dans sa lutte avec le christianisme*, 2 vols. [in one], Lyon and Paris, 1843; Jules Simon, *Histoire de l'école d'Alexandrie*, 2 vols. Paris, 1844, 1845; Jules Barthélemy-Saint-Hilaire, *De l'école d'Alexandrie. Rapport à l'Académie des sciences morales et politiques, précédé d'un Essai sur la Méthode des Alexandrins et le Mysticisme, et suivi d'une traduction des morceaux choisis de Plotin*, Paris, 1845; Étienne Vacherot, *Histoire critique de l'école d'Alexandrie*, 3 vols. Paris, 1846–51.

6. Heinrich Moritz Chalybäus, *Historische Entwickelung der speculativen Philosophie von Kant bis Hegel. Zur näheren Verständigung des wissenschaftlichen Publikums mit der neuesten Schule dargestellt*, Dresden,

1837, further editions. Leipzig, 1839, 1843, 1848, 1860; Ludwig Feuerbach, *Geschichte der neuern Philosophie von Bacon von Verulam bis Benedict Spinoza,* Ansbach, 1833, 2nd edition Leipzig, 1844; Karl Ludwig Michelet, *Geschichte der letzten Systeme der Philosophie in Deutschland, von Kant bis Hegel,* 2 vols. Berlin, 1837, 1838 [repr. 1967]; in English: Dugald Stewart, *A general view of the progress of metaphysical, ethical, and political philosophy, since the revival of the letters in Europe,* 2 vols. Boston, 1817, 1822, 2nd edition Edinburgh, 1842 (as *Preliminary dissertation* in *Encyclopaedia Britannica,* vol. I); John Daniel Morell, *An Historical and Critical View of the Speculative Philosophy of Europe in the Nineteenth Century,* 2 vols. London, 1846; London, 2nd edition; Edinburgh, 1847; New York, 1847, 1848; in French: Jean Philibert Damiron, *Essai sur l'Histoire de la Philosophie en France au XIXe Siècle,* Paris, 1828, further editions in 2 vols. Paris, 1828, 1834; Bruxelles, 1829, 1832, 1835; Adolphe Franck, *Philosophes modernes, étrangers et français,* Paris, 1879.

7. Johann Josef Ignaz von Döllinger, *Die Universitäten einst und jetzt,* Munich, 1867, 44.

8. U. J. Schneider, "A Bibliography of Nineteenth-Century Histories of Philosophy in German, English, and French," in *Storia della Storiografia* 21 (1992), 141–69; slightly revised also in *Philosophie und Universität* (see below n. 12), 317–55.

9. Friedrich Wilhelm Joseph Schelling, "Allgemeine Übersicht der neuesten philosophischen Literatur" [first published in *Philosophisches Journal* 1797 and 1798], in *Schellings* Werke, ed. Manfred Schröter, vol. 1, Munich, 1927, 379.

10. Letter by Johannes Schulze quoted in Max Jacobson, "Zur Geschichte der Hegelschen Philosophie und der preußischen Universitäten in der Zeit von 1838 bis 1860," in *Deutsche Revue* 30 (April 1905), 120.

11. Friedrich Adolf Trendelenburg, *Historische Beiträge zur Philosophie,* 3 vols., Berlin, 1852, 1855, 1867.

12. U. J. Schneider, *Philosophie und Universität. Historisierung der Vernunft im 19. Jahrhundert,* Hamburg, 2000.

13. Wilhelm Wundt, *Erlebtes und Erkanntes,* 2. Auflage Stuttgart, 1921, 314–22.

14. U. J. Schneider, "Philosophy teaching in nineteenth-century Germany," in *History of Universities* XII, ed. L. Brockliss, 1993, 197–338; with revisions now also in *Philosophie und Universität* (n. 12), 41–150.

15. Jean Paul [Friedrich Richter], "Brief über die Philosophie. An meinen erstgeborenen Sohn Hans Paul, den er auf der Universität zu lesen hat [1799]," in *Sämtliche Werke,* ed. Norbert Miller, Abt. I, vol. 4, Munich, 1962, repr. 1996, 1014; Karl von Raumer, "Kathedervortrag. Dialog," in *Die deutschen Universitäten,* Stuttgart, 1854 (Geschichte der Pädagogik

vom Wiederaufblühen klassischer Studien bis auf unsere Zeit, part 4), 207; Ernst Troeltsch, "Meine Bücher," in *Die deutsche Philosophie der Gegenwart*, ed. R. Schmidt, vol. 2 (1921), 13.

16. Arthur Schopenhauer, "Über die Universitätsphilosophie" [first published 1851], in *Sämtliche Werke*, vol. 4, Stuttgart and Frankfurt am Main, 1986, 173–242; Friedrich Nietzsche, "Über Universitäts-philosophie" [written 1867f.], in *Werke und Briefe* (Historisch-Kritische Gesamtausgabe), ed. H. J. Mette and K. Schlechta, vol. 3, Munich, 1935, 395.

17. Cf. Heinz and Ingrid Pepperle, eds., *Die Hegelsche Linke. Dokumente zu Philosophie und Politik im deutschen Vormärz*, Leipzig, 1985, 200–11 (Ruge), 235–372 (Bauer); *Philosophie und Universität* (n. 12), 281–85 (Fischer).

18. This rubrification follows in fact the titles as announced in printed lecture programs that were published first in Latin giving the names of the professors for all faculties, arranged according to seniority, with their respective courses, published in the mid century also in German, and later only in German, detailing the disciplines within faculties by a systematic order of courses, with names of professors attached.

19. *Philosophie und Universität* (n. 12), 81–103; universities in German territories from 1800 to 1900: Berlin (founded 1810), Bonn (f. 1818), Breslau (f. 1821), Erlangen, Freiburg, Giessen, Göttingen, Greifswald, Halle, Heidelberg, Jena, Kiel, Königsberg, Leipzig, Marburg, München, Münster (only 2 faculties), Rostock, Strassburg (f. 1872), Tübingen, and Würzburg. Münster and Strassburg were not considered for statistical evaluation.

20. The lecture programs clearly show that professors took turns in teaching to avoid individual specialization and to cover the canon for the students on a regular basis. Big philosophy departments could not avoid doubling and tripling courses on offer, whereas small departments omitted some canonical courses for a single semester but rarely longer.

21. F. Paulsen, *Die deutschen Universitäten und das Universitätsstudium*, Berlin, 1902, 561: "Die Gesamtheit der deutschen Universitäten bildet eine nach außen abgeschlossene, nach innen zusammengeschlossene Welt; ein beständiger Wechsel der Studenten, aber ebenso auch der Dozenten durchrinnt sie, wie den Körper der lebendige Blutstrom. Den ausländischen Universitäten, namentlich denen des englischen Typus, ist diese Erscheinung fremd."

22. Albert Peip, *Die Geschichte der Philosophie als Einleitungswissenschaft. Eine Antrittsvorlesung*, Göttingen, 1863.

23. Julius Deuschle, "Über den Unterricht der Philosophie auf Universitäten," in *Zeitschrift für das Gymnasialwesen* 9 (1855), 118: "So ist nach meinem Bedünken die beste Grundlage des philosophischen

Unterrichts ein wohlgeordnetes Studium der Quellen selbst—eine Art Quellenstudium."

24. J. B. Meyer, *Deutsche Universitätsentwicklung. Vorzeit, Gegenwart und Zukunft,* Berlin 1875 (*Deutsche Zeit und Streitfragen* 48), 84.

25. *Seminars* in German universities meant in most cases that there was (a) a room with books and a table to study them together, (b) a course held in such a room, and (c) sometimes also a budget for books and scholarships for excellent students. Seminars in the institutional sense (a) and (c) were established early for philological and historical disciplines, whereas in philosophy there were only three at the end of the 19th century. But seminar teaching (b) was common even before, taking place in lecture rooms or at the professors' houses. Cf. Wilhelm Erben, "Die Entstehung der Universitäts-Seminare," in *Internationale Monatsschrift für Wissenschaft, Kunst und Technik* 7 (1913), 1224–64, 1336–48; E. Pfleiderer, "Philosophische Seminare," in *Im Neuen Reich* 7 (1877), 147; cf. *Philosophie und Universität* (n. 12), 114–19.

26. Edmond Dreyfus-Brisac, *L'université de Bonn et l'enseignement supérieur en Allemagne,* Paris, 1879, 157; Gabriel Séailles, "L'enseignement de la philosophie en Allemagne," in *Revue international de l'enseignement* 6 (1883), 972; Louis Léger, "Les programmes des universités allemandes," in *Revue des cours littéraires de la France et de l'étranger,* Année 6, no. 44 (Oct. 1869), 735 sq.

27. E. v. Hartmann, "Wie studiert man am besten Philosophie?" in *Nord und Süd* 51 (1889), 61: "Erst derjenige kann philosophisch gebildet heißen, der mindestens eine Periode der Geschichte der Philosophie in fremder Darstellung und mindestens ein philosophisches System aus den Originalwerken gründlich bis in alle Falten kennengelernt und durchgedacht hat. Daß keiner hierbei stehenbleiben kann, der in der Philosophie ernstlich weiter kommen will, versteht sich von selbst; aber ein solcher ist dann genügend vorbereitet, um sich seinen Weg allein zu suchen."

28. See Martin Heidegger, *Beiträge zur Philosophie (Vom Ereignis)* [written 1936–39], Frankfurt am Main, 1989 (Gesamtausgabe vol. 65), 213 sq.

29. G. W. F. Hegel, *Vorlesungen über die Geschichte der Philosophie,* 3 vols. [first published 1833–36], repr. in *Werke in zwanzig Bänden,* Frankfurt am Main, 1970, vols. 18–20, see vol. 20, 466; cf. the manuscript edition of Hegel's introduction: Hegel, Vorlesungsmanuskripte vol. 2: 1816–31, ed. Walter Jaeschke (*Gesammelte Werke* 18), Hamburg, 1995, 38.

30. Imannuel Kant, "Lose Blätter zu den Fortschritten der Metaphysik" [notes concerning the question if there had been any progress in metaphysics since Leibniz and Wolff, published first by Friedrich Theodor Rink, Königsberg, 1804], in *Kants Werke* (Akademie-Ausgabe),

vol. 20 (Kants handschriftlicher Nachlaß, vol. 7), Berlin, 1942; cf. Giuseppe Micheli, *Kant Storico della Filosofia,* Padua, 1980; "Filosofia et storiografia: la svolta kantiana," in *Storia della Storiografia* (n. 4), vol. 3/2, 879–957; *Die Vergangenheit des Geistes* (n. 3), 297–309.

31. About Hegel's claim to have read the history of philosophy philosophically, cf. Ludwig Feuerbach, "Hegels Geschichte der Philosophie," in Feuerbach, *Sämtliche Werke,* ed. Wilhelm Bodin and Friedrich Jodl, vol. 2, 2nd. edition, Stuttgart, 1959, 4; Rudolf Haym, *Hegel und seine Zeit. Vorlesungen über Entstehung und Entwicklung, Wesen und Wert der Hegelschen Philosophie,* 2nd edition, ed. Hans Rosenzweig, Leipzig, 1927, 448, 454.

32. Walter Jaeschke pointed out this discrepancy in his introduction to Hegel, *Geschichte der Philosophie. Orientalische Philosophie,* Hamburg, 1993 (Philosophische Bibliothek 439), cf. xxiii, xxvii, cf. *Philosophie und Universität* (n. 12), 212–46.

33. *Philosophie und Universität* (n. 12), 223.

34. Karl Rosenkranz, *Hegel als deutscher Nationalphilosoph,* Leipzig, 1870, 218: "Hegel will sagen, dass die Philosophie, so gut als jede andere Wissenschaft, mit einem Namen, oder wie man auch spricht, mit einer Autorität einen notwendigen, ewig wahren Begriff in Erinnerung bringen könnte... Der elatische Standpunkt und der Begriff des sich selbst gleichen Seins, Plato und der Begriff einer wahren affirmativen Dialektik, Aristoteles und der Begriff der Teleologie usw. sind identisch."

35. Coleridge lectured in a London tavern about the history of philosophy: Kathleen Coburn, ed., *The Philosophical Lectures of Samuel Taylor Coleridge,* hitherto unpublished, London and New York 1949; cf. *Philosophie und Universität* (n. 12), 158–80.

36. Cousin lectured several times about the history of philosophy; his course of 1828 gained him a widespread audience, having been, shortly before, reinstated as professor at the Sorbonne: *Cours de l'histoire de la philosophie* [first published 1828], repr. 1991 (Corpus des Oeuvres philosophiques en Langue Française); cf. *Philosophie und Universität* (n. 12), 180–212; Patrice Vermeren, *Victor Cousin—Le jeu de la philosophie et de l'État,* Paris, 1995.

37. Hegel, "Differenz des Fichteschen und Schellingschen Systems der Philosophie," in *Gesammelte Werke,* vol. 4: *Jenaer Kritische Schriften,* ed. Hartmut Buchner and Otto Pöggeler, Hamburg, 1968, 9; also in *Werke in zwanzig Bänden,* Frankfurt am Main, 1970, vol. 2, 16.

38. Hegel claims his own introduction was a "justification" of the history of philosophy: cf. Werke, vol. 18 (n. 29), 18.

39. Johann Eduard Erdmann, "Die deutsche Philosophie seit Hegels Tod," in *Grundriß der Geschichte der Philosophie,* vol. 2, 2nd edition, Berlin, 1870, 839. In 1861 Karl Rosenkranz counted altogether 71 German Hegelians,

among them 24 professors of philosophy; cf. Rosenkranz, *Alphabetische Bibliographie der Hegel'schen Schule*, in *Der Gedanke* 1 (1861), 77–80, 183–263.

40. Cousin, *Cours de l'histoire de la philosophie* (repr. edition, 1991), 23. "Il faut d'abord, Messieurs, que nous sachions si nous sommes amenés ici, vous par une curiosité vaine, moi par une simple habitude, ou si en effet nous mettons nos efforts en commun, non pour tourmenter plus ou moins ingénieusement des chimères, mais pour satisfaire un besoin plus élevé."

This text has been published, in a slightly different version,
in *Rivista di Filosofia* 2 (2003), p. 231–246.

Response to Ulrich Johannes Schneider

KARL AMERIKS

IN SUMMING UP his very vivid and well-documented account, Ulrich Schneider stresses two important points with which I certainly agree: that in the 1800s the study of the history of philosophy was an ever-growing part of philosophy itself, especially in courses at German universities, which aimed at perpetuating the legend that there is something like a timeless idea of philosophy that we need to learn through its history and that this approach was impressively, although not uniquely, stimulated by Hegel, who argued that "history represents the coming into being of our science [philosophy]" (9).

Schneider also notes that Hegel's approach involves stressing historical claims about the "main" "principles" present in various works and eras and ordering them in terms of a narrative of "development" and "progress." And he seconds the Hegelian idea that "a truly philosophical history of philosophy is possible only if the term *history* is replaced by the term *development*" (11). I propose to assess this idea critically by carrying Schneider's reflections a bit further. Along the way, I will also present a response to the challenging question he ends with and that Victor Cousin raised but did not himself answer: what, if any, is the "higher need" (12) behind our growing interest in the history of philosophy?

My own account, which can be sketched only very briefly here, would involve incorporating Schneider's findings in a broader context. If one steps back just a bit, it seems clear that the growing attention given to the history of philosophy in the 19th century is part of a much broader pattern, one in which disciplines and lifestyles of *all* sorts had become explicitly historical even earlier—most notably, toward the end of the 18th century.[1] Once one reflects on this *general* process of historicization, however, developments in *philosophy in particular* take on an especially complex appearance. In other recent work, I have called this phenomenon the mystery of the *historical turn* in philosophy—that is, the remarkable fact that precisely at the time of the original post-Kantian era, historical considerations *suddenly* became *central* to *mainstream* philosophy.[2] I believe that this turn in philosophy takes on its most interesting form at two key moments: at its birth, right before the 19th century, and then in our own time. Note that these periods flank the 19th-century developments that Schneider catalogs. He catches the rise in historical interest when it has already established itself—and, I would say, already started to decay in the mid-1800s—and then, understandably enough, he leaves off at the round figure of 1900. One cannot help but ask, What is the "higher need" that originated the historical turn *even before* 1800, and what is it that makes it still seem so relevant to us now, *long after* 1900?

The major clue for responding to this problem is, in my view, connected with a theme that does *not* come up directly in Schneider's talk of "progress" or "development," although it may be hinted at in passing in his reference to Harold Bloom. What I have in mind is that side of our interest in history that has to do primarily with themes such as historicism, relativism, "strong reading," and deconstruction —and with some of the more provocative ideas associated with figures such as Bloom, Paul Feyerabend, and Richard Rorty. That is, for some of us now, what the word *history* conjures up at first is not a linear image of ascent or decline or a cyclical return of eternal "principles," but instead a process that may be even more disorderly than whatever Nietzsche, Heidegger, or Foucault outlined, for the work of these figures, after all, still offers what is at least a genealogy with fairly distinct periods and clear, dominant directions.

This threat of a *radically historicist* conception of history is especially relevant for the history of *modern philosophy* for the following reason. Recall the general fact, just noted, of a historicization of disciplines *throughout* the modern university and the fact that this was accompanied by an intense interest in, and an exhibition of, the phenomenon of so-called progressive development. This is a remarkable fact, but note that all of this is still compatible with the practice of a complex of disciplines and a view of knowledge that in a sense remains basically *non*historical in nature. In the exact sciences, the objects of the disciplines, as well as the findings of the specialists themselves, involve change in all sorts of ways—and yet there still remains strong confidence that here we have gained possession of a core set of *constant* principles or methods that are *clearly* agreed upon and that can be adequately approached by focusing simply on *current* techniques. For these disciplines, despite what some readers of Kuhn might contend, history is an incidental background and not a fundamental problem.

With areas such as philosophy, however, historical concern takes on a very different character—one involving the disquieting modern worry that the discipline itself, despite what figures such as Hegel and Kant insist, is not—and never will be—a science at all, in any strict English sense. This worry took on an extremely pressing character in the later 18th century. Right at that time, two highly disturbing developments were occurring. First, there was a growing decline in relatively easy moves back and forth between the new exact sciences and philosophy—moves that Leibniz and Descartes once made with eerie confidence, in both their basic principles and their day-to-day scholarly life. (Hence it seemed more and more odd for physicists to be called professors of "natural philosophy.") The modern achievement of highly developed exact sciences forced most philosophers to acknowledge that what they are doing as such is not science in the new strict (and paradigmatically clear, at least in practice) sense; Hume is *not* "another Newton."

Second, and simultaneously, an explosion of social, economic, and religious changes made leading thinkers more sensitive than ever to the diversity of human cultures as a kind of variety that is not a matter of easily charted steps on a progressive chain (as in natural science) or an illustration of principles that are eternal and such that their temporal instantiation is merely incidental. I take *Herder* to be the thinker who expressed historicist notions along this line in the most vivid and influential manner in the 18th century.[3] The crucial implication of Herder's work is that philosophy is on the whole more like art than science. Different eras, and the different leading thinkers who crystallize the principles of these eras, simply think *differently* and not necessarily better or worse than others. Herder emphasized that ancient (and even pre-Greek) art and thought are remarkable in their own manner and are not mere forms of pre-modernism or even pre-Socratism. This liberating but also corrosive idea worked its way through Schlegel, Dilthey, Nietzsche, and

Heidegger to Rorty and our own time; no wonder we are debating its ramifications here and now at Princeton.

Herder's work was very well-known at first—especially to Kant, Reinhold, and Hegel—but their reactions tended to smother signs of his direct influence. Kant notoriously rejected the views of Herder—his former student—altogether, as he aimed to protect a classical vision of philosophy as an eternal science, still very much like mathematics. What Reinhold and Hegel (and others such as Schelling) attempted was something more ambitious. They did not move from Kantian ahistoricism to radical Herderian historicism but instead initiated a way of doing philosophy that expressly presents itself as a synthesis of *both* the ahistorical systematic intentions found in figures such as Plato, Leibniz, and Spinoza *and* the deeply historical insights stressed by Herder (and somewhat kindred figures such as Montesquieu and Rousseau). In contrast to what they took to be Kant's overreactionary ahistoricism and Herder's overly relativistic historicism, they invented a model of a philosophy that is at once historical and systematic. Its original aim was to display itself as nothing less than a complete solution to the whole dialectic of fundamental problems that had arisen in the extremes of earlier philosophies. In integrating a historical *Auseinandersetzung* with their predecessors into the basic structure of their systematic writing, the German idealists claimed to have found a way of presenting the sequence of Herder's diverse "main" "principles" as not a mere colorful cavalcade but a necessary—and necessarily argumentative— sequence, a *Bildungsgeschichte* that has to be *philosophically experienced* if we are truly to know others and ourselves.

On one hand, against the ahistoricists, this approach, in its stress on the difficulties of interpretation and contextual understanding, can mark out a way in which philosophy is something supposedly deeper and more complex than natural science, something not to be measured or threatened by science's merely contingent and predictive improvements in our knowledge of natural fact. On the other hand, against the historicists, this approach can insist that it was backed by systematic arguments, by demonstrations that— despite the conflict of historical doctrines—there exists a grand evolving and meaningful pattern hidden in the maze of options that philosophy presents.

My hypothesis is that after Hegel's *Phenomenology* and by the time of his *Logic* and his ascension to a professorship, this uniquely ambitious attempt at a synthesis had already outlived its high point: despite the "legend" of a progressive history of philosophy presented throughout mainline 19th-century universities, most leading thinkers did not really believe it. We can now see that the key process was rather an initially off-the-main-track radicalization of the deep Leibniz/Herder split that had arisen just prior to the unique synthesis proposed by the idealists from Reinhold to Hegel. Thus there arose the revolution in philosophy, led by neo-Leibnizians from Bolzano to Russell and Carnap, that formed the dominant analytic departments of the 20th century that still tend to turn their back on the notion that the history of philosophy has an essential significance.[4] And there also arose the opposed underground movement of neo-Herderians—not only Isaiah Berlin, but all of the anarchists, historicists, existentialists, radical particularists, and postmodernists who seem more at home in a literature, history of ideas, or sociology department than in a mainline philosophy seminar.

In contrast to these long-opposed extremes, a significant third party has again arisen. It retains the *core* feature of Reinhold and Hegel's "turn"—namely, the idea of a *basic linkage* of historical and systematic thought while adding a new and more modest element. This new element—which I find in most of the most exciting philosophy of our time, such as in the Cambridge-ideas-in-context projects of figures such as Jerry Schneewind, Quentin Skinner, and Raymond Geuss—is the practice of combining historical and systematic considerations *without* assuming, as Reinhold and Hegel did, that there is an *evident pattern of unified progress* to be plotted out in all of our basic ways of thinking, from aesthetics to epistemology. In other words, philosophical thought might be able to be fundamentally systematic and historical at once without *remaining* either historicist or naively linear, even in a complex dialectical fashion.

The move to history, on this perspective, involves not a proof of development, in any clear scientific sense, but, rather, a disclosure of *significant dependence* in a way that is both conceptual and contextual. What makes earlier philosophical views on key topics—such as Aristotle's and Kant's views on virtue—specifically historical and relevant to us (despite their not leading to a science) must be something more than the mere fact that these figures are different and not here. If that were all there is to it, we might as well be looking at an exotic bird through a telescope. What is crucial is that we acknowledge figures such as Aristotle and Kant as our own *argumentative* but *distant ancestors*. The bet here is that we can understand ourselves as who we basically are only by figuring out better how we can become true to the notions that past *thinkers* introduced as the main, even if highly nontransparent, guides to the self-defining culture that we have become and will continue to be.[5]

If these figures were not thought of as *argumentative* ancestors, we could appropriate their ideas without systematic consideration in the way that a weather reading from an old manual might be taken over by a later scientist—without any philosophical reflection. And if they were not *distant* ancestors, we would not have to engage in the special hermeneutical work that (as Herder, Schleiermacher, and others taught us) is required if we are to remain genuinely open to uncovering a philosophy that may be *deeply* different, perhaps more world disclosing now than ever before, and not simply a crude form of what we already believe. And if they were not *our* main predecessors, we would not always have to keep attentive to the idea that in some ways they may be closer to our very selves— that is, more revelatory of our own fundamental nature—than anything contemporary.

In sum, even if (contra Hegel and perhaps Schneider) our concern with philosophy and its history need *not* be a matter of philosophy's ever literally becoming a science, it still can be the case that the idealists were right to turn us toward a genuinely philosophical concern with our own conceptual history, a concern that is more than a matter of merely understanding what is other.[6] The "higher need" that we are satisfying then is not to confirm, whiggishly, what our great "progress" supposedly has already been but, rather, to learn— by argument and not mere *Einfühlung*—how much the past can still reveal to us of what we must yet do to *know ourselves*. This is always in large part a matter of becoming truer to our own *philosophical origins*—just as any proper descendants may seek best to realize themselves, as well as their ancestors, by uncovering the deepest and most "sacred" "charges" that have not yet been fulfilled in their own "family" (a family that can, of course, always become further extended).

A final note—from Notre Dame, so to speak. That so many intellectuals, from 1800 until now, look for these charges more and more in the history of *philosophy* and *not* in *literally sacred* traditions is another explanation of where, as Hegel surely knew, *our* "higher need" to turn to history comes from: it is not a merely academic task but a deeply personal project—one that, for better or worse, obviously has taken on an ever-greater intensity to compensate for the decline in the way that standard religious sources appear to be capable of satisfying our historical thirst. In history we all can seek, as believers *or* nonbelievers, a "higher" common ground—and as philosophers we can find it even in endless controversy.[7]

NOTES

1. The participants in this conference (Teaching New Histories of Philosophy, Princeton University Center for Human Values [www. Princeton.edu/values], April 4–6, 2003) have documented this point extensively in their own work. See especially Schneider, *Die Vergangenheit des Geistes. Eine Archäologie der Philosophiegeschichte*, Frankfurt, Germany: Suhrkamp, 1990, and *Philosophie und Universität. Historisierung der Vernunft im 19. Jahrhundert*, Hamburg, Germany: Felix Meiner, 1999. A highly relevant work on this topic has just been completed by the Princeton scholar Theodore Ziolkowski. His *Clio: The Romantic Muse. The Historicization of the Faculties in Germany*, Ithaca, N.Y.: Cornell University Press, 2004, traces the path that this process takes at the beginning of the 19th century in fields such as religion, law, and science as well as philosophy.

2. See my *Kant and the Fate of Autonomy*, Cambridge, England: Cambridge University Press, 2000; "Text and Context: Hermeneutical Prolegomena to Interpreting a Kant Text," in *Kant verstehen/Understanding Kant*, ed. Dieter Schönecker and Thomas Zwenger, Darmstadt, Germany: Wissenschaftliche Buchgesellschaft, 2001, 11–31; and "Reinhold über Systematik, Popularität und die 'Historische Wende,'" in *Philosophie ohne Beynamen. System, Freiheit und Geschichte im Denken Karl Leonhard Reinholds*, ed. Martin Bondeli and Alessandro Lazzari, Basel, Switzerland: Schwabe Philosophica, 2004, 303–33. On the issue of the interdependence of philosophy and history, I have been especially influenced by writers such as Alasdair MacIntyre, Robert Pippin, Allen Wood, Gary Gutting, Dieter Jähnig, Nicholas Boyle, Tzvetan Todorov, Charles Larmore, Dieter Henrich, Manfred Frank, and Charles Taylor. Heinrich Heine anticipated (and stimulated) the most influential contemporary attitudes on this topic in his prototypical "Nietzsche/Rorty" tract, *The History of Religion and Philosophy in Germany* (1834).

3. Herder's charm is that he does not do this consistently, and he is occasionally still caught in "progressivist" (or "retro") or "eternal" presumptions of his own. See Michael Förster, ed. *Herder: Philosophical Writings*, Cambridge, England: Cambridge University Press, 2002.

4. Sometimes this is done with the thought that a unified systematic philosophy may be possible after all, for example, as Michael Dummett has suggested, under the heading of a general theory of meaning. Alternatively, sometimes this is done with no metaphilosophical thought or simply with the idea that it is sufficient for philosophy to be a formal discipline that points out technical infelicities in the arguments of others or that constructs clarifications in new regional disciplines, such as the

semantics of natural language, that have not yet settled into the steady path of a "normal science." The main error here, I believe, is to keep thinking of philosophy as a typical science—or otherwise simply a kind of art or literature. The error is understandable because philosophy is like art, since there is a part of it that essentially involves the signature of individual creativity, and it is also like science because it essentially involves commitment to intellectual progress. But neither art nor science essentially requires a turn to history, whereas there is now, I believe, a central strand of philosophy that, as an unrestricted discipline of universal critical reflection, cannot avoid focusing on the influence of history as such.

5. In speaking in terms of what we need to be true to, I am anticipating the notion that doing philosophy can be at once a matter of achieving a form of self-determination (with international as well as individual implications) and of gaining insight into one's culture and the real world. (Hence it is not simply a matter of understanding a topic but can also be a way of *becoming* one's true self, as when, for example, a contemporary Jew learns Hebrew not as a mere scholarly exercise but as part of a process of identity formation that reveals and realizes basic truths that would otherwise lie dormant.) These are not two separate projects, but one complex interconnected enterprise. The project of self-defining ourselves now is not a matter of independently legislating a new identity but is, rather, an issue of simultaneously appreciating our background and actualizing what we see that we can do with it in our current situation. Analogs of this process would be the efforts of poets such as Eliot and Heaney to define their own language and world in terms of a fitting expression of their premodern inheritance. Examples of it in philosophy would be the attempts of thinkers as diverse as Nietzsche, Heidegger, Foucault, and Williams to define themselves—and the best philosophical orientation of our era—in terms of a critical appropriation of the fundamental ideas of ancient and even pre-Socratic thought and practice.

6. My own—largely Kantian—position is not that this historical approach is the only proper path or the one that is clearly the best for philosophy but that it definitely has a special value and should be accepted as at least one of the most important ways of doing philosophy now. It does regard philosophy as one way of overcoming the repressed, but it does not have to be committed to any particular theory that this repression is conspiratorial or intentional or psychological in any ordinary sense.

7. For recent discussions on these issues, I am very indebted to the participants at the conference and to my colleagues from Notre Dame: Paul Franks, Gary Gutting, Vittorio Hösle, Lynn Joy, Patrick Kain, Fred Rush Jr., Mathias Thierbach, James Turner, and especially Anja Jauernig.

Comment: Philosophy in Practice

LORRAINE DASTON

MY CHARGE is to comment on the entire conference, including papers, commentaries, and ensuing discussions. I intend nothing like a summary but, rather, a reflection on what seem to me, a historian of science, to be some of the most striking themes to emerge in the past days. First, an echo of your own voices, as caught by the eager ethnographer:

"Teaching philosophy is as much a matter of orientation as accuracy." (Susan Neiman)

"Part of the charge of philosophy is to explain how we got from there to here." (Alexander Nehamas)

"History of philosophy tries to break the link between past and contemporary philosophy." (Daniel Garber)

"History of philosophy is an invitation to dialogue." (Mark Larrimore)

"Only reading can break the authoritarian relationship between lecturer and student." (Ulrich Schneider)

"The main thing an introductory philosophy course should do is to teach students to think philosophically." (J. B. Schneewind)

"The history of philosophy course is central to the major." (Jeffrey Edwards)

"Pretty much the same history of philosophy course is taught in departments of the most diverse orientations." (Knud Haakonssen)

"Devotion to the use of reason used in a certain way is philosophizing. Every philosopher knows what I mean." (John Cooper)

Historians of philosophy, at least within the context of this conference, seem to be victims of their own indispensability. The survey course in the history of philosophy almost always serves as the introduction to philosophy as a discipline and, I shall argue, to *philosophizing*. Hence the conflicts aired at this conference are not just variants on the familiar themes of how to reconcile teaching with research, or even how to bridge undergraduate and graduate teaching—though both themes have been present in discussion. Rather, the conflicts are about what philosophy is, and how to do it. No wonder historians of philosophy feel their decisions about what to teach and how to teach it are not entirely their own: the stakes are too high for them or their colleagues to be insouciant about such choices. Changes in the introductory history of philosophy courses would not only have a "ripple effect," as Jerry Schneewind put it; they could unleash a tsunami. Or so some of you seem to hope.

Several papers and commentaries have remarked upon the ways in which an enriched history of philosophy sheds light on the key problems in the field, how they come into being and pass away. A few people have gone further and suggested that the normative aims of philosophy—for example, truth or certainty—also have a history. What I would like to suggest on the basis of the papers and the discussions they have stimulated is that the doing of philosophy, its characteristic practices, also merits historical inquiry. History of philosophy courses don't so much trace that history as exemplify *current* practices; indeed, they are the principal means for instilling these practices, and that is why they are so gratifyingly and oppressively indispensable.

While reading the precirculated papers for this conference, I was struck by a paradoxical contrast between the ways in which philosophers and historians confront their respective historical traditions. Fledgling historians may encounter the classics of their discipline in a graduate seminar on historiography, but there exists no consensus among professors of history concerning the necessity of studying Herodotus or Gibbon, Thucydides or Mommsen, Tacitus or Fustel de Coulanges—much less a belief that students would or should learn (to adapt an oft-repeated phrase in the papers for this conference) how to "do history" by analyzing these texts. Students ambitious to master the ways of history are sent first to the most recent secondary literature, then to the primary sources, and, ultimately, to the archives for their professional initiation in how to think and work like a historian. Sometimes beginners are assigned a vade mecum like E. H. Carr's *What Is History?*, a genre of books notorious for eliciting blather from even the most eminent historians.

But almost no novice is assigned Bayle or Macaulay (or for that matter, Leibniz on the House of Guelph or Hume on the history of England) to read, debate, and, above all, argue with. The works of these authors are part of the history of the discipline but not of the tradition of history. Philosophers of science and ethicists, political philosophers and logicians, all have likely cut their teeth on Descartes and Kant. How many historians have served their apprenticeship with Livy or Casaubon? Hence the paradox: in this sense, the teaching of history and the training of historians is far less historical than that of philosophers—even philosophers of the most stridently anti-historical, analytic persuasion.

In this attempt to take stock of the conference as a whole—including the papers, the commentaries, and the discussions they inspired—I would like to explore the significance of this surprising contrast. I do not think that it is purely a matter of institutional contingency that, as Ulrich Schneider's paper shows us, since at least the 19th century and, arguably, before that, the prevailing method of introducing students to philosophy has been historical, and overwhelmingly through an encounter with classic texts—however mediated by textbooks or informed by historical context and however elastic the definition of the canon of classic texts. Dan Garber's students will certainly read Descartes in a more richly populated context than French students accustomed to the splendid isolation of the text described in Denis Kamboucher's paper would, but all will read Descartes. Students in Nancy Tuana's or Ian Hunter's or Susan Neiman's classes will read different texts (and different genres of texts) from those taught in warhorse Descartes-to-Kant surveys, but they will still read and analyze and argue about texts, be they Barbeyrac, Wollstonecraft, or Pope. My suggestion is that what history of philosophy courses teach is a set of practices as well as a set of problems and that the practices are even more constituitive of philosophy than the problems are. Practices are not mechanical techniques; there is nothing algorithmic about knowing how to argue, knowing how to evaluate the arguments of others, and (above all) identifying an interesting philosophical problem. These classes provide students with exemplars of not only what counts as philosophy but also what counts as *doing* philosophy. They initiate students into philosophy as a tradition, even though their disciplinary formation may come considerably later, when they encounter the latest work by the current doyens of the field in specialist seminars.

What are these practices, and how does a tradition differ from a discipline? The first point to make is that traditions, despite their reputations, may be continuous without being conservative. Several papers remark on significant innovations in the multimillennial career of philosophy, and there is no reason to think that novelty is at an end. Some of these innovations have had a profound, if usually unremarked, impact on the practices of philosophizing. Take, for example, the shift (noted en passant by Donald Kelley) from a striving for wisdom to a quest for truth. The etymology of *philosophy* enshrines the former; the Greeks did not pursue *philo-alytheia* (though it is, arguably, the goal of certain ancient natural philosophical works, like Aristotle's *Physics*). A second, related shift is underscored by Knud Haakonssen: the eclipse of philosophy as a way of life, as opposed to a way of acquiring and certifying knowledge. A whole set of practices disappeared along with the shift from wisdom to truth and from way of life to search for genuine knowledge. As Haakenson notes, lives of philosophers ceased to be of philosophical interest by the end of the 18th century, although they continued to play a not insignificant role in the mythology of the discipline—in the form of often apocryphal but oft-repeated anecdotes. Although stories about Kant's daily walk, Newton's apple, Einstein's lackluster high school grades, and the like persist, they no longer serve as exempla of the *vita contemplativa*, because life and works, *vita* and *contemplativa*, have been put asunder.

Along with these shifts, genres of philosophical writing and thinking disappeared—for example, the dialogue and the spiritual exercise—to be replaced by the treatise and, eventually, the article. Since philosophy was no longer about the perfection of the self in order to receive wisdom and also no longer structured as a relationship of master to disciples in the Socratic mode, the practices that crystallized these aims and relationships lost their meaning. Philosophy was no longer envisioned as a forum of competing schools, each with its own masters, in which initiates purified their souls through meditation and concourse with a spiritual guide (of whom the Socrates as portrayed by Alcibiades in the *Symposium* was the model for centuries), but, rather, as an architectural tour of *Gedankengebäude*. (The prevalence of the architectural metaphor in 19th- and 20th-century history of philosophy merits a study in its own right, evocative as it is of the vision of philosophy as free-standing, structural, and internally coherent.) These *Gedankengebäude* were attached to names (Aristotle, Descartes, Locke, Kant, Schopenhauer) but were otherwise as empty of personal presence as a building hit by a neutron bomb. The practices that accompanied architectural philosophy are still very much with us— so much so as to enjoy the invisibility of self-evidence. These are the practices that are instilled first and foremost through the teaching of the history of philosophy, and they define what it is to do philosophy. More than that, they have established the doing of philosophy as more authentically philosophical than the being of philosophy; in other words, primarily the practices rather than the problems specify the philosophical tradition.

What are these practices? Here I can give only the barest sketch: although we now have a voluminous literature on the history of scientific practices, we have only the rudiments of a history of practices in the humanities. Except for some older work on hermeneutics (mostly translated from other languages and traditions) and one notable study of the history of footnotes (by Anthony Grafton), there is almost nothing on the epistemology and practices of humanists. Historians of science have written about how biologists learned to see under the microscope, how botanists learned to characterize plants in succinct Latin, how physicists learned to abstract from messy phenomena to mathematical models. But how do art historians learn to see, historians learn to read, philosophers to argue? What is the history of the art-historical slide collection, the initiation into archival research, the graduate seminar? These are questions barely posed, much less answered, but I nonetheless find the contributions to this conference to teem with hints about such a history, at least for philosophy since the late 18th century. Despite the diversity of subject matter and approach, the practices of explicating, arguing, making coherent, and creating ideal communities surface again and again. Let me very briefly explain what I mean by each, on hand from examples drawn from the papers.

Explicating: As Knud Haakonssen acutely observes, a signal function of the history of philosophy since the late 18th century has been to make contemporary philosophical initiatives intelligible by showing the point of worrying about this particular problem and "to overcome and go beyond the problems that had made up the history of philosophy". The precondition for overcoming was explication: what was the meaning of this problem and this proposed solution, and why were both significant? The kinds of explication can be very different, ranging from close attention to context (the 17th-century battles against Aristotelian natural philosophy, the 18th-century preoccupation about providence, the 19th- and 20th-century assimilation of the new physics and mathematics) to an exclusive focus on the text itself as a self-sufficient entity à la Gueroult to a genealogy of ideas à la Lovejoy. But the alpha and omega of all of these forms of explication constitute the text itself—always as explanandum and sometimes allegedly also as explanans—and the techniques of slow, questioning, gimlet-eyed reading applied to those texts, so different from the forms of close reading applied to poetry or even to historical documents. As a philosopher friend from graduate school (it might have been Dan Garber) put it to me, "After every sentence I read, I stop and ask myself whether I understood it, and whether I agree with it." This is not just *Verstehen*; it is *Verstehen-mit-Widersprechen.*

Arguing: Philosophy has always been about argument with one's predecessors (think of Aristotle's brisk way with Plato and the pre-Socratics in the *Physics* and *Metaphysics*), but argument as conveyed by the history of philosophy is a very particular species of this genus. One is required first to master the argument before refuting it, and mastering the argument means not just piecemeal but as part of an architecture, a whole. The whole *Gedankengebäude* may be flawed (indeed, it is the point of the exercise to detect these flaws), and its flaws may be made clear by attending to this colonnade or that cupola, but to miss the building for the column is the mark of the rank beginner. A student who nowadays argues scattershot in the style of Aristotle, however cleverly, is unlikely to get above a B in the course. Almost nothing about Aristotle's way of arguing required that Heraclitus or even Plato dwell in a *Gedankengebäude;* almost everything about the form of argument modeled by history of philosophy courses and honored far beyond their confines presupposes that arguments connect to other arguments like the thigh bone connects to the hip bone. (The simile is used advisedly; philosophical argument abounds with anatomical metaphors and ambitions.) In logic and the philosophy of science it is perhaps possible to stake one's reputation on a single argument or paradox, but even here the argument is unlikely to be an isolated one—something, preferably a good deal, must be seen to hinge upon it. It is this hinging, the discovery and forging of hinges, that is characteristic of modern forms of philosophical argument, and it is not an accident that the hinging habit is usually first acquired through the history of philosophy.

Making coherent: There is no reason philosophy should be likened to architecture or anatomy—in short, to be viewed as a coherent whole. Nor is it self-evident that avowedly systematic philosophers actually succeeded in realizing their dreams of coherence—Spinoza perhaps, but the idea of making everything Leibniz wrote fit together makes one's head ache. Yet there is a decided bias in favor of the book-length, systematic treatment of a problem—a taste imbued once again with the history of the philosophy course. As Nancy Tuana and Susan Neiman point out, stimulating philosophy can be found in many genres, from the maxim to the letter to the novel, but it is rather the exception to encounter these sorts of texts in any kind of philosophy course and, consequently, in any recent philosophical bibliography, except perhaps as the jeu d'esprit of an éminence grise. There is a decided preference for texts that repay the effort of architectonic analysis, the practice of making coherent. Once again, these tastes and skills are first and probably best cultivated through the teaching of the history of philosophy, exercised upon texts chosen not only for their influence (a fluctuating index, depending on which historical period one chooses to assess) but still more for their connectivity, both internal to themselves and with other texts in the curriculum. Once acquired, the practice of making coherent extends from the reading of other philosophers' works to the crafting of one's own.

Creating ideal communities: So far, all of the practices I have mentioned concern texts, and texts in their most disembodied form: whether the text in question is presented in the original or translation, in critical edition or inexpensive paperback, by itself or with the works with which it was originally written, or in paper or electronic form is tacitly assumed to make little difference to its identity and meaning. But there is a material side to the practices of philosophy, albeit one that ultimately shades into the most immaterial realms imaginable, from the depths of time to the breadth of space. These are the efforts to create ideal communities that cross boundaries of geography and historical period, race and gender, even species, such as Kant's "all rational beings," which included angels and probably Martians. Ideally, one's interlocutors can be anywhere, anytime, anyone; all that counts is the ability to participate in the tradition, for which reason is a necessary but perhaps not sufficient condition. This community-building is itself a historical effort and ongoing—for example, it was and is evidently considerably easier to transcend nationality than gender—and it is hardly unique to philosophy. (One thinks of the Republic of Letters in early modern Europe.)

But the means philosophy uses to achieve its ideal communities are arguably unique and oddly concrete and embodied. In Ulrich Schneider's paper there is a footnote reference to the original definition of the seminar as a room with books and a table at which to study them together, as well as a course given in such a room. Historians such as Steven Turner, Bonnie Smith, Kathryn Olesko, and William Clark have shown the vast significance of seminar teaching for the history of science and scholarship starting in the late 18th century, and philosophy is no exception here. The teaching of the history of philosophy, even if it is done in lecture form, approximates the seminar with its communal table via the challenge to discuss— and to discuss simultaneously with the flesh-and-blood professor and classmates *and* the corporeally absent but intellectually very present author of the text at hand. Whereas students in seminars on history or literature are encouraged to analyze the texts before them, students in philosophy seminars are invited to *converse* with the text, as they converse with the other people gathered around that all-important table, that shared and leveling space. A peculiar process of distillation results, in which all interlocutors are concentrated, again ideally, into nothing more (or less) than interlocutors. If there is something séance-like about this meeting of minds, quick and dead, around a table, that may in part account for its moral as well as intellectual force: witness the vehement taboo against ad hominem arguments in post-18th-century philosophy and the cultivation of an epistemological perspective that approximates a "view from nowhere." Like all communities, this one is knit together by an ethos and instantiated by practices.

By this point, I have probably managed to alienate, or at least mystify, both the historians and the philosophers with all of this talk about the practices fostered by the way in which the history of philosophy is taught. The historians will be wondering what all of this has to do with, as Ian Hunter puts it, "descriptive enquiry oriented to an empirical historical investigation of the rival conceptions" extant in a particular cultural-political context; philosophers will be skeptical as to whether this could have anything to do with the quest for truth and universals. I would like to conclude with preliminary replies to both sorts of doubt. First, to the historians: just as history can illuminate how a philosophical problem can come into being and pass away—I think, for example, of Jerry Schneewind's proposal to treat "past moral philosophers as responding to large-scale practical problems that were urgent in their time"—these practices and their emergence, diffusion, and decline are themselves potential objects of historical inquiry. And they arguably do as much or more to shape the philosophical tradition—indeed, the very idea of what such a tradition can and should be and how it is to be transmitted. To the philosophers: These practices are woven into the warp and woof of doing philosophy. They are not extraneous or supplementary to standards of judging good philosophy and bad; they are constituitive of them. They are imbibed, if not with mother's milk, then in that first history of philosophy course that models what philosophy is and how it is done. Practices do not define truth, but they define the acceptable ways of finding truth—ways that are neither inevitable nor self-evident. They merit the attention of both historians and philosophers and, above all, of historians of philosophy. In wonder is the beginning of philosophy; in history is the beginning of philosophizing.

A Note from inside the Teapot

ANTHONY GRAFTON

THIS CONFERENCE is an event. To a historian of my generation, indeed, it seems almost a miracle. In the antediluvian days when I set out on my career as an intellectual historian, philosophers and historians rarely met, and when they did, they were more likely to generate critical mass than to engage in a critical discussion of texts and issues. When I arrived as a new instructor at Cornell University in the fall of 1974, I rapidly discovered that the local historians were brilliant loners. They had stayed in Ithaca because they enjoyed hiking, shooting, and long hours of solitary reading and writing. The philosophers, by contrast, cultivated a well-developed tradition of discussion. They read and argued about papers, attended one another's seminars, and spent hours talking about their work in Ithaca's counterpart to the Café des Philosophes: Johnny's Big Red Grill. In their kindness, they even allowed a young historian to join them—a historian whose memories of an early engagement with Wittgenstein were tempered with the memory of the speed with which he had flown from philosophy when he discovered that his professor and the graduate students in his class did not consult the German original of the texts they analyzed.

Cornell gave me the chance to listen to wonderful conversations— about Wittgenstein and his famous visit to Ithaca, about issues in the philosophy of language and science, about pretty much everything. But my experiences with the philosophers, in the end, left me with very mixed impressions. Attending the seminars of Norman Kretzmann and Lisa Jardine, I learned something, for the first time, about the history of formal argumentation in the Middle Ages and the Renaissance. Kretzmann's precision and learning impressed us deeply. The care with which he wrote out every word of his lectures, in blue ink, the jokes carefully entered in red, was the sign of a master teacher. But his deep knowledge of manuscripts and

317

paleography, the history of university learning and the transmission of texts, and the dexterity with which he connected these, in teaching, to the analysis of particular arguments revealed a great scholar at work. His model of advanced teaching and scholarship helped shape my own, much less formidable efforts.

But most other Cornell teachers and students of philosophy showed considerable less interest in the refinements of humanistic scholarship. One old friend from undergraduate days, now finishing a thesis in the department, explained to me that Cornell had one specialist in Continental philosophy because someone had to clean the drains. A newer friend glossed her refusal of a good job at a liberal arts college with what seemed to her a perfectly adequate explanation: "They wanted me to teach a survey of the history of philosophy. To do it I would have had to teach history of ideas. Of course I couldn't go there." When Paul Oskar Kristeller came to lecture on his studies of the philosophical tradition, historians, literary scholars, and art historians thronged the hall. Of the philosophers, though, only Kretzmann made an appearance. And when I ventured to ask Kristeller about this at a party, he indicated that anyone interested in the history of philosophy could expect little more in the United States. Admittedly, historians fully reciprocated the philosophers' lack of interest. Of my immediate colleagues at Cornell, only one, a historian of science, even seemed to know that the university had a philosophy department. And when I arrived at Princeton a year later, I found a similar situation—even to the famous notice, "Just say no to the history of ideas," that adorned one door in 1879 Hall.

A quarter century later, the world has changed. Philosophers write erudite, richly contextualized and informative intellectual biographies of Descartes, Spinoza, Wittgenstein, and others who have no place in the old official canon. The Cambridge histories of philosophy and Companions to the work of individual philosophers have yoked philosophers and historians, who seem to pull their wagons in complete harmony. As surprising, historians do systematic work on the history of philosophy, and the philosophers seem to take it seriously. Many recent works exemplify the new situation, but I'll cite only one exemplary text: Stephen Menn's dazzling survey of Renaissance thought in the *Cambridge History of Seventeenth-Century*

Philosophy, which, like the magnificent book it appears in, exemplifies the new order of things at its best.[1]

This new scene of amity and collaboration, a peaceable kingdom replacing the *bellum omnium contra omnes*, affords a pleasing spectacle. Today, though, I'll suggest that there are still ways in which the collaboration could go farther. In particular, I suspect that the historians have still more to offer the philosophers—and that historians would benefit more than anyone if philosophers reacted, in a formal way, to some of their recent innovations in method. I have in mind the texts of a particular place and time: Rome and Florence in the 1480s. For generations, historians of philosophy have studied the work of Marsilio Ficino and Giovanni Pico della Mirandola. They have examined the two men's use of ancient sources, have traced the outlines and excavated many details of their philosophical systems, and have provoked some fascinating debates. In particular, they have inspected very closely the forms of natural magic that Ficino and Pico practiced and recommended, but their results have been oddly contradictory.

Ficino, for his part, called for a magic that could unlock the *vires occultae* of particular plants, animals, and stones by using only natural knowledge. Some scholars have argued that this vision of licit magic was traditional. Ficino, they have noted, repeated arguments advanced long before by such respectable authorities as Thomas Aquinas. Others have pointed out that Pico's magic relied on a set of sources new to the Western tradition—the Jewish Kabbalah, as revealed to him by such informants as the brilliant con man Flavius Mithridates and the erudite neo-Platonist Johanan Alemanno—and have claimed that this novelty above all explained why a papal commission found him guilty of heretical and suspect statements and refused to allow him to hold a public debate over his 900 theses. Some have seen Ficino as praising the magic of the ancient Egyptians, which enabled them to draw spirits down into statues that spoke and moved. Others have seen him as condemning the same practice.[2]

My problem here is simple. I'm not sure that approaches like these—approaches that concentrate on the formal arguments made by early modern philosophers, assuming that they were constructed, coherently, like buildings designed from scratch—actually do justice to some highly significant formal features of their writing—to some of the ways in which they used sources and constructed arguments from them. Ficino and Pico, like many of their contemporaries, composed their books chiefly from other books, weaving and patching quotations and longer passages together. Often, as Ann Blair pointed out in her groundbreaking study of Jean Bodin, learned writers deployed the same facts and anecdotes in more than one setting.[3] The same anecdote could serve apparently opposite purposes or could support apparently contradictory theses in a single text. In his treatise *On Drawing Life from the Heavens*, for example, Ficino described with apparent admiration a series of feats carried out by magi, who drew on the *logi spermatikoi* distributed throughout the natural world.

> Besides, some people by warming eggs even without animals win over to them life from the universe; and often, by seasonably preparing certain materials, they procreate animals even without any eggs or perceivable seeds, for example, the scorpion from basil, bees from an ox, a bird like a blackbird from sage, that is, they supply them with life from the universe by particular materials at the right time. Like all these, our wise man—when he knows what or what sort of materials (partly begun by nature, partly completed by art, and, although they had been dispersed, grouped together) can receive what or what sort of influence from the heavens—assembles these materials when that influence is most dominant, he prepares then, he brings them to bear, and he wins through them celestial gifts.[4]

In the *Apology* that Ficino appended to this text, however, he cited one of the same examples, this time as an instance of a bad sort of magic. While a demonstration of spontaneous generation rested on a true understanding of nature, it served no serious purpose and therefore deserved condemnation.

> Of this profession [natural magic] there are also two types: the first is inquisitive, the second necessary. The former does indeed feign useless portents for ostentation: as when the Magi of Persia produced a bird similar to a blackbird with a serpent's tail out of sage which had putrefied under manure, while the Sun and Moon occupied the same degree in the second face [decan] of Leo: they reduced the bird to ashes and poured it into a

lamp, whereupon the house seemed as a result to be full of serpents. This type, however, must be avoided as vain and harmful to health.[5]

Ficino drew this example of magical practice from the *Picatrix*. But it seems quite likely that he did not retrieve it directly from the original text.

From early in the 15th century, humanist teachers counseled their pupils to keep notebooks—or, if their social position made it impossible to take notes themselves, to hire poor students to keep notebooks for them. Erasmus, in his widely read manual *On copiousness in words and ideas*, told students that "anyone who wants to read through all types of authors (for once in a lifetime all literature must be read by anyone who wishes to be considered learned) will collect as many quotations as possible for himself." The student, he explained, should devise a complex, all-inclusive set of headings and subheadings, under which he could enter his extracts.

> Then, after having chosen yourself headings, as many as will be adequate, arrange these in the order you want, then add to each its parts, then under these subheadings you will at once note the *loci communes* or *sententiae*, whatever you meet with in any author and particularly in the better ones: *exemplum, casus novus, sententia*, joke or marvel, proverb, metaphor, or parable. This method will have the result of fixing in your mind what you read and will accustom you to use the wealth of your reading. For there are some people who keep many things as it were laid up for use, but when they come to speak or write they are remarkably poverty-stricken and bare. And in this way you will have, whenever occasion demands, a whole apparatus for speaking, ready pigeon-holed, from which you can draw.

Many scholars turned their whole libraries into elaborate mechanisms for the retrieval of bits of text. Reading, in normal humanist practice, meant writing: one examined texts pen in hand, marked or copied salient passages, compiled them into notebooks organized by categories, and finally recombined them in one's own work. Complex systems of annotation could identify the significant passages in books. Splendid reading machines made it possible to consult several books at once while making notes on a particular subject. The library melted imperceptibly into each new book that its owner produced.

Ficino, presumably, kept a notebook or notebooks, into which he entered larger conceptual structures and smaller technical details. The *Picatrix*'s story of the blackbird could easily have found a place under more than one heading: as evidence of the way *occultae virtutes* worked to bring about a genuinely preternatural occurrence and as an instance of the way that even true magic could be abused to put on an impressive but empty show. This method of compilation seems problematic now: it clearly presupposed a notion of authorship different from the modern one. But it also clearly fitted the needs of writers who believed, as Ficino did, that every significant text had glittering fragments of one shattered great revelation embedded in it. Most important, this method made it possible—even easy—for Ficino and other magi to produce works that mirrored their own intellectual insecurities about magic, for it enabled them either to deploy, side by side, stories about the magical speaking statues that the Egyptian priests and magi had devised and condemnations of these or to use the same story to highly different argumentative effects.

The fact that some philosophers compiled their texts in this fashion certainly does not mean that they had no original arguments to offer when doing so, for they used the stories, images, and arguments that they stockpiled in highly independent ways, deliberately showing the careful reader that only they decided how to deploy any particular quotation or anecdote. Here too, practices of argument used in substantial treatises derived from what their authors had learned as boys. Schoolmasters always encouraged their students not just to copy what the ancients had said, but to change it. Those who recommended making notebooks could quote Macrobius, who told students to emulate bees and carefully select the best bits of what they read for precise, unaltered reuse in new texts. But they could also quote Macrobius's source, Seneca. He told students to emulate bees and produce honey, the original source of which could no longer be identified, since they had digested and made their own what they had found in other authors.[6]

No one gave more explicit instructions on this point than Gasparino Barzizza, the influential Paduan teacher whose pupils included Leon Battista Alberti. In a short, punchy treatise "On imitation," he explained in a strikingly frank way how the young Latinist should go about his basic task: "Imitation can be understood and carried out in four ways—by addition, subtraction, transferral and transformation"—but not, of course, by direct copying. Sometimes, relatively simple changes could make a classical sentiment new without debasing its currency: "If Cicero says, '*Scite hoc inquit Brutus* [Brutus said that neatly],' I will add, '*Scite enim ac eleganter hoc inquit ille vir noster Brutus* [Our friend Brutus said that neatly and elegantly].'" More ambitious tactics included the inversion of the classical source: "If Cicero, whom we wish to imitate, praised someone to the skies, we could blast him to the depths."[7] Renaissance philosophers mastered these textual tricks at school and practiced them in later life, self-consciously and effectively.

One passage—a very famous one—illustrates the central role that the practices of humanism played in constituting the new natural philosophy of the Renaissance. Pico, in his 1487 *Oration* and the *Apology* in which he defended it, drew a famous distinction between two forms of magic.

> I have also put forward magical theses, in which I have shown that magic takes two forms. One of these consists entirely in the work and authority of demons, a horrid and terrifying thing. The other, when rightly understood, is the absolute consummation of natural philosophy. The Greeks mention both. Considering the former unworthy of the name of magic, they name it *goeteia*. But they call this by the proper and individual term *mageia*, as if it were the perfect and highest form of wisdom.[8]

Every learned man who felt the need to defend magic recycled Pico's eloquent formulations—starting with Ficino. He stated in his own *Apology* of 1489: "There are two kinds of magic. The first is practiced by those who unite themselves to demons by a specific religious rite, and, relying on their help, often contrive portents.... But the other kind of magic is practiced by those who seasonably subject natural materials to natural causes to be formed in a wondrous way."[9]

Many others followed Ficino. It's not surprising to see Henry Cornelius Agrippa follow his example in his *De occulta philosophia,* the

16th-century magician's desk reference. But the case of Gabriel du Puy-Herbaut is more striking. He drew up a detailed manual on how to censor heretical books, in which he explained to his readers that the books Paul had told the Ephesians to burn were "magical," and he noted that "Augustine says, in the *City of God*, that magic was created by demons." He treated magical books as even more vile than Rabelais's *Gargantua and Pantagruel*, which he also condemned. Yet even he made an exception for "the Platonic and philosophical magic, which is said to be the absolute consummation of natural philosophy."[10] The Jesuit Benito Pereira came to the study of magic with firm prejudices against it, since he had commented at length on the passages in Genesis that portray magic as the weaker opposite of the true religion of Moses. Yet he too accepted that—as he wrote, again recycling Pico's words—the true *mageia* was not just licit but also the consummation of natural philosophy.[11] Pico's sharp distinction between licit and illicit magic, with its Greek terminology borrowed from Porphyry, seems to offer strong support for the least radical reading of Pico and Ficino's dealings with magic: the one that holds that their magic derives from late antique sources that they knew, and that represented magi like Hermes and Zoroaster as using magic to work wonders, and that it is "supported by a cosmology which is supposed to make it both scientifically and religiously sound."[12]

But the text that really occupied Pico's thoughts as he defined the two forms of magic was one far better known—and far more authoritative—than Porphyry's lost writings. And its shadowy presence behind Pico's text calls for comment. In *The City of God*, Augustine devoted several chapters to drawing a contrast between the true Christian religion and false magic. Like Pico, he cited Porphyry, but he did so to refute his source and the distinction he had tried to draw between different forms of magic, some licit and some not. Augustine described the Christian attack on pagan idolatry in Alexandria.

> These things and others like them, which it would take too long to record here, were done to commend the worship of the one true God and to prohibit that of the many false ones. They were done with simple faith and trust in piety, not with incantations and songs composed with the art of forbidden curiosity, which they call either *mageia*, or by the more detestable name of *goetia*,

or by the more honorable one of theurgy, by which they try to distinguish between them. They want to show that of those dedicated to forbidden arts, some, whom the ordinary people call *malefici*, are damnable (for they say that these belong to *goetia*), but that others are praiseworthy, to whom they ascribe theurgy. Yet both are bound by the deceptive rites of demons, under the names of angels.[13]

When Pico made his distinction, he deliberately reversed Augustine's verdict. He could expect few readers to have read Porphyry, but he knew that every learned man had read Augustine—as he had, pen in hand. In this case, he made clear to all who shared his mastery of allusion, the pagan philosopher Porphyry was right, the Father of the Church wrong. Like many humanists—such as Maffeo Vegio, who added a 13th book to Virgil's *Aeneid* to show that Virgil had gone wrong by making the original 12 end so unhappily, and Leon Battista Alberti, who made his own treatise on architecture into a massive attack on the ancient one by Vitruvius—Pico used allusions to signal that he was not only drawing on but also rebutting ancient authorities. More dangerously still, he made clear that his cosmology implied a rejection of Augustine's.

At least one of Pico's readers showed, as subtly as Pico, that he recognized Pico's true source. Giambattista della Porta, in the beginning of his own treatise on magic, distinguished between natural magic and "that infamous sort, created by invocation of unclean spirits, and described as the product of illegal curiosity, which the more recondite Greeks call *goetia* or theurgy." By inserting bits of Augustine's terminology—the phrase *illegal curiosity* and the reference to theurgy—della Porta delicately revealed what Pico had done—without ever saying that either Pico or he challenged the preeminent authority of Augustine, but perhaps implying exactly that.[14] Late in the 16th century, Giordano Bruno and Tommaso Campanella would take magic as the basis for a sweeping attack on Christianity itself. One wonders whether they—like their fellow southerner della Porta—found inspiration in Pico's defiance of Augustine.

This little story has several consequences for the history of philosophy. It confirms that, as Menn and others have pointed out, many early modern thinkers did not limit their engagement with the philosophical tradition to texts and ways of working with them that are currently classified as philosophical. More important, it shows that influential ways of dealing with tradition as a whole could range from systematic applications of dialectic to purposeful misquotation. It makes clear that some readers, at least, were conscious of these tactics and accepted them but does not tell us how many, even at the time, actually fell into this category. It invites philosophers to assess the value and import of forms of argument that did not come from the realm of formal dialectic. And it suggests that early modern visions of intellectual traditions and early modern forms of argument could evidently embrace stronger challenges to reigning systems of belief than some current histories of philosophy seem to accept. Perhaps more occasions like the present one will make it possible to explore these issues at greater length—and at more leisure.

Notes

1. Stephen Menn, "The Intellectual Setting," *The Cambridge History of Seventeenth-Century Philosophy*, ed. Daniel Garber and Michael Ayers, Cambridge, England, 1998.

2. For an excellent survey of the issues, see Brian Copenhaver and Charles Schmitt, *Renaissance Philosophy*, Oxford, England, 1992.

3. Ann Blair, *The theater of nature: Jean Bodin and Renaissance science* (Princeton, 1997). See also *Die Praktiken der Gelehrsamkeit in der frühen Neuzeit*, ed. Helmut Zedelmaier and Martin Mulsow, Tübingen, 2001.

4. Marsilio Ficino, *De vita coelitus comparanda*, III.26; *Three Books on Life*, ed. and trans. John Clark and Carol Kaske, Binghamton, N.Y., 1989, 386–89: "Praeterea sicut nonnulli foventes ova, etiam sine animalibus vitam illis ex universo conciliant, et saepe materias quasdam opportune parantes, absque ovis manifestisque seminibus animalia procreant, ut ex ocimo scorpionem, apes ex bove, ex salvia avem merulae similem, vitam videlicet a mundo materiis certis opportunisque temporibus adhibentes: sic et ille sapiens ubi cognovit quae materiae sive quales partim incohatae natura, partim arte perfectae, etsi sparsae fuerint congregatae, qualem coelitus influxum suscipere possint, has eo regnante potissimum colligit, praeparat, adhibet sibique per eas coelestia vendicat."

5. Ficino, *Apologia*, ibid., 398–99: "Illa sane ad ostentationem supervacua fingit prodigia, ceu quando Persarum Magi ex salvia sub fimo putrefacta, dum Sol et Luna secundam Leonis faciem occuparent, eundemque gradum ibi tenerent, generabant avem merulae similem serpentina cauda, eamque redactam in cinerem infundebant lampadi, unde domus statim plena serpentibus videbatur. Hoc autem tanquam vanum et saluti noxium procul effugiendum."

6. See Ann Moss, *Printed commonplace-books and the structuring of Renaissance thought*, Oxford, England, 1996.

7. Gasparino Barzizza, *De imitatione*, in G. W. Pigman, "Barzizza's Treatise on Imitation," *Bibliothèque d'Humanisme et Renaissance* 44 (1982), 341–52, at 349–351: "Omnis bona imitatio fit aut addendo, aut subtrahendo, aut commutando sive transferendo, aut novando. Addendo ut si invenirem aliquam brevem latinitatem in Cicerone vel in alio aliquo libro, adiungam ei aliqua verba ex quibus videbitur illa latinitas aliam accipere formam et diversam a prima. Exemplum. Si ponatur quod Cicero dixerit, 'Scite hoc inquit Brutus,' addam ac dicam, 'Scite enim ac eleganter hoc inquit ille vir noster Brutus.' Ecce quomodo videtur habere diversam formam a prima."

8. Giovanni Pico della Mirandola, *Oratio; Discorso sulla dignità dell'uomo*, ed. Giuseppe Tognon, Brescia, 1987, 46–47: "Proposuimus et Magica theoremata, in quibus duplicem esse magiam significavimus, quarum altera daemonum tota opere et auctoritate constat, res medius fidius execranda et portentosa. Altera nihil est aliud, cum bene exploratur, quam naturalis philosophiae absoluta consummatio. Utriusque cum meminerint Graeci, illam magiae nullo modo nomine dignantes *goeteian* nuncupant, hanc propria peculiarique appellatione *mageian*, quasi perfectam summamque sapientiam vocant." See also Pico, *Oeuvres philosophiques*, ed. Olivier Boulnois and Giuseppe Tognon, Paris, 1993, 54–57.

9. Ficino, *Apologia*, ed. Clark and Kaske, 398–99: "Denique duo sunt magiae genera. Unum quidem eorum, qui certo quodam cultu daemonas sibi conciliant, quorum opera freti fabricant saepe portenta. Hoc autem penitus explosum est, quando princeps huius mundi eiectus est foras. Alterum vero eorum qui naturales materias opportune causis subiciunt naturalibus mira quadam ratione formandas."

10. Gabriel du Puy-Herbaut, *Theotimus, sive de tollendis et expungendis malis libris*, Paris,1549), 9–11, 180–83.

11. Benito Pereira, *De magia, de observatione somniorum et de divinatione astrologica, libri tres* (Ingolstadt, 1591), I.9, 49–50.

12. I cite Menn's condensed exposition, 65–66.

13. Augustine *Civitas dei* 10.9: "Haec et alia multa huiuscemodi, quae omnia commemorare nimis longum est, fiebant ad commendandum unius Dei veri cultum et multorum falsorumque prohibendum. Fiebant autem simplici fide atque fiducia pietatis, non incantationibus et carminibus nefariae curiositatis arte compositis, quam vel magian vel detestabiliore nomine goetian vel honorabiliore theurgian vocant, qui quasi conantur ista discernere et inlicitis artibus deditos alios damnabiles, quos et maleficos vulgus appellat (hos enim ad goetian pertinere dicunt), alios autem laudabiles videri volunt, quibus theurgian deputant; cum sint utrique ritibus fallacibus daemonum obstricti sub nominibus angelorum."

14. Giambattista della Porta, *Magiae naturalis sive de miraculis rerum naturalium libri iiii*, Lyon, France, 1561, I.1, 8 vo-9 ro: "Ipsam [sc. magiam] bipartitam faciunt, infamem alteram, ac immundorum spirituum incantationibus concinnatam, et nephariae curiositatis esse afformatam, quam reconditioris literaturae Graeci *goeteian* vel Theurgias vocant, cui omnes adversantur, ut quae praestigia et phantasmata porrigat, quorum mox vestigium non remaneat. Naturalem alteram, quisque veneratur, et colit, ut nil altius, nilve bonarum literarum candidatis plausibilius: nec aliud esse putent, quam naturalis Philosophiae consummationem, summamque scientiam."

Philosophy, History of Philosophy, and l'Histoire de l'Esprit Humain: A Historiographical Question and Problem for Philosophers*

JONATHAN ISRAEL

NUMEROUS intellectual and cultural innovations were introduced in western Europe during the early Enlightenment period, roughly during the 80 years from 1660 to 1740, in the wake of the rise of Cartesianism and the so-called mechanistic worldview. Many of these, such as the new Bible criticism of Spinoza and Richard Simon and such innovative mathematics such as Newton's and Leibniz's calculus, are well-known; other innovations, though, are less so. In recent years, a number of scholars, including Donald Kelley and several German colleagues, have drawn attention to a hitherto remarkably little discussed phenomenon in the history of European thought— namely, the advent, or invention, of a new and (for a time) highly controversial scholarly field of research called history of philosophy and sometimes also, more vaguely, *historia philosophica*.[1]

The *érudits* who wrought this change in the scholarly landscape were often extremely scathing about the efforts of earlier scholars, from Lorenzo Valla and Ficino onward, to investigate the history of philosophy, very possibly too much so. Nikolaus Hieronymus Gundling (1671–1729), for example, a Halle professor dubbed by

---

*If what follows has any merit, I must thank a number of colleagues with whom I have had the benefit of an extremely stimulating series of conversations in Princeton over the past two years, discussion without which I would not have been able to develop this line of argument. In particular, I wish to thank Martin Mulsow, Donald Kelley, Jerry Schneewind, Morton White, Malcolm de Mowbray, Jonathan Sheehan, and Tony Grafton.

his German colleague Heumann a master of the new *historia philosophica*, a man swayed neither by *praeiudicium antiquitatis* nor *autoritatis*,[2] having closely investigated the topic, concluded, like Jean Le Clerc (1657–1737) and the Kiel "Polyhistor" Daniel Georg Morhof before him, that the humanists had wholly mismanaged the task of analyzing the history of Platonism and that Ficino, in particular, despite his zealous efforts in this area, had got himself hopelessly confused.[3] But if they were excessively disdainful of their humanist predecessors, the basic point of these early Enlightenment scholars was surely correct—namely, that Renaissance thought, despite a continuous and growing tension in the fraught unity it forged between Christian Revelation and ancient pagan thought, could never truly detach itself from writing about ancient philosophy as it thought it ought to be, selecting and adjusting its themes to fit Christian criteria rather than studying it for what it was.[4]

There can be little doubt, moreover, that in this field there took place during the early Enlightenment a truly decisive break and one intimately connected with the new concept of text criticism that evolved in several western European countries in the closing decades of the 17th century. While it is true, therefore, that much of the research that fed the new discipline of history of philosophy was carried out in the wake of the pioneering efforts of Leibniz's teacher Jakob Thomasius (1622–84), mostly in Protestant Germany, it needs to be borne in mind that this development was in many respects a response to, and inseparable from, the wider intellectual context in northwestern Europe at the time. In particular, the advent of history of philosophy received much of its impetus from the broad Thomasian reaction against Cartesianism, Spinozism, and Bayle.[5] At the same time, as we have said, a vital element in the methodology of this soon predominantly German initiative was supplied by the new conception of text criticism, and this was forged, above all, in the Netherlands by Spinoza, Bayle, and Le Clerc, the last being admired in Germany as everywhere as one of the prime architects of the new *critique*.[6]

In this present paper, my aim is to highlight three specific questions, each of which, though it may not appear so at first, seems on closer consideration to cut integrally across the disciplines of both history and philosophy, linking them in what, to us, is a highly unfamiliar manner. First, what exactly is the nature of the change in thinking involved in the transition from what—if I might be allowed the expression—could be called the precritical phase of thinking about the history of philosophy to history of philosophy as conceived by the expounders of the new *critique* and the scholars who, in the early 18th century, built up the new area of study? Second, why did the scholars and thinkers who engineered this shift from precritical thinking about history of philosophy to the new critical inquiry into history of philosophy regard the old approach as fundamentally unphilosophical and the new approach as philosophical in some allegedly crucial sense with far-reaching implications for the practice of philosophy itself?

Third, and finally, I shall ask—even though from the perspective of 20th-century philosophers, and especially the Anglo-American analytic and pragmatic schools (which tend to reduce most history of philosophy to the history of error), this is likely to seem to many today wrongly conceived and even perhaps ridiculous— whether the critical thinkers of the early Enlightenment can conceivably have been right in claiming that only through study of *historia philosophica*, or what Fontenelle and the great French (crypto-Spinozist) scholar and critic Nicolas Fréret (1688–1749) called *L'Histoire de l'esprit humain*,[7] can we grasp what philosophy is and how to define it. Furthermore, could they possibly be right that it is only through studying history of philosophy that the practice of philosophy itself assumes meaningful sense and direction. Their position amounted to claiming that any and all philosophy not firmly anchored in the study of *L'Histoire de l'esprit humain* must ipso facto be false, irrelevant, and useless. Does such a stance deserve our consideration, and if so, might it be a proposition admissible not just by assorted neo-Hegelians and Nietzscheans but perhaps also, on the Anglo-American side, by proponents of a holistic pragmatism applied to the entirety of human culture?[8]

In any case, endeavors to explore the history of philosophy undertaken prior to the late 17th century struck practitioners of the new *critique*, such as Le Clerc and Bayle, and expounders of the new discipline of history of philosophy, such as Bayle, Buddeus, Gundling, Heumann, Fréret, Lévesque de Burigny, and Brucker, as ungrounded and inadequate. They thought this for two main reasons: first, as already noted, they perceived a fatal gap in the critical methodology of the humanists. While granting the latter were well equipped with philological and language skills, they held that even the very best of them, such as Henri Estienne, Casaubon, Lipsius, and Scaliger, failed to understand how to reconstruct the historical context in which a particular text, idea, or belief arose or even, in the main, the need to do so.[9] Second, and no less damning, they thought their predecessors had shown themselves incapable of uncoupling philosophy from theology.

The gap between mid-17th-century notions of history of philosophy and the new concept did indeed appear vast. Christoph Adolph Heumann (1681–1764), one of the principal promoters of the new history of philosophy, found something to praise in the *Historiae philosophicae libri septem* (Leiden, 1655) by his German-Dutch predecessor Georgius Hornius (1620–70) but only as regards his intentions. He lauded him for being the first person since ancient times who "proposed to bring *historiam philosophicam* into a proper system," an enterprise on which this scholar embarked as young man, in 1640.[10] Hornius, moreover, turned out to be the first of a batch of mid-17th-century writers of ambitious survey accounts of the history of philosophy, the other main contributors being Gerardus Vossius (1577–1649), whose widely consulted *De Philosophia et philosophorum sectis libri II* appeared posthumously at The Hague in 1658; Holsteiner Johann Jonsius (1624–59), author of *De Scriptoribus historiae philosophicae* (1659); Englishman Thomas Stanley; Dutchman Abraham de Grau at Franeker; and Leiden Cartesian Johannes de Raey (1622–1707).[11] But overall, the result struck Le Clerc, Buddeus, Heumann, and so forth as mainly indicative of the vast intellectual gulf scholars had to subsequently cross to escape their limitations. Except perhaps for Vossius, these authors struck the men of the new *critique* as being marked by positively astounding naïveté, credulity, and preoccupation with demonology, magic, and theological mysteries.

If Heumann entertained a poor opinion of Jonsius, who seemed to him to have absolutely no conception of what history of philosophy is,[12] he considered Hornius's volume scarcely less disastrous. Complaining of the latter's "many useless digressions" and numerous inaccurate statements as well as damaging omissions, he saw the underlying problem as one of complete lack of historical-critical sense. Hornius's effort to compose the first systematic history of philosophy since ancient times foundered, it seemed to him, on his inability both to understand the historical contexts of the systems he sought to discuss and to sift critically the early sources and authorities on which he relied. Hornius, declared Heumann, "examines almost nothing but simply throws together everything which he has learnt or has read."[13] Being totally destitute of the proper critical apparatus, Hornius, he held, had done nothing but sow confusion wherever he went.

Only marginally better was the major English contribution to precritical history of thought: Thomas Stanley's *History of Philosophy* (3 vols., 1655–60). A Royalist poet, translator, and scholar, Stanley (1625–78) at least dispensed with Hornius's demonology and focused more or less systematically on the actual content of Greek and Roman philosophy as well as on the conceptual differences between the schools. Stanley, moreover, while basing himself chiefly on Diogenes Laertius, realized at least that "there is much more to be found" about the Greek philosophers "dispersed amongst other authors."[14] But even though his history of philosophy continued to be consulted until well into the 18th century and was reissued not only in further English editions in 1687 and 1701 and in Dutch translation (1702), also, for the benefit of German scholars, in a Latin translation published at Leipzig in 1711,[15] his contribution too seemed to the new men totally inadequate as philosophy of history. While Stanley was rightly following Casaubon in dismissing the idea that Plato had been inspired by Hermes Trismegistus and encouragingly referred to the "forgery of those books which seem by some impostor, to have been compiled out of the works of Plato, and the Divine Scripture,"[16] Heumann complained that he otherwise displayed scarcely any sign of independent critical judgment. He was particularly scornful of Stanley's failure to dismiss the long-established belief, cherished by many humanists, that "Plato received some light from Moses": indeed, he seemed to give the notion fresh currency by remarking that it was backed "with much greater authorities" than were humanist claims about Hermes Trismegistus, and he listed Aristobulus, Josephus, Justin Martyr, Clement

Alexander, Eusebius, and Saint Augustine as being among these "authorities" as well as cited Numenius as exclaiming, "What is Plato (saith he) but Moses speaking Greek?"[17]

Again and again, Heumann objected to Stanley's lack of historical analysis and uncritical adherence to his sources. Deriding him as the "English Laertius," he pronounced him an author sufficiently versed in Greek and Latin scholarship who, however, "lacks judgment both historical and philosophical" and, further, "yields nothing to Laertius in *Leichtgläubigkeit* (credulity)."[18] This was as damning a judgment as one could make in the early Enlightenment period, Diogenes Laertius *dont l'ouvrage est écrit sans méthode comme sans critique*,[19] as Fréret put it, having become the measure of everything deemed defective in precritical history of philosophy and all the more so in that the new men, Le Clerc foremost among them, dismissed all of the existing Renaissance humanist editions of that unique ancient source as completely uncritical and almost useless.[20]

Yet no less fatal than lack of critical judgment, as it seemed to the practitioners of the new discipline of history of philosophy, was their predecessors' inability to conceive of history of philosophy other than as something closely linked, and subordinate, to theology. Whether explicit or not, until the late 17th century, theological premises undoubtedly continued to shape the landscape within which the subject was conceived and explored. Hornius's account of philosophy's history begins with Adam and takes it for granted that a major role was played by supernatural forces.[21] What seemed to him the impious and atheistic tendencies in much of ancient Greek philosophy he deemed essentially demonic in inspiration, indeed as having been directly introduced by Satan himself.[22] Furthermore, as Heumann notes with undisguised contempt, one of his chief aims was to play down the contribution of the pagan Greeks,[23] the seeds of sound philosophy, according to Hornius, like De Grau and De Raey later,[24] having been passed down by Noah and his sons via the Hebrews, Egyptians, Babylonians, Assyrians, Persians, and Indians, with the role of Moses being regarded as especially pivotal.[25] De Grau, leaning heavily on such Church Fathers as Clement of Alexandria and Eusebius, later reaffirmed the supposed dependence of Thales, Pythagoras, and other early Greek thinkers on the Hebrews and Egyptians as well as the presiding role of Moses.[26]

Finally Hornius—unlike De Raey, whose Cartesianism prompted him to attack both Aristotelianism and the new Eclecticism[27]—added insult to injury particularly in Cartesian eyes by venerating Aristotle as *princeps philosophorum*, indeed asserting Aristotle's superiority over all other thinkers on the grounds he had collected the diverse elements of philosophy "into one body and system," which could then be thoroughly approved by Christian theologians.[28] It was indeed only with the rise of the new history of philosophy that theological premises and supernatural agencies became eradicated from ideas about the evolution of human thought, which was now conceived in increasingly secular and nonsupernatural terms. Exponents of the new history of philosophy pointed out that Moses had undoubtedly been a great prophet but not a philosopher and that far from philosophy having been handed down from Noah via the Hebrews, Egyptians, and Babylonians, it was in fact the Greeks—just as Diogenes Laertes and other ancient authors claimed—who invented the discipline.[29] Furthermore, by *philosophy* they made clear that what was meant was not so much, or not only, astronomy or natural science but still more metaphysics, logic, and moral philosophy. Eulogizing Socrates, Heumann categorically insisted that ancient Greece was *die Mutter der Moral-Philosophie.*[30]

The new men, then, were right to claim that a very wide gulf separated them from the notions of history of philosophy prevailing in Europe from the rise of philological *humanisme érudit* down to the third quarter of the 17th century. What was now conceived of as history of philosophy arose, though, out of an exceptionally fraught intellectual atmosphere, a veritable war of philosophies, and from the outset was considered not just a reference aid but, rather, a weapon and principal working tool of philosophers. Jakob Thomasius thought systematic research into *historia philosophica* indispensable to his scheme for a modernized Eclecticism intended to reform the old Aristotelian scholasticism while retaining its best points; at the same time, his new historicoeclectic system was from the outset designed to repulse libertinism, Cartesianism, and Spinozism as well as all forms of uncritical, indiscriminate syncretism, "which mixes truth with what is false."[31]

By contrast, Bayle's extensive contributions to the new study of history of philosophy were closely tied to his philosophical battle with the *rationaux*—that is, the type of philosophizing represented by Le Clerc, Jacques Bernard, Isaac Jaquelot, and in some respects Locke— writers who argued that an essentially empiricist philosophy like Locke's could and should be systematically joined to a rational theology (such as Le Clerc's). But at the same time as he sought to demonstrate that reason cannot support faith, Bayle's researches into past philosophers also had much to do with his elaborate critiques of Arisotelianism, Malebranche, and Spinoza and, in particular, his notorious claim in his *Dictionnaire* and *Continuation des Pensées Diverses* (1705) that proto- and quasi-Spinozist tendencies permeate pre-Socratic Greek thought and Stoicism, as well as Stratonism and diverse other schools of Hellenistic philosophy besides Averroism and diverse strands of Islamic and Christian medieval and Renaissance philosophy.[32] Meanwhile, Buddeus, Heumann, and Brucker developed their Thomasian Eclecticism with history of philosophy as a central component. For them too, history of philosophy was an essential tool of philosophizing *and* a weapon against Cartesianism, Spinozism, and Bayle, as well as Leibniz and Wolff. Meanwhile, Gundling, though a pupil of Christian Thomasius, veered in a different direction and seems to a considerable extent to have followed Bayle, whose criticophilosophical method and pursuit of toleration and freedom of opinion he much admired and from whom he admitted having learned much.[33] Gundling employed history of philosophy in a scholarly but yet also rather subversive fashion somewhat in the manner of Fréret, Lévesque de Burigny, and Boureau-Deslandes's *Histoire Critique de la philosophie* (3 vols., Amsterdam, 1737). Among his more disturbing claims were his insistence, against Buddeus, that Hobbes was not an atheist and his contention not only that was Bayle right to identify Plotinus as a proto-Spinozist but also that even Platonism itself is, at bottom, essentially monist and ultimately Spinozistic.[34]

That the eclectic impulse to draw on successive stages in the evolution of philosophy in order to shape a viable new philosophy was a shared feature of both the conservative and Radical enlightenments and was more than a merely temporary feature of the latter, is shown by the example of Diderot, who during the 1740s and 1750s developed not only into a skilled encyclopedist but simultaneously into an exponent of a monistic, evolutionary, materialistic hylozoism that he himself considered to be related to strands of ancient Greek thought as well as Spinoza: *"Selon moi,"* he wrote to an ally in October 1765, *"la sensibilité, c'est une propriété universelle de la matière."* [35] This, he knew, widely separated him from the bulk of his contemporaries and the entire legacy of Christian thought while simultaneously, or so it seemed, connecting him to a venerable tradition reaching back via Lucretius and the Hellenistic age to the Presocratics besides strands of ancient Indian and Chinese philosophy.[36] The shifting, provisional nature of his formulations and his preference for keeping his system open to all influences and as inclusive as possible led him to cultivate what might be termed a radical non-Christian eclecticism that borrowed extensively from the Eclectic and anti-Spinozist Brucker.[37]

What all of this boils down to is that the new discipline of history of philosophy simultaneously played a crucial role in developing and refining one of the chief blocs of the European conservative Enlightenment—namely, Thomasian Eclecticism—and, from Bayle onward, in shaping the Radical Enlightenment. What these two conflicting initiatives had in common was also something that, in both cases, stimulated the new field of study—namely, the conviction that theology must be uncoupled from philosophy, and reason and faith kept separate. This was combined with the notion that philosophical truth is to be found widely scattered among mankind, albeit also usually obscured by myth and theology, so that, however vaguely, glimpses of it are to be garnered everywhere and in all systems of thought. The task of the historian of philosophy and of the philosopher, therefore, in their eyes tended to converge. This meant that philosophers were thrust into a forum in which scholars dusted down—and revealed to view—previously half-submerged and concealed fragments of truth scattered across human history and had little choice but to relate their systems to this new activity. The German "enlightened" Eclectics and such radicals and crypto-Spinozists as Fréret and Diderot alike believed that philosophers ignorant of history of philosophy cannot meaningfully philosophize, since all of the grounding and proofs of any viable philosophy lie in what Brucker called *historia intellectus humani* itself.

The two opposing blocs agreed that history of philosophy had become doubly vital in being both an instrument for "doing philosophy" and a prime tool of education and publicity. In a world visibly being remade, in which the reeducation of the public and the public sphere became so bitterly contested an arena, guiding the young in the "right" direction seemed increasingly vital. Hence, in introducing his journal the *Acta Philosophorum*, in 1715, Heumann offered among his reasons for promoting *historia philosophica* his conviction that it was now urgent to teach young Germans how to classify and evaluate philosophical concepts so as to more effectively counter the atheistic, deistic, and Spinozistic tendencies vitiating the scholarly world of his time.[38]

Hitherto, he reasoned, there had been scant need to teach the ordinary layman to distinguish "good" philosophical ideas from "bad," and constructive concepts from those that are harmful, since practically everyone, in the most vital matters, adjusted to the guidance of the Church. But since the late-17th-century philosophy wars had erupted, young people were frequently misled by "bad" ideas so that they had to be taught to distinguish between viable and unfounded concepts, and to do this, he urged, the best aid was precisely history of philosophy because this study reveals the pedigree and hence true character—good or evil, Christian or un-Christian—of all of the diverse philosophical schools and traditions. The new *historia philosophica*, he believed, lit the path to sound philosophizing, for as he saw it, only the modern Eclectics who comprehensively examine—with judgment, scholarly skill, discernment, and a Christian conscience—the whole range of what is available know how to steer between the multiple pitfalls of Aristotelianism, Cartesianism, Spinozism, Malebranchism, and Bayle's radical fideism.[39] The supreme teacher of contemporary society, the Luther of philosophy, as he calls him, was precisely his revered teacher, Christian Thomasius, who, with his father, had been the first to grasp the vital importance of this.

Radical thinkers, meanwhile, also envisaged truth as widely scattered and as appearing over the ages in a succession of outward forms that exercised a powerful hold albeit only temporarily within specific historical contexts. *"Le progrès des connaissances humaines est une route tracée,"* held Diderot, *"d'où il est presque impossible à l'esprit humain de s'écarter. Chaque siècle a son genre et son espèce de grands hommes."*[40] But where for the Eclectics progress in philosophy includes harmonizing philosophy with theology, for the radicals there remains an ancient, coherent, and in a special sense eternal inner core that finds no legitimate expression in theological terms and that for those who think independently and venerate only reason remains unalterably and always a guiding force. On these grounds, Diderot placed the Eclectics high among those *philosophes* "*qui sont les souverains sur la surface de la terre, les seuls qui soient restés dans l'état de nature, où tout étoit à tous.*"[41]

Evidently, then, the new discipline of history of philosophy simultaneously played a crucial role in developing and refining one of the chief blocs of the European conservative Enlightenment— namely, Thomasian Eclecticism—and, from Bayle to Diderot, simultaneously in shaping the Radical Enlightenment. For both, the key tasks of the historian of philosophy, and the philosopher, tend to converge. This meant that philosophers were thrust into a new forum where scholars dusted down, and revealed to view, previously half-submerged and concealed fragments of truth scattered across human history. From the perspective of both the Thomasians and the Radical Enlightenment, philosophers were left with little choice but to incorporate this new activity in integral, creative, and dynamic ways into their own thought. Eager to attack philosophers who refused to adjust in this manner for their obscurantism and ignorance, they claimed that philosophers ignorant of history of philosophy cannot competently philosophize, since all of the grounding and proofs of any meaningful philosophy can and need to be located in the full context of Diderot's human progression or what Brucker called *historia intellectus humani.*

From the mid 18th century onward, by contrast, the prestige of history of philosophy appeared to recede, particularly on the conservative right. While during the 18th century the moderate mainstream with the support of governments, churches, and most opinion could with some justification claim to have defeated the Radical Enlightenment, it was far from clear that it had won the battle on purely intellectual grounds. On the contrary, one of the strongest claims of the rival Counter-Enlightenment in the late 18th century and during the early 19th was precisely that the moderate mainstream were deluding themselves if they think there is a philosophical middle path and that, in fact, there is no purely philosophical reply to Spinozistic radicalism. It was for this reason, urged the Counter-Enlightenment, that the radical wing had managed to appropriate the concept *l'esprit philosophique* and turn this into such a dangerously subversive force. Consequently, for conservatives, philosophy had to necessarily evolve into something quite different from late-18th-century *esprit philosophique,* which, after Diderot, Helvétius, and Mably exclusively meant the application of materialist, naturalistic, and democratic republican philosophical principles in a consistent fashion to the whole of the human reality. Philosophy as such, held Jacobi, cannot answer or defeat Spinozism in Diderot's broad sense; that is, the claim that the whole of reality consists of a single coherent structure, governed by a single set of rules, in which contingency has no part, all cause and effect being mechanistic but also hylozoic so that Nature evolves, creating itself without any external Providence, and accordingly that philosophy's province is everything. In the 20th century, Einstein described this Spinozistic conception, which he admitted was also his own as postulating the unity and "orderly harmony of what exists" without any divine or supernatural intervention.[42]

What this implied, the men of the Counter-Enlightenment and the post-1815 Restoration appreciated, was that philosophy can neither prove the truth of miracles, supernatural forces, disembodied spirits, free will, and life in the hereafter, nor justify monarchy and aristocracy, nor uphold ecclesiastical authority. This meant that there is no means, via philosophy, to counter the republican, anti-hierarchical, and anticlerical principles of the republican democrats, *nouveaux Spinozistes,* and radical *philosophes.* Consequently, if governments and society aspire, as in the early 19th century they most assuredly did, to uphold revealed religion, monarchy, and aristocracy and to repel democracy and individual freedom, then there was no alternative but to drastically narrow the scope of philosophy itself and repudiate all efforts to equate philosophy with what the radical *philosophes* called *l'esprit philosophique.*

Hence, from the perspective of scholars immersed in the philosophical wars of the Enlightenment, the insistence of most of 19th- and 20th-century Anglo-American philosophy—with the possible exception of a holistic pragmatism applied to all human culture[43]—that the subject should be further and further narrowed and turned into as technical a discipline as possible inevitably makes a very strange impression. It is no doubt vital to explore the limits of reason. But whether based on reason alone, or faith, Man cannot dispense with some kind of account of reality as a whole—even if that account is purely nihilistic or totally irrational. Restricting philosophy's scope so that it is reduced to efforts to explain a small slice of reality can only mean abandoning the rest to what lies outside philosophy in its Enlightenment sense—namely, theological explanations and Counter-Enlightenment. Yet whether Anglo-American analytic philosophy dominates the discipline in the future or not, there will still be secular minds wanting secular, naturalistic explanations of the cosmos who, without wishing to espouse Marxism or some other secular quasi-religion or Nietzsche's Weltanschauung, remain committed to the quest for this-worldly principles that are universal, coherent, and persuasive enough to justify modern antihierarchy, democracy, toleration, and equality. That being so, it would appear there is no alternative to reincorporating philosophy of history as a key tool of philosophizing.

NOTES

1. Michael Albrecht, *Eklektik. Eine Begriffsgeschichte mit Hinweisen auf die Philosophie- und Wissenschaftsgeschichte*, Stuttgart, 1994, 493–96, 507–8, 539–58; Ulrich Schneider, "Eclecticism and the History of Philosophy," in D. R. Kelley, ed., *History and the Disciplines: The Reclassification of Knowledge in Early Modern Europe*, Rochester, N.Y., 1997, 83–102; Donald R. Kelley, *The Descent of Ideas. The History of Intellectual History*, Aldershot, 2002, 141–68.

2. Christoph August Heumann, *Acta Philosophorum, das ist: Gründl. Nachrichten aus der Historia philosophica*, 18 vols., Halle, Germany, 1715–27, vi (1716), 1033.

3. Nikolaus Hieronymus Gundling, *Vollständige Historie der Gelahrheit*, 5 vols., Frankfurt-Leipzig, 1734–36, i, 933–41; C. Blackwell, "The Logic of History of Philosophy. Morhof's *De Variis Methodis* and the *Polyhistor philosophicus*," in Françoise Waquet, ed., *Mapping the World of Learning: The Polyhistor of Daniel Georg Morhof*, Wiesbaden, Germany, 2000, 106–9.

4. Jean Jehasse, *La Renaissance de la critique. L'essor de l'humanisme érudit de 1560 à 1614*, Paris 2002, xiv, xvii, 114, 668–70.

5. See Jonathan Israel, *Radical Enlightenment. Philosophy and the Making of Modernity 1650–1750*, Oxford, England, 2001, 442–43, 546–47, 628–36, 652–53.

6. Herbert Jaumann, *Critica. Untersuchungen zur Geschichte der Literaturkritik zwischen Quintilian und Thomasius*, Leiden, Netherlands, 1995, 95, 176–80, 191, 213.

7. The term, of course, reappears in the title of Jean Dagen, *L'histoire de l'esprit humain dans la pensée française de Fontenelle à Condorcet*, Paris, 1977.

8. See, in this connection, Morton White, *A Philosophy of Culture: The Scope of Holistic Pragmatism*, Princeton, N.J.: Princeton University Press, 2002.

9. Gundling, *Vollständige Historie* i, 909–20; Jean Le Clerc, *Ars Critica, in qua ad studia linguarum Latinae, Graecae, et Hebraicae via munitur*, 2 vols., Amsterdam, Netherlands, 1697, ii, 449–50.

10. Heumann, *Acta Philosophorum* vi, 1716; Kelley, *Descent of Ideas*, 85.

11. Heumann, *Acta Philosophorum* vi, 1716, 1049, 1054; Jakob Brucker, *Historia Critica Philosophiae*, 2nd edition, Leipzig, 1767, i, 35–38.

12. Heumann, *Acta Philosophorum* iii, 1715, 161.

13. Ibid., vi, 1716, 1046–49.

14. Thomas Stanley, *The History of Philosophy containing the Lives, Opinions, Actions and Discourses of the Philosophers of every Sect*, 3 vols. 2nd edition, London, 1687, i, preface; Heumann, *Acta Philosophorum* iii, 1715, 537–38; Kelley, *Descent of Ideas*, 97–98.

15. Heumann, *Acta Philosophorum* iii, 1715, 529.
16. Stanley, *History of Philosophy* i, 160.
17. Ibid.
18. Heumann, *Acta Philosophorum* iii, 1715, 538–39; Gundling, *Vollständige Historie* i, 919.
19. Nicolas Fréret, *Oeuvres complètes,* 20 vols., Paris, "an IV," 1796, ii, 38.
20. Le Clerc, *Ars Critica* ii, 449–50.
21. Georgius Hornius, *Historiae philosophicae libri septem. Quibus de origine, successione, sectis et vita philosophorum ab orbe condito ad nostram aetatem agitur,* Leiden, 1655, 47–49, 52, 57–59; Kelley, *Descent of Ideas,* 97.
22. Hornius, *Historiae Philosophicae,* 49.
23. Ibid., 135.
24. Abraham de Grau, *Historia Philosophica,* 2 vols., Franeker, 1674, i, 19–35, 40, 120. Nikolaus Hieronymus Gundling, *Sammlung kleiner teuscher Schriften und Anmerckungen,* Halle, Germany, 1737, 169–70.
25. Hornius, *Historiae philosophicae libri,* 59–61, 104, 127–30, 139; see also Malcolm de Mowbray, "What Is Philosophy? *Historia Philosophica* in the Dutch Republic, 1640–1669," paper given to the Early Modern Workshop, Institute for Advanced Study, Princeton, N.J., on November 27, 2001 (forthcoming).
26. De Grau, *Historia philosophica* i, 32–3, 40, 120.
27. De Mowbray, loc. cit.
28. Hornius, *Historiae philosophicae libri,* 194.
29. Heumann, *Acta Philosophorum* ii, 1715, 286–97, and vi, 1716, 24–32, 1038–39; Kelley, *Descent of Ideas,* 162.
30. Heumann, *Acta Philosophorum* ii,1715, 286.
31. Albrecht, *Eklektik,* 297–300; Francesco Tomasoni, "Critica al Cartesianesimo nella filosofia eclectica di Christian Thomasius," in M. T. Marcialis and F. M. Crasta, ed., *Descartes e l'eredità cartesiana nell'Europa sei- settecentesca,* Lecce, 2002, 151; Kelley, *Descent of Ideas,* 148–53; Martin Mulsow, *Moderne aus dem Untergrund. Radikale Frühauklärung in Deutschland,* 1680–1720, Hamburg, Germany, 2002, 259, 291–99.
32. Guido Canziani, "Les philosophes de la Renaissance italienne dans le Dictionnaire," in Hans Bots, ed., *Critique, Savoir et Érudition à la veille des Lumières,* Amsterdam-Maarssen 1998, 143–64; Gianluca Mori, *Bayle philosophe,* Paris, 1999, 133–88.
33. Gundling, *Vollständige Historie* i, 913; Jaumann, *Critica,* 218; Albrecht, *Eklektik,* 576–77; Mulsow, *Moderne aus dem Untergrund,* 297.
34. Nikolaus Hieronymus Gundling, *Gundlingiana. Darinnen allerhand Jurisprudenz, Philosophie, Historie, Critic, Litteratur und übrigen Gelehrsamkeit gebörige Sachen abgehandelt werden,* 5 vols, Halle, Germany, 1715–28, ii, 312–15, and v, 189–91, 222–44; Gundling, *Vollständige Historie* i, 919–36,

and iv, 4907–8; Mulsow, *Moderne aus dem Untergrund*, 235, 288–91, 300–313.

35. I. Mihaila, "L'*hylozoïsme* de Diderot," in B. Fink and G. Stenger, ed., *Être matérialiste à l'âge des lumières. Hommage offert à Roland Desné*, Paris, 1999, 189.

36. Ibid., 191–93.

37. Dagen, *L'Histoire de l'esprit humain*, 455–56; Albrecht, Eklektik, 562–66.

38. Heumann, *Acta Philosophorum* i, preface.

39. Albrecht, *Eklektik*, 495.

40. Diderot, *Oeuvres complètes* xiv, 140.

41. Donini, "History," 19.

42. R. W. Clark, *Einstein. The Life and Times*, New York, 1971, repr. 1994, 502.

43. White, *Philosophy of Culture*, 185–87.

History and/or Philosophy

Donald R. Kelley

> For what man, in the natural state or course of thinking, did ever
> conceive it in his power to reduce the notions of all mankind exactly to
> the same length, and breadth, and height of his own?
>
> —*Jonathan Swift*

HISTORY AND PHILOSOPHY have had a love-hate relationship—a mutual admiration/detestation society—for centuries despite the defection of some scholars and the emergence in the 17th century of a new discipline based on a problematic alliance between them, that is, the history of philosophy. Does this have something to do with the fact that though each discipline claimed to be a form of wisdom, philosophy was a product of largely oral culture, and history, of largely written culture—one based on intellectual exchange and the other on storytelling? In any case, the traditional point of difference, or conceptual casus belli, was simple, for as Johann Jonsius wrote in 1659, "History considers singulars [*singularia*], and philosophy considers universals [*universalia*]," thus recalling the medieval problem of universals.[1] In fact, the history of philosophy, rational if not empirical or "positive" philosophy, has continued to be plagued by this disjunction—this "inner contradiction," as Hegel called it—in a number of ways.[2]

As a practice, the history of philosophy began in antiquity, especially in the doxographical work of Diogenes Laertius (third century B.C.E.), with many later editions and commentaries, reinforced by the rival genres de viris illustribus and vitae sanctorum.[3] As a modern discipline, the history of philosophy emerged in the wake of Renaissance scholarship, was received into the universities from the 17th century, and was summarized and codified in J. J. Brucker's *Critical History of Philosophy* (1741–43), which established the first version of the canon of academic philosophy down to the derivative handbooks of Tennemann, Cousin, Windelband, and Ueberweg (which is just now appearing in a new edition). The first theoretical justification for the history appeared in the context of modern Eclectic philosophy, which assumed the name from the ancient Eclectic school reported by Diogenes Laertius but assumed new form under the influence of Lutheran thought and which was largely responsible for the aforementioned canon.[4]

The new Eclecticism took its stand on the principle of "the liberty of philosophizing" (*libertas philosophandi*)—that is, the liberation of scholars from dependence on one sectarian view, the right to select from many, and the assumption that history, not metaphysics, was "first philosophy," so that, as Christian Thomasius wrote in the 17th century, "History and philosophy are the two eyes of wisdom; if one is missing, then one is half-blind" (*einäugy*).[5] Yet it also bound them to tradition in the sense that one of its premises was that truth was the product not of individual but of collective effort. According to Bacon (admitted posthumously into the Eclectic canon), "The perfection of the sciences is to be looked for not from the swiftness and ability of one inquirer but from a succession."[6] This assumption owed something not only to Bacon's program of cooperative research but also to the skeptical view of individual genius. As Francisco Sánches had asked, "But, after all those great men, what fresh contribution can *you* possible make? Was Truth waiting for *you* to come upon the scene?"[7] This intellectual humility also entailed examining philosophical error, so that wisdom could be distinguished from falsity, *sapientia* from *stultitia*, as historians of theology have long done and as historians of philosophy still do.[8] So the aim of Eclecticism was to join the old, unreflective, doxographical tradition and its philological extension with the scientific search for truth in order to give philosophical legitimacy to history and, conversely, historical legitimacy to philosophy.

But the eclectic, or electric, method, as it was called, also marked the beginning of a rupture in modern academic philosophy, which was (at least in retrospect) that between the old encyclopedic view, according to which philosophy was the study of everything knowable (*philosophia est omnis scibilis cognitio*, in the words of Johann Alsted),[9] and the newer view that would reduce philosophy to matters of logic, pure reason, and perhaps mathematics. Both parties claimed to be critical, but the first was closer to philological criticism, while the second inclined to the standards of mathematics. The latter had little use for the doxographical tradition and what Leibniz regarded as the merely external aspects of philosophy, and indeed Leibniz himself praised his teacher (and Christian Thomasius's father) Jakob Thomasius for turning away from the distractions of unreflective learning. "Most of the others are skilled rather in antiquity than in science and have given us lives rather than doctrines," Leibniz wrote in his famous letter of 1669.[10] "You will give us the history of philosophy, not of philosophers."

In this same spirit, suspicions of the encyclopedic approach were growing in the generation before Kant as it was introduced into the universities through massive textbooks assigned as introductions to philosophy. For example, in an early Latin essay on the history of philosophy, Kant's friend Christian Garve described his early enthusiasm for the subject and then its disappointing aftermath. "How can I describe how much my hope was disappointed?" he asked. "Out of that great and splendid apparatus nothing has issued except the lives of philosophers and the listing of dry opinions."[11] As Kantian J. C. A. Grohmann believed—a prediction heard more than once over the next two centuries—"The history of philosophy is the end of all philosophizing."[12] "The history of philosophy," remarked Jules Michelet more radically, "kills philosophy," and indeed the shrinking canon of Western philosophy was strewn with the corpses, so to speak, of philosophers discredited or cast out into intellectual oblivion by later truth-seeking critics.

This theme was taken up more directly by Hegel, who argued that the history of his science was not a mere gallery of opinions, as presented in the tradition of textbooks (such as Brucker's), which he rejected, but rather a rational enterprise whose essence must be followed logically and not chronologically. Recalling the formula cited earlier, Hegel dismissed erudition as merely "knowing a mass of useless things...without any substance or interest in themselves." Moreover, the past remained a "foreign country" to historians, for as Hegel put it, in a striking anticipation of contemporary presentist hermeneutics, "The course of history does not show us the Becoming of things foreign to us, but the Becoming of ourselves and of our knowledge." For Hegel, in other words, history was transformed—that is, philosophized—into a theory of development that transcended the Laertian "lives and opinions of philosophers" and that subjected the human past to the universal solvent of Hegel's integral idealism, producing a specific version of Enlightenment conjectural history (as Dugald Stewart called it)—that is, that familiar oxymoron (as many historians regard it), the *philosophy of history*. In retrospect, Hegel's system suggested, and was taken by some to be, the "end" both of history and of philosophy.

The Eclectic legacy and the learned history of philosophy, which Garve deplored and which Kant and Hegel rejected, were illustrated by the very first journal devoted to the history of philosophy—that is, the *Acta Philosophorum*, founded in 1715 by C. A. Heumann and exploited by Brucker. This journal, modeled on the *Acta Eruditorum* (if not the *Acta Apostolorum*), featured not only monographs but also reviews of the mushrooming "literature" in the field. In his extensive introduction, Heumann declared of its modern counterpart that it was "the best method of philosophy and, furthermore, that no one deserved the name *philosopher* who was not an Eclectic." In the *Acta*, Heumann offered a comprehensive survey of the history of philosophy (term, concept, and discipline) from its origin through all stages of succession and growth.[13] Heumann naturally aimed at truth, but he recognized a difference between logical and historical demonstrations, between the truth guaranteed by reason and that offered by probability and authority. What is remarkable is that unlike Leibniz, Heumann believed that philosophical understanding required not merely inward-looking speculation but also inquiry into the external conditions of philosophizing, since, as Heumann aphorized, "Philosophers are made, not born" (*Philosophi fiunt, non nascuntur*). This reversal of the condition of the poet (*nascitur non fit*) suggests another major theme of the *Acta*, which is the philosopher's character or genius, and here Heumann's emphasis on temperamental balance anticipates the observation of William James that "The history of philosophy is to great extent that of a certain clash of temperaments."[14]

Beyond psychological factors, Heuman inquired into the influence of such factors as environment, climate, the stars, and historical periods. Was there a *genius locorum* or a *genius seculi*? This was an insight summed up more concisely in Glanvill's famous phrase *climates of opinion.*[15] The point in any case was that historians had to take factors of history, race, psychology, and nationality into account and had to study the special quality of philosophizing in all of the modern nations. This was the principle followed, too, by Brucker, who declared, "We have carefully remarked those personal circumstances respecting any author, which might serve to throw light on his opinions, such, for example, as his country, his family, his education, his natural temper, his habits of life, his patrons, friends, or enemies."[16] Brucker was also concerned with questions of anachronism, which were of little interest to philosophers, so that, "We have been particularly careful, not to ascribe modern ideas and opinions to the ancients, nor to torture their expressions into a meaning which probably never entered into their thoughts, in order to accommodate them to a modern hypothesis or system."[17]

Nevertheless, the history of philosophy became a major and indeed a subsidized object of study in 18th-century Germany. In particular, it was one of the four subjects encouraged by the Prussian Academy of Sciences first headed by Leibniz (the others being metaphysics, moral philosophy, and natural law). The publications of the so-called French colony sponsored by Frederick the Great contributed to the larger effort to form a national school to compete with the schools of England and France.[18] It was hospitable to Eclectic philosophy as well as to the history of philosophy and featured the work of scholars involved in both enterprises, including those of Brucker and his epigones.[19] In German universities in the 19th century, as Ulrich Schneider has shown, courses on the history of philosophy increased steadily (rising from 19 percent of all philosophy courses in 1825 to more than 80 percent in 1955) and became a regular part of the teaching of philosophy, and this trend continued until recently, when analytic philosophy has made significant inroads. Yet the problem deplored by Hegel remained, and as Schneider also points out, many philosophers complained that the history of philosophy was confusing to students because of its doctrinal indecisiveness and distracting emphasis on research.

One central problem inherent in the history of philosophy may be seen by analogy with the history of science, which also emerged into prominence in the 18th century, and this is the difference between logical and historical progression. As J. S. Bailly wrote in his pioneering history of astronomy, "A science is a sum of truths. To link [*enchaîner*] them, to present them in their order from the simplest to the most complex is the object of elementary exposition, but the chain of these truths is not the order of their discovery."[20] This insight was also present in the great enterprise of the French *Encyclopédie*, which likewise added a historical dimension to the chain of sciences envisioned by D'Alembert in his preliminary discourse, and it received definitive expression in Auguste Comte's distinction between a historical and a dogmatic or systematic approach.[21] This was clearly the case, too, with philosophy, which developed out of the complex relationships between masters and disciples, their disputes and proofs over ideas and methods, and the conflicts between the schools, ancient and modern. Kant's so-called a priori history of philosophy would express this development in regular and rationalize terms—turn it into a sort of "conjectural history," in the words of Dugald Stewart—but this could not do justice to the order of discovery and debate, for it would still be "doing philosophy" and not writing its history.

The conceptual role of history in philosophy came under scrutiny in the late 18th century, especially as a result of the debate over the philosophy of the history of philosophy (*Philosophie der Philosophiegeschichte*), in which several questions were posed along the lines of Thomas Kuhn's exploration of the role of history in scientific discovery.[22] Was philosophy accumulated and inherited wisdom, or was it the work of an elite of master thinkers? Was history, as Eclectics argued, essential in the pursuit of wisdom? Was the history of philosophy actually a part of philosophy, as Kant himself wondered? Was the history of philosophy merely the history of *opinion* (an unexamined term that has served mainly as a pejorative way of referring to the ideas of other people).[23] Were philosophy and its history separate disciplines, as Christian Weiss asked in 1799, or identical sciences, as C. Hippeau insisted in 1837 and as Croce suggested in the next century? These problems have never been resolved and indeed are still being debated in much the same terms today in gatherings like this one and resultant volumes, a wave of which appeared in the 1980s. I have at least six volumes in English alone concerning this problem—though few of them paying attention to the deeper background suggested here—and there are others in German, Italian, and French.[24]

One question that has separated philosophers and historians is that of the accessibility of the past, a question revived a generation ago by Quentin Skinner and reflecting the older literary problem of what was ungrammatically called the intentional fallacy. The past was a foreign country in other words, and so were its languages and psychologies. Nor, according to the critique of Gadamer, was it possible to rethink the bygone thoughts of past authors as Dilthey and other champions of Romantic hermeneutics and the older historicism held, so that, despite the assistance of a semantic continuum, there can be no literal recovery of past meaning—no retrospective mind reading—but only a reformulation of meaning in present and dialogical terms.[25] Indeed, dialogue itself must be strictly limited because of the conditions of writing and what Paul Ricoeur has called the semantic autonomy of the text, according to which, as all teachers come to learn, the message received is never quite the message sent.[26] These are conditions of interpretation, which historians have lived to accept, whether or not they can be absorbed into the projects of philosophy, especially the teaching of philosophy, which have always depended on assumptions concerning the stability of terms, linguistic structures, and meanings.

Another less subtle question is that of truth, which has also depended on these assumptions about conditions of logical exchange. In the 17th century, Thomasius and others tried to throw light on this question by distinguishing between certain and probable truth and in effect between absolute and moral certainty, but the tides of Cartesian rationalism and the natural science model in the following century tended to exclude, between the extremes of truth and error, considerations of probability, prejudice, and especially opinion, private and public. The human conditions of judgment recognized by Heumann and others were regarded as irrelevant to the attainment of objective truth. "The mind has no sex," as Poullain de la Barre put it—and, similarly, no class, no nationality, nor any other cultural limitation.[27] Moreover, such a conception of truth was projected over the entire history of Western philosophy, thus segregating it from other forms of wisdom, whether pre- or post-Socratic, and losing appreciation of the ancient Greek assumptions, recently recalled by Marcel Detienne, about the intellectual privilege and hegemony of qualified "masters of truth"— wise men whose place was inherited or appropriated by the "philosophers" (and later, I might add, by historians).[28] In any case, the notion of truth as socially constructed is deeply embedded in philosophical tradition, even though it was long neglected in the history of philosophy. Ever since the time of the ancient Greek *Aletheia*, philosophers have developed a conception of and a monopoly over truth, which was reinforced by modern natural and mathematical philosophy by modern "masters of truth" and then projected back over philosophical tradition as a meta-historical category.

Among the enemies of truth, 18th-century philosophers, including the Eclectics, targeted in particular the vice of prejudice, which ostensibly (in the spirit of Descartes) could be avoided as an act of will, as suggested by Joseph Glanvill in his attack on dogmatizing, opinions divorced from experience, and "the prejudice of custom and education."[29] Such prejudice, however, included not only identifiable errors but also what Heidegger called "forestructures of understanding" and the grounds of meaning, including languages and cultural environment; and as Hans-Georg Gadamer has pointed out, the Enlightenment's naive "prejudice against prejudice" has actually undermined rational as well as historical criticism.[30] In fact, he concluded, prejudice is not an obstacle to but a condition of understanding, though I do not see that this insight has been followed up by philosophers outside the hermeneutical tradition.

The history of philosophy is often told as a succession of master thinkers (Heidegger's self-serving term) who, in the words of Dugald Stewart, taken from Lucretius and Plato, passed the lamp of Enlightenment down through the ages with the help of reason and "criticism." But there has been a rival tradition, associated with Protagoras and the Sophists, which has emphasized the primacy of language in philosophy, and this position, taken up by Renaissance humanists, was resumed in the age of Kantian criticism by scholars like Hamann and Herder in the name of "metacriticism" and the importance of history to the practice of reason itself. Three years after the publication of Kant's first *Kritik*, Hamann issued his *Metakritik* of the "purity of reason," which for him involved the partly misconceived, partly unsuccessful attempt to make reason independent of all custom, tradition, experience, and even language.[31] Ultimately, Hamann's deepest concerns were religious, but his arguments rested on empirical, linguistic, anthropological, and historical grounds—what Kant called *kat' anthropon* arguments, which were not universally valid but which were convincing to a limited audience, such as the audience aimed at by men of letters and the so-called popular philosophers.

Herder shared Hamann's religious motives and Kant's philosophical ambitions, and his point of departure, too, lay in language and literature, since he regarded these fields of study as truly foundational for the formulation of rational arguments and philosophical criticism. (Of course, Kant would reject this, and it was no compliment when he suggested that Herder's true calling lay in "philosophical poetry" like that of Pope.) In fact, Herder would agree with Pope's formula about the "proper study of mankind"— which itself recalled the Protagorean "Man is the measure of all things." For Herder and others of his persuasion, the main question was not, What is Enlightenment? but rather What is humanity?—and anthropology rather than logic, metaphysics, or epistemology was the key discipline. On this topic there was a vast debate, including hundreds of doctoral dissertations and journal articles, and Herder himself expanded metacriticism into a systematic review and rejection of Kant's critique of pure reason.[32] For Herder, space and time are not absolutes but derivations from experience, the calendar of nature and the conventions and tenses of language. There is no a priori knowledge, and self-knowledge is empty without awareness, a posteriori and from concrete experience, of the Other—that is, of the historically remote as well as the culturally different. For grasping this sort of alterity was also part of the Enlightenment project, and this was what led to Herder's own turn to what he called the philosophy of history and then cultural history (*Kulturgeschichte*), which was the path he chose to understand reason not just in its allegedly pure form but also in its human development.[33]

Nobody reads Herder's *Metakritik* these days, and this is not a connection I've seen made, but I believe that what he offers, in his rejection of late-18th-century philosophical fashion, is not only an epistemological metacritique of the empty abstractions of critical philosophy but also a justification of cultural history as the more comprehensive and human way to a critique of reason—for *human* reason is indeed all we can know. To suggest the folly of philosophical schemes Herder quoted at length from Swift's *Tale of a Tub*, which situated philosophers in the "academy of modern bedlam." "For what man, in the natural state or course of thinking, did ever conceive it in his power to reduce the notions of all mankind exactly to the same length, and breadth, and height of his own?" asked Swift. "Yet [answering his own question] this is the first humble and civil design of all innovators in the empire of reason." Swift meant Descartes, but Herder turned the ridicule on Kant and his followers.

Herder's arguments, however, were ruled out of court by academic philosophers both then and in the philosophical canon ever since. In the two centuries since, Kantian professional philosophy, especially in Germany, has continued mainly along the yellow brick road of internal reflection to the Emerald City of pure reason and pure apriorism, as in the early Husserl's vision of philosophy as "rigorous." At most there are distant echoes of Herder from philosophers on the margins of their profession, such as Gadamer, who remarked that, "In phenomenology, then, the same abysmal forgetfulness of language, so characteristic of transcendental idealism, was repeated, thus appearing to confirm, albeit belatedly, Herder's ill-fated criticism of the Kantian transcendental turn"[34]—and, further away, Derrida, who asked in his commentary on Husserl, "Did not Herder [in *Metacritique of Pure Reason*] already reproach Kant for not taking into consideration the intrinsic necessity of language and its immanence in the most a priori act of thought?"—suggesting also that Derrida goes on to add that this "unhistorical naïveté may be the basis of Husserl's supposed methodological revolution."[35] But of course Husserl himself came to appreciate the subversions that history could work on the Enlightenment project in his later work on the crisis of the cultural sciences. In general I have been struck by the extent to which modern discussions of the role of history in philosophy have repeated the debates over the *Philosophie der Philosophiegeschichte* in the 18th century. Jonathan Bennett's study of Spinoza, according to Daniel Garber, was aimed at "finding philosophical truth and avoiding philosophical falsehood—which was precisely the aim of Eclectic philosophy." [36] The question, unanswered by the Eclectics, remains: what are the criteria of "philosophical truth"—or in Garber's rendition, "what we have come to think of is true"—and its opposite? In his derivative entry for the *Encyclopédie*, virtually a translation of Brucker, Diderot emphasized the freedom of Eclectic philosophy from tradition, authority, and prejudice and its attempt "to restore the clearest general principles, to examine and to discuss them without admitting anything beyond the testimony of experience and reason," but of course this was to subject the history of philosophy to current conceptions of experience and reason, and so the old criticism also remains: why bother with the rest of what history has to offer that is either false, irrelevant, or of mere antiquarian interest? Since the time of the ancient Greek *Aletheia*, philosophers have developed a conception of and a monopoly over truth, which was reinforced by modern natural and mathematical philosophy by modern "masters of truth" and then projected back over philosophical tradition as a timeless and universal category, first (as with the Eclectics) guaranteed by faith in religion and later by an equally dogmatic faith in secular reason.

Philosophy is notoriously an internalist enterprise, and perhaps these admittedly externalist considerations are too far beyond the horizons and discourse of philosophers, especially for the purposes of teaching. It is certainly the case that the critiques of philosophers like Rorty and Derrida have not been welcomed by everyone within the academic fold, and there is little reason to believe that the views of historians will be much attended to either. The main impediment to dialogue in this area, it seems to me, is the hermetically disciplinary, or even superdisciplinary, character of modern academic philosophy and its attendant history, especially in the United States. The common phrases *doing philosophy* and *being a philosopher* are indications of the notion that when philosophers are talking or writing, they are doing more than this; they are participating in a transcendent exchange of ideas and arguments that are not privy to laypersons or subject to extradisciplinary criticism. But for historians, talk by "masters of truth" is still talk, philosophical writing is still writing, "doing philosophy" still requires verbal exchange (and so does interpretation), and professional or disciplinary taboos cannot apply to these aspects of the human condition. I do not mean this as a philosophical position, of course, but only to suggest that residual spiritualism is inappropriate to the craft of the historian or the critic (as a writer if not a teacher).

I recall a conversation with John Rawls years ago, just when he was making his own way "back to Kant," and the distinction he made between writing philosophy and doing philosophy I'm sorry I did not have the presence of mind to pursue this very (it seems to me) Kantian line about the purity of thought detached from the vulgar constraints of the written word—another version, perhaps, of the problem of universals. In any case, I began to appreciate the emphasis perversely placed on writing (*Écriture*) by Derrida, and I did pursue the issue with philosophers, especially my late colleague, also a devout Kantian, Lewis Beck, who was in no way impressed with my simplification of Derrida's arcane line of argument. I also recall reporting to Lewis with some satisfaction the election of Derrida to the American Academy of Arts and Sciences, though I was subdued—though at the same time justified—by his response that this had been achieved only under the rubric of "literary criticism (including philology)."

In this connection I also came to understand why historical and literary critics of Kant like Herder and Meiners, who have been virtually read out of the history of philosophy, turned to the history of literature and the history of culture in the later 18th century— and not without parting shots at what they saw as the unhistorical and vacuous tendencies of Kantian and post- (or neo-)Kantian philosophy. My recent book *The Descent of Ideas* was in part an account of this divergence and of the separation, incomplete as it has been, of intellectual history (or the history of ideas) from the history of (philosophical) ideas, and it may suggest some reasons for what might seem my antiphilosophical attitude toward the history of philosophy.[37] In fact, I do not think we can do without either discipline, or, rather, any of the three disciplines, but I have no philosophical prescription for a perfect union or even peaceful coexistence. At their best they continue to provide, if not agreement about truth, at least alternative paths to wisdom.

NOTES

1. Jonsius, *De Scriptoribus historiae philosophiae libri I* [1659], Jena, Germany, 1716.
2. *Introduction to the Lectrures on the History of Philosophy*, trans. T. M. Knox and A. V. Miller, Oxford, England, 1985, 11.
3. Diogenes Laertius, *Lives of Eminent Philosophers*, trans. R. D. Hicks, Cambridge, Mass., 1972, and see Richard Hope, *The Book of Diogenes Laertius: Its Spirit and Method*, New York, 1930, and Allen Brent, "Diogenes Laertius and the Apostolic Succession," *Journal of Ecclesiastical History*, 44, 1993, 367–89.
4. Michael Albrecht, *Eklektik: Eine Begriffsgeschichte mit Hinweisen auf die Philosophie- und Wissenschaftsgeschichte*, Stuttgart, Germany, 1993, reviewed by Ulrich Schneider in *Journal of the History of Ideas*, 59 1998, 173–82, and "Das Eklektizismus-Problem in der Philosophiegeschichte," in *Johann Jacob Brucker (1696–1770): Philosoph und Historiker der europäischen Aufklärung*, ed. Wilhelm Schmidt-Biggemann and Theo Stamm, Berlin, 1998, 135–58.
5. *Cautelae circa Praecognita jurisprudentiae in usum auditorii Thomasiani*, Halle, Germany, 1710, 84, cited by Schmidt-Biggemann, Topica Universalis, 283.
6. *De Sapientia veterum*, "Prometheus," in Works, II, 654. In general, see Steven Shapin, *The Social History of Truth: Civility and Science in Seventeenth-Century England*, Chicago, 1994.
7. *That Nothing Is Known*, ed. and trans. E. Limbrick and D. Thomson, Cambridge, England, 1988, 169.
8. See Martial Gueroult, *Histoire de l'histoire de la philosophie* I, Paris, 1984, 87, and *Zwischen Narretei und Weisheit*, ed. Gerald Hartung and Wolf Peter Klein, Hildesheim, Germany, 1997.
9. Jonsius, *De Scriptoribus historiae philosophiae libri I* [1659], Jena, Germany, 1716.
10. Preface (20/30 April 1669) to Nizolio, *De Veris Principis et vera ratione philosophandi contra pseudophilosophos libri IV*, Frankfurt, 1670, fol. 2v ("non philosophorum, sed philosophiae historia"); also in *Philosophical Papers and Letters*, trans. Leroy E. Loemker, Dordrecht, Netherlands, 1969, 93. For Leibniz's and Thomasius's exchanges on the history of philosophy, see *Leibniz-Thomasius: Correspondence 1663–1672*, ed. and trans. Richard Bodéüs, Paris, 1993.
11. *De Ratione scribendi historiam philosophiae*, Leipzig, Germany, 1768; cf. G. G. Fülleborn, ed., *Beiträge zur Geschichte der Philosophie*, Züllichau, Germany, 1791, XI, 88, and see below, ch. 9.

12. Lutz Geldsetzer, *Die Philosophie der Philosophiegeschichte im 19. Jahrhundert,* Meisenheim, Germany, 1968, 30.

13. *Acta Philosophorum,* I, 567–656, "Von dem Ingenio Philosophico." Cf. William Ringler, *"Posta nascitur non fit:* On the History of an aphorism," *JHI,* 2 (1941), 497–504. The formulas *Criticus non fit, sed nascitur,* attributed to David Ruhnken, and *interpres not fit, sed nascitur,* are reported by Phillip August Boeck, "Theory of Hermeneutics," in *The Hermeneutics Reader,* ed. Kurt Mueller Vollmer, London, 1986, 139.

14. *Pragmatism, a New Name for Some Old Ways of Thinking,* New York, 1907, 6.

15. *Vanity of Dogmatizing,* London, 1661, 227.

16. Brucker, I, 15, Enfield, England, I, 27.

17. Brucker, I, 28, Enfield, England, I, 19: "nec ad nostrorum temporum habitum et sapientiae inter nos cultae ideam philosophia vetus exigenda est."

18. See Christian Bartholmèss, *Histoire philosophique de l'Académie de Prusse depuis Leibniz jusqu'à Schelling,* Paris, 1850, I, 405; II, 63.

19. Ibid., II, 123, and see *Johann Jacob Brucker (1696–1770),* ed. Schmidt-Biggemann and Stamm (with comprehensive bibliography), especially the contributions by Schmidt-Biggemann, Longo, Blackwell, and Jehl; and Gregorio Piaia, "Brucker versus Rorty? On the 'Models' of the Historiography of Philosophy," *British Journal for the History of Philosophy,* 9 (2001), 69–81.

20. *Histoire de l'astronomie ancienne,* in *Sur l'Histoire des sciences,* ed. M. Fichaut and M. Péchaux, Paris, 1969, 143.

21. *Cours de philosophie positive,* ed. Ch. Le Verrier, Paris, n.d., I, 145.

22. Geldsetzer, *Philosophiegeschichte,* 22, "Ob die Geschichte der Philosophie selbst ein Teil der Philosophie sein könne"; 43, "Geschichte darf nicht Philosophie und Philosophie darf nicht Geschichte werden"; and 122, "Nous sommes de ceux qui regardent la philosophie et l'histoire de la philosophie comme deux sciences identiques."

23. See Kelley, "Philodoxy: Mere Opinion and the Question of History," *Journal of the History of Philosophy,* 34 (1996), 117–32.

24. Richard Rorty, J. B. Schneewind, and Quentin Skinner, ed., *Philosophy in History,* Cambridge, England, 1984; A. J. Holland, ed., *Philosophy, Its History and Historiography,* Dordrecht, Netherlands, 1985; Bernard P. Dauenhauer, ed., *At the Nexus of Philosophy and History,* Athens, Ga., 1987; Peter H. Hare, ed., *Doing Philosophy Historically,* Buffalo, N.Y., 1988; T. Z. Lavine and V. Tejera, ed., *History and Anti-History in Philosophy,* Dordrecht, Netherlands, 1989; and also Jorge J. E. Gracia, *Philosophy and Its History: Issues in Philosophical Historiography,* Albany, N.Y., 1992.

25. *Philosophical Hermeneutics*, trans. David E. Linge, Berkeley, Calif., 1976, 57.

26. *Intepretation Theory: Discourse and the Surplus of Meaning*, Fort Worth, Tex., 1976, 32.

27. Londa Schiebinger, *The Mind Has No Sex? Women in the Origins of Modern Science*, Cambridge, Mass., 1989.

28. *The Masters of Truth in Archaic Greece*, trans. Janet Lloyd, New York, 1996.

29. *Scepsis scientifica*, ed. John Owen, London, 1885, 106; 2nd edition of *The Vanity of Dogmatizing*, London, 1660; and see Werner Schneiders, *Aufklärung und Vorurteilskritik*, Stuttgart, Germany, 1983.

30. *Truth and Method*, trans. Garrett Barden and John Cumming, New York, 1975, 241.

31. *Schriften über Sprache, Mysterien, Vernunft* 1772–1788, Vienna, 1951, 283–89, trans. in Gwen Griffith Dickson, *Johann Georg Hamman's Relational Metacriticism*, Berlin, 1995, 519–25 ("Metacritique of the Purism of Reason" [1784]). See also Isaiah Berlin, *The Magus of the North: J. G. Hamann and the Origins of Modern Irrationalism*, London, 1993.

32. *Verstand und Erfahrung: Vernunft und Sprache, Metakritik*, in *Sämtliche Werke*, Stuttgart, Germany, 1853, xxxvii; and see Ulrich Geier, *Herder's Sprachphilosophie und Erkenntniskritik*, Stuttgart, Germany, 1981.

33. D. R. Kelley, "The Old Cultural History," *History and the Human Sciences*, 1996, 101–26, and "Intellectual and Cultural History: The Inside and the Outside," *History of the Human Sciences*, 15, (2002), 1–19.

34. *"Destruktion* and Deconstruction," trans. Geoff Waite and Richard Palmer, in *Dialogue and Deconstruction: The Gadamer-Derrida Encounter*, ed. Diane P. Michelfelder and Richard Palmer, Albany, N.Y., 1989, 102.

35. *Edmund Husserl's "Origins of Geometry": An Introduction*, trans. John P. Leavey, Pittsburgh, 1978; and *Of Grammatology*, trans. Gayatri Chakravorty Spivak, Baltimore,1974.

36. Hare, 28.

37. *The Descent of Ideas: The History of Intellectual History*, London, 2002.

Historians Look at the
New Histories of Philosophy

PANELISTS

Lorraine Daston, *Chair*
Anthony Grafton
Jonathan Israel
Donald R. Kelley

Harold Helm Auditorium
Princeton University
Princeton, New Jersey
Sunday, April 7, 2003

After opening remarks by Jonathan Israel, the following discussion took place:

Peter Hylton: I want to respond to something Tony Grafton said, but also more generally to say something, because it seems to me that there's a dog that hasn't barked at this conference, and I don't quite know where to begin.

But those of us who teach in philosophy departments must be aware that most of our colleagues regard philosophy as simply in the pursuit of truth and not, for the most part, truth which is of a historical nature.

Now, this is a very odd situation, because, on one hand, there are science and the history of science, and they are not the same. And you don't even expect that your scientists will know any history of science; I mean, perhaps it's nice if they do, especially the historians of science who know some science. But that's another matter.

And some people at this conference, it seems to me, have actually suggested that philosophy departments should be split off from history of philosophy departments. I don't know. It doesn't seem to me an accident. I mean, I don't think it's a good thing, but it's not incomprehensible that 1879 Hall should have it on the sign saying, Just say no to the history of philosophy.

And I guess what I'm saying is that we don't understand the relationship between philosophy and history. It's not the relationship between science and history. I think there is an integral relationship, but I think it's very hard to give an account of.

I think one kind of account which has been floating around—in particular I think of things that Karl Ameriks said—has to do with an understanding of the formation of one's own philosophical position.

But that certainly is not all there is to philosophy, at least not all philosophy says there is to it. I mean, that would be very odd if all there was to a subject was the understanding of one's own position in doing that subject which consisted entirely in an understanding of one's own position in doing that subject which consisted, and so on.

So it's certainly not all there is to philosophy. And neither can it be said that it's a necessary feature of philosophy. There are, after all, very good philosophers who are astonishingly ignorant of the formation of their own tradition.

Hume was 26 when he wrote the *Treatise of Human Nature*. How much of the history of philosophy had he had time to absorb?

There are more recent examples, but I don't wish to insult anybody by calling them ignorant, although those are not people that you're likely to find at this conference.

Anthony Grafton: One possible answer would be that, in effect, the history of philosophy serves some of the same purposes for philosophy that disciplinary history serves in science. That is, scientists do learn a form of the history of their discipline. It comes in first lectures, in the prefaces to textbooks, in glancing remarks, and it is not historical. It is not designed to be. It is designed to be part of their preparation for the current practice of the discipline.

Many people's comments have suggested that though history of philosophy is infinitely more sophisticated than disciplinary history, it occupies a bigger space than disciplinary history does in science. It is though perhaps a little to the side of the center of things, not the way that the guy in the math department who knows about the history of number theory is really off to the side.

Nonetheless, my impression from most of what I have heard is that structurally speaking, the history of philosophy serves mostly as preparation for philosophy. And in that regard in a sense it's indifferent whether it's done in the new way or the old way, as long as it serves to produce people who are good philosophers in a modern sense.

Daniel Garber: I was going to raise something very similar to what Peter just raised, but I think, Tony, you may not be understanding what this means to somebody who teaches in the philosophy department.

First of all, you know, as I think that a number of us have been saying—you know, over by the coffee urn—one of the real differences between what we do and what you do, as a consequence of Peter's observation, is, we are teaching in a department where what we do principally in our professional work is significantly different from what others do in our department.

We are preparing students to do something other than what we do, as opposed to historians of ideas, for example, who are working in one sector of generally historical confines. You do history. You do a different kind of history from your colleagues, who maybe do military history or social history or who work on Chinese history, or something like that. But it's still history.

What we're doing as historians of philosophy professionally and in our teaching careers is to prepare students to go on to do something that is in many ways very different. And I think a lot of the discussion that we have had here—I think very, very interesting discussion—is over the question—really the very contested question—of what philosophy should be.

I think what Peter said reflects the realities of many philosophy departments, particularly the graduate departments in the prestigious universities. But I think that part of the dissatisfaction, part of the subversiveness of what it is that we're doing has to do with perhaps a dissatisfaction with that conception of philosophy and an interest in changing that. And in that respect it's very interesting to look at the history of analytic philosophy as a way of underscoring the fact that where we are today itself has a history.

Donald Kelley: I just wanted to say one thing about this.

It seems to me that teaching philosophy in particular, but writing philosophy, requires an allegiance to the notion of textural reading,

reading of discrete texts, and not asking the kinds of questions that historians would: Why was this important at a certain point and not later? Why is this particular text better than another one?

The importance of analyzing a text and getting into the arguments and doing good philosophy of major figures, maybe three or so, this undercuts the program of historians, which is to ask irrelevant questions, maybe about the character of philosophers, and it seems to me that there are a lot of inarticulated differences between historians and philosophers that don't always come to the surface.

Knud Haakonssen: Well, I would like—as somebody who is most deeply into the historicized mode of doing history of philosophy— to deal in the sort of answer to Peter's question, which is a very good one, and one way of answering it is that it's exactly because one is in pursuit of truth that one wants history to read it as a spoiler of the monopoly of ways of seeking the truth that we have seen in the departments for a very long time.

In other words, there is one way of defending this, which I alluded to in my paper, a sort of union, and Don alluded to this, a union kind of true skepticism as evidence of doing history in the interests of pursuing who is after truth.

And that certainly is a reason for having a professionalized history of philosophy, which can do this at the highest level of our professionalism, so that we have a division that Dan indicates here, which means, on one hand, the professional history of philosophy that we have to pursue at the research level but which informs us as a component in our curriculum that has exactly the spoiler's purpose—that is, to try to show that there are other ways of doing philosophy than those that are part of the so-called mainstream, the epistemological paradigm, etcetera. But it's all, of course, in the interest of an idea of searching for truth.

I do not see what conflict there is, unless one has decided beforehand that there is a high road to truth and that that is philosophy.

Mark Larrimore: I would just like to register as violent as possible a protest as I am capable of at the idea that philosophers or philosophy departments have any monopoly on the teaching of critical thought or any monopoly on the pursuit of truth.

The history of philosophy is conducted by people in a number of disciplines: in political science, in comparative literature, in religion, in theology, in history, and in English.

I think it's most unfortunate that we allow the concentrations or the fixations of a particular deformation of the discipline of philosophy in the United States at this point to prevent us from thinking about the things that you might do if all of these disciplines worked together rather than all the other disciplines working round those analytic philosophers whose conception that only they are in command of some particularly sacred approach to things. It actually interferes seriously with the doing of responsible history and philosophical inquiry.

John Cooper: I wanted to respond or add some thoughts in relation to what Dan was saying in response to Peter's question. But I hope I'll be permitted to say much more than that, if that's OK, because I want also to bring into it some reference to what Tony said just before I came in the room. He was using some kind of stalking horse, but I'm not quite sure.

But, at any rate, it seems to me that however much it's true and however much we might welcome the expansion of the study of philosophy and its history in all kinds of other departments, including religion departments, it's also true, without claiming some sacred authority of any kind at all, it's also true that a philosophical study of the history of philosophy is different from a historical one, a religious one, and other very important points of view, for example, whatever goes on in English departments and whatever goes on in politics departments. And this is not because, at least according to my understanding, we are imposing some conception of philosophical work drawn from analytic philosophy of the 20th century at all.

My understanding of philosophy is an ancient one. That is, my understanding of philosophy is really the understanding you get from Socrates, which is that it's a devotion to a certain use of reason understood in a certain way—namely, a philosophical way.

I could say a lot more about what that is, and maybe I would succeed, maybe I wouldn't succeed, in getting someone who wasn't already into philosophy to understand what I was talking about, but every philosopher knows what I mean. Every member of a philosophy department knows what I mean. And that's why I disagree with Dan in thinking that what we do when we teach the history of philosophy in a philosophy department is to prepare students for something else.

What I'm doing when I teach the history of philosophy to my students is teaching them philosophy and teaching them how to think philosophically and how to live philosophically. And what they then go on to do with it, well, that's up to them. If they then go on to study Gil Harman's epistemology or somebody else's ethics, metaethics, stuff about which I might have no interest at all, that's fine by me.

What I'm interested in is reading these philosophical texts in a philosophical way where my conception of that is responsibility to the basic conception of philosophy laid down by Socrates and the Greeks, which is both a certain kind of thinking, a certain kind of responsibility, not just argument, but arguments included in it. It's an approach to how to think and live.

And that's why I do philosophy. And the reason I do the history of philosophy is that I find not just for Socrates and Plato and Aristotle and maybe Kant, if those are the ones you thought I had in mind, that's four, but equally Chrysippus is at least as great a philosopher as any modern philosopher, and Carneades as well, and not to mention Epicurus, not to mention Plotinus. These are all people who had the same conception that derived from Socrates of what philosophy is, and there's a tremendous amount to learn.

Of course, my field, as you know, is ancient philosophy. But what I'm saying I would apply to lots and lots of medieval philosophy, lots and lots of early modern philosophy, and lots and lots of 19th-century philosophy.

Wherever you can find for teaching purposes materials of a philosophical kind understood that way, then you should teach them, or you're invited to teach them. And if you can find in Pico, which I can't, but if you can find in Pico philosophical things to do, understood in this way, then I think we ought to encourage people to do more of that.

Anthony Grafton: Well, I think, John, that's exactly what I meant when I said I thought there were really quite different notions here of why one does the history of philosophy. And I really did mean that I thought you represented exactly that, a very firm statement about it as a philosophical enterprise. And I guess I feel a little bit like Ernst Gellner when he got the analysts mad at him many years ago that I have provoked exactly the kind of statement I wanted.

It seems to me, though, that there really is a question here. There is no question that at one time the main line of philosophy departments, and especially the elite philosophy departments, seemed to outsiders, and, you know, of course, I speak as an outsider, even a refugee, seemed to be undergoing a development which was in many ways parallel to that of other disciplines which had one tad of substantial historical and humanistic content and which were redefining themselves as highly technical and defining that out.

The parallel that strikes me quite forcibly in Princeton is economics, which was a very strong historical discipline here at one time, hard though that is to believe, and has simply extruded that from its definition of what economics does.

I can't tell you how wonderful it is to hear you and Dan and others protest against this version of philosophy and insist that, no, it is a humanistic discipline in its historical content. The history not only can't be extruded but is, as Knud said, a vital part of it because it tells you things you don't know otherwise. And that is, after all, I think, what philosophy is all about: the pursuit of those things.

Nonetheless, it seems to me I hear, and I know that John, not in my parodic version, but in the version of him I read, has brought authors back into the canons that weren't there before. So, honor is satisfied, I hope.

I still hear different versions here. I do hear one which, like John says, there is a thing which is philosophy, and it's great to find that Carneades lives up to that.

And I hear another version: there is a thing that was called philosophy, and history of philosophy is about reconstructing that. I think it's a good tension to have both things in the discipline, and it seems to me I have heard both positions represented very forcefully here. That's a good thing.

My question remains about teaching, because it seems to me that the ideal, from an outsider's standpoint, would really be to have historical teaching that represented both of these standpoints in a very powerful way. Since, though, most individuals are somewhere between these posts on a continuum, I suspect, it would be really good to have a student have a historical course that said there is philosophy. And a way of doing it is confrontation with the way these guys did it.

And there is a case for saying there was philosophy and it was historically contingent and it was this combination of things, institutions, intellectual developments, theological changes, and social history that made it that, and it would be good for students to hear both of those and come up with their own choices and their own voice by hearing both of them and working between them.

The thing that I remain skeptical about is whether there is the space pedagogically for allowing that or whether, in fact, the real pedagogical problem isn't that you are confined to an angle where you're going to be lucky to get a student to get one version or the other.

And that, it seems to me, is the point where I would love to see a kind of revolution in the garden take place and the standpoints both widely represented. But as a historian, I think each of them could be represented usefully heuristically, if not perhaps in an ultimate sense.

Jonathan Israel: Yes. I also wanted to say something about this fascinating juxtaposition between these two paradigms of the ancient Greek model of philosophy as setting the scene and defining what the philosopher is and what he does and the problematics for the historian of philosophy, who feels that he is teaching something which is an important preparation and is integrally related but nevertheless is not the same thing as what most philosophers in philosophy departments are actually doing.

Now, of course, both paradigms are strongly represented, as Tony has just said. Both have great relevance, and both are part of the reality that we are discussing, but I would just like to connect what John was saying with the rise of the history of philosophy linked to the new critique, the new history of philosophy of the late 17th century, as distinct from what passed for history of philosophy before.

Of course, both the Renaissance and the mid-17th-century historians of philosophy didn't think philosophy began with the Greeks, and a lot of what they were saying was trying to detract from the achievement of the Greeks.

One of the great differences between these two sages—when you get into Heumann and people like this in the beginning of the

18th century—is the enormous emphasis which starts with Bayle. One could mention various people that I link to this important change who would say you can't even begin to discuss philosophy until you realize that the Greeks invented philosophy and the Greeks set the scene by defining all the main categories and contours and issues, and if you don't realize that, if you don't appreciate that, if you don't study that, and if you're not able to historicize about it, then you can't discuss philosophy at all. I think that that is a central part of the message.

Socrates is the inventor, as far as Heumann is concerned, of moral philosophy, and so on and so forth. And they were enormously interested; it's not only the supreme greats—Socrates and Plato and Aristotle—but the discussion of the pre-Socratics, of all the different Hellenistic schools, of the very elaborate discussions of stoicism.

And then Bayle, of course, loved to bring up Hellenistic schools that everyone else had totally forgotten about. Strato and Stratonism was a favorite of his. He made it a major issue in European philosophical debate, when it hadn't been raised by anybody for hundreds and hundreds of years.

But it seems to me that although both paradigms are strongly represented, somebody might ask, let's say it's a student, or somebody else, or an interested member of the public, "Well, which of these is better, and which shall I give preference to?" And it seems to me that that's a valid question.

And I think it's interesting how these early Enlightenment guys, at least it seems to me, would respond to that question. They would say, "Well, let's go look at our universal values, the sort of things that we want to develop, inculcate, or exercise people's minds around—moral, political, universal issues, which affect everybody—and then they would go back to what John has just been saying and say that on that basis it's self-evident that training a philosopher in this way, to have a universal conception and questioning of what the human reality is, is the better model of philosophizing and the nature of philosophy than the more restrictive paradigm.

Peter Hylton: Tony Grafton was saying roughly, well, there's this way of doing history of philosophy and that and that they should both happen, and that's great. But I want to know how I should think about it. I've been doing the subject for 30 years, and I still don't know.

Susan Neiman: Well, it's a wonderful discussion, and there are so many ways to go that I'm in danger of not putting them all together, because we have raised lots of points here.

The most important one, though, strikes me: the very first one you all began with, which I found truly astonishing. And this is not the first time in my life that I've been involved in a discussion with world-class historians who have said things like, "Gee, I'm so grateful," or "Thank you for allowing me to participate in your discussion."

No, I don't think he was, actually. Alas, he ought to have been, perhaps, because I always go away from these conversations feeling, Gee, did I just pull one over.

I mean, just simply by getting my Ph.D. in Emerson Hall, here is some unbelievably eminent historian who is 15 years older than me saying, "Well, gosh, I'm not a philosopher, but…"

And I think it's an extraordinary phenomenon, particularly by virtue of the fact that Tony himself mentioned his contempt for people who read Wittgenstein with the original, or Don, who, I gather, is my paradigm student, who walked in and said, "This is just too boring; it's not what I thought it was going to be about."

And so this is an extraordinary mixture of emotions between intimidation and contempt, and I wonder where it comes from and how one can get past it, because one of the things that I first want to do is second Mark's claim that, I have learned increasingly over the past few years, more from people in fields sort of contiguous to philosophy than, I'm afraid, from almost anybody in philosophy, maybe because the work I've been doing has been so non-mainstream, that I have benefited enormously from people who are contiguous, and I think it's wrong to suggest that we've got some monopoly on critical thinking or deep stuff, right.

On the other hand, there are important differences, and I'm trying to—there's two ways to go. One would be to—and I've been trying to make a list here as you've been talking of historians' virtues and philosophers' virtues, the stuff that we learn, and I'm not clear what they are. I mean, one thing seems to be historians read whole books, OK, and historians—right?

Jonathan Israel: An interesting theory.

(Laughter)

Susan Neiman: All right. Maybe you don't. Historians know more.
(Laughter)

The other thing is one of the reasons I regret having spent this vast amount of time reading the same things over and over, while you guys actually were expanding your horizons. One of the things you know more than we do is languages. But that's a point on which I have to add a question mark.

So that would be one way to go in trying to set out the things.

But the other way to go I think would be the way that John Cooper was going. I got into history of philosophy because I simply thought that Kant was better than anybody I was reading in 20th-century philosophy. And then you can say, "Well, how many Kants are there, or how many Platos?" It turned out that Bayle was better, too.

I mean, it turned out that everybody—well, nearly everybody—in the 18th century was, it seemed to me, better, deeper, richer, you know, spoke more to the problems that I was really concerned about than people in the 20th century. So, I think the big difference is maybe something like that.

And the last sentence, just because this has been an extremely fruitful and productive conference, Jerry: many thanks, and maybe one ought to think about some form of a follow-up.

Lorraine Daston: Any responses to the claim that the 18th century is the best of all possible centuries?

(Laughter)

J. B. Schneewind: I want to ask Don Kelley for a clarification of something I think you said.

It seemed to me that you were saying that you philosophers do textual reading, and if you're serious about that, you can't ask the kinds of questions historians ask, like, Why does this question matter? Is that what you were saying?

Donald Kelley: No. I think I was partly responding in terms of the teaching of philosophy, where you don't have time to drift off into antiquarian questions.

All I mean is that the historian's impulse would be to ask questions that you probably think are irrelevant, because you want to find a line of argument and...

J. B. Schneewind: Yes, but if that's true, I can't let it go unchallenged, because it seems to me one of the defining features of what I think of as the new history is that we try to situate the arguments at a point where the argument doesn't fully explain itself.

I'll give you just one example. Sidgwick says in the *Methods of Ethics* that he's not trying to examine the commonest systems of moral thought. I couldn't understand why he was doing that. And the book doesn't explain why he's doing that. To find out why he was doing that, I had to go outside it and look at his life, look at his religious doubts, look at the peculiar constellation of ideas that led him to think that maybe he could find an increasing ethics of love in commonsense morality and that that might be a kind of progressive revelation. None of that is in the book. It's the only thing that makes sense of that particular enterprise.

When I teach Sidgwick, I have to tell them that. I think that one frequently runs up against questions like that in doing just the kind of argumentative work Cooper wants done because the arguments aren't fully explanatory of what the philosopher is doing.

So if you were right, then the whole new histories project is wrong.

Donald Kelley: I'm not setting up a competing paradigm. I'm just saying that following this rational curiosity and following the arguments are not necessarily what moved historians who might want to look at the literary side or the rhetorical side and not care about what the philosopher was moving—arguing from A to B.

J. B. Schneewind: Well, I agree with that. My only point is that caring about the argument does not exclude you from caring about what led to those arguments and from teaching it as part of the history of philosophy.

Donald Kelley: We should teach a course together, and I should be as perverse as possible to show you what…

J. B. Schneewind: Don, we've been working together for 15 years, and you always have been.

(Laughter)

Cornel West: What we love about Cooper is that he's so honest, candid, and not always right. And what I mean is this: take, for example, a person in political theory or religion, and so forth; Socrates can be an inspiration. The example of Socrates is undetermined. We can start with Socrates and end up with Erasmus,

372

we can start with Socrates and end up with Herder, we can start with Socrates and end up with Kant. So we'd have that same Socratic spirit: concern with philosophical argument but with different twists, turns, and so forth.

Now, if that's the truth, then the question is, What is the difference for a philosopher to invoke Socrates so that the philosopher's philosophical orientation makes him somehow distinct from what we're doing in the religion department or what a person would do in literature if Kafka invoked Socrates, if Chekhov invoked Socrates, all these despotic generals as what people enlist in their armies. Socrates didn't want them. He wanted something else. He was suspicious of those sects—the Platonists, the Aristotelians, the kind of fun that Lucian makes of them, right?

Now, that's a Socratic spirit. You would agree with that? So what is the real difference that we're talking about here?

I mean, that's what gets me. Maybe it's because we share a certain reference to Socrates and someone else doesn't. But it's still unclear to me.

And then, if you take history seriously, the historicity of reason, the dynamism of reason, then Herder looks more convincing, and, therefore, you end up with art and poetry.

In Greco, the imagination strikes you as much as interesting as rationation, and so forth.

Where do we disagree, though, John, on that?

John Cooper: We don't disagree at all.

Anthony Grafton: I see philosophy and the history of philosophy as really more closely and tightly related than I do the practice of art and the history of art, which doesn't mean that experience and the practice of art don't have a tremendous impact on some art historians.

I mean, Lawrence Gowing is a great art historian because he's a remarkable artist, and he does a very particular kind of art history.

I'd like to reply to your rebuttal and say, I don't think that's right, because, like John, I feel about historians that there is something that historians are, which doesn't prevent you and John, and virtually everyone I see out there, from doing historical work that I profit from.

I have read a great many of you, and I will read some of you that I haven't read because I'm inspired by this conference. Your work will have an impact on the way I teach and probably in projects I'm embarking on, on the way I work on certain texts in my research.

I still think historians do things in a distinctive way that is difficult to describe and difficult to characterize. But in the history department we have certain things in common in the way we do things, which we really don't feel we share with all people who do really important historical work in other disciplines.

I think we are stuck with border definitions that we have inherited from a long time ago that don't particularly express our intellectual affiliations, but they do still express something. There is still a sense in a history department of some sort of consensus about what's important history, what's serious history, and what isn't.

And the only way I can really identify that is by pointing to what we do in the history department, and it just isn't exactly what you do. It doesn't mean the two things can't fruitfully interact. But I don't think they are the same. One point is, we can't say this is really cool and expect credibility from our audience. That's a real difference—and I don't mean this as trivial.

When Robert Graves was studying English at Oxford, he went to his tutor one day to read an essay, and the tutor said, "Mr. Graves, it appears to me that you prefer certain authors to others." And he was given to understand that this was a bad thing. In the purely historicist Oxford English school of the 1920s, preference was not acceptable. That would never have been true in Oxford philosophy. It wouldn't have been true then, it wouldn't be true now, it wouldn't have been true—though Oxford philosophy's preferences would have gone from Hegel to very different authors in that period. I think that that sense of the tremendous importance of what you're working on, not just for then, but for now, is something that the occasional historian runs into. But, on the whole, it's not a necessary feature of our practice. It's wonderful when it happens, but it is not, I think, necessary in the way that I just don't see why you would be a historian of philosophy if you didn't have some of that sense that John expressed.

Ian Hunter: Just by way of bringing in an example of what I think illustrates the kind of thing that Tony Grafton has been saying: Sometimes the fissure between the historical and the philosophical approach to a question can be quite sharp, and in a sense, it's very difficult to work out whether a mediating position is possible at all.

And the example I have in mind is from Kant studies today, and it's what's called the difference—and many of the people in the room, of course, have very strong views on this, which is the point I'm making. It's the difference between what's called the two-world viewpoint and the two-standpoint viewpoint with regard to Kant's practical philosophy.

Now, a lot of contemporary American Kantian moral philosophy insists on the two-standpoint reading. OK? And that insistence is doctrinal. The two-world viewpoint is unacceptable.

Now, that to me is a philosophical response to Kant. It's also a part of the way in which Kant was domesticated for American teaching purposes. That's a historical point.

If we were to look at people—at Kant scholars in Germany in the prewar period, like Max Wundt or a major figure like Heinz Heimsoeth, and go through the war into the modern period, you will find, in fact, a version of the two-world reading of Kant. I mean Kant as a classical metaphysician. Those people can't really fit into the American teaching of Kant.

Now, a historian's viewpoint is that it's true to say what I have just said about that history, but a philosopher who accepts the two-viewpoint reading will simply insist on it and is not really interested in that relativizing mood whereby you say we can construct Kant differently; he has been read differently. But it's true that the Germans did read Kant differently in this particular regard.

But here is an example, I think, of the fissure. I'm not putting it forward because I see a way around it, but simply to exemplify. It's simply an example.

Michael Friedman: Yes. I wanted to follow up on what Tony was saying, and I had a question for him.

I think he's put his finger beautifully on it with his minor-versus-great issue, because I think to be a philosopher who does history of philosophy is, in part, to know, as it were, who is greater and who is less great. That is kind of definitive of what we do. So I wanted to talk specifically about the Ficino, Pico in early modern philosophy talk problem, and I want to do it concretely by mentioning Cassirer and kind of get your thoughts about that, because he's one of the first people, at least in philosophy and probably in intellectual history, to really take these people very, very seriously as an essential part of modern thought. But he also handles the minor-and-great thing in a certain way because he takes Kant, of course, to be the greatest. He takes it to be obvious, as I think we all do, that Descartes, Leibniz, etcetera, Kant, are greater than Ficino and Pico, as all professional philosophers do.

And to read Ficino and Pico with those eyes, I mean, not necessarily so crude, you know, it's all leading to Kant etiologically, but he has in his mind that really the important thing about modern thought finally is that it culminated in Kant in some way or other.

Now, taking account of the fact that this is a hundred years ago, and, of course, we've made lots of mistakes and we didn't know things that we know now, what do you think about that both as intellectual history—and I take it that it's unacceptable by the current standards of intellectual history to operate that way.

We just take it as self-evident that Kant is greater than—and by greater, we don't mean he was, in fact, just more important or more influential either. Philosophers don't mean that.

But what do you think of it also as an acceptable way of doing history of philosophy? I mean, accepting, I think, your very clear and beautiful way of characterizing what the difference is.

If you are a philosopher, is it acceptable to handle the great, the minor the way Cassirer does, magnifying everything he says but that way?

Anthony Grafton: I think the Cassirer work is absolutely acceptable, as long as you're as self-conscious as he is about what he's doing and see it as a way of trying to shed light on these people, which is anachronistic, but may still put a shade of light on them which hasn't seen.

I would actually make the case for Pico and Ficino. And here the reading I do comes out in terms of a philosophy of self-cultivation, and I think they have very interesting things to say that put them within the Greek tradition, but also add to it.

And that's very much, obviously, from reading history of ancient philosophy for the past 20 years that those issues have arisen as such central ones in the philosophical tradition and that Hadot and others have brought them downstream to our period as well.

I think it's fine, as long as it's done self-consciously. And people who denounce Cassirer tend to be saying, "But he was assuming you would know that he was writing as a Kantian and with a sense of the Kantian revolution as what he's looking for."

But, yeah, I think it's acceptable, absolutely. It makes you rethink the text; it makes you ask yourself, at the very least, why you don't believe this. And that's what I found myself doing with it. And it forces someone who is—my own preference is very much: what was this thing, what were they doing, what can we see that they didn't know they were doing, what they were also doing, because they had institutional and other constraints.

But Cassirer really helps you see that, I think, by saying, Well, what if you do it this way. And again, that's not a historical standard method. It's the kind of—it is much more hypothetical and heuristic than the kinds of methods we comfortably apply.

Jonathan Israel: Yes. I just wanted to tie together some of the remarks—Tony's remarks about history and philosophy, the remarks about art history—because I didn't entirely agree here.

I think that both of the key differences in philosophy are universal. I don't see how anything cannot have both historical and philosophical dimension. One couldn't say the same about art history, I think, or the practice of art.

And I don't entirely agree that although all scholars must be historical at some point or other in what they're doing and that you can't totally eliminate the historical dimension from any form of the humanities or, for that matter, science, any other kind of scholarship.

And history, of course, is widely practiced by many colleagues in many disciplines. But it's something different that we do in the history departments; I'm not sure I really agree with that.

There are a tremendous variety of approaches, of course, and many different conceptions of what history is, usually—certainly where I come from in England—without very much philosophical dimension of it.

It's simply perhaps more awareness of the variety of approaches, the methodologies that professional historians have used, and that in terms of the technique and in terms of methodology, one could say, OK, professional historians are likely to know about these things and others not. But, otherwise, I didn't see any very vast differences.

But just if I may add a word on Pico and Ficino, with their marvelously rich methods of allusion and hinting, it seems to me that this is one of the most important episodes in the history of mankind, and one of the strands that grew out of it, which is hinting in perhaps a more subversive and seditious way, *libertinage érudit*, from the 16th century through to the beginning of the 18th, this has very profound philosophical implications, but I'm not sure that it's philosophy.

Going back to what John was saying before, it seems to me there's a difference between living in a theological climate which you oppose for profound philosophical reasons, but you're forced to use a language of allusion and hints in order to begin the work undermining it, which is tremendously important philosophical work. But I don't see that as philosophy. I think there is an important difference. And that's exactly what is the difference between I think the older tradition of *libertinage érudit:* what is implied were often many of the same concepts, those that are being directly stated at the end of the 17th century and then the 18th.

But there is a difference between arguing the case systematically and hinting or suggesting implications that might go in that direction.

Donald Kelley: The only thing I'd say is while agreeing that this is not philosophy, I would insist that it's a form of argument employed by philosophers, including even some philosophers in this period, and that it, like the philosophical kind of training Dan talked about, is not only forced upon them by theological constraints; it's also ingrained in them by the kind of intellectual and pedagogical training that they have gone through, and that to that extent, though it is not philosophy on its own, it's part of the way they do philosophy in just the way that any other form of argumentation is.

John Cooper: I just want to say that there is a larger intellectual tradition—larger than philosophy—in which Pico and Ficino and others are working, and that is wisdom. Wisdom of philosophy is a Western kind of wisdom. Wisdom encompasses what Pico and others, pre-Greek religious movements, and in one sense it would make more—we can't talk about history and wisdom, but that it the larger framework within which philosophy was placed in the early modern period. Pico is an example of that.

Juliet Floyd: Well, as someone who always read the German of Wittgenstein, I was very stimulated by this remark, and many people have said many things that I fundamentally agree with.

I guess I can only report from the field of the attempt to try to think historically and philosophically about the construction of the present situation in philosophy departments in the United States primarily. I need every skill I can get when I read a text. This is the model of the book, that everything a man says can be said in three words. This is a very—there are a lot of ancient allusions there. It's packed, it's intended to be packed. There is no way to understand the text if you aren't able to go backward in a literary or a rhetorical fashion from that.

So, part of our situation today in analytic philosophy departments is an echo of the 18th-century debates between, say, Herder and Kant. It's extremely important to understand that. I think that many of the originators of analytic philosophy actually understood that.

It's important when you read Frege's *Grundlagen* to understand the attack on your predecessors that go back to Aristotle and who self-consciously formulated that.

However, it's also important to understand what mathematically is going on. And one of the reasons philosophy departments are in the position they're in now is that there were people who got tenured positions in philosophy departments who were producing mathematics—mathematics that the math department was not willing to produce. And there are institutional, sociological, and intellectual reasons why a certain couple of generations felt it was extremely important to have that knowledge produced. Logic is still an extremely marginal subject in the mathematics department.

So I think you have to look very carefully both at history and at philosophy. There is no way to understand philosophical text without doing so. And I can only report as a historian of the 20th century why this is self-evident to me. And I don't feel conflict, and maybe that's just because it's closer in time. But I think that when we discuss paradigms like there is argumentation versus literary and rhetoric, we really can't be too schematic, because it doesn't make sense, in general, to use those categories.

And even more in the *Investigations*, which I'm teaching right now. It's impossible. You must know Plato, you must know Augustine, you must know it all. And, in fact, Wittgenstein is writing specifically about the problem we have in this room that we cannot define a priori what philosophy is in this particular modern world we live in.

So I don't see in some sense, in principle, a barrier to systematic argumentation versus historical detail. I think it all depends on the particular way it is presented.

Steven Nadler: Something became crystal clear to me this morning, finally, and this is that when historians speak of the new history of philosophy, they mean something that's about 400 or 500 years old, and when philosophers speak about new history of philosophy, it's about 15 or 20 years old.

What I want to do is second John Cooper's sentiment in the following way. In 1984, in what is admittedly a very interesting book on Spinoza's *Ethics*, in the very first paragraph Jonathan Bennett writes, "I find Spinoza's political writings of no use whatsoever in understanding Spinoza's *Ethics*." And what the new history of philosophy means to philosophers is that you could never say that again, or you could never take that approach.

And I think John is absolutely right, and what the new history of philosophy means is that in doing philosophy historically, you want to make sure that the person you're engaged in dialogue with, although long dead, I think that's a difference between history of philosophy and philosophy, is that the people you were in dialogue with just happened to be dead, or dying, I guess, that you really want to make sure you have some very good understanding of what they take themselves to be saying. And that's where I think the history comes in—at least for doing history of philosophy in a philosophy department.

Daniel Garber: I think your characterization of the teaching of history of philosophy and the role that it plays in inculcating students into current practice allows me to state, I think very succinctly, exactly the kind schizophrenia that I felt as a historian of philosophy teaching in a philosophy department, which is to say, on one hand, that exactly what these courses are supposed to do is to initiate students into the practices of current philosophy.

On the other hand, I see an important role for myself as a historian of philosophy in explicating precisely how it is that those practices were not shared by previous generations and how it is that they came to be. And I think that that's exactly the conflict that I feel between in a certain sense: my life as a historian of philosophy and my life as a teacher of philosophy in a philosophy department.

Lorraine Daston: May I ask you a question in return?

Daniel Garber: Sure.

Lorraine Daston: As a historian of science, I am also in the position sometimes of actually teaching young scientists as well as young historians of science, and it's perfectly clear to all of us that what I am teaching no longer counts as current, acceptable practice and content of science.

Nonetheless, the act of self-consciousness, which learning about the history is considered to be, I think, by all parties, including the fledgling scientists, is another arrow in their quiver, another conceptual and analytic tool which they can then apply to the here-and-now subject matter.

Do you think that's true for philosophy?

Daniel Garber: Yes. Absolutely. But this is perhaps the difference between the introductory course—the Descartes-to-Kant course— which really is very much initiating students into current practice, and slightly more advanced courses, where I feel that I can bring in this other perspective, because I do think understanding that there are alternative conceptions of what the subject is and has been is an important part of educating philosophers to do contemporary philosophy, to understand the contingency of our conception of philosophy in just the way that I think that educating scientists to understand the contingency of our conception of physics or science in general is important. But they are different functions.

Lorraine Daston: I wonder sometimes whether *contingency* is the right word, because I think that although one can imagine it being otherwise, there is a great deal of conceptual space between the absolutely contingent and the absolutely determined. There is a reason why it turned out the way it did, and the reason may be a good reason.

Daniel Garber: Or not.

Lorraine Daston: Or not. But at least it should be argued.

Daniel Garber: But it's a question, yes?

Lorraine Daston: Michael?

Michael Friedman: Yes. Thanks.

I think the distinction between discipline and tradition is extremely helpful here, and I think it's helpful to explain why we, historians and philosophers, sometimes become frightened and angry at each other, why historians, you know, especially get frightened by and angry at Kant and contemporary analytic philosophy and why historians of philosophy get sometimes frightened by and angry at historians.

It's because philosophy, I think, isn't a disciplinary tradition; it's just a tradition in the end. We don't have a subject and a method that are clear and unproblematic.

There is a philosophy that all of these things are in question. We don't ever have anything like normal science in philosophy. I mean, that doesn't make sense, because that would be to take things for granted in an unquestioned way, and the nature of philosophy is not to do that. Although temporary, you can have little local ones, but still nothing like it.

So, for example, I was reading Dan Garber, the most historical of all of us, who says I can't do archives. That's not what I want to do. Right?

Now, to do history, most recent literature, the primary source is archives. This is what you do. This is what you learn. Primary sources don't scare us. Most recent literature can be scary, archives can be scary.

I have my friend. I thought, for a philosopher, I'm pretty knowledgeable about the literature and history of science. No. Because I am not up-to-date.

I mean, I'll talk to D'Amico, Bertolinonelli, and I'll say, Gee, I read this interesting book, you know, from 1986 or 1993. Yeah, that's pretty good for an older work. How am I ever going to keep up? How am I ever going to know what's happening in the history of science. Right? You know, let alone you have to go to an archive. I've never learned how to go to an archive. Occasionally, I've gotten some photocopies from some archives.

So, you know, that's scary because we don't have an agreed-upon disciplinary. I mean, philosophy is not a *Wissenschaft*, not even a *Geisteswissenschaft*. History is a *Geisteswissenschaft*.

Philosophy, on the other hand, you know—because this is such a problem—has occasionally tried to be, you know, a *Wissenschaft* in the strictest sense, not to worry, even a mathematical *Wissenschaft*.

So, Kant once said that philosophy on this particular path of a science is not a humanistic discipline anymore. Right? This is what makes historians upset.

Now, you know it makes Kant great, but, of course, it makes Kant wrong in that you can't do that. Right? Analytic philosophy thought we could make philosophy into mathematical logic. What a fantastically great idea, superimportant. Of course, you can't do that. Right?

So, it scares historians; it makes them mad. You're trying to make something humanistic not humanistic. But here it's necessary that philosophy try to do that, although it never succeeds, you know.

And so I think that the issue about, is it a science, is it a discipline, is it a tradition, these are all very important.

Lorraine Daston: I'd just like to explain something that Susan remarked on earlier, which is why so many of us—I think all of us at this table—have a kind of unrequited love affair with philosophy. You know, we are like lovers spurned.

Cornel West: When Kant calls on a philosophical poet like Pope, this is an etiological and political and philosophical claim. It was his status. But he is a popular philosopher, and I'm a professional philosopher. So it might be a tradition. But every tradition was mediated with certain forms of institutionalization in the academy; it is a discipline.

You know, when I arrived at graduate school, it was a discipline, right, and I was disciplined, and it was beautiful.

And so, this notion somehow that philosophy has not normalcy. My God, schools of thought, neo-Kantianism, not pushing out other—trying to get Nietzsche on the curriculum, trying to get Schopenhauer's essays included, trying to get Rorty in the philosophy department: I mean, these are serious battles going on.

We had to separate etiological self-understanding of philosophers with the practices of the discipline that are actually examined historically. That's all. That's the question I'm raising, you see. Peirce did some of the pieties here.

Karl Ameriks: To pick up directly on Michael's point and also Peter's opening question and then on your remarks about what philosophy is about: So I've been thinking, if we want to figure out what the new histories of philosophy are, we have to think of what the history of philosophy is, and then today we're getting into the simple question of what makes philosophy distinctive and what philosophical knowledge we might come to, and I have been very influenced by thoughts like Michael's that even if it's a discipline, philosophy isn't a science in the hard sense of having a clear kind of progression to it.

So that even if we love Socrates, and so forth, and go back to study Socrates, there's something a little strange about it, because in science you wouldn't go back. If you were a scientist, you wouldn't go back and study some ancient scientist with the same enthusiasm that we philosophers do. And so it's a mystery.

I was trying to figure out the relationship between philosophy and history—the special relationship between philosophy and history—and I thought it might have something to do with, is philosophy an art or a science. But then it occurred to me: that's not really an issue at all because we found out today there's a big distinction between art and music, or whatever, and the history of art and music, and they're not the same thing. They are very different.

It also seems to me that science and the history of science, those are just different things. If you're a scientist, you're doing one thing. If you're doing history, you're doing another. There might be a little overlap in the classroom. But those are just very different.

So my proposal is that what you have to think about, maybe, and you might not like the specific way I'm going to phrase it, but I think what we have to think about maybe is that philosophy, whatever it is, is definitely neither an art nor a science; it's just a third, different kind of thing.

And my suggestion, and others may have other suggestions, is that this kind of unrestricted critical reflection that Michael was also talking about: there's a lot of critical reflection in other disciplines, but somehow with philosophy there is this aim of system and it's going deeper to whatever foundation is offered in mathematics, or whatever; the philosophy of mathematics is different from the mathematical foundation of mathematics within mathematics; and so forth and so on. But it's just a proposal.

I think unless we start thinking about philosophy distinctively as a third enterprise, other than art and science, it's hard to figure out why history has to have a special role.

And the final proposal on that is that history really doesn't have to have a special role in philosophy if it is a universal reflective critical discipline. I wouldn't agree that we always do or philosophers come to philosophy through history courses.

But precisely since it's a universal critical discipline, it's always open to philosophy to consider our historical prejudices and arguments from the perspective of, well, what are the hidden premises or the influential premises that people are blinded to by not considering history enough. And there Socrates may be valuable in a number of different ways, for example.

Jonathan Israel: Just a few off-the-cuff responses. And this perhaps straight out of Spinoza, Bayle tradition.

It seems from one philosophical perspective, almost by definition, that philosophy can't be a science, and it can't be one of the humanities because precisely its purpose is to try to look at the whole and say what it is. Nothing else looks at the totality and tries to make sense of it.

For those people, that's the point of philosophy. Others see philosophy as having a more restricted role. But that tradition or conception, which I think has more in common than other modern traditions of philosophy, what John was saying before, with the Greek conception of what philosophy is, which is not only about understanding, but it's about shaping life and shaping both private life and civic life.

I think that philosophy then must stand on its own, and it can't be classified with any of the sciences or any of the humanities. And even the question of what is the division between sciences, if there is a division, which Spinoza would probably deny, because he would say that man is part of nature and that history, he speaks of *historia naturalis*, and he would say that ultimately this is a false distinction we make between science and the humanities. Whether there is a distinction and the nature of the distinction, that's the proper task of philosophy.

So I think that, by definition, and in a very special way, it must be quite outside the sciences. And what scientist working in science today tries to sum up the findings of science and tells you where Kant is going? Is that a task for a scientist? I think that's a philosophical question. I suspect it's actually not a task for a scientist.

Peter Hylton: I'd like to add my voice to the voices of admiration for Jerry Schneewind for organizing this conference, and I'd like to remind everybody that the first word in the title of the conference is *Teaching* New Histories of Philosophy, and I find that in much of the discussion I've had the privilege to hear so far, the emphasis has been on the different ways of understanding philosophy as something that could be taught but also specifically something that could be written about.

I'd like to bring it back to teaching a little bit, and particularly what I would dare to call almost a crisis of undergraduate history of philosophy teaching in the American college and university.

My remarks will basically be threefold, and I'll try to keep them as brief as possible. First, I'd like to say some general things about the relationship of the history of teaching philosophy to the American university and American society in general; second, having to do with where the history of philosophy stands within the discipline, the professional discipline of philosophy; and third, a plea for more of an approach to the teaching of the history of philosophy that is interdisciplinary in its dimensions.

In the first case, I think that I'm gong to imagine being an undergraduate, not a philosophy major, which is the general situation for most undergraduates facing courses in the history of philosophy.

As much as it may gall people in this room, I want to remind all of us that most undergraduates who take a course in the history of philosophy are not philosophy majors. Most of them are not approaching the subject at the most elite universities in the country, but often at very good colleges and universities where they might take a course in Kant or maybe early or later modern history of philosophy, and I want to suggest that for the most part, undergraduates who take courses in the history of philosophy are not by a long shot history of philosophy majors or philosophy majors going on to Ph.D. programs in philosophy. We know this. The demographic is clear.

I suggest that one of the elements of the discussion of teaching the history of philosophy that has so far been somewhat absent in the program that I have heard so far is the importance of the custodial duty in the teaching of the history of philosophy.

We could go on at length about these matters. So I'm going to be very brief in saying that both the impact of postmodernism and its various understandings on the undergraduate curriculum and the graduate curriculum and, of course, the constant background buzz of the mass media have created in the undergraduate student—and even the bright undergraduate student who will go on in many cases to professional school—a kind of invitation to cultural amnesia. The postmodernism invites relativism, which we're all familiar with and all its painful implications.

The mass-media background, which our undergraduates are listening to all the time, creates a kind of a sense that the world really didn't begin until roughly the end of the Vietnam war for most of our undergraduates. And this creates, I think, a complexity for teaching the history of philosophy to undergraduates who are not going to be professional students in philosophy or in the humanities in general.

And my strongest sense is that undergraduate courses in the history of philosophy should be taught in such a way that they can be serviceable to those students who are going on to Ph.D. programs in philosophy and the humanities, but also they should be taught in such a way that they can be appreciated and enjoyed by non-philosophy majors who will also be populating those courses.

To simply see the history of philosophy courses as service courses for philosophy majors in the vast landscape of higher education in this country is to basically disconnect the discussion from many able students who don't have the background or the ambition to pursue additional courses or majors in the history of philosophy. So I think this puts very great demands on the instructor.

And I agree with John Cooper that we can model the teaching of the history of philosophy to undergraduates—even those who are not majoring in philosophy—in such a way that we can show by the doing of philosophy in the class the sense of the disinterested spirit of Socratic inquiry and the sense also that what we have to teach in this course is of importance for both majors and nonmajors.

And I'd like to have a little honesty from the panel on the point that most students taking courses in the history of philosophy are not philosophy majors and will not go on to Ph.D. programs in philosophy.

And I think that this leads me to my second matter—that of the place of teaching the history of philosophy within the discipline of philosophy.

In the teaching of the discipline of philosophy, it seems to me that many students are looking, in effect, for the wisdom side of the discussion, the wisdom side of the great books and ways in which it can be applied to practice, and I think that every teacher of the history of philosophy should make an effort to connect the historical person and the situation that they are exploring in the classroom to what is going on in contemporary culture, because these connections can give students a sense of the aliveness of philosophy, that it's not just a tour into some antiquarian museum that is best reserved only for people who want to be observers and not participants in the discussion and conversation of philosophy.

Finally, just to say that for the interdisciplinary side of the teaching of the history of philosophy and not talking about the nuances of its historiography, I think that every effort that can be made in the teaching of the history of philosophy that can introduce biography, and, specifically, the background of the man or woman who is the philosopher that is being examined, can give life and substance to the subject in a way that can take it well beyond the academic categories that have been framed for us through professionals going to the conferences that we attend, such as these.

For example, in the teaching of Descartes, all students are fascinated by the meditations, but they're even more fascinated by sections of the discourse where he kind of drops his professional mask and says, you know, it was through many of his travels that he learned most of what he had learned as an undergraduate, that it was outside the university and not in the classroom that he found most enlightenment.

These are things that our students need to learn—the human—to humanize these great men and women and not just to see them as museum pieces for future philosophers who will pursue Ph.D. programs and later enshrine them in their professional life.

Thank you.